THE MIDDLE EAST IN TURMOIL

THE MIDDLE EAST IN TURMOIL

Conflict, Revolution, and Change

William Mark Habeeb

Contributions by
Rafael D. Frankel and Mina Al-Oraibi

 GREENWOOD

AN IMPRINT OF ABC-CLIO, LLC
Santa Barbara, California • Denver, Colorado • Oxford, England

Copyright 2012 by William Mark Habeeb

All rights reserved. No part of this publication may be reproduced, stored in a
retrieval system, or transmitted, in any form or by any means, electronic, mechanical,
photocopying, recording, or otherwise, except for the inclusion of brief quotations
in a review, without prior permission in writing from the publisher.

Library of Congress Cataloging-in-Publication Data

Habeeb, William Mark, 1955–
   The Middle East in turmoil : conflict, revolution, and change / William Mark Habeeb ;
contributions by Rafael D. Frankel and Mina Al-Oraibi.
      p. cm.
   Includes bibliographical references and index.
   ISBN 978-0-313-33914-1 (hardcopy : alk. paper) — ISBN 978-0-313-08514-7 (ebook)
   1. Social conflict—Middle East. 2. Revolutions—Middle East.
3. Democratization—Middle East. I. Frankel, Rafael D. II. Al-Oraibi,
Mina. III. Title.
   HN656.A8H33   2012
   303.60956—dc23   2011037132

ISBN: 978-0-313-33914-1
EISBN: 978-0-313-08514-7

16 15 14 13 12   1 2 3 4 5

This book is also available on the World Wide Web as an eBook.
Visit www.abc-clio.com for details.

Greenwood
An Imprint of ABC-CLIO, LLC

ABC-CLIO, LLC
130 Cremona Drive, P.O. Box 1911
Santa Barbara, California 93116-1911

This book is printed on acid-free paper (∞)

Manufactured in the United States of America

CONTENTS

PREFACE

As this volume goes to press, the decks are being shuffled in virtually every Middle Eastern state, and change is occurring rapidly in a region that many had thought was immune to it. But despite the daily headlines, the underlying factors that have shaped the broad outlines and direction of Middle East politics endure, as have many of the elements of conflict and division within individual states. And although the decks are being shuffled, the cards remain the same: Increasingly young, vocal, and technologically connected publics; entrenched regimes and power centers whose supporters are fighting to hold on to economic and societal privileges; monarchies seeking new ways to maintain their legitimacy; transnational, but locally flavored, religious movements; ethnic and sectarian minorities; and strong military establishments who often are more concerned about internal security and regime defense than about external threats. The focus of this book is these enduring elements of Middle East politics.

After an introductory chapter that describes the critical factors that have shaped Middle East politics over the past half century, the subsequent chapters will look at individual countries (or subregions, such as the Maghreb), assessing that country's potential sources of internal conflicts and division as well as its external conflicts. In some instances, the internal conflicts may be played out via civil violence or even civil war; in other instances, via the ballot box. The external conflicts may lead to everything from open warfare, terrorism, and arms races to diplomatic agreements and peace accords. What will become clear is the indelible link between many of the internal and external conflicts.

Two of the chapters were written by experts with a uniquely deep understanding of the country in question: Rafael D. Frankel wrote the chapter on Israel, and Mina Al-Oraibi the chapter on Iraq. Samuel Dolbee made extensive updates and revisions to the entire manuscript and contributed important insights. Maxine Taylor of ABC-CLIO ensured that the manuscript made it to publication.

I alone bear responsibility for all errors of fact and omission.

INTRODUCTION: THE EVOLVING MIDDLE EAST

The Middle East erupted in 2011 as a wave of revolutionary fervor spread from Tunisia to Egypt and then throughout the Arab World. The events of early 2011 were truly a "black swan"[1] occurrence, a regionwide chain of events that not even the world's top Middle East scholars had foreseen or predicted and yet will change the social, political, and economic dynamics of the Middle East in fundamental ways. Everything can be explained retroactively, and the events that rocked the Middle East in 2011—and will not fully play out for many years to come—are no exception. The growing youth population, endemic unemployment, stagnant economic growth, income disparities, the spread of information technology and its social networking tools, the rising global cost of food, the sclerotic regimes—all of these factors had been evident, and discussed, for years. But the regionwide uprisings that began when a Tunisian vegetable vendor set himself on fire after being harassed by the local police still came as a complete surprise.

The tumultuous events that ushered in 2011 took on different characteristics in different countries, were met with different responses by the various regimes in power, and will produce different long-term outcomes. Yet if one steps back and takes a macrohistorical perspective, the events that began in the Arab world in 2011 (some might say they began with the Green Revolution in Iran in 2009) were simply the latest developments in a process that started with the collapse of the Ottoman Empire—a process of forging states and creating national identities, often within multiethnic and multisectarian boundaries; of negotiating the role of Islam in public life; of determining the distribution of political power and economic benefits within societies; of jockeying for leadership within the Arab world; and of defining the Arabs' role on the world stage.

The Middle East state system as we know it has existed for less than 100 years. When the Ottoman Empire collapsed following World War I, new states emerged—or rather, were created by the victorious European powers—in a region where transnational

empires and caliphates had ruled for centuries. With only a few exceptions—principally Iran and Egypt—the new states of the Middle East had no history as nation states
or even national entities (Israel is a unique case in that its establishment was the process of a dispersed nation—the Jewish people—seeking to create a state in their an-
cestral homeland). Many were merely collections of tribes and clan groups that lived
in close proximity with one another. These new states' boundaries were delineated to
fit the needs and strategic agreements of the European powers, not the ethnic, sectarian, or communal loyalties that characterized their societies. Much of the violence
and conflict that has scarred the Middle East is reflective of this fact.[2] Moreover,
the inherent tensions and contradictions caused by the way in which the modern Middle East was born are still being played out, and the most likely future conflicts in the
region—domestic as well as interstate—continue to reflect the regional state system's
troubled birth.

In the immediate years following World War II, most Middle Eastern states secured
full independence from their European mandatory powers. Since that time, regional politics in the Middle East have been shaped by several critical factors, all of which derive from the region's complex history and many of which exist in tension with one or
another:

CONCERTED AND OFTEN RUTHLESS EFFORTS AT STATE BUILDING BY CENTRAL GOVERNMENTS

The ethnic and sectarian diversity that characterizes many Middle Eastern states,
and the fact that few of them enjoy any historical sense of national identity, have led to
the rise of authoritarian (often military-based) regimes that were capable of maintaining central state control and suppressing dissent. In some cases, such as the Baathist
governments of Syria and Iraq, the ruling regimes were controlled by ethnic or sectarian minorities. In the Arabian Peninsula, the state-building regimes were generally
controlled by family or tribal dynasties that had seized power from rivals. Until the
early 1990s, these regimes often relied on external lifelines of support from one or another great power, usually the United States or the Soviet Union. After the end of the
Cold War, many continued to enjoy U.S. economic and military support.

These authoritarian state-building regimes are now under attack by processes of
political change. In some cases, such as Egypt, the state will survive the processes of
change intact. In others, such as Iraq and Syria, transition from authoritarian regimes
may lead to the dismemberment of the postcolonial state, or at least to a marked devo-
lution of central power.

THE LURE OF TRANSNATIONAL MOVEMENTS, BOTH SECULAR AND RELIGIOUS IN NATURE

From the time of the Islamic conquest of the Middle East in the seventh century
until the fall of the Ottoman Empire, most of the peoples of the Middle East lived as
members of a larger transnational unit, even if loosely structured, as in the waning days
of Ottoman rule. While the postindependence central governments made great strides
in forging national identities within their new nation states, the lure of transnational
movements continues to attract support, especially when popular opposition to local

authoritarian regimes grows. In the 1950s and 1960s, the most popular transnational forces were secular (Nasserism and Baathism, for example). Since the late 1970s, transnational Islamism has posed the greatest threat to central national governments. At its most worrying, transnational Islamism has been coupled with violent terrorism.

The revolutions of 2011 introduced a new transnational force in the Middle East, although one that is less ideologically defined than socialism or Islamism. Optimists term this force *democratization,* but that term assumes a certain outcome. *People power,* which denotes a demand for greater popular representation in government and an end to authoritarianism, is a vaguer but more accurate term and does not necessarily imply that the end result will be Western-style liberal democracy. In fact, Western-style liberal democracy is perhaps the least likely end result; more probable are forms of managed democracy, as in post-Soviet Russia; the dissolution of the central state in favor of self-ruling subnational identities (which may or may not be democratic in nature); or the emergence of a new, if more enlightened, form of authoritarianism.

To the degree that Middle Eastern states experience political opening that includes a role for Islamist political parties, the threat of transnational Islamism may actually decrease, for national Islamist parties will by electoral necessity focus on national and local issues. And the most extreme and violent forms of Islamism, such as characterized by al-Qaeda and like-minded groups, will see their power and popularity wane in a transition from authoritarianism to more representative government.

THE ENDURING INTEREST AND INVOLVEMENT OF FOREIGN POWERS IN MIDDLE EASTERN POLITICS

Foreign powers started competing for influence in the Middle East as soon as the Ottoman Empire began showing signs of fragility and decay in the 19th century. Even though the Ottoman Empire was formally sovereign over much of the Middle East until after World War I, Britain, France, and Russia all carved out spheres of influence as the Ottoman rulers' grip weakened. After these European powers were forced to retreat following World War II, the United States and the Soviet Union emerged as the dominant external actors, operating principally through client states and regional military bases. With the end of the Cold War, the United States assumed the position of the dominant external power but soon found itself unable to control events or determine outcomes at will. Moreover, in the economic arena, Europe never ceded its influence in the region, and in the 21st century, China increasingly has become a critical economic and commercial actor in the Middle East. Fueled by its massive oil and gas revenues and its yearning to resume a prominent role on the world stage, Russia also has reemerged as a potentially influential external player in Middle East affairs.

The bottom line is that while the identity of the foreign actors may fluctuate and change over time, the stakes at play in the Middle East guarantee that the region will continue to experience keen foreign interest in its political developments—and, more ominously, continued foreign efforts to determine or shape the outcome of Middle East political dynamics. The stakes for foreign actors include both elements of attraction—such as energy, strategic geography, and market access—as well as those of aversion—such as emigration and Islamic extremism.

The 2011 revolutions pose a challenge to foreign actors, who no longer can be guaranteed of compliant client regimes among authoritarian and monarchical governments. Foreign actors seeking to direct events in the region will not have as easy a time as before and will see their influence curtailed in those states where more representative and accountable governments are established. The great powers—the United States foremost—long favored stability over unfettered popular rule; the luxury of predictability and pliability that this policy produced has come to an end. In its place will come more assertive and independent regional actors, as well as more overt competition among such regional power centers as Cairo, Baghdad, Riyadh, and Tehran.

THE PROMINENT ROLE OF NONSTATE ACTORS IN MIDDLE EAST POLITICS

As mentioned, the traditional state system is a relatively new—and relatively insecure—feature of Middle East politics, while transnational tendencies remain an enduring force. As a result, nonstate actors always have played important roles in the Middle East and frequently are at the center of conflict. They are almost universally feared by the region's central governments, because they are inherently incompatible with a strong state system (although central governments frequently have tried to use and manipulate these nonstate actors to their advantage). Nonstate actors in the Middle East include national liberation movements, such as the Palestine Liberation Organization (PLO); transnational political movements, such as the Muslim Brotherhood; militant political parties, such as Hamas and Hezbollah; and terrorist organizations, such as al-Qaeda and Islamic Jihad. Increasingly, they also include civil society groups, such as the April 6 Movement in Egypt and the Green Movement in Iran, who may or may not seek political power. Their goal is political change and an end to authoritarian rule.

Moreover, many Middle Eastern countries contain traditional sociopolitical associations that predate the formation of the state and hold significant power and influence, and in some cases maintain armed forces or militias. These may be sectarian communities, such as the Maronite Christians of Lebanon, or tribal and family groups with ancient and enduring bonds. When the state system is under pressure or facing collapse—as in Lebanon during that country's long civil war and in Iraq following the U.S. invasion of 2003—there is a marked tendency among populations to seek security within these traditional associations and identities.

The role and influence of nonstate actors will rise concomitantly with the increase in representative government. This may have positive consequences—such as civil society and multiparty politics—or less positive ones—such as civil war.

THE INABILITY OF MOST MIDDLE EASTERN STATES TO GENERATE SUSTAINED ECONOMIC GROWTH AND JOB CREATION

With the exception of Israel, most states in the Middle East have yet to develop an economic system that produces sustained growth, job creation, and innovation (and even in Israel, growing economic disparity has become a serious problem). The economies of those Middle Eastern states endowed with energy resources have certainly experienced boom years, depending upon the international price of oil and gas, but these periods of economic excess should not be mistaken for a successful economic system. As with most rent-based economies, the energy-rich states of the Middle East suffer from extreme economic imbalance and inequality, and often from un- or underemployment. Those with relatively small populations, such as Qatar, can better endure commodity price fluctuations than those, such as Saudi Arabia and Algeria, with relatively large populations.

But the vast majority of people in the Middle East live in non–oil producing states based on highly localized subsistence economies and in societies that feature glaring extremes of poverty and wealth. The existence of large middle classes—widely believed to be the prerequisite for sustained economic growth as well as for democratic development—is rare. The exceptions are Israel, Tunisia, and within some of the larger urban areas, such as Cairo, Beirut, and Dubai.

The relative economic stagnation of most Middle Eastern states has had a significant effect on the nature and extent of conflict in the region, both internal and interstate. The Lebanese civil war, the Iraqi invasion of Kuwait, the Iranian Revolution, and the revolutions of early 2011 all had economic underpinnings among their multiple causes. The appeal of Islamic extremism also to a large extent is based on economic factors, principally economic inequality, corruption by elites, and perceptions of overly intrusive foreign economic (and with it, cultural) influence.

At the same time, the widespread conflict that has plagued the Middle East in recent decades has had a significant (and universally negative) impact on economies. Regional conflicts have required states to spend inordinate amounts of resources on military forces and defense, thus directing resources away from more productive uses. Lebanon and Algeria during their long civil wars, Iraq since the 2003 U.S. invasion, and the Palestinian territories since 2000 are prime examples of the devastating economic effects of conflict. The ability of countries in the region to attract foreign capital and investment has been severely restrained by perceptions of political risk, which is one of the downsides to the mass political unrest that began in 2011.

While these five factors may be enduring features of Middle East conflict in the modern era, they have not been *equally* influential at any given time. As a result, the nature and manifestation of conflict in the Middle East has evolved and transformed over time to reflect both global realities as well as changing regional dynamics. From the 1950s through the 1980s, conflict in the Middle East principally took the form of interstate war, most related to the question of Palestine (the Arab-Israeli wars of 1948, 1956, 1967, and 1973). This period also witnessed two Israeli invasions of Lebanon and a virtual civil war in Jordan in an effort by each state to crush the PLO (a nonstate actor) as well as a struggle between secular transnational movements such as Nasserism and Baathism, and the more conservative, traditional regimes such as Saudi Arabia and the Hashemite Kingdom of Jordan. This struggle produced low-level conflict between Egypt and Saudi Arabia and between Jordan and Syria, conflicts that likely would have developed into open war had it not been for the overriding conflict between the Arab states and Israel. The Iran-Iraq War in the early 1980s, a long and extraordinarily destructive interstate war, was related to geostrategic competition and secular authoritarian fear of transnational Islamism.

Overlaying these conflicts and regional tensions was the Cold War. The U.S.-Soviet competition for influence and strategic access in the Middle East led to propped-up regimes and massive arms shipments, two factors that served to rigidify the state system and strengthen the power and influence of regional militaries. More positively, both the United States and the Soviet Union had a clear interest in preventing widespread conflict from breaking out in the region, lest it spiral out of control and lead to a direct superpower confrontation (this phenomenon is seen most clearly in the U.S. efforts to halt the 1973 Arab-Israeli war, despite Israeli protestations, out of fears of a superpower escalation). Both superpowers also shared an interest in preserving the state system and defending their allies from external or internal threats. It was in neither superpower's interests to have the Middle East state system fail or to see the region collapse into chaos.

But even during the Cold War, one could see not far beneath the surface of the state system the elements for different types of conflict. Lebanon's long and bloody civil war (1975–1990) was in many ways a harbinger of future conflicts. Those participating in Lebanon's agony included first and foremost the country's own sectarian groups and traditional family and clan associations, but also regional states (Syria and Israel) and powerful nonstate actors (such as the PLO). Ultimately, even the United States became a brief direct actor in Lebanon's drama. Similarly, the Iranian Revolution of 1979 propelled a volatile new element into Middle East politics—the revolutionary Islamic state that was aligned with neither superpower (in fact, hostile to both) and sought to export its ideology. Although many factors contributed to the war between Iraq and Iran, a powerful underlying cause was the threat posed to a secular nation-state (Iraq) by the transnational revolutionary movement represented by the Islamic Republic of Iran.

The end of the Cold War removed one element of tension from the Middle East (that of superpower rivalry) but also removed an important element of stability: the shared commitment of the United States and the Soviet Union to the regional state system and to certain restraints on conflict. The fact that the Cold War ended with the political collapse of one of the superpowers (the Soviet Union) also made it easier for the remaining superpower (the United States) to consider direct military intervention in the Middle East. During the Cold War, direct intervention by either superpower would have risked a potentially cataclysmic confrontation.

The conflicts that have plagued the Middle East since the end of the Cold War have been decidedly different in nature from the mostly interstate wars of the earlier decades. Nevertheless, they still reflect the five enduring elements of Middle East conflict in the modern world. Among the most significant post–Cold War conflicts are the Palestinian intifadas (1989 and 2000), popular uprisings that demonstrated the growing power of nonstate actors and popular discontent. While the first intifada led to the first serious Israeli-Palestinian peace process, the second, more violent uprising—coming in the wake of the collapse of the peace process—led to the destruction of the Palestinian economy and increased the influence of extremist elements on both sides.

Iraq's 1991 invasion of Kuwait, which had its roots in the nations' British-delineated borders, was significant on several counts. First, it was the first full-scale attack by one Arab country against another. This is not to say that the Arab states had lived in neighborly peace for the preceding decades—skirmishes and confrontations had occurred between Algeria and Morocco, Jordan and Syria, Egypt and Libya, Saudi Arabia and Yemen—but none of these incidents compared to Saddam Hussein's naked military invasion of Kuwait and his claims that Kuwait was Iraqi territory. For not only was Saddam openly invading a fellow member of the Arab League, he also was challenging the sanctity of the region's borders as they were drawn by European powers.

Saddam's recklessness was met by a rare unified opposition among most Arab states and a U.S.-led counterattack that both drove Iraqi forces out of Kuwait and started the process of bringing down Saddam's Baathist regime (a process completed in 2003 with the U.S. invasion of Iraq). The Iraqi invasion and the U.S. response highlight both the enduring elements of Middle East conflict as well as the changes brought about by the end of the Cold War. The enduring elements were the fragile state system and the ongoing tension between transnational movements (in this case, the secular Baathist movement) and more conservative or traditional regimes (the Kuwaiti sheikhdom). The most significant change brought about by the end of the Cold War was the reduced risk of superpower confrontation, which allowed the United States to do what would have been unthinkable a mere five years earlier: attack an Arab state (one that had been a loyal Soviet ally, no less) and station thousands of troops in the Persian Gulf region.

The first decade of the 21st century brought an outbreak of new conflicts in the Middle East, all of which reflect the enduring elements of regional conflict but also reveal changing realities. The Israeli-Palestinian conflict was renewed in 2000 as a much more violent uprising, with a growing religious component, especially after the marginalization and death of the secular PLO chairman Yasser Arafat in 2004 and the continuing rise of religious and ethnonationalist parties in Israel. Israel's attempts to respond to what was in effect a popular uprising by using conventional military means led to thousands of civilian deaths and massive destruction but failed to create conditions for a peaceful resolution. It also helped solidify the growing power of the Islamic movement Hamas.

The second U.S.-Iraq war in 2003, this time launched to bring about the overthrow of the Saddam Hussein regime, was in part a U.S. reaction to the terrorist attacks of September 11, 2001 (attacks conducted by a nonstate actor, al-Qaeda, but with no Iraqi involvement). It succeeded in overthrowing the Baathist regime but at the cost of triggering a sectarian civil war in Iraq and leaving U.S. forces stuck in an unwinnable conflict. While Iraq later established a representative government and a modicum of day-to-day stability, it is far from certain that Saddam's former realm will remain a unified and peaceful state. More significantly for the future, the fall of the Baathist regime paved the way for an electoral takeover of Iraq by the majority Shia, who are religiously allied with and supported by Iran. For the first time in centuries, the Middle East is confronted by a possible Sunni-Shia confrontation, as the major Sunni powers—Saudi Arabia, Egypt, and Jordan—have vowed to prevent Iranian influence from expanding and to protect their Sunni co-religionists in Iraq.

Israel's invasion of Lebanon in 2006 in response to provocations from Hezbollah, a heavily armed Lebanese Shia political party, demonstrated the power of nonstate actors to control the agenda. Although the war was between Hezbollah and Israel, it was the Lebanese state system that suffered the most damage. Similarly, the Sunni-dominated

Palestinian Hamas Party (a nonstate actor, albeit one that controls the Gaza Strip) has become Israel's principal opponent in its struggle with the Palestinians—and also the opponent of Palestinian moderates led by the Fatah Party, despite the fact that Hamas and Fatah have tried to negotiate a coalition agreement. Israel has been forced to come up with a way to respond to Hamas's provocations and rejectionist positions without completely undermining the Fatah leadership, lest it destroy the last elements of Palestinian secular moderation.

After the Israeli-Palestinian conflict, the longest-running major confrontation in the Middle East is between the United States and Iran. This conflict, like other Middle Eastern conflicts, has multiple causes, starting with the anti-U.S. theme of the 1979 Iranian Revolution. But the underlying cause is U.S. opposition to the rise of a regional hegemon that is pursuing a nuclear weapons capability, especially one that is led by a theocratic regime hostile to the United States, Israel, and moderate Arab regimes. Indeed, one of the major themes of U.S. foreign policy in the Middle East in the post–Cold War era has been the desire to prevent the rise of *any* regional hegemon, be it Iraq's secular regime or Iran's theocratic one, as well as to prevent the rise of any power that might pose a threat to Israel.

The most powerful current trend in Middle East conflict is its growing ethnic, intercommunal and religious characterization—in short, issues of identity. Not surprisingly, perhaps, as identity politics tends to arise out of "the disintegration or erosion of modern state structures, especially centralized, authoritarian states."[3] The transformation of the Israeli-Palestinian conflict is a case in point: in its early years, this conflict was one between nation states; today, it has transformed into an intercommunal and, increasingly, a religious conflict. As part of this trend, nonstate actors and political movements are in some instances becoming more powerful than states and are challenging state authority. The clearest examples are the Shia Hezbollah movement in Lebanon; Moqtada al-Sadr's Shia movement in Iraq; the Sunni Hamas Party in Palestine; and the Kurdish nationalist movement in northern Iraq (some scholars argue that Al Jazeera, the pan-Arab television network based in Qatar, serves as a nonstate actor with considerable influence[4]). States no longer have a monopoly on violence, one of the defining elements of sovereignty, nor on social services, one of the defining elements of centralized state systems. Islamic groups, especially, have built countersocieties to challenge the state indirectly by providing services traditionally offered by central governments, including health care and education.[5] Even more significantly, nonstate actors have appeared to be more successful in confronting perceived threats and provocations from the West and Israel, demonstrating that "movements can do what states failed to do."[6]

In August 2006, the Ibn Khaldoun Center in Cairo polled 1,700 Egyptians on the question, "Who is the most important leader in the Middle East?" The top five answers were: Haasan Nasrallah, leader of the Lebanese group Hezbollah; Mahmoud Ahmadinejad, president of Iran; Khaled Meshal, leader of Hamas; the late Osama bin Laden, mastermind of al-Qaeda; and Mohamed Mahdi Akef, leader of the banned Egyptian Muslim Brotherhood. Only one of the top five—Ahmadinejad—was leader of a state. As the center noted in releasing the poll results:

> While subject to future fluctuations, these Egyptian findings suggest the direction in which the region is moving. The Arab people do not respect the ruling

regimes, perceiving them to be autocratic, corrupt and inept. They are, at best, ambivalent about the fanatical Islamists of the bin Laden variety. More mainstream Islamists with broad support, developed civic dispositions and services to provide are the most likely actors in building a new Middle East. In fact, they are already doing so through the Justice and Development Party in Turkey, the similarly named PJD in Morocco, the Muslim Brotherhood in Egypt, Hamas in Palestine and, yes, Hezbollah in Lebanon.[7]

Clearly, Middle East conflict is taking on an increasingly religious cast. But this does not mean that religious dogma or theocratic debates are at the root of conflict. As French Middle East scholar Gilles Kepel has noted, "perhaps religion is only the crystallization of far larger conflicts: the language in which to express, for lack of a better alternative, the vast disquiet in the civilization of Muslim societies."[8] More broadly, Clement Henry claims that the Middle East has become "the new battle ground for contending visions of the new global order," in which fears that globalization represents a new form of imperialism will create tension both within societies and between global cultures.[9]

A final element of instability—and thus a potential source of conflict—that has arisen in the 21st-century Middle East is the people power movement, both internally driven as well as externally promoted. The regional uprisings that began 2011 have been widely described as democracy movements, but mere opposition to antidemocratic leaders or regimes does not make one a democrat, and it is not yet clear whether the revolutions of 2011 will lead to forms of government that will mirror liberal Western democracies; they could just as easily lead to new autocracies (of a secular or theocratic model) or to civil wars. Nevertheless, there is no doubt that the clamor for more representative government and less suppression of personal freedoms is genuine, especially among the region's younger generations, and is motivated by widespread and deep discontent—over economic prospects and corruption, in particular. And even if these movements do aspire to establish democracies, not only are "democratizing states more prone to instability than are authoritarian ones,"[10] but the very process of democratization can be wrought with instability and violence. The greatest risk, perhaps, is that new more representative governments prove unable to remedy the urgent problems so many Middle Eastern societies confront, resulting in cynicism and renewed discontent (and quite possibly a return to some form of authoritarian rule). Democratization processes also may empower transnational movements that have questionable commitment to sustaining democracy over the long term, even if they are eager participants in electoral processes in the short term. In particular, the assumption among many scholars that Islamism and democracy are incompatible—an assumption that has proven wrong in Turkey and Indonesia—will be tested in the Middle East.

Authoritarian regimes in the Middle East are committed to the twin and related goals of preserving the nation-state as well as their own elite position within it. It is no surprise that they have traditionally resisted democratization processes that risk undermining both goals. But their ability to resist popular opposition is being threatened by the growing widespread use of technological means of communications, such as social networking, and the access many ordinary people have to satellite television broadcasts, even in countries where satellite dishes are officially prohibited. The unrest in Tunisia and Egypt in early 2011 that led to the stunningly rapid (and amazingly peaceful) demise of the Ben Ali and Mubarak governments demonstrated how fundamentally fragile authoritarian governments may be, despite outward appearances of strength, and how effectively modern technology can be used as a tool of mobilization for disaffected populations. Even the rigidly authoritarian regime of Bashar al-Assad in Syria could not suppress a popular movement that was well aware of developments in Tunisia and Egypt and, despite tight strictures, was able to use communication technology effectively.

Taken together, these new characteristics of Middle East conflict—which reflect the changing dynamics of the post–Cold War Middle East—mean that it will become increasingly difficult to distinguish between internal and external conflicts; between terrorist groups and legitimate nonstate actors; between national and sectarian interests; and between state and clan. It also is likely that more black swan events will characterize the Middle East in coming years, events that are unforeseen but develop rapidly and with enduring and sometimes profound consequences.

Subsequent chapters will look at each country in the Middle East, from Morocco to Iran, and assess the conflict situations, both internal and external, that characterize the respective society and polity. Some of these conflicts will be exacerbated by democratization processes; others will become more stable under conditions of more representative government and increased personal freedoms. The Middle East never has been accurately predictable and is even less so today. The best we can do is to understand the factors that have shaped the region's history, the conflicts that have ensued from them, and the unique variables that characterize each state; doing so will at least allow us to speculate on how regional change might play out.

NOTES

1. The concept of a black swan event is developed by Nassim Nicholas Taleb in his brilliant book, *The Black Swan* (New York: Random House, 2007).

2. For an excellent overview of the creation of the modern Middle East, see Arthur Goldschmidt, *A Concise History of the Middle East,* 7th ed. (Boulder, CO: Westview Press, 2002).

3. Mary Kaldor, *New and Old Wars: Organized Violence in a Global Era* (Stanford, CA: Stanford University Press, 1999), 78.

4. See Mohammed Zayani, ed., *The Al-Jazeera Phenomenon* (Boulder, CO: Paradigm Publishers, 2005).

5. See Raymond Hinnebusch, "The Politics of Identity in Middle East International Relations," in *International Relations of the Middle East,* ed. Louise Fawcett (New York: Oxford University Press, 2005).

6. Mamoun Fandy, "Beware the 'Contagion' Spreading in the Middle East," *Financial Times* (October 10, 2006).

7. Quote from Saad Eddin Ibrahim, *Washington Post* (August 23, 2006). Poll information from Ibn Khaldoun Center website: www.eicds.org.

8. Gilles Kepel, *Bad Moon Rising* (London: Saqi Books, 2003), 11.

9. Clement Henry, "The Clash of Globalizations in the Middle East," in Fawcett, *International Relations of the Middle East,* 106–7.

10. Augustus Richard Norton, "The Puzzle of Political Reform in the Middle East," in Fawcett, *International Relations of the Middle East.*

1 EGYPT

Egypt is the largest and arguably the most important country in the Arab world. It also is one of the few nations in the Middle East whose identity and rough boundaries have been established for many centuries—dating back to 3000 BCE and the unification of upper and lower Egypt. As the Egyptian diplomat Tahsin Bashir once said, "Egypt is the only nation-state in the Arab World; the rest are just tribes with flags."[1] This perception gives Egypt a certain aura of stability and consistency in a region better known for rapid and often unpredictable change. But this aura of permanence and stability sometimes obscures the fact that Egypt has been heavily influenced by outside forces, beginning with the Arab conquest in the seventh century CE, which introduced Islam to what was then a largely Christian country (a large minority of Coptic Christians continues to live in Egypt). The Arab conquest also introduced the Arabic language to Egypt and, through centuries of intermarriage, transformed the country into an Arab nation.

The Ottoman Empire took control of Egypt in the 16th century and, at least officially, was the sovereign power until the time of World War I. In reality, however, the Ottoman Empire suffered a long and slow decline, and, as it did, other European powers—France and Britain, in particular—secured dominant roles in Egypt. In 1914, Egypt became a British protectorate, and in 1922 it was granted formal independence. But British troops remained in Egypt, concentrated along the strategically important Suez Canal (which was operated by a joint Anglo-French company), and British influence was ubiquitous throughout Egyptian government institutions.

In 1952, a group of Egyptian army officers staged a coup against the government of King Farouk, an ineffectual monarch propped up by British support. By 1954, Col. Gamal Abdel Nasser had maneuvered into the top position and became president of the new Egyptian republic. Nasser was a charismatic and idealistic leader whose ambition was to lead not only Egypt but the entire Arab world in a new revolutionary

Arab nationalist movement aimed at removing the vestiges of colonial control (which included the State of Israel) and instituting a strong statist and socialist economic system. He negotiated for the withdrawal of British troops from Egypt, and once this was accomplished, he nationalized the Suez Canal in 1956. This action led to war when Egypt was attacked by a joint British-French-Israeli coalition intent on regaining control over the canal, but under U.S. and international pressure, the coalition withdrew its forces, thus solidifying Egyptian sovereignty over the canal. Nasser's victory against the coalition also solidified his position as the leader of Arab nationalism, and his popularity soared not only in Egypt but throughout the Arab world.

Egyptian troops had fought alongside other Arab forces against the new State of Israel in the 1948 Middle East war, but it was not until Nasser's rise to power and the subsequent 1956 war that Israel became the bête noire of Egyptian foreign policy—and the focus for Nasser's movement to unify the Arab world. To Nasser, Israel represented the last vestiges of colonialism in the Arab world, and his rhetoric grew increasingly hostile to both Israel and the United States. Egypt became a de facto ally of the Soviet Union, and by the late 1960s, thousands of Soviet military advisers were stationed in the country. Nasser's popularity spread far beyond Egypt's borders, and Nasserist movements and political parties were established in a number of other Arab states.

In June 1967, Israel responded to perceived Egyptian provocations by launching a surprise attack against Egypt, Syria, and Jordan that ended in a humiliating defeat for the Arab armies and for Nasser personally; when the dust settled after a mere six days, Israel had seized control of Egypt's Sinai Peninsula right up to the Suez Canal, as well as Syria's Golan Heights and the West Bank of the Jordan River.

Nasser died suddenly in 1970 and was succeeded by his vice president, Anwar Sadat. Although a member of the 1952 military junta, Sadat was far less ideological than Nasser and less interested in a broader Arab world leadership role. He quickly came to the conclusion that resolving the conflict with Israel would better allow Egypt to address its serious economic and social problems, which Nasser's socialist economy had failed to solve. Sadat also was suspicious of Soviet intentions and shocked Moscow by demanding a withdrawal of Soviet military personnel from Egypt. He also took steps to liberalize the economy and reverse some of the statist policies that had characterized the Nasser years. After unsuccessfully extending some peace feelers, Sadat determined that the only way to bring about the return of Egyptian territory would be to launch another war—not with the goal of destroying Israel but rather to regain Egyptian honor and to force the international community to address the issue.

Sadat's 1973 surprise attack in the Sinai—in collaboration with Syria's surprise attack in the Israeli-occupied Golan Heights—was only partially successful on the battlefield. But it succeeded brilliantly in attracting the interest of the United States and the Soviet Union and led to direct U.S. engagement in Arab-Israeli peacemaking. Sadat shocked the world in 1977 by flying to Israel and addressing the Israeli Knesset (parliament). Two years later, after intensive U.S. mediation under President Jimmy Carter, Egypt and Israel signed their historic peace agreement.

The peace agreement with Israel brought to an end the single greatest external military threat to Egypt and greatly reduced the prospects for Egypt's involvement in an interstate war. But it also led to Egypt's rejection by and subsequent isolation from the broader Arab world—a 180-degree change from Nasser's regional leadership role. Moreover, internal sources of conflict were growing, as evidenced by the assassination of Sadat in 1981 by members of a radical Islamist group who had infiltrated the Egyptian armed forces. Egypt had been the home to an important Islamist movement—the Muslim Brotherhood—since the 1920s. The Brotherhood took the form of a political party in 1939 but was banned and oppressed by Nasser in 1954. From 1984 until 2011, the Brotherhood was allowed to operate as a religious and social organization but not as a political party; Brotherhood sympathizers, however, ran for the Egyptian parliament as independents.

The 1979 Iranian Revolution inspired Islamist activists throughout the Middle East and led to the formation of several new radical groups in Egypt, including the Islamic Jihad, the group that claimed responsibility for the assassination of Sadat. Thus, the signing of the peace agreement with Israel and the assassination of Sadat marked a turning point in Egyptian security concerns: from external (war with Israel) to internal (the threat from Islamist radicals). It also marked the end of the Nasser era of regional secular nationalism. While other countries, such as Syria and Iraq, tried to assume the mantle of secular regional leadership, no other nation had Egypt's status and power, or Nasser's charisma. This phenomenon left a void in terms of pan-Arab secular politics that regional Islamist movements have attempted to fill ever since.

Sadat's successor, Hosni Mubarak, ruled Egypt from 1981 until he was ousted by the military following several weeks of mass popular unrest in early 2011. Mubarak sought to repair ties with the Arab world that had been broken with the signing of the peace treaty with Israel while simultaneously maintaining relations with Israel; in this he was largely successful. In the face of a growing number of terrorist attacks by Islamist radicals, he also launched a severe crackdown against Islamist groups in the 1990s. This crackdown largely succeeded, but not before more than 1,000 people were killed. By 2000, Mubarak appeared to have achieved internal security, but it was based on the existence of a pervasive security service, electoral manipulation, and the suppression of opposition voices (secular as well as Islamic).

Egypt's underlying social, demographic, and economic problems—combined with a political system that allowed little room for legitimate opposition—created conditions that proved ripe for unrest. Rumors that the elderly President Mubarak was laying the ground for his son, Gamal, to succeed him became a further source of frustration and resentment. With the rapid overthrow of Tunisia's president Ben Ali in January 2011 serving as an inspiration, Egyptian activists—mostly young, urban, and college educated—launched a nonviolent protest movement that grew rapidly. The Egyptian military, the backbone of the regime's political power since the 1952 revolution and an institution whose principal concern is security and order, refused to act against the protesters. Faced with this opposition from his erstwhile colleagues, Mubarak begrudgingly resigned.

While Egyptians take pride in calling the events of early 2011 a revolution, what occurred in fact more resembles a soft military coup. But regardless of how the events are termed, there is no doubt that the resignation of Mubarak ushered in a new era, one that is driven by advocates of democratization as well as by supporters of an Islamic polity. The Supreme Council of the Armed Forces (SCAF), a wholly military-run

Egyptians protest in front of an army tank in Cairo's Tahrir Square in January 2011, just days before Hosni Mubarak stepped down as president. Egypt's revolution helped launch the "Arab Spring." (AP Photo/ Ahmed Ali)

body, secured a modicum of order after the initial revolutionary fervor dissipated. But as Egyptians debated the timing and mechanisms of democratic elections, the SCAF came to be seen with growing distrust. Indeed, a key issue hovering over Egypt's political future is the degree to which the military will eventually return to the barracks and allow a civilian, popularly elected government to run the country; by late 2011, this issue had become the most heatedly debated of all of Egypt's unanswered questions. Even after multiparty parliamentary elections in November 2011, one thing seems certain: the Egyptian military will not in the immediate future become a disinterested actor under civilian institutional control.

Whatever form of government eventually emerges in Egypt, it will have to negotiate a number of internal conflicts, redefine Egypt's regional role, and address economic frustrations.

COPTIC-MUSLIM CONFLICT

Coptic Christians make up about 9 percent of Egypt's total population of just over 80 million.[2] The Coptic denomination traces its roots to the earliest years of Christianity, and its liturgy is closely related to those of the Ethiopian and Eritrean Christian Churches. Until the Arab Muslim invasion in the seventh century, Copts were the predominant organized religion in Egypt. The Arab invasion launched a slow process of Arabization and Islamization that transformed Egypt into the nation it is today; but a sizeable Coptic minority has continued to thrive (the ancient Coptic language, however, has been replaced by Arabic, except for liturgical purposes).

The Coptic community has experienced ups and downs in its relationship with the Muslim majority. Although the Egyptian constitution guarantees freedom of religion, it also declares Islam as the official religion of Egypt and Islamic law (or sharia) as the basis of Egyptian law. Many Copts, especially those living in Egypt's more cosmopolitan cities such as Cairo and Alexandria, have been successful in business and politics. Among Egypt's most prominent Copts is Boutros Boutros Ghali, former Minister of State for Foreign Affairs and later secretary general of the United Nations. Copts always hold several seats in Egypt's parliament, although these usually are seats appointed by the president, not the result of popular election. But even Copts who have risen to high levels in Egyptian society often complain about glass ceilings and other informal prejudice against them.

Many of the key leaders of Egypt's nationalist movement in the 1920s and 1930s, who fought for true independence from Britain, were Coptic. During the Nasser years, Copts fared well, benefiting from Nasser's emphasis on secular socialism and his suppression of political Islamist groups, such as the Muslim Brotherhood. But the relationship between Copts and Muslims took a new and darker direction with the rise of radical political Islam in the late 1970s. In an effort to temper the rising power of political Islam, President Sadat allowed the Muslim Brotherhood to reorganize, at least unofficially, and parliament passed a law reaffirming sharia as the basis of Egyptian law. Muslim activists started to accuse the Copts of building illegal churches (under Egyptian law, churches can be constructed only with the approval of the government).

Sadat's visit to Jerusalem in 1977, followed in 1979 by the overthrow of the shah of Iran in an Islamic Revolution, led to open hostility toward the Sadat government among Islamists. Much of the hostility was expressed by attacks against the Coptic community, which was accused of being pro-Western and anti-Islam. In the summer of 1981, a riot broke out in a mixed Coptic-Muslim area of Cairo when rumors spread that Coptic Christians were planning to build a church on a site intended for a mosque; scores of people were killed before security forces took control. Sadat responded by arresting leaders of both the Coptic church as well as the Muslim Brotherhood.

For the ensuing 30 years, clashes between Muslims and Copts have occurred periodically, often reflecting the state of relations between the government and Islamist radicals. In periods during which Islamist extremists have been active, Copts have frequently been targeted—especially in certain rural areas of the country, where Muslims and Copts live in close proximity and where the government's control is less tight than in the cities. It is not uncommon for churches to be attacked by Islamist extremists.

A few of these incidents have been quite serious: in 1998 and again in 2000, sectarian clashes in the town of El-Kosheh left over 20 people dead and hundreds arrested. Many of the Copts who were detained by police claimed that they were tortured. Conflict usually is sparked by accusations of conversion—both Copts and Muslims accuse the other side of trying to convert its believers[3]—as well as reactions to attempts by Copts to build or rehabilitate churches. Economics may play a role as well: in much of rural southern Egypt, Copts in the towns work as merchants selling goods to the local Muslim farmers. Even cultural issues may cause sectarian friction: in Alexandria in 2006, thousands of Muslims protested outside the main Coptic church, where a play about religious conversion was being performed.

Coptic-Muslim relations took a dramatically new turn for the worse on January 1, 2011, when a car bomb detonated in front of a Coptic church as worshippers left a service, killing over 20 and injuring scores more. The Mubarak government quickly condemned the attack and blamed it on foreign elements—and indeed, the nature of the attack did bear resemblance to al-Qaeda operations—but Copts throughout Egypt used the tragedy as an opportunity to express their fears and frustrations.

The revolution that overthrew the Mubarak government was initially celebrated as a unifying event, as Copts and Muslims participated together in the mass protests at Tahrir Square. But over the course of 2011, several incidents, most involving attacks on churches by Islamic extremists (see below), raised the specter of sectarian strife. In October 2011, the Egyptian Army aimed lethal fire on Copt protesters, further elevating tensions.

Relations between Copts and Muslims will likely remain tense at times, although the majority in each community will generally remain immune from direct confrontation. The degree to which violent incidents continue to erupt will depend largely upon Egypt's ability to deal with the Islamist extremist movement and groups inside the country as well as the risk posed by foreign terrorist groups. Any rise in Islamist radicalism (such as the *salafist* movement, see below), or even significant electoral success by the more moderate Muslim Brotherhood, will have an immediate and direct impact on the Copts' sense of security and on Coptic-Muslim relations. A new Egyptian constitution almost certainly will carve out a prominent role for Islam (which would merely be a recognition of social reality), but Egypt's Copts hope that the constitution also includes strong civil liberties and a commitment to religious tolerance. If it doesn't, the Coptic community will feel further anxiety and some of its more wealthy members may seek to emigrate.

Support for Copts in the United States—especially among members of Congress—will mean that violence directed against them may also have a negative effect on U.S.-Egyptian relations. Ironically, public support for the Copts by U.S. politicians may actually serve to worsen their relations with Muslims, who may view such support as a sign of Coptic collusion with the United States.

IRAN

Egypt and Iran have never, and are unlikely to ever, come into direct conflict due to the great physical distance between the two nations. Nevertheless, the two states have shared a relationship of mutual animosity ever since the 1979 Iranian Revolution; the roots of the enmity stretch back even further, to an ancient historical competition for influence in the broader Middle East. As the two largest and most influential Middle Eastern states, Egypt and Iran are destined to view each other in a wary and competitive way, regardless of their respective forms of government. Both states will continue to strive for leadership on such issues as Israeli-Palestinian peace as well as for influence with the energy-rich Gulf states.

The fissures in Egyptian-Iranian relations are many: Egypt is Arab, Iran predominantly Persian; Egyptians are overwhelmingly Sunni Muslims, Iranians Shiite Muslims; since the late 1970s, Egypt has been an ally of the United States, while Iran has been America's arch enemy in the region since 1979; Egypt supports moderate and conservative governments in the Middle East, Iran is the self-anointed leader of many of the region's most radical movements; Egypt has been victimized by Islamist extremist terror, Iran is a state supporter of many terrorist organizations. Clearly, the Egyptian-Iranian relationship is not one based on trust and friendship.

For a very brief period—from around 1974 to 1979—Egypt and Iran shared an alliance with the United States, opposition to the Soviet Union, and a moderate political agenda in the region. But this affinity was short-lived. The 1979 Iranian Revolution, whose leaders vowed to export their revolution to the entire Islamic world, greatly concerned the Egyptian leadership, which already was dealing with a resurgence of Islamist radicalism in Egypt. Relations between the new Islamic Republic of Iran and Egypt took an immediate negative turn when President Sadat granted asylum to the deposed shah of Iran. Iran broke diplomatic relations with Egypt in 1980 and condemned Egypt's signing of the Camp David Accords with Israel. Some Iranian leaders called for Sadat's overthrow and later openly celebrated when Sadat was assassinated in 1981. A street in the Iranian capital of Tehran was named after one of Sadat's assassins.

When Iraq invaded Iran in 1980, thereby launching a bloody eight-year war, Egypt openly sided with the Iraqis and provided support to the government of Saddam Hussein (as did the United States), further embittering the Iranian regime. Egypt repeatedly accused Iranian agents of facilitating Islamist extremist activities in Egypt and claimed that Iran was harboring and training Egyptian terrorists.

A brief rapprochement occurred in 2000, when President Mubarak and Iranian president Mohammad Khatami conducted a telephone summit, followed by several meetings of the two countries' foreign ministers and a face-to-face meeting between Mubarak and Khatami in late 2003. Khatami was a moderate, at least by the standards of the Islamic Republic of Iran, and was taking concerted efforts to patch up Iran's frayed ties in the region.

The election of the radical Mahmoud Ahmadinejad as president of Iran in 2005 initially put Egyptian-Iranian relations back on ice. And as the situation in Iraq worsened following the 2003 U.S. invasion, Iran's support for that country's Shia forces further concerned Egypt, which, along with Saudi Arabia and Jordan, views itself as a defender of Iraq's Sunni community. Egypt opposed the U.S. attack on Iraq, in large part because it correctly foresaw that the fall of Saddam would most likely usher in a Shiite-dominated government, which in turn would increase Iranian influence in an important Arab country. As that fear comes true, Egyptian officials worry about the resulting shift in regional power to Iran.

Egyptian officials also are concerned about Iran's influence over the Palestinian Sunni Islamist group Hamas as well as the Lebanese Shiite political movement Hezbollah. Both of these groups are opposed to the more politically moderate forces in their respective societies that Egypt supports. Relations with these organizations also bear implications for the regional leadership roles that both Iran and Egypt seek. While Iran's prestige in the Arab world has grown as a result of its patronage of these groups, Egypt's image has suffered, particularly due to the perception of its complicity in the Israeli blockade of the Hamas-controlled Gaza Strip. On one level, the Egyptian government is concerned with Hamas and Hezbollah as harbingers of the rising power of

Islamist political movements in the region; the Mubarak regime feared that such organizations represent an indirect threat to the Egyptian government as potential role models and inspiration for Islamist movements in Egypt. On another level, there were indications that Iranian-backed agitation was more directly aimed at the Egyptian regime. In April 2009, the Egyptian government claimed to have uncovered a Hezbollah cell operating along the border with Gaza, allegedly supplying Hamas with Iranian arms.[4] President Hosni Mubarak responded with an address in which he issued a warning to any regional powers—widely understood to mean Hezbollah and its Iranian backers—interfering in Egyptian affairs.[5]

Egypt also has expressed concern over Iran's alleged attempts to develop nuclear weapons. While Egypt would be unlikely to be a target of an Iranian nuclear attack, Iran's possession of nuclear weapons would vastly expand the Islamic Republic's influence, prestige, and ability to persuade (or coerce) other actors in the region. It is possible that Egypt would seriously consider the development of a nuclear weapons program in the event that Iran becomes a nuclear power, although officially Egypt still advocates for a nuclear-free Middle East and is a signatory to the Nuclear Non-Proliferation Treaty (NPT). Any movement by Egypt away from the NPT or any indications that Egypt is developing a nuclear weapons program would have serious implications for Egypt's relations with Israel and other states in the area, and indeed could spark a regional nuclear arms race. The desire to avoid such a development is the primary motive behind Egypt's opposition to Iranian acquisition of nuclear weapons.

Because Egypt and Iran do not share a border and neither country possesses a navy capable of distant deployment, a direct military confrontation between the two countries is unlikely (the acquisition of nuclear weapons or long-range missiles by either side, however, would render a direct military confrontation possible, if unlikely). In April 2011, the interim Egyptian government that was installed after Mubarak's ouster announced a reopening of diplomatic relations with Iran. This move was more likely a signal that post-Mubarak Egypt would pursue an independent foreign policy (and one less tied to U.S. and Israeli interests) than was the case under Mubarak. The exchange of ambassadors will not remove the underlying tensions in the relationship, although it will create a better atmosphere and reduce the chances of misunderstanding. The cold war between the two Middle Eastern powers, fought largely via diplomacy and, at times, proxy conflicts (such as in Lebanon or Palestine, or internally within Egypt through Iranian support of extremists) will likely continue regardless of the ultimate victor in Egypt's leadership contest,[6] and there remains the danger that this regional cold war could become a nuclear standoff in the event that both countries pursue nuclear weapons programs.

INTERNAL CONFLICT WITH ISLAMIST RADICALISM

Political Islam has a long history in Egypt. The Organization of the Muslim Brothers—known informally as the Muslim Brotherhood—was established in 1928 by Hassan al-Banna. The Brotherhood grew rapidly and, by the 1940s, was one of the most powerful political movements in Egypt. The Egyptian monarchy—and, more importantly, the British—tolerated the Brotherhood and even cooperated with the group on certain issues. The Brotherhood was incensed by the creation of Israel in 1948, and many of its members volunteered to fight in Palestine during the 1948–1949 war. Although the Egyptian armed forces also fought against Israel, Egyptian leaders were concerned by the radicalization and militarization of the Brotherhood; the organization was banned in 1948.

Brotherhood leaders supported the 1952 coup that put Nasser in power, and briefly they were allowed to operate openly. But before long, Nasser's goals of secular Arab nationalism and socialism led the Brotherhood into opposition, and, in 1954, the Brotherhood was once again banned. But Nasser's regime went far beyond merely banning the Brotherhood: it launched a repressive campaign against the group's leadership and members, leading to thousands of arrests and executions. Instead of destroying the Brotherhood, however, this campaign against it only further radicalized its members, many of whom spent years in jail.

One of these imprisoned brothers was Sayyid Qutb. While in prison awaiting execution, Qutb developed a new theory of political Islam that would become influential not only within the Islamist movement in Egypt but throughout the Middle East. Qutb claimed that the world is divided into two groups—Muslims and nonbelievers—who will be in conflict until Islam reigns supreme. More significantly, Qutb claimed that none of the existing Arab governments were true Muslim regimes because of their westernization and pursuit of such non-Islamic ideologies as capitalism and socialism. Qutb called on Muslims to launch a holy war—or jihad—against these false Muslim governments, beginning with the government of Egypt. Qutb was executed in 1966, but his ideas have lived on.[7] Many, perhaps even a majority of Muslim brothers, continued to support a peaceful form of Islamist politics. But Qutb's ideas resonated with a minority that started to espouse violence as the only means to crate a truly Islamic state.

In 1971, President Sadat released many of the Brotherhood prisoners in an attempt to reach out to the more religious elements in Egyptian society as well as to counter the still powerful influence of the Nasser-era socialists. But the Brotherhood's members were unhappy with Sadat's growing allegiance to the United States after 1974, and Egypt's peace treaty with Israel. Moderate members of the Brotherhood—the majority—responded by trying to create a political network to challenge the government. But the more extremist followers of Qutb—some of whom had broken from the Brotherhood and formed new, more radical organizations—began a campaign of violence and terrorism that lasted for over two decades.

Starting around 1974, Egypt experienced regular terrorist incidents committed by Islamist extremists. Perhaps the most spectacular such incident was the 1981 assassination of President Sadat by Islamist militants who had infiltrated the armed forces. Attacks against Copts and their churches also frequently occurred. The ranks of the radical Islamists were boosted in the late 1980s by Egyptians who had volunteered in Afghanistan's war against invading Soviet forces. These volunteers returned to their native land inspired by the success of the Islamist resistance in defeating the Soviet Red Army.

The most intense period of Islamist violence in Egypt was between 1992 and 1997, when Islamist extremists conducted a series of violent attacks against foreign tourists, including the killing of 58 tourists in an attack at the ancient site of Luxor in November 1997. By attacking tourists, the extremists were not only expressing their animosity toward Western influences, they also were attempting to undermine one of Egypt's most important sources of revenue, the tourism industry.

Mubarak (who had succeeded Sadat in 1981) responded forcefully, declaring a national state of emergency and conducting a massive campaign to round up and detain Islamist activists. A loose coalition of Islamist groups declared a unilateral cease-fire in 1997—in part because of general public opposition to their tactics and in part because of the government's successful effort at suppression.

Egypt has been largely free of significant Islamist extremist activity since 1997, but Mubarak kept the state of emergency in force (a fact that became a target of criticism by antiregime activists, who believed he used it to suppress all opposition), and Egyptian security forces maintain a close watch over suspected activists and institutions such as al-Azhar, the renowned Islamic university in Cairo. Although terrorist acts have been on the decline in Egypt, the sources of frustration that first attracted some segments of Egyptian society to the extremist movements remain, even after Mubarak's ouster. A series of violent attacks against Coptic Christian targets in the early months after the revolution were blamed on *salafists*, followers of a strict interpretation of Islam similar to the Wahhabism of Saudi Arabia.

The Muslim Brotherhood avoided being in the forefront during the protests of early 2011 and participated fairly in November 2011 elections as a legitimate political party. But a failure by Egypt to successfully transition into a democracy, the failure of a democratic government to meet the needs of Egypt's frustrated and discontent populace, or a severe economic crisis that further expands the number of Egyptians living in poverty and economic distress could conceivably catapult extremist elements to power (perhaps via a second revolution of the economically disenfranchised). Indeed, the salafist Nour Party won a larger than expected vote in the November 2011 elections.

Even if the Brotherhood were to participate in democratic politics (and all indications are that this is their preferred route), other more extremist and violent Islamist elements— such as the *salafist* movement—could be emboldened by a crisis. But the fact that the Brotherhood was legalized in April 2011, thus giving moderate Islamists a voice in politics, will help to minimize the influence of more extremist elements. Moreover, ever since its legalization, the Brotherhood has wrestled with a degree of internal discord and differences of opinion over political strategy, thus showing how movements previously perceived as monolithic often are revealed to be much more diverse when their members are allowed to publicly express themselves and compete legally for political power.

CONFLICT WITH HAMAS IN THE GAZA STRIP

The seizure of political control of the Gaza Strip by the Palestinian Islamist Hamas Party in July 2007 created a serious problem for Egypt. Between 1948 and 1967, Egypt controlled the Gaza Strip, although Gaza's population was overwhelmingly Palestinian, many of whom lived in refugee camps after fleeing or being expelled from their homes in what is now Israel during the 1948 war; Gaza was intended to be part of the Palestinian state envisioned in the 1947 United Nations Partition Plan. Israel seized

Gaza from Egypt in the 1967 Six-Day War and established military rule and a number of civilian Israeli settlements. When Egypt and Israel signed their historic peace treaty in 1979, Egypt renounced all claims over the Gaza Strip and recognized it as Palestinian territory whose future status would be negotiated between Israel and the Palestinians.

Hamas was established in 1987 during the first Palestinian intifada, or uprising, against the Israeli occupation. Hamas's founding leaders had close political and ideological links with the Egyptian Muslim Brotherhood, who had gained influence and contacts in the Gaza Strip during the period of Egyptian control. Hamas, in fact, often is described as an offshoot of the Egyptian Muslim Brotherhood and is known to receive financial and material support from Brotherhood members in Egypt. For this reason, the Mubarak government always regarded Hamas warily. Moreover, Hamas's charter calls for the establishment of an Islamist state in all of historic Palestine, including Israel, and Hamas leaders oppose the Egyptian-Israeli peace treaty. Ironically, in its early years, Hamas received clandestine support from the Israeli military and intelligence agencies, who considered their primary enemy to be Yasser Arafat's Palestine Liberation Organization (PLO). Some Israelis believed that fostering Hamas would weaken the PLO and lead to internal dissent within Gaza; at the time, they did not understand the growing power of Islamist movements in the region.

Hamas's power grew dramatically with the advent of the second intifada in 2000, which coincided with the failure of the Camp David summit between Palestinian Authority (PA) president Yasser Arafat and Israeli prime minister Ehud Barak. Israel's subsequent attempt to destroy the PA and isolate Arafat only further strengthened Hamas, which conducted a series of terrorist attacks against Israel and was seen by many Palestinians—both secular and religious—as the only Palestinian organization that was putting up resistance to the Israeli occupation. Moreover, Hamas was able to provide social services to the people of Gaza that the PA was unable to provide, thanks in large part to financial assistance from Saudi Arabia and Muslim activists from across the world who shared Hamas's objective of establishing an Islamist state in Palestine.

When Israel withdrew from Gaza in 2005, it turned over responsibility for the Egypt-Gaza border to Egyptian and PA security forces, along with a team of European monitors. This development put Egyptians, for the first time since 1967, in direct contact with Gaza, and opened up the possibility for confrontation and conflict.

In 2006, Hamas achieved a major political success when it won the Palestinian legislative elections. The presidency, however, was in the hands of Mahmoud Abbas of the secular Fatah Party. The two parties tried to form a national unity government, but by the summer of 2007, fighting had broken out between forces loyal to Fatah (and armed by the United States) and Hamas militants. In July 2007, Hamas seized control of the Gaza Strip and declared itself rulers of the territory. Egyptian officials regarded this development with concern and feared that Hamas's victory in Gaza would embolden its own Islamist activists.[8]

At the same time, however, Egypt felt it necessary to deal with Hamas and attempted to broker an agreement between Hamas and Fatah that would end their conflict and return Gaza to the control of the PA, but these efforts proved fruitless. This failure transpired as the balancing act between Egyptian government policy toward Hamas and pro-Palestinian sympathies of the Egyptian populace became increasingly tenuous. Israel, with the support of the United States, had imposed a blockade of Gaza when Hamas seized control, and Egypt closed its border with Gaza as a sign of support for the PA. On the one hand, Egypt was loath to deal with Hamas; the government reasoned that legitimizing the Islamist group in the eyes of the Egyptian people could embolden the Brotherhood to demand equal recognition within Egypt as a legitimate political party. But on the other hand, Egypt did not want to appear to be supporting Israel's blockade of Gaza, and Egyptian leaders were aware that Hamas and its charismatic leaders were extremely popular on the streets of Egypt.

The danger that Hamas's rule in Gaza poses for Egypt became clear in January 2008, when over 100,000 Gazans forced their way through the border fence between Egypt and Gaza in a desperate effort to secure food and supplies. Egyptian border police allowed the incursion—which was a brief economic boon to the Egyptian border town at Rafah, whose shops sold out of goods in a matter of hours—but eventually forced the Palestinians to return to Gaza. Israel was concerned about the incident, fearing that Hamas activists acquired new weapons caches in Egypt (Israel had complained for years about weapons being smuggled into Gaza from Egypt). But some Israelis, including its deputy defense minister, suggested that Israel should relinquish all responsibility for Gaza to Egypt. Egyptian leaders strongly rejected this proposal, having no desire to "rescue" Israel by assuming control for the 1.5 million Palestinians in Gaza.[9] Egypt secured the border, sent in border patrol reinforcements, and pledged to prevent such incursions in the future.

Continued hostilities in Gaza have kept the Egyptian government in the very uncomfortable position of acting as border guard for the impoverished population of Gaza. The most notable example of this awkward dynamic occurred in late 2008 and early 2009, when the Israeli military initiated Operation Cast Lead, a ground and air assault intended to root out Hamas militants firing rockets at Israeli towns. The offensive resulted in extensive Palestinian civilian casualties, generating widespread international outcry. Within the Arab world, protests were not singly aimed at Israel, however, but at Egypt as well due to its perceived complicity in the operation, underscoring the widening chasm between Egyptian policies and popular sentiments within the region.[10] In the wake of the conflict, Israel and the United States ratcheted pressure on Egypt to seal the border with Gaza more tightly, particularly with respect to the smuggling of both humanitarian and military goods through tunnels underneath the border. As public outcry over the conditions of Gaza has intensified—for example, in the wake of the Israeli military's lethal raid on a convoy of Turkish ships carrying aid to Gaza in May 2010—Egypt occasionally opened its border with Gaza. However, concerns over both sentimental and literal spillover from Gaza—whether manifested in Hamas's encouragement of Egypt's own Islamist groups or the migration of a large Palestinian population to the Sinai in the event of a humanitarian emergency—continued to figure prominently in Egyptian handling of the situation.

Egypt's military-appointed interim government proved much more responsive to the popular will (the Mubarak regime's perceived close ties with Israel had become a common complaint of opposition activists, although this issue was not a significant motivation behind his ouster). The interim government succeeded in April 2011 in brokering a peace agreement between Fatah and Hamas, to the consternation of Israel, and responded to popular calls by reopening the Gaza border at Rafah. Moreover, the legalization of the Muslim Brotherhood in Egypt lessened the fears of a Hamas "contagion."

The issue of Gaza and Egypt's relationship with Hamas reveals the degree to which Egypt, despite its 30-year peace with Israel, can still be drawn into the unresolved Israeli-Palestinian conflict. It is not inconceivable that Egyptian and Israeli forces could find themselves in direct confrontation in the event that Israel launched another major military operation in Gaza that was combined with an attempt by Gazans to flee to Egypt.

RENEWED CONFLICT WITH ISRAEL

Between 1948 and 1973, Egypt fought four declared wars with Israel, as well as a "war of attrition" and periodic border skirmishes. After President Sadat's surprise visit to Jerusalem in 1977 and the signing of the Camp David peace agreement in 1980, the countries have lived in peace—although a peace that some commentators, mostly Israelis, describe as a "cold peace." Despite multiple potential provocations—Israel's several invasions of Lebanon, the Palestinian intifadas, terrorist attacks—Egypt and Israel have avoided military confrontation and maintained diplomatic relations (during the second intifada from 2000 to 2005, Egypt withdrew its ambassador from Israel in protest but did not sever official relations). The two nations even enjoy a degree of economic and commercial cooperation, and Israeli tourists frequent Egyptian beach resorts and historical sites. This is not to say that a future military conflict is out of the question, but once Israel returned all the Egyptian territory it captured in 1967 in exchange for Egyptian recognition, the most immediate sources of direct conflict were removed. Even during the extremely volatile situation in Gaza in 2007 and 2008, the two nations were careful to avoid a confrontation and to remain in communication about each other's actions.

The biggest risk factors in terms of potential conflict between Egypt and Israel are dramatic changes in government in either or both countries that would lead to a de facto, if not de jure, abrogation of the 1979 peace treaty. For example, were Israel to elect a radical right wing government that chose to pursue a violent program of ethnic cleansing of Palestinians from Gaza and the West Bank, no Egyptian government would be able to stand idly by. While this scenario is not a likely possibility, neither is it an altogether impossible one. Avigdor Lieberman, who assumed the position of minister of foreign affairs after the 2009 elections, has previously advocated the transfer of Israel's Arab population to the West Bank and Gaza.

On the Egyptian side, the political opening that followed the ouster of Hosni Mubarak has allowed anti-Israel voices to speak more freely. There is no question that the Egyptian public never supported the relationship with Israel to the same degree that the Mubarak regime did, and this became apparent in the early days of the post-Mubarak period, when Egyptians began to call for an investigation into the agreement negotiated under Mubarak by which Egypt provides Israel with natural gas supplies at favorable prices. Egypt's policy toward Gaza, which essentially was supportive of Israeli policy, also was called into question. Free and open elections in Egypt could bring to power a government either run by, or beholden to, Islamist groups. The Muslim Brotherhood, which is considered by most analysts to be a moderate Islamist movement, has officially rejected the Egyptian-Israeli peace treaty as well as Israel's right to exist. At a bare minimum, such a government in Egypt would initiate a period of frosty relations between the two countries.

But perhaps the greatest cause for concern when considering the possibility of renewed Israeli-Egyptian conflict is the fact that most Egyptians do not approve of their country's peace with Israel and are outraged at Israel's policies toward the Palestinians.[11] Particularly in the wake of the Israeli assault on the Gaza Strip in January 2009 (Operation Cast Lead), the lethal botched Israeli raid on a Gaza-bound aid boat in 2010, and the August 2011 Israeli attack on a militant gang operating on its southern border with Egypt that left five Egyptian soldiers dead, popular animosity toward Israel could be used as a rallying call by political parties, secular or religious. And if a party that openly opposes the peace treaty—such as the Muslim Brotherhood—were to come to power, it would know that popular opinion already is in support of its position.

But the possibility of a war with Israel is extremely slim. A country cannot fight a war without the army's willingness, and there is no indication that the Egyptian army has any interest in an armed conflict and would be unlikely to take any actions that would risk it. Moreover, the United States is the principal arms supplier to Egypt, and the military would risk severing this relationship if it were to take a hostile stance

Egyptian soldiers stand guard outside the Israeli embassy in Cairo as protesters wave the Palestinian flag. Democratic freedoms in Egypt will lead to more vocal opposition to Israeli policies. (AP Photo/Mohammed Abu Zaid)

toward Israel. The most likely outcome of a more democratic Egypt is an increase in anti-Israel rhetoric and diplomacy but no change in the country's basic position of peace with the Jewish state.

SINAI BEDOUINS (TAWHID WA JIHAD)

The Sinai Peninsula, a triangular-shaped territory strategically located between the Suez Canal and Egypt's borders with Israel and Gaza, has since 1956 been the focal point of three wars—all of which involved Egyptian-Israeli conflict. Since 1982, when Israel returned the Sinai to Egypt, the peninsula has been largely peaceful. Under the terms of the Egyptian-Israeli peace treaty, Egypt is allowed to maintain only limited numbers of troops in the Sinai, and both countries have strenuously avoided actions that could be seen as hostile by the other.

But in 2004, a new threat to Egypt emerged in the Sinai in the form of disgruntled Bedouin groups who resorted to terrorism to express their opposition to the Egyptian government. Sinai is home to around 350,000 people, many of whom are Bedouin, a traditionally nomadic people whose family origins are in the Arabian Peninsula. In addition to the Sinai, Bedouin live in the desert areas of southern Israel and Jordan and do not always respect contemporary national borders. Other residents of the Sinai include a substantial Palestinian community that identifies with other Palestinians in Gaza and other parts of Palestine. The Egyptian government has been accused of ignoring the economic development of the Sinai, other than the resort areas along the Gulf of Aqaba, and devoting insufficient sums to the social welfare of the peninsula's inhabitants.[12]

Between October 2004 and April 2006, a series of terrorist bombings in the Sinai killed 123 people and injured hundreds more. All of the attacks took place in resort towns along the Gulf of Aqaba, and the dead and injured included Israeli and European tourists as well as Egyptians. Egyptian authorities initially blamed the attacks on al-Qaeda, but after an investigation and several arrests were made, it was determined that the attacks were in fact carried out by a previously unknown group of Bedouins and Palestinians from the Sinai. The group, known as Tawhid wa Jihad ("Oneness and Struggle"), was found to have connections with—and most likely had received training from—Palestinian extremist groups in Gaza.

Egyptian security forces launched a massive sweep of the Sinai, killing dozens and arresting thousands of people believed to be members or supporters of Tawhid wa Jihad. But the root causes of the radicalization of some of Sinai's populace have not yet been addressed. It is perhaps no coincidence that the terrorist group chose to attack those resort areas of Sinai where the Egyptian government had invested the most money, mostly for the benefit of foreign tourists and Egyptian private-sector firms that ran the hotels and resorts. The indigenous residents of the Sinai reaped few benefits from this investment, and resentment toward Cairo had grown over the years.

Until and unless the Egyptian government undertakes serious economic development in the Sinai, the region's Bedouin and Palestinian population will continue to feel marginalized and discriminated against. Given the close proximity of Gaza, with its abundance of extremist activity, disgruntled residents of the Sinai will have a ready source of inspiration and weapons. While terrorist attacks in the Sinai are unlikely to pose an existential threat to the Egyptian state or even to the Egyptian government's hold on power, such activity could have a devastating impact on the critical revenue Egypt receives from foreign tourism. The most serious future scenario would result from violent or anarchic conditions in Gaza spilling over into Sinai, rendering greater and sustained contact between Sinai's population and Palestinian extremist groups.

CONFLICT WITH SUDAN

Relations with Sudan are considered of critical importance in Egypt. The two countries share a long border and a longer history, and Egypt's economic dependence on the Nile River means that whoever controls Sudan—from where the Nile flows into Egypt—will always be of great interest to Egypt. For a time beginning in 1820, Egypt ruled northern Sudan. The two countries were subsequently both under British sway for many years, and they shared a king prior to Nasser's 1952 takeover in Egypt. Egypt and Sudan flirted with unification during the Nasser years but eventually pursued separate paths. Nevertheless, the two nations enjoyed generally good relations in the postindependence period until the early 1990s, when a military coup in Sudan brought to power a radical Islamist government with connections to terrorist organizations throughout the Middle East, including Egypt.

In 1995, Islamist militants attempted to assassinate Egyptian president Mubarak during an African summit meeting in Ethiopia; Egyptian security forces accused Sudan of involvement in the plot, and Egypt broke diplomatic relations with its southern neighbor. Relations were tense for several years as Egypt, which was fighting Islamist radicals at home, remained hostile to Sudan's government. Among other allegations, Cairo accused the Sudanese government of harboring Egyptian extremists. A thawing in relations occurred in 2000, when Egypt agreed to reestablish relations. By this time, Sudan had become more focused on its long-running civil war in the south and a growing rebellion in Darfur; the Khartoum government could not afford to maintain a hostile relationship with Egypt.

Egypt has avoided criticism of Sudan over the humanitarian crisis and civil war in Darfur, despite pressure from the West for Egypt to play a more active role. Egypt's primary concern about the crisis in Darfur is its potential spillover effect—specifically, the prospect of a flood of Sudanese refugees seeking sanctuary in southern Egypt. A significant number of Sudanese refugees already reside in Egypt. Egypt, however, has traditionally been opposed to large numbers of foreign troops being stationed in Sudan, fearing that this would impinge on Egypt's perceived sphere of influence in the region.[13]

The Egyptian-Sudanese relationship could become conflictual under three conditions: the return of a radical government in Khartoum could reignite hostility with Egypt, especially if this were combined with a resurgence of Islamist extremism within Egypt. A complete collapse of Sudan due to the Darfur crisis and continuing tensions between Sudan's Muslim north and Christian south (which became an independent state in July 2011) also could create new sources of conflict, especially if such a collapse led to a refugee crisis. Finally, disagreement over the rights to Egypt's most crucial natural resource—the Nile River—might threaten Egyptian-Sudanese relations. However, grumbling about the injustice of existing water-sharing agreements is typically located further upriver, pitting Sudan and Egypt against central and east African nations rather than against each other.[14]

NOTES

1. Quoted in Hisham Melhem, "Arab Despotism's Second Act," *The Middle East Channel* (March 17, 2011), http://mideast.foreignpolicy.com/.

2. *CIA World Factbook, 2007*. Various other sources place the number of Copts as anywhere between 6 and 15 percent of the population. Population estimates often are motivated by political interests.

3. In Islam, conversion is considered a crime, often punishable by death.

4. Will Rasmussen, "Cairo Accuses Hezbollah of Planning Egypt Attacks," *Reuters* (April 8, 2009), http://uk.reuters.com/article/idUKL8213444.

5. "Mubarak to Iran and Hizbullah: Beware the Wrath of Egypt," Agence France Presse, April 23, 2009.

6. Mohammad Abdulsalam, "Is There a Cold War between Arabs and Iran?" Al-Ahram Center for Strategic and Political Studies, November 2006.

7. See Gilles Kepel, *Le Prophete et pharaon: Les mouvements islamistes dans l'Egypte copntemporaine* (Paris: La Decouverte, 1984).

8. Tariq Hassan, "The Muslim Brotherhood Is Trying to Reproduce Hamas' Experience in Gaza," *Al-Ahram* (June 23, 2007).

9. Michael C. Dunn, "Egypt's Quandary over the Gaza Border," *MEI Commentary* (January 30, 2008).

10. "Cast Lead in the Foundry," *Middle East Report Online* (December 31, 2008), http://www.merip.org/mero/mero123108b.html.

11. Khaled Moussa Al-Omrani, "Egypt: Israel Recognized by Government, Not by People," *Inter Press Service* (December 19, 2007).

12. See "Egypt's Sinai Question," *International Crisis Group Middle East/North Africa Report*, no. 61 (January 30, 2007).

13. "Egypt to Launch a New Peace Plan on Darfur," *International Herald Tribune* (May 9, 2007).

14. Jack Shenker, "Egypt's Nile: Nation Puts Great River at Heart of Its Security," *The Guardian* (June 25, 2010), http://www.guardian.co.uk/world/2010/jun/25/egypt-nile-security-cut-water-supply.

2   GULF STATES

The small states along the Persian Gulf share many, although not all, of the same security concerns and threats. The principal shared external threat is Iran—more explicitly, Iranian efforts to dominate the Gulf region militarily and politically. But the tide of popular discontent that spread throughout the Arab world in 2011 did not leave the Gulf states untouched, and Bahrain in particular faces serious internal challenges due to its large Shia majority and minority Sunni ruling class. Bahrain, Oman, Qatar, and the United Arab Emirates—along with Kuwait and Saudi Arabia—all are members of the Gulf Cooperation Council (GCC), a political, military, and economic organization founded in 1981, just two years after the Islamic Revolution in Iran, with the goal of creating a regional bulwark against the spread of Iranian influence.

The military component of the GCC includes a mutual defense pact (an attack on one is considered an attack on all) and extensive military cooperation, such as joint maneuvers and efforts to create equipment compatibility. The wealthier members of the GCC, such as Kuwait and Saudi Arabia, have provided economic assistance to less wealthy members, such as Oman, to purchase advanced military equipment and defense systems. Anthony Cordesman, a prominent authority on Middle Eastern military forces, has argued that in a conventional conflict with Iran, the GCC states would "almost certainly win."[1] The greatest threat from Iran, however, is not conventional war but nonconventional tactics such as proxy war through support of terrorist groups; subversion through infiltration and incitement of the Shia populations in the Gulf states; interference with the shipping lanes of the Gulf; and, potentially, the development of a nuclear warfare capability.

Another shared threat is potential instability in Iraq (which, in turn, is linked to the Iranian threat given Iran's influence among Shia groups in Iraq). Civil war and terrorist violence in Iraq would over time likely spill over into neighboring states and would threaten the economic growth of the region.

But the existence of perceived common threats has not erased all tensions between and among the GCC states. Some of these tensions have interfered with the GCC's ability to expand and deepen its activities or to better coordinate its national militaries. This chapter will assess the specific security concerns and threats to the smaller Gulf states: Bahrain, Oman, Qatar, and the United Arab Emirates (see chapters 7 and 10 for analyses of Kuwait and Saudi Arabia).

BAHRAIN

Bahrain is a small (290 square miles) island nation in the Persian Gulf with just over 1.2 million people. Although Bahrain lies just off the coast of Saudi Arabia and to the west of Qatar, it lacks its neighbors' vast oil and gas reserves. Instead, Bahrain's economy is based on refining and processing its neighbors' crude oil as well as on financial and commercial services and trading. Another significant source of income derives from tourism, largely in the form of weekend visitors from religiously strict Saudi Arabia (the two countries are connected by a 15-mile-long causeway) who come to enjoy Bahrain's restaurants and bars.

Archaeological finds indicate that Bahrain has been inhabited for millennia and has been predominantly Arab and Muslim since the seventh century despite periods of Portuguese and later Persian rule. In 1783, the Khalifah family from the Arabian Peninsula gained control, and a long line of Khalifah sheikhs has ruled the island country ever since. In 1820, the Khalifahs signed a treaty granting the British control over defense and foreign policy; Bahrain's status as a British protectorate came to an end in 1971, after British forces withdrew from the Gulf region, and Bahrain became an officially recognized sovereign state.

Bahrain is just over 80 percent Muslim, but unlike neighboring Arab states, a majority are Shia (the ruling Khalifah family, however, is Sunni). Around 10 percent of the population is Christian, and there are smaller communities of Jews, Hindus, and Baha'is. Like most of the Gulf states, Bahrain relies on foreign workers for much of its labor, and non-Bahrainis make up about 38 percent of the population. The presence of a large foreign population, combined with Bahrain's history as a trading nation and its outward orientation, has made for a cosmopolitan and open society, at least in comparison to nearby Saudi Arabia.

Bahrain enacted political changes early in the 21st century after several years of unrest and tension between the Shia and Sunni communities. Following a 2001 national referendum, the country became a constitutional monarchy with a 40-member Council of Deputies whose members are directly elected by the people; an upper chamber, the Consultative Council, is appointed by the king.

Bahrain is a member of the GCC and generally follows Saudi Arabia's lead on defense and foreign policy issues. Bahrain strongly supported the U.S.-led coalition in the 1990–1991 war to evict Iraq from Kuwait and also served as a staging base for the 2003 U.S. war against Iraq. Although Bahrain's defense forces are small, it receives military equipment from the United States, and its port and airfields have been made available to U.S. forces in the Gulf, including the U.S. Fifth Fleet.

Tension with Iran

Iran poses the greatest threat to Bahrain and is the most likely source of international tension and conflict. Throughout much of the 18th through 20th centuries, Iran periodically claimed Bahrain as part of its territory, although the British protectorate over the island nation prevented any direct Iranian action to seize Bahrain. In 1970, the shah of Iran repudiated these territorial claims after a United Nations–conducted survey in Bahrain indicated strong preference for independence, which Bahrain declared in 1971.[2]

But the 1979 Iranian Islamic Revolution again raised tensions between the two countries. Bahrain's leaders, who are Sunni, feared that the radical government in Tehran would seek to incite Bahrain's large Shia community, which already had been expressing grievances against the Khalifah family and complaining about political and social discrimination. In 1981 and again in 1996, Bahrain accused Iran of seeking to orchestrate a Shia-led coup, which Tehran denied. In a July 2007 newspaper interview, a close advisor to Ayatollah Khomeini, the spiritual leader of Iran, renewed Tehran's claim to Bahrain. This led to an immediate denunciation by Bahrain and other GCC states, and within weeks Iran had sent its foreign minister to Bahrain to reassert Tehran's recognition of Bahrain's independence. But in 2009, another advisor to Ayatollah Khomeini described Bahrain as Iran's "14th province," again causing an uproar in Bahrain.[3]

Bahrain's development of close security ties with the United States, which began prior to its independence, can be explained in large part by the perceived threat of Iranian influence and Iran's periodic territorial claims to Bahrain. The Bahraini relationship with the United States, however, also has further angered Iran, and has placed Bahrain clearly in the pro-Western camp. Despite the periodic tensions and the underlying sense of threat, however, Bahrain and Iran maintain positive commercial and trade links.

As long as Bahrain maintains close defense ties with the United States, it has little to fear from Iran in terms of a direct military attack. Bahrain remains vulnerable, however, to Iranian influence in its internal political affairs. Moreover, in the event of a regional conflict—such as could be caused by a U.S. and/or Israeli attack on Iran's nuclear facilities—Bahrain could become the target of Iranian-sponsored subversion, terrorism, and economic warfare.

Bahrain's leaders have long been concerned about Iran's potential development of a nuclear weapons program, as this would dramatically alter the regional balance of power. In late 2010, leaked U.S. diplomatic cables indicated that Bahrain's leaders had encouraged the United States to take action against Iran to prevent the Islamic Republic from developing a nuclear weapons capability.

If political unrest in Bahrain were to lead to the overthrow of the monarchy and the establishment of a popularly elected government—one almost certain to be Shia-dominated—the country's relationship with Iran could transform from one of mistrust into one of alliance. This eventuality would in turn have profound consequences for Bahrain's relationships with the other Gulf states—especially Saudi Arabia—as well as with the United States.

Internal Sectarian (Shia-Sunni) Tensions

Bahrain has long been plagued by periodic tension between its Shia and Sunni communities, dating back at least to the 1920s. In 1999, Sheikh Hamad bin Isa Al-Khalifa became the country's new ruler upon the death of his father. In an effort to address the simmering sectarian tensions, Sheikh Hamad released a number of Shia activists who had been imprisoned and initiated the process that led to the 2001 referendum and the development of a new national charter (or constitution) that, in addition to making Bahrain a constitutional monarchy, also declared equal rights for the Sunni and Shia communities.

These political changes helped to ease tensions, but in 2005 new unrest broke out as members of the Shia community protested against social and economic inequities. And despite the formal political changes implemented with the new constitution, Shia leaders felt that their community still was excluded from top government positions. The police often responded harshly to the protests, further embittering the Shia community.

In the 2006 assembly elections, Shia candidates won 17 seats (out of 40) amid allegations that election districts had been drawn in a way to favor Sunni candidates. King Hamad selected 20 Shia to sit in the upper chamber, along with 19 Sunni and 1 Christian; he also appointed a Shia as deputy prime minister.[4]

By 2008, Shia-Sunni tensions were becoming more public and more widespread, with each community's mosques becoming the centers of agitation and protest. The Shia now were demanding a greater role in politics and more Shia members of the cabinet; they also wanted fewer absolute powers for the ruling Khalifah family, which controlled about half of all cabinet posts including all of the most critical positions. King Hamad (under the new constitution, his title became king instead of emir) tried to ease tensions by releasing more Shia prisoners who had been detained during protests. The government also enforced stricter laws on alcohol consumption and entertainment in response to criticism from both Shia and Sunni religious leaders.

The 2011 uprising in Bahrain's capital, Manama, was inspired by events in Tunisia and Egypt but was fundamentally different in that it reflected the country's sectarian division: most of the protestors were Shia, and the grievances related more to their resentment over Sunni political and social dominance than to economic hardship. The king responded with force and eventually called in troops from other GCC states, led by Saudi Arabia, to maintain control; this succeeded in quelling the demonstrations but did nothing to address the underlying grievances. Bahrain will continue to face internal discord until power in its political, business, and social systems is more reflective of the majority population. The king's heavy-handed response to the Shia uprising—which included mass arrests and allegations of torture—will make it hard for him to survive unless power is devolved and a form of constitutional monarchy is established. But, as noted above, any popularly elected government in Bahrain would be dominated by Shia parties, who may then reject a Sunni monarch (even one with limited constitutional powers). Saudi Arabia, in turn, would be loathe to see a Shia-controlled (and possibly Iranian-influenced) Bahrain in such close proximity to the kingdom.

Protesters march toward Pearl Square in Manama, Bahrain's capital, in February 2011. Most of the protesters in Bahrain were supporters of the Shiite-led opposition. (AP Photo/Hasan Jamali)

It is no coincidence that sectarian tension in Bahrain began to increase at the same time as the Shia of Iraq were solidifying their position as that country's dominant political group following the U.S. invasion of 2003 and national elections.[5] Bahrain mirrors Iraq in that the Shia community is in the majority but, like in Iraq prior to the overthrow of Saddam Hussein, most levers of government control are in the hands of Sunnis. But this is not to equate Khalifah rule with that of Saddam: The Shia in Bahrain have not experienced the type of suppression that their Iraqi cohorts suffered, and King Hamad has taken concrete steps to address many of the Shia grievances. Still, the response to the 2011 demonstrations was harsh, and by calling in GCC troops, King Hamad was, in effect, acknowledging that his own forces were unable to maintain order against a restive population. The Shia community of Bahrain will continue to look to developments in Iraq as a potential model of democratic evolution and could very well become more assertive in its demands. As such, it is developments in Iraq more than potential meddling by Iran that may have the greatest impact on internal political stability in Bahrain.

Territorial Dispute with Qatar

For over 200 years, the ruling families of Bahrain and Qatar were locked in a territorial dispute involving several islands and reefs in the Persian Gulf, the most important of which are the Halwar Islands, as well as a town on the Qatari mainland that the Khalifahs claimed. In 1986, the dispute escalated when Qatar landed troops on a disputed reef and took several Bahraini prisoners. But in 1991, Qatar agreed to refer the dispute to the International Court of Justice (ICJ), which ruled in 2001 mostly in favor of Bahrain (the Halwar Islands, in particular, were granted to Bahrain). Both countries accepted the ruling. Since the ICJ ruling, relations between the two countries have improved substantially. In 2010, work was set to begin on a 25-mile-long "friendship causeway" linking the two countries.

SULTANATE OF OMAN

Background

Located on the southeast coast of the Arabian Peninsula, Oman covers a large area of desert and mountain terrain but is sparsely populated, with fewer than 3 million people. The population is concentrated along the lush northern coast, where the land is fertile. A small area of Omani territory, the Musandam Peninsula, is geographically separated from the rest of the country by the United Arab Emirates. This peninsula, however, overlooks the strategic Strait of Hormuz and is critical to maintaining fee passage of ships through the strait.

The Omani population is more diverse than that of any other country in the Arabian Peninsula. Although a majority is Arab, there are large communities of ethnic Baluchs (from modern-day Pakistan and Iran), Persians, and Africans. Like most of the Gulf countries, Oman has a sizable population of expatriates, mostly South Asians and Filipino/a laborers and Western businesspeople. The Ibadi branch of Islam—closely related to the Sunni—is followed by around 75 percent of the population; there are smaller communities of Shia and Hindus.[6]

Oman was first settled by Arabs in the second century CE, and, except for periods of Portuguese (1507–1650) and Persian (1737–1749) rule, has been ruled by local tribal leaders—from 1749 until today by the Al Bu Said dynasty. Beginning in the late 18th century, the Al Bu Said sultans increasingly had to rely on British support to secure their control against opposition tribes from the interior of Oman. After two attacks on the capital city of Muscat, in 1895 and 1915, British mediators negotiated a compromise agreement in which the Sultan would recognize tribal sovereignty in the country's interior regions but would remain the sovereign of all Oman. Tribal opposition continued until the 1950s and periodically required British military intervention to subdue.

In the 1960s, the sultanate faced a new threat from Marxist guerillas in the southern province of Dhofar; the guerillas received support from the Soviet Union, China, and South Yemen. The sultanate received military support from Britain, Jordan, and Iran and financial support from the United Arab Emirates and Saudi Arabia. By 1975, the Dhofar rebellion had been largely defeated.

In 1970, during the height of the Dhofar rebellion, the sultan was overthrown by his son, Qaboos. The new sultan launched a modernization program designed to open Oman to foreign investment and end its relative isolation. Oman was a charter member of the GCC when the organization was formed in 1981 and has followed a generally pro-Western foreign policy, including participation in the 1990–1991 Gulf War.

Domestic Unrest

The popular unrest that spread across the Arab world in 2011 affected Oman as well, where the focus was on unemployment and accusations of corruption by ministers and businessmen. Unlike in Tunisia and Egypt, however, the sultan remained personally popular, and there were few calls for his overthrow. The sultan responded to the protests by increasing the powers of the legislature and granting cost-of-living wage increases for public-sector employees. Despite his personal popularity, the sultan retains virtually all decision-making powers, so ultimately he could become a target of protests if economic conditions do not improve. Moreover, the sultan, who is in his 70s, has no children and thus no crown prince; his succession could thus be an occasion of further unrest, perhaps targeted more directly at a change in government.

Repercussions from an Attack on Iran

Oman has followed a policy of stable relations with Iran ever since the Islamic Revolution in 1979. The two countries control either side of the Strait of Hormuz and have historic cultural ties due to the ethnic Persian population of Oman. In 2009, the sultan visited Tehran for the first time since the Islamic revolution and conducted talks on trade and security cooperation.

Like other Gulf states, however, Oman does not relish the thought of an Iranian nuclear capability, and to balance its policy toward Iran, the sultanate has maintained close ties with its GCC allies—especially Saudi Arabia—as well as defense relationships with the United States and the United Kingdom. Oman is in the unique position of having close ties to both the West and Iran, which could potentially place the sultanate in a role as mediator or bridge between the two conflicting sides.

The greatest threat to Oman would be fallout from an Israeli or coordinated Western attack on Iran. If Iran attempted to close the Strait of Hormuz in retaliation, Oman—as guardian of the strait's southern coast—would be compelled to act or forced to cooperate with Western militaries. And like all the other regional states, Oman's economy would suffer from a protracted conflict between the West and Iran.

Civil War in Yemen

Political unrest and civil war in Yemen poses another threat to Oman. Omanis remember well the guerilla war it fought in Dhofar against rebels supported by the former South Yemen. While that particular conflict appears to have been resolved, Omanis are aware of the cross-border influences that could emanate from Yemen. For this reason, the sultanate has publicly supported the continued unification of Yemen and has cooperated with its GCC allies in efforts to stabilize the situation in its southern neighbor.

QATAR

Qatar occupies a small peninsula that extends into the Persian Gulf off of the Arabian Peninsula; it shares a border with Saudi Arabia. The original settlers were nomadic tribes from the Arabian Peninsula. Qatar was controlled briefly by the Al-Khalifa family, who used the peninsula as a launching point for their eventual conquest of neighboring Bahrain, where they still rule. The Al Thani family has ruled Qatar since the 19th century, although the country was officially part of the Ottoman Empire from 1871 until after World War I, when Britain signed a treaty with the Al Thanis that gave London control over Qatar's foreign policy in return for protection. Qatar became fully independent in 1971.

Qatar is sparsely populated, with just 850,000 people, a large majority of whom are non-Arab guest workers; only about 180,000 are Qatari citizens.[7] Nearly 80 percent of the population is Muslim (with Hindus and a small Christian community making up the rest), and a majority of them are Sunni. Qatar is extremely wealthy, controlling one of the largest reserves of natural gas in the world as well as extensive petroleum reserves; energy resources account for over 50 percent of Qatar's gross domestic product. On a per capita income basis, Qatar is the second-wealthiest country in the world.[8]

Qatar is an emirate with a hereditary leadership and only minimal aspects of democracy. Under the new 2005 constitution, a new legislative body was created—a 45-member Majlis al-Shura—but it is to serve essentially as an advisory body to the emir. The emir has the power to appoint 15 members of the Majlis, with the other 30 elected by Qatar's small voter base; women will be allowed to vote and run for office, but there are no political parties. The first elections were originally scheduled for 2008 but have since been pushed to 2013. Despite few aspects of democracy, there is little opposition to the emir's rule. Because of its small population and vast wealth, the government can guarantee that Qataris enjoy economic security.

Qatar was a founding member of the GCC and has generally followed a pro-Western foreign policy. Qatari forces participated in the 1990–1991 U.S.-led war against Iraq, and air bases in Qatar were used by U.S. and French forces to stage bombing sorties on Iraq. Qatar continued its close cooperation with the U.S. military during the 2001 U.S. military operation against Afghanistan and the 2003 U.S. invasion of Iraq and has signed a Defense Cooperation Agreement with the United States. The country's close military relationship with the United States, and the presence of U.S. military personnel in Qatar, has made the emirate a stated target of various regional terrorist groups.

Qatar, despite its small size and dependence on outside support for protection, has pursued a surprisingly independent foreign policy since the early 1990s. Although it supported the 1990–1991 war against Iraq, Qatar was quick to restore ties with Saddam's government after the fighting. In 1995, the emirate funded the creation of Al Jazeera, a regional (and today, global) satellite television network that has covered political developments in Arab states in a way that often has angered Qatar's regional allies. Qatar has also taken a lead diplomatic role in addressing Lebanon's internal political crises and in pushing for Israeli-Palestinian peace talks, and in April 2011, the emirate contributed fighter jets to the NATO-led military operation against Libya's Mu'ammar Gadhafi.

The Terrorist Threat

Qatar is a potential target for regional terrorist groups due to its close defense and security ties with the United States. But with one exception—in 2005, an Egyptian extremist carried out a car bombing of a theater in Doha (the Qatari capital) that was frequented by Westerners, killing one British citizen and wounding a dozen others—Qatar has avoided terrorist attacks. Some U.S. government officials have accused Qatari officials, including some members of the ruling family, of providing safe haven and free transit for known terrorists, including individuals who were implicated in the September 11, 2001, attacks on the United States.[9] The Qatari government has denied these allegations, but if true, they may be signs of a balancing act by Qatar, in which close ties with the United States is combined with a laissez-faire policy toward certain extremist leaders, thus providing immunity for the emirate from terrorist attacks.

Qatar's selection as site of the 2022 World Cup finals will require the government to demonstrate in the intervening years that it is capable of maintaining security against terrorism.

Tensions with Saudi Arabia

Living next door to the Arabian Peninsula's largest and most powerful state, Saudi Arabia, has not been easy for Qatar. The ruling Al Saud family in Saudi Arabia long regarded Qatar as within its orbit, if not under its sovereignty, and has worked to maintain strong ties to pro-Saudi families and even sympathetic members of the Al Thani family. A dispute over border demarcation led to an armed clash in 1992; the border was demarcated to both sides' satisfaction in 1999.

Saudi Arabia also has been the most vocal Arab state in lodging complaints about Al Jazeera's programming. In 2002, the kingdom briefly withdrew its ambassador from Qatar following an Al Jazeera report that was critical of Saudi Arabia's founder, King Abdul Aziz al Saud.[10] In 2006, Saudi officials objected to a proposed natural gas pipeline connecting Qatar and the United Arab Emirates; the Saudis claimed that the pipeline would traverse Saudi territorial waters. A similar Saudi protest had prevented construction of a proposed pipeline from Qatar to Kuwait. A rapprochement occurred in 2007 when the two heads of state paid visits to each other's capitals, after which the Saudis returned their ambassador to Qatar.

In all likelihood, Qatar-Saudi tensions will continue to flare from time to time, given the emirate's independent foreign policy, but it will be played out on the diplomatic front. The border skirmish that took place in 1992 was a rare occurrence and quickly resolved. The importance of GCC unity in the face of regional threats—especially from Iran—will ensure that any disagreements remain carefully contained.

Potential Conflict with Iran

Qatar and Iran have traditionally maintained cordial relations, perhaps the strongest bilateral relations Iran has with any GCC state. Within the GCC, Qatar is a frequent advocate for improved ties between Iran and the GCC states. This state of affairs is largely explained by the close commercial cooperation that forms the basis of the bilateral relationship: Qatar and Iran amicably share the vast North Field/South Pars natural gas deposit that lies off the Qatari coast.

In 2006, Qatar opposed a United Nations Security Council Resolution that would have imposed sanctions on Iran if it did suspend its nuclear enrichment and reprocessing activities, and in 2007 Qatar's emir invited Iranian president Mahmoud Ahmadinejad to attend the annual GCC summit, which Qatar hosted that year. In December 2010, the emir visited Tehran and met with President Ahmadinejad and other Iranian leaders in an effort to convince Tehran that Qatar would not allow its territory to be used in a potential U.S. military strike against Iran.

Despite the cordial ties between Qatar and Iran, the emirate could still be subject to an Iranian attack aimed at U.S. military installations in Qatar. For this reason, Qatar has opposed talk of a U.S. or Israeli preemptive attack against Iran. The emir has repeatedly called on the United States to engage Iran in negotiations.

UNITED ARAB EMIRATES

The United Arab Emirates is a federation of seven emirates located along the eastern coast of the Arabian Peninsula. The largest and economically most important of the seven emirates are Dubai and Abu Dhabi—the former a major global financial and logistics hub, the latter one of the world's largest producers of oil and natural gas.

For centuries, the area that is now the United Arab Emirates was the domain of disparate rival tribal factions whose economic activity was based primarily on fishing, pearling, and trading. In the late 18th century, one tribal group—the al-Qasimis—became the dominant power along the coast. But when the al-Qasimis began extending their reach and attacking British naval vessels and India-bound ships in the region, they provoked a British attack that led to their downfall.

Power shifted to a confederation of smaller tribal groups, the Abu Dhabi–based Banu Yas, who signed a series of treaties with other groups throughout the early 19th century, culminating in a perpetual truce in 1853; from that time, the area was referred to as the Trucial States. In 1892, the Trucial States agreed to allow Britain to make foreign policy and defense decisions for the region; representatives of the Trucial States, however, met regularly to discuss internal affairs.

Oil was discovered in Abu Dhabi in 1958, thus beginning a historic transformation of the economies of all seven emirates. Despite the new oil discoveries, Britain announced in 1968 that it would withdraw its forces from the region by the end of 1971. The Trucial States—along with Bahrain and Qatar—began discussions about forming a confederation after the British withdrew. Bahrain and Qatar ultimately decided to go it alone, but in 1971 six emirates formed the United Arab Emirates (the seventh, Ras al Khaymah, joined the following year). Throughout the 1970s, the United Arab Emirates worked at creating a more centralized federal government. Not surprisingly, Dubai and Abu Dhabi were the key actors during this process; as the two most dominant emirates, their concurrence on major decisions was vital. In 1976, the seven emirates agreed to merge their armed forces, a significant step in the development of a unified sovereign nation. Nevertheless, rivalries between the ruling families of Dubai and Abu Dhabi have frequently led to political tension, although the basic federated structure of the United Arab Emirates has not been challenged.[11]

The United Arab Emirates' oil wealth helped to fund a development boom in the 1970s. Abu Dhabi, where most of the country's oil and natural gas reserves are located, also has provided over 50 percent of the federal budget in most years. In addition to

Dubai's meteoric rise as a global trading and financial center has been fueled by the UAE's oil wealth. (Nigel Spiers)

defense, the federal budget has financed extensive growth in infrastructure, housing, and services, so that today the United Arab Emirates has a literacy rate of over 80 percent and Western standards of medical care.[12] Although its energy reserves are small, Dubai developed as a financial and logistics center, and in the 1990s as a tourist destination not only for other residents of the Arabian Peninsula but for vacationers from Europe and Russia as well. Dubai became world famous for some of its more dramatic developments, such as an indoor ski slope and the world's tallest skyscraper. The other emirates also have pursued growth and development strategies that have greatly improved the standard of living of their inhabitants, although their pace of development has been much slower than that of Dubai and Abu Dhabi.

As Dubai's prosperity and global role grew, so did its sense of independence from the rest of the United Arab Emirates and its sense of parity with oil-rich Abu Dhabi. But when the world financial crisis erupted in late 2008, Dubai was confronted with the reality: its remarkable growth had been highly leveraged, and, as global credit markets collapsed, Dubai World, one of the emirate's largest flagship companies with close links to the ruling family, found itself on the verge of bankruptcy in late 2009. Abu Dhabi came to the rescue, injecting the necessary funding to keep Dubai World—and, indirectly, Dubai—afloat. Although Dubai's pride may have been wounded by the neighborly bailout, the incident in fact may have served to strengthen the United Arab Emirates' unity by creating more financial coordination between the two dominant emirates.[13]

Because of the United Arab Emirates' location—across the Persian Gulf from Iran and along the route that oil tankers follow to enter the Indian Ocean—and its peoples' long history as traders, its society is considerably more cosmopolitan and its borders more porous than those of countries such as Saudi Arabia, where society was tradition-ally more centered on oases communities within a vast desert. The United Arab Emir-ates' cosmopolitan nature has been strengthened by its rapid economic growth, which has brought to the nation millions of foreigners to work in jobs that citizens of the emirates either do not wish to perform are or not trained to perform. While completely accurate figures are not available (due to the flows of in- and out-migration), most ob-servers estimate that less than 20 percent of the population are Emirati citizens. Of the remaining 80 percent, the majority hail from South Asia (India, Pakistan, and Bangla-desh), Iran, and other Arab states. This mix has created concerns about the country's underlying identity and its concept of nationhood.

Simmering Tensions with Iran

The United Arab Emirates lies just across the Persian Gulf from Iran, arguably the region's most powerful state and one with which the emirates that compose the United Arab Emirates have shared a long history. Although Iranians are not Arabs and are pre-dominantly of the Shia branch of Islam, the flow of people, goods, and ideas across the relatively narrow Persian Gulf has occurred for centuries. This proximity and interac-tion has profited the peoples on both sides of the Gulf, but it also has led to tensions and conflict.

The disparity in relative size—Iran has a population of 67 million compared to the United Arab Emirates' 5 million, only about 1 million of whom are Emiratis—would suggest that Iran always would be the winning side in conflicts or disagreements. In fact, other realities serve to create more balance in the relationship. For one, the United Arab Emirates has important allies, not the least of which are the United States, other Western powers, and Saudi Arabia, and thus access to advanced weaponry. The na-tion's economic power also is an asset, not only by providing the funds for the purchase of advanced weaponry but also by creating linkages between the United Arab Emir-ates economy and those of the West (while the United Arab Emirates has only around 8 percent of Iran's population, its economy is nearly 30 percent as large in terms of gross domestic product[14]).

The principal causes of tension between the United Arab Emirates and Iran are a territorial dispute; the Iranian regime's support for terrorist groups and its export of radical Islamic ideology; Iran's nascent nuclear program; and the free flow of goods between the United Arab Emirates and Iran. Underlying these specific elements of ten-sion is the overall regional power balance between the majority Sunni Arab states of the Arabian Peninsula (and their Sunni brethren in Iraq) and the majority Shia Irani-ans (and their Shia Arab brethren in Iraq). And all of the tensions are complicated by the fact that up to 20 percent of the residents of the United Arab Emirates are Iranian nationals.[15]

Territorial Dispute

The territorial dispute between Iran and the United Arab Emirates centers on three sparsely inhabited islands in the Persian Gulf: Abu Musa, Greater Tumbs, and Lesser

Tumbs. Iran seized control of the islands in 1971 (during the reign of the shah), after the British withdrew their military forces from the region. Iran claimed at the time that the islands were historically Iranian, contrary to the United Arab Emirates' claim that they belonged to the emirate of Sharjah. The Arab world protested Iran's seizure of the islands, but the United States did not try and stop the move, out of deference to the shah, who was one of the West's most important allies in the region. Iran and Sharjah reached an agreement that kept Abu Musa—the most important of the islands—under Sharjah's sovereignty but allowed Iran to base troops there; revenues from oil wells surrounding the island were to be shared. In 1992, however, Iran, now an Islamic republic, declared full sovereignty over the islands. The United Arab Emirates repeatedly has called on Iran to take the dispute to the International Court of Justice or submit it to international arbitration, but Teheran claims that its sovereignty over the islands is nonnegotiable.

Despite their small size and sparse populations, the three islands are of economic and strategic significance. Abu Musa contains offshore—and possibly on-shore—oil reserves and is the emirate of Sharjah's principal energy resource. The islands' strategic significance is due to the fact that they are located near the Strait of Hormuz, one of the world's most vital waterways through which passes 20 percent of the world's oil supplies. Any effort to close or blockade the Strait of Hormuz—as well as any effort to forcefully reopen it—would be greatly enhanced by the military control of Abu Musa and the Tumbs.

Given their strategic importance, it is unlikely that Iran would agree to withdraw from the islands. At the same time, the United Arab Emirates and its regional allies lack the military capability to seize and control the islands, rendering a military solution a remote possibility at best. Nevertheless, in the event of a broader regional conflagration involving Iran and Arab states (such as an Iranian military move into Iraq in support of its Shia allies), the islands would be very likely to come into play. As noted, whoever controls them has an important advantage in terms of controlling access to the Strait of Hormuz, and thus they would play an vital role in the economic warfare component of any regional military conflict.

Short of a broader regional conflict, the disagreement over the islands will most likely remain an irritant and a source of distrust in United Arab Emirates–Iranian relations but will not be allowed by either side to escalate into an open conflict or to lead to a breach in diplomatic relations.

Iran's Nuclear Ambitions

Iran's nuclear program is another cause of tension and conflict between the United Arab Emirates and Iran, for several reasons. Most important is the fact that an Iranian regime in possession of nuclear arms would substantially tilt the balance of power in the Gulf region—and indeed the entire Middle East—in Iran's favor. Having a non-Arab, majority Shia nation as the region's dominant political power is anathema to the majority Sunni Arab nations of the Arabian Peninsula. Tehran would feel emboldened to interact more directly with the Shia communities in these Arab countries and could more directly challenge U.S. interests and facilities in the region. Iran's bargaining power on a host of issues—from the contested islands to trade issues to the price of oil—would be magnified. This potential regional strategic shift in the balance of power, more than the threat of actual Iranian use of nuclear weapons, is the greatest fear of the United Arab Emirates' leaders. Their most likely response would be to pursue nuclear capability of their own, perhaps in concert with Saudi Arabia or other members of the Gulf Cooperation Council or to seek a binding mutual defense agreement with the United States. The United Arab Emirates already has taken the lead among Arab states in announcing plans for a domestic nuclear reactor program, although its leaders have stated unequivocally that, as signatories of the Nuclear Non-Proliferation Treaty, they have no intention of enriching uranium and will open their facilities to full inspection.[16]

Iran's nuclear ambitions are the cause of other concerns as well. For example, many Emiratis believe that Iran does not possess the capability to safely operate advanced nuclear facilities or quickly respond to a nuclear accident. Of particular concern in this regard is the Iranian nuclear reactor facility at Bushehr on the coast of the Persian Gulf. Rashid Abdullah, the United Arab Emirates' foreign minister, has publicly expressed concern that "we do not have any protection in case of a radioactive leakage [from Bushehr]."[17] Moreover, the specter of Iranian nuclear weapons, or even an advanced nuclear program, could damage the United Arab Emirates' role as a major global trading center and growing tourist destination.

The degree of the United Arab Emirates' concern about Iran's nuclear plans was expressed starkly in July 2010 by Yousef Al-Otaiba, the country's ambassador to the United States, who was quoted by a writer for the *Atlantic Monthly* magazine as saying that the United Arab Emirates would prefer a military strike on Iran by the United States despite the fallout such an action would have in the region and the potential for Iranian retaliation. The writer, Jeffrey Goldberg, went on to quote Al-Otaiba as saying: "Our military, who has existed for the past 40 years, wake up, dream, breathe, eat, sleep the Iranian threat. It's the only conventional military threat our military plans for, trains for, equips for, that's it, there's no other threat, there's no country in the region that is a threat to the U.A.E., it's only Iran. So yes, it's very much in our interest that Iran does not gain nuclear technology."[18]

Despite the high level of anxiety caused by Iran's nuclear program, it is unlikely that Iranian possession of nuclear weapons would lead to a shooting war. For one thing, Iran would still lack the ability to launch a significant conventional military attack against its neighbors, and the GCC states taken together in fact have superior conventional military forces (although the Islamic Republic does possess intermediate-range missiles that could strike the Arabian Peninsula).[19] In the event that Israel or the United States (or both, in concert) were to militarily attack Iranian nuclear facilities, Iran's most likely response would be to increase regional subversive activities and support for terrorist groups. The possibility of open conflict would hinge on whether Tehran chose to respond by attempting to close the strategic Strait of Hormuz, or even by attacking tanker traffic in the Persian Gulf, thus threatening global energy supplies and causing severe damage to the Gulf states' economies. But even in this scenario, the United Arab Emirates and other Gulf states would rely on the United States to participate in the response.

Nevertheless, the United Arab Emirates has taken steps to ensure that it is capable of self-defense in the event an open conflict with or direct intimidation by Iran were to occur. In early 2009, for example, the United Arab Emirates announced the purchase of $5 billion of advanced weaponry, including an antisubmarine warship.[20] This purchase came on top of a $6.95 billion deal with the United States that was reached in 2008, which included air defense systems and Black Hawk helicopters.[21] However, the increased militarization and proliferation of advanced weapons in the region also increases the chance of an unintentional conflict.

Border Tensions with Saudi Arabia

The United Arab Emirates and Saudi Arabia have had a long-standing border dispute, which periodically becomes a source of tension between the two Arabian Peninsula nations. The dispute concerns a small corridor of land between the United Arab Emirates and Qatar that was declared part of Saudi territory in the 1974 Treaty of Jeddah.[22] The corridor gave Saudi Arabia access to the Persian Gulf as well as control of the Shaybah oil field, which at the time was not being exploited. The United Arab Emirates, however, never formally ratified the treaty and has not revoked its claims to the territory, which would give the United Arab Emirates a border with Qatar.

The issue lay relatively dormant until 2006, when the United Arab Emirates publicly laid claim to the territory and began to publish maps that depicted the corridor as part of the United Arab Emirates. In the intervening three decades, Saudi Arabia had begun to exploit the Shaybah field, generating 550,000 barrels of oil per day.[23] In addition, Saudi control of the corridor complicated the planned Dolphin Gas Transmission Project, a multi-billion-dollar joint venture among the United Arab Emirates, Qatar, and Oman that would allow Qatar to supply natural gas to its two partners.[24] Saudi Arabia has protested the United Arab Emirates' claims and called on the government to respect the 1974 treaty. The Saudis also have denied entry to Emiratis who try to enter the kingdom using their national identity cards instead of their passports—normally an acceptable practice among GCC member states—because the identity cards depict the disputed territory as part of the United Arab Emirates.[25]

The chances of this conflict developing into a violent confrontation are slim. Both the United Arab Emirates and Saudi Arabia are members of the GCC, a fact that would likely serve as a brake on a serious escalation of tensions. Moreover, the countries have considerable interests in common—not the least of which is a shared fear of Iranian hegemony—that they would not want to put at risk by allowing the border issues to get out of control. Nevertheless, the stakes are more serious than the size of the corridor might suggest—including oil revenues from Shaybah and the Dolphin Project—and the conflict could take on a higher profile in the event that the Iranian threat were to recede or one of the two states were to make a reckless move.

Instability in Iraq

Political instability in Iraq has direct and indirect effects on the United Arab Emirates' stability. Although it is hard to envision a scenario in which the nation becomes militarily involved in Iraq—other than perhaps the dispatching of soldiers as part of a broader GCC peacekeeping mission—negative developments in Iraq could increase the risk of terrorism in the Arabian Peninsula and could enhance Iranian strategic power in the region.

In the worst-case scenario, in which Iraq descends into civil war and disorder, the regional Sunni-Shia rift grows even wider, the presence of a sizable Shia population in the United Arab Emirates could lead to internal tensions. In the event that the Sunni community in Iraq appeared to be losing an internal civil war or power struggle, the leaders of the United Arab Emirates—along with the other GCC states—would feel compelled to provide assistance. This would not only exacerbate internal tensions in the United Arab Emirates but could also become another source of tension with Iran, whose allies in Iraq are among the Shia parties.

Finally, and most ominously from the United Arab Emirates' perspective, there is a danger that the internal destabilization of Iraq could lead to direct Iranian intervention in that country, especially if the Iranians were invited to intervene by one of the Iraqi Shia parties. While this would be highly unlikely to occur while U.S. forces are stationed in Iraq, it is certainly possible after a complete U.S. withdrawal. A direct Iranian presence in Iraq—or even a strongly pro-Tehran government in Baghdad—would have a pronounced impact on the Persian-Arab and Sunni-Shia balances of power and influence in the Gulf region.

Internal Issues

Although real economic disparity exists among the seven emirates, in general the United Arab Emirates is an extremely wealthy country that provides extensive social services for its citizens. None of the emirates have ever been a hotbed of religious extremism, or indeed of any form of political radicalism. Although the country does not have a democratic form of government, traditional tribal and clan relationships provide a certain level of access to leaders. The popular protests that occurred across much of the region in 2011 had no noticeable impact on the nation.

The greatest internal threat comes not from native-born Emiratis but rather from the large number of foreign workers who live in the United Arab Emirates and are estimated to make up more than 80 percent of the population.[26] Many of the guest workers live in substandard housing, do not have the same access to services as do Emirati citizens, suffer from poor working conditions, and frequently have suffered from debt bondage or involuntary servitude. During the economic boom period of the 1990s and 2000s, there generally were many jobs available, and, despite the hardships, guest workers could still earn enough money to send back to heir home countries to make the effort worthwhile. But in an economic slowdown, the jobs that guest workers usually perform are often the first to go, raising the danger of creating a large and disgruntled noncitizenry.

Terrorism

The United Arab Emirates, and especially the emirates of Dubai and Abu Dhabi, faces a serious terrorism threat for several reasons. First, it is one of the most open, cosmopolitan, and pro-Western countries in the region, if not the entire Middle East.

The population contains a large number of noncitizens, some of whom are undocumented and many of whom are non-Muslims (and thus may be perceived as potential targets by Islamic extremist groups). Moreover, at any given time, there are many Westerners in the country, either on business or, increasingly, as tourists, making prime targets for anti-Western extremist groups such as al-Qaeda. Dubai in particular features a number of high-profile potential targets—including the world's largest skyscraper, hotels and restaurants that serve alcohol, and port facilities—that, if attacked, would render serious damage to the region's economy and have long-term psychological effects. The United Arab Emirates' long and mostly deserted coastline, along with vast areas of desert, provide potential terrorist groups with access and sanctuary. The use by terrorists of small suicide boats, which are almost impossible to defend against, could wreak havoc with shipping in the Gulf, which in turn would be devastating to the country's economy.

Several factors, however, have served to mitigate the United Arab Emirates' risk of a terrorist attack. Most important, there is no local network of al-Qaeda sympathizers or Islamic religious extremists within the population. While it is not always easy to determine the sympathies of the large expatriate population, the vast majority are in the United Arab Emirates to work, and any sign of extremism would likely be dealt with harshly by the security services, which are rated as among the most efficient in the Middle East.

The United Arab Emirates also has developed extensive and sophisticated counterterrorism measures, beginning with guidelines to prohibit extremist preaching in mosques and prevent radical influences from affecting the education system, and laws that criminalize the use of the Internet by extremist groups. Authorities also have taken steps to minimize the use of the banking system by terrorist groups, although this goal has sometimes conflicted with the goal of developing a banking system that will attract foreign depositors and investors. In 2005, the emirate of Dubai created the Container Security Initiative in partnership with the U.S. Customs and Border Protection Service. The initiative examines and reviews shipments and transshipments from Dubai's two major ports to ensure that terrorist groups do not use containers to ship materiel or explosives. In 2008, the United Arab Emirates created the national Emergency and Crisis Management Authority to manage and coordinate the national response to a security crisis, terrorist or otherwise.

Despite these efforts, the United Arab Emirates remains vulnerable to a terrorist attack. The nature of terrorism is such that a tremendous amount of damage—in terms of lives, expense, and psychology—can be inflicted with just one successful attack. To a certain degree, the likelihood of a terrorist attack on the United Arab Emirates will depend on the country's relationship with Iran and the nature of developments in Iraq.

NOTES

1. Anthony Cordesman, "The Conventional Military Balance in the Gulf," *Summary: Gulf Roundtable Series*, Center for Strategic and International Studies, July 8, 2010.

2. Kenneth Katzman, "Bahrain: Reform, Security and U.S. Policy," *Congressional Research Service* (April 26, 2010), 8.

3. Ibid., 9.

4. Ibid., 3.

5. See William Walls, "Iraq Sectarian Conflict Reverberates beyond Borders," *Financial Times* (February 23, 2006).

6. Central Intelligence Agency, "Middle East: Oman," *The World Factbook,* https://www.cia.gov/library/publications/the-world-factbook/geos/mu.html.

7. Central Intelligence Agency, "Middle East: Qatar," *The World Factbook,* https://www.cia.gov/library/publications/the-world-factbook/geos/qa.html.

8. Ibid.

9. Christopher Blanchard, "Qatar: Background and U.S. Relations," *Congressional Research Service* (January 24, 2008), 11–13.

10. Ibid., 16.

11. For a good history of the United Arab Emirates, see Malcolm Peck, *The United Arab Emirates: A Venture in Unity* (Boulder, CO: Westview Press, 1986).

12. Central Intelligence Agency, "Middle East: United Arab Emirates," *The World Factbook,* https://www.cia.gov/library/publications/the-world-factbook/geos/ae.html.

13. See, for example, Rhoula Khalaf, "Long Term Test of Unity for UAE," *Financial Times* (June 28, 2010).

14. Central Intelligence Agency, "Welcome to the World Factbook," *The World Factbook,* https://www.cia.gov/library/publications/the-world-factbook/index.html.

15. Central Intelligence Agency, "Middle East: United Arab Emirates."

16. For an overview of Arab states' reactions to Iran's nuclear program, see "Nuclear Programmes in the Middle East: In the Shadow of Iran," in *Strategic Dossier,* ed. John Chipman, International Institute for Strategic Studies, May 2008.

17. Simon Henderson, "The Elephant in the Gulf: Arab States and Iran's Nuclear Program." *Washington Institute for Near East Policy: Policy Watch* (December 22, 2005).

18. See Jeffrey Goldberg, "UAE Ambassador Endorses and American Strike on Iran," as posted on the blog site of the *Atlantic Monthly Magazine* (July 6, 2010), http://www.theatlantic.com/jeffrey-goldberg/.

19. Anthony Cordesman, *Security Challenges and Threats in the Gulf: A Net Assessment* (Washington, DC: Center for Strategic and International Studies, 2008), 4.

20. "Iran Neighbor UAE Spends $5 Bln on Arms Deals," *Reuters,* February 26, 2009.

21. *Middle East Online* (September 13, 2008), www.middle-east-online.com.

22. For a text of the treaty, as it was filed with the United Nations, see "Agreement between the Kingdom of Saudi Arabia and the United Arab Emirates on the Delimitation of Boundaries," *United Nations—Treaty Series* 1733, no. 30250 (1993), http://untreaty.un.org/unts/120001_144071/16/2/00012854.pdf.

23. Simon Henderson, "Map Wars," *Policy Watch,* no. 1069, Washington Institute for Near East Policy (January 19, 2006).

24. Justin Dargin, *The Dolphin Project: The Development of a Gas Initiative,* Oxford Institute for Energy Studies (UK), 2008.

25. Souhail Karam, "Saudi and UAE Border in Dispute over ID Cards," *Reuters,* August 23, 2009.

26. Central Intelligence Agency, "Middle East: United Arab Emirates."

3   IRAN

Iran rivals Egypt as a nation with an ancient and rich history and an identity that pre-dates Islam. Iranians trace their lineage to the ancient Persians, whose first great empire, under Cyrus the Great, was established in the sixth century BCE. Islam did not spread to Iran until 637 CE, when Arab armies defeated the Persian Sassanid Empire at the battle of Qadisiyya. Iranians subsequently played a large role in the cultural and religious dominance of the Abbasid Empire. But it was not until the 16th century that Iran began to reestablish its identity as a distinct political and national entity, when Ismail Safavi declared Persia's independence from the Ottoman Empire and founded what became the Safavid Empire. He also declared Shiism the state religion of the empire. From this point on, Iranians pursued a distinct identity in the broader Middle Eastern and Islamic contexts, one that continues to guide Iran's policies and the perception of Iran by its neighbors.

By the 18th century, the Safavid Empire was in decline, subject to attacks from Afghanistan and Russia, but Iran remained independent, if weak. Near the end of the 18th century, a new dynasty, the Qajars, came to power, but throughout most of the 19th century Iran struggled to maintain its sovereignty while playing off the great powers (Russia, Britain, and the Ottoman Empire). When the Ottoman Empire collapsed after World War I, and with Russia in the throes of revolution, the British were left standing and assumed the dominant role in Iran in the early 20th century, turning the country into a virtual protectorate. The discovery of large oil reserves in the early 20th century only enhanced Iran's attraction to Britain as well as to both British and U.S. oil companies.

The Qajar dynasty was overthrown in 1925 by its defense minister, Reza Khan, who anointed himself Reza Shah (or king) and established the Pahlavi Dynasty. Iran's new ruler sought to modernize the country, still woefully backward even by regional standards, and to weaken the British grip over the national economy and especially the oil sector. Reza Shah tried to counter British influence by employing the traditional Iranian tactic of playing off global powers: he developed friendly relations with both the Soviet Union and Nazi Germany. When World War II broke out, Iran declared its neutrality, despite British pressure to break with Germany. When Hitler attacked the Soviet Union, British pressure increased, for Iran was the only land route available to send Allied supplies to the Red Army. Eventually, British and Soviet troops moved on Tehran in 1941 and deposed Reza Shah in favor of his 22-year-old son, Mohammed Reza, who became the second Pahlavi shah.

After the war, Iran entered a tumultuous phase marked by surging anti-British nationalism, reflecting the nationalist movements that were arising throughout the Middle East. The target of popular ire was the Anglo-Iranian Oil Company, which had monopoly control over the country's energy resources and refused to share profits with the state. Responding to this popular sentiment, in 1951 the shah appointed Mohammed Mosaddeq as prime minister; one of his first acts was to nationalize the oil sector. Two years later, the U.S. Central Intelligence Agency staged a coup against Mosaddeq and, with the cooperation of the shah, crushed popular opposition. The shah now ruled as an autocrat, and the United States, having demonstrated its ability to intervene in Iranian affairs, now replaced Britain as the foreign overseer.

The shah was determined to transform Iran into a powerful modern nation and a dominant regional power, and he realized that, in order to bring this about, he would have to strike a tacit deal with the United States. He thus combined an aggressive modernization and industrialization program with close military ties to Washington; Iran became one of the United States' top markets for military equipment, particularly after the 1973 surge in oil prices filled Tehran's coffers. Thousands of U.S. military advisors flocked to Iran, and U.S. forces were given base rights in the country. Despite the outward display of Iranian nationalism and power, the shah was, in fact, a dependent ally, and members of the secular and prodemocratic opposition began to speak out. The shah, however, responded by ruthlessly oppressing all secular opposition, leading Iran to be cast as one of the worst human rights violators in the world.

The shah dared not, however, crack down on the Shiite clergy, who became the voice of opposition against a regime that was increasingly seen as despotic and too closely tied to the United States. By 1978, protests had become daily occurrences, and even the shah's vaunted security services were having a hard time keeping the situation under control. From Paris, where he lived in exile, the Ayatollah Ruholla Khomeini sent taped messages to his followers in Iran. Khomeini, a prominent Shiite cleric, had been an outspoken critic of the shah since the early 1960s, when he served time in jail for supporting protests against some of the shah's modernization plans (including giving women the right to vote). He also was strongly opposed to the highly visible U.S. presence in Iran, which he believed to be corrupting of Iran's core Islamic values. The shah sent him into exile in 1964.

As the shah's regimes crumbled in the face of massive protests—a forerunner, in many ways, to the spring of 2011—Khomeini prepared for his triumphant return, which took place on February 1, 1979, a mere two weeks after the shah fled the country. It was unclear at first what direction the revolution would take. The first prime minister appointed by Khomeini (who at the time had no official position or title) was

Mehdi Bazargan, a liberal secularist more akin to Mosaddeq than to the religious mullahs. But he lasted only nine months, succumbing to a continued revolutionary fervor that culminated in the seizure of the U.S. embassy by radical students, who proceeded to hold U.S. diplomats hostage for over two years. The students and their supporters among the clergy feared that the United States was planning to orchestrate another coup, as it had done against the reformist Mosaddeq 25 years earlier.

Iran could easily have descended into political turmoil at this stage of the revolution: The Kurdish region of the country was in open revolt, an armed opposition to the mullahs had formed (the Mujahedine-e-khalq), and the man who won presidential elections, Abulhassan Bani Sadr, fled to France after being impeached by the parliament and fearing that his arrest, and possible execution, were to follow. Bani Sadr was initially an ally of Khomeini's and won election with nearly 80 percent of the vote, but he soon fell into conflict with Khomeini and the other clerics over the issue of clerical power.

But Iran was spared a descent into political chaos in large part thanks to Saddam Hussein in neighboring Iraq. Fearing that Khomeini and his followers planned to extend the Iranian Revolution to Iraq's majority Shiite community, Saddam launched a war against the fragile Islamic Republic in 1980, perhaps hoping to nip in the bud the Shiite Islamic fervor that he believed posed such a threat to his continued control of Iraq. The Iraqi invasion served the purpose of unifying Iranians behind Khomeini and allowed the clerical leaders to postpone addressing the difficult issues the country faced, about which there were significant differences within the leadership.

If the war with Iraq was politically helpful to the Islamic regime, in all other respects it was disastrous for the nation. In eight years of fighting, Iran lost an estimated 1 million lives; many were children as young as 13 who were drafted into the army with promises of the glories of martyrdom. The Iranian economy, already reeling after several years of revolutionary turmoil, virtually collapsed, saved only by the fact that, as an oil exporter, Iran maintained a source of hard currency (and due to the war, oil prices rose appreciably). Iranians suspected, with good reason, that the United States was quietly finding ways to assist Saddam, despite the traditional animosity between the West and Iraq's Baathist regime. This only reinforced the Iranian fear that the United States would continue to try and orchestrate a political change in Tehran to its liking, a fear that dated back to the overthrow of Mosaddeq.

In 1988, Iran and Iraq accepted United Nations Security Council Resolution 598, which brought the war to an end. Khomeini did so only reluctantly, but his country was exhausted and running out of manpower. He died a few months later and was succeeded as supreme leader by Ali Khamenei. After eight years of brutal fighting and over 1 million fatalities on each side, the two countries returned to their prewar borders; nothing tangible had been accomplished except destruction, although internally both nations were now more unified. In just a few years' time, Iraq would launch another military adventure against Kuwait. But for Iran, the end of the long war meant a turn inward—and the landscape was not a pretty one. A stagnant economy kept afloat thanks to oil revenues was facing a host of U.S. trade and investment sanctions—including sanctions against any oil company, domestic and foreign, that invested in Iran's decaying energy infrastructure—and the loss of able-bodied men in the war.

At the same time, Iran's population had boomed, from around 40 million in 1980 to 57 million in 1990, and the number of Iranians under the age of 15 represented nearly one-third of the population.[1] Within a decade, the bulging youth population would begin to have consequences for Iranian political developments.

In 1997, Mohammed Khatami was elected president with significant support from young voters (the voting age in Iran is 16) and women. Khatami was regarded as a reformist and was not the candidate of choice of the conservative religious community. But Iran had changed, and unlike Bani Sadr—whose struggles with the clerics led to his ouster and exile—Khatami served for two terms. But his administration was marked by almost constant struggle to implement reforms against the will of the religious leadership of the country, which still wielded overwhelming power (under the constitution of the Islamic Republic, the supreme leader controls the army, including the powerful and loyal Revolutionary Guards, as well as the judiciary and the media). Despite his popularity, Khatami's room for maneuver was severely restricted. Near the end o the Clinton administration in the United States, there were rumors that the United States and Khatami were holding behind-the-scenes dialogue to attempt a reconciliation, or at least to moderate the mutual hostility in the bilateral relationship, although Khamenei and the clerical establishment remained opposed to establishing ties with the United States.

In 2005, Mahmoud Ahmadinejad, a political newcomer, was elected president. Ahmadinejad had served for two years as the appointed mayor of Tehran, where he had reversed many of the previous mayor's reform initiatives. He campaigned as a conservative and received the backing of the religious leadership, including Khamenei. He claimed to be a "common man" and pledged to direct more of the state's oil revenues to working-class Iranians. He also vowed not to pursue reconciliation with the United States and to continue developing Iran's nuclear power, although he claimed the program was for peaceful purposes only. He won in a runoff election with 62 percent of the vote.

Ahmadinejad immediately became a controversial figure, both inside and outside Iran. Many of his public statements attracted international attention—especially his denial of the Holocaust and his extreme animosity toward Israel. And despite his pledges, the economy continued to stagnate (in part because of Western sanctions) and inflation soared; life for the average Iranian, 20 percent of whom lived below the poverty level, did not improve in Ahmadinejad's first term. Ahmadinejad faced three challengers when he ran for reelection in 2009—all presidential candidates in Iran must be approved by the cleric-controlled Guardian Council, and 476 had applied for candidacy. One of the approved candidates was Mir-Hossein Mousavi, a former prime minister who was seen as a reform candidate with strong support among moderates and youth; he also was endorsed by former president Khatami. Mousavi ran on a platform of more free-market economic policies, including privatizations of state-owned assets. He also promised a less combative tone in foreign affairs than Ahmadinejad had displayed, although he too supported Iran's nuclear program.

Ahmadinejad won handily in the first round, garnering 62 percent of the vote. The opposition immediately claimed election fraud and pointed to numerous incidents throughout the country. The Western press and governments generally supported allegations of electoral fraud, as did several academic observers.[2] In a harbinger of the spring of 2011, pro-Mousavi supporters took to the streets soon after the election results were in and accusations of fraud had been voiced. The protests quickly became the largest such demonstrations since the 1978–1979 Iranian Revolution. At first Mousavi urged his followers to remain calm, but after a few days he appeared before them at a rally attended by up to 3 million protesters.[3] As the protests spread and grew, the movement was coined the Green Revolution, a reference to the Mousavi campaign's colors; like the revolutions that would rock the Arab world in two years' time, many of the protesters communicated with each other by cell phones and Twitter. Supreme Leader Khamenei declared the elections to be fair but also ordered an investigation into the claims of irregularities.

The protests were met by violent responses from the police and the Basij, a paramilitary force that operates under the guidance of the Revolutionary Guards in support of the clerical establishment, and scores of people were killed and wounded. Pro-Ahmadinejad supporters also were rallied to challenge the Green Movement for control of the streets. For a brief period, it appeared that Iran was on the verge of political change, but government forces regained control of the streets after several weeks of unrest. It is important to recognize that the protests in Iran were directed at what was perceived to be a fraudulent election—as well as at the underlying economic situation—and not at the overthrow of the Islamic Republic. It was more of a civil rights movement and a protest against perceived corruption than it was a revolution; the common chant among protesters was "Where is my vote?" not "down with the regime," although there were some isolated calls for an end to theocratic rule. Nevertheless, it began a process of popular political activism that would soon be seen in the Arab world as well.[4]

Iran faces a number of potential conflicts, both internal as well as against foreign foes. The internal conflicts are not only related to demands for more political openness by groups such as the Green Movement, but also to intraregime struggles. Moreover, Iran's population of 78 million is only 51 percent ethnic Iranian; other large groups include Azeris, Kurds, Arabs, and Turkmen, and at various times these minority groups have demanded greater freedoms. Another internal challenge could come from Iran's Sunni population, which represents just under 10 percent of the population,[5] and members of the armed antirevolutionary movement Mujahedine-e-khalq. Externally, Iran faces potential conflicts with Israel and the West over its nuclear program and against Saudi Arabia and the Gulf Cooperation Council (GCC) states over dominance of the Gulf region. For most of the 21st century, Iran has literally been surrounded by conflicts—in Afghanistan and Iraq—that involved the heavy presence of U.S. troops. As these conflicts wind down, Iran may feel less encircled but no less threatened.

INTERNAL SOURCES OF CONFLICT

While Western observers often portray Iran in monolithic terms, the creation of the Islamic Republic of Iran in 1979 did not create an internally unified nation, and Iran's often baffling policies do not reflect the behavior of a unitary actor. In the republic's early days, signs of discord were evident in the impeachment and exile of President Bani Sadr, the arrest and execution of many political figures who initially had been aligned with the clerical government, the appearance of armed resistance in the form of the Mujahedine-e-khalq and other groups, and the voluntary exile of thousands of secular Iranians. Were it not for the war with Iraq, which served to unify Iranians behind the government, the revolution may very well have taken a different and uncertain course.

Iranian leaders long have used external threats—in particular, the United States and Israel—to rally the populace and dampen internal opposition. But not far beneath the surface are a number of serious conflicts that, alone or in combination, could threaten the stability of the government.

Regime Infighting and Succession

From its establishment, the Islamic Republic has wrestled with a complicated power structure, enshrined in a constitution (which was approved in a national referendum in December 1979) that features overlapping authority and places significant power in the hands of unelected religious leaders. The ultimate authority in the country is the unelected supreme leader, a religious figure, of which there have been but two: Ayatollah Khomeini and Ali Khamenei. Although the president and parliament are elected, candidates must be approved by the Guardian Council, an unelected institution made up of clerics and religious scholars, and the supreme leader officially ratifies the president's election. The Guardian Council has the power to veto any laws passed by parliament if it deems them to be counter to Islam. Although popularly elected, Iran's presidents have limited power and very little leverage over the religious leadership.

This inherent tension in the Iranian system almost ensures that infighting will occur within the regime. The reformist president Khatami, for example, considered not running for reelection in 2001 due to the fact that so many of his initiatives during his first term were rejected or foiled by the clerical establishment, and many of his supporters were arrested or assassinated. Even when Khatami decided to run—and proceeded to win overwhelmingly—the conservative religious leaders continued to successfully block his efforts at reform.

Unlike Khatami, Mahmoud Ahmadinejad ran for president with the support of the conservative religious leaders, who strongly backed him after the controversial 2009 elections. But he too has clashed with the clerics, and the conflict came to a head in 2010 and 2011, when conservatives accused the president of trying to usurp powers, in both domestic and foreign policies, that rightfully belonged to the supreme leader. Ahmadinejad also began channeling state funds to sectors of Iranian society, such as the urban poor, in an effort to broaden and expand his constituency; conservatives and clerics saw this as an attempt by the president to go over their heads and create a power base of his own. Some conservatives accused him of trying to ensure his own influence after 2013, when his second term ends (presidents are allowed to serve only two terms), by designating an heir apparent. This act alone was an affront to the clerics, who always have believed that presidential candidates must be approved by the Guardian Council and endorsed by the supreme leader.

The religious leadership expressed its strong disapproval of Ahmadinejad. The Guardian Council refused to allow him to fire his intelligence minister and revoked

Iran's mercurial president Mahmoud Ahmadinejad
speaks under a portrait of Ayatollah Ali Khamenei,
the country's religious leader who holds immense political power. (AFP/Getty Images)

his appointment of himself as oil minister. Ahmadinejad's chief advisor, who
many believed he was grooming to succeed him in 2013, was squeezed out of
power and then arrested.[6] By the middle
of 2011, there was no doubt that the balance of power in Iran remained in favor
of the supreme leader and the Guardian Council. At best, Ahmadinejad faces
two more years of declining power and
influence, possibly even irrelevance; at
worst, he could be impeached by the
parliament.

Ahmadinejad's travails reflect a phenomenon that will be an ongoing tension
in Iranian politics. Elected leaders, especially when they have a popular base
of support, will continue to be inclined
to challenge the clerical authorities by
trying to expand presidential power.
This will be true of conservative presidents, such as Ahmadinejad, as well as
of reformist presidents, although the latter will have the additional challenge of
trying to advance policies that the cler-
ics ideologically oppose. The clerics will, no doubt, continue to resist, and continue to
enjoy the leverage, power, and constitutional authority to do so. The title supreme leader
is indeed appropriate, so perhaps the biggest question in Iran is not who will succeed
Ahmadinejad in 2013, but rather who ultimately will succeed the elderly Khamenei.

Iranian foreign and domestic policies likely will continue to reflect this tension
between the weak elected government and the powerful unelected one. But like all political tensions based on inherent contradictions, there ultimately will be a resolution.

The Green Movement

Following the controversial 2009 election and subsequent unrest, Mir-Hossein
Mousavi, the presidential candidate defeated by Ahmadinejad, formed an association
called the Green Path of Hope, popularly known as the Green Movement (he emphasized that he was not starting a political party, an illegal move that would have subjected him to possible arrest). Mousavi's goal was to maintain nonviolent pressure on
Ahmadinejad and, by extension, on the clerical establishment that had backed him. He
particularly aimed to motivate Iran's youth. The movement was immediately subject
to repressive actions by the government, and Mousavi and some of its other founders
were placed under virtual house arrest. The Green Movement called for demonstrations to be held on February 11, 2010, the anniversary of the founding of the Islamic

Republic, but the regime succeeded in thwarting any action through preemptive arrests and a visible presence on the streets.

The revolutionary tide that struck the Arab world in early 2011 did not reverberate strongly in Iran, other than in a few sporadic and uncoordinated street protests, despite calls by the Green Movement and other reformist groups for action. The forces of coercion in Iran—the army, the Republican Guard, and the Basij—remain loyal to the supreme leader and under his control, and they took preemptive steps to prevent mass action (and forceful responses to the actions that did occur). The Green Movement's inability to generate a response was indicative of both its failure to evolve into a mass organization as well as the continuing power of the government. In fact, Khamenei initially issued several statements in support of the Arab revolutionaries, both to position himself on the right side of history as well as out of genuine animosity toward the pro-U.S. leaders who were the targets of unrest. His tone changed, however, when the events of spring 2011 erupted in Syria, Iran's closest ally in the Arab world.

A significant difference between Iran and the Arab states that witnessed political revolutions is that there is at least a façade of electoral choice in Iran. While the supreme leader has authoritarian powers, and the opaque Guardian Council makes many decisions that affect the electoral process, political campaigns have been competitive and candidates have offered truly contrasting positions on issues. Moreover, Iran is a deeply religious nation, which grants a certain degree of legitimacy to the supreme leader that an authoritarian military leader such as Egypt's Mubarak or Tunisia's Ben Ali never enjoyed. Iran, like all countries, will experience political change over time. But unlike some of its neighbors in the region, such change is likely to be evolutionary (and reflective of struggles among political elites) rather than revolutionary, with spikes of unrest and possible violence.

The 2012 parliamentary elections and the 2013 presidential contest could again create conditions (or electoral outcomes) that arouse public opposition, and the massive demonstrations after the 2009 vote are evidence that Iranians are willing to take to the streets—and also evidence that the regime is not hesitant to respond with force. Despite uncertainty about its effectiveness and the regime's determination to suppress it, the Green Movement has the potential to coalesce into a legitimate opposition force against the regime, connected as much by social networking technology as by any discreet actions.

Mujahedine-e-Khalq

The Mujahedine-e-khalq was established in the 1960s as an armed opposition movement against the shah, with the goal of overthrowing his regime. In the 1970s, it launched several armed attacks against Iranian government targets as well as U.S. targets in Iran. Although a leftist-secular organization, the Mujahedine-e-khalq initially supported the Islamic Revolution, but by 1981 it was at odds with the Khomeini regime and sought its overthrow. In 1997, the U.S. State Department designated the Mujahedine-e-khalq a terrorist organization (principally for actions it had undertaken in the 1970s) and refused all contact with it. In 2009, the European Union removed the group from its list of terrorist organizations, and the group's leaders have requested that the U.S. State Department follow suit.

The Iranian regime accused the Mujahedine-e-khalq of involvement in the 2009 unrest, but this may have been an attempt to discredit the popular uprising by linking it to a terrorist organization. The Mujahedine-e-khalq undoubtedly supports the Green Movement, but there is no evidence that the groups coordinate their activities or are even in contact; Green Movement leaders have reiterated that they wish to achieve the goal of regime change by peaceful means.

The exact number of Mujahedine-e-khalq fighters is unknown, although U.S. forces encountered several thousand at a camp in eastern Iraq during the U.S. invasion in 2003. U.S. forces confiscated the fighters' weapons but allowed them to remain in Iraq. It is unlikely that there are many Mujahedine-e-khalq fighters inside Iran, and the group has not claimed responsibility for any armed actions in many years.

Ethnic Insurgencies

Just over 50 percent of Iran's population is ethnic Persian. The remainder is a mix of various ethnic groups, the largest being Azeris (around 25 percent); other groups include Kurds, Arabs, Baluchs, and Turkmen. Many members of these communities feel alienated from the Islamic Republic government in Tehran, for a range of reasons. For some, alienation is based on religious differences (the Baluchs and many Kurds, for example, are Sunni Muslims). For others, it is based on the fact that the Islamic Republic is a highly centralized government, with major decisions made in Tehran with little input from non-Persians or residents of other ethnic regions. Economic disparity is also a feature of modern Iran, with outlying regions more likely to suffer from economic underdevelopment and fewer state resources. Moreover, all of Iran's minority groups have compatriots living across the country's borders in Iraq, Azerbaijan, Afghanistan, Turkmenistan, and Pakistan. Some analysts have compared Iran to the former Soviet Union, another multiethnic state with a dominant ethnic group (Russians) and severe disparities among regions.[7]

Iran long has accused outside powers of fomenting unrest among its minority groups. One of Tehran's concerns during the eight-year war with Iraq was that Iran's Arab population, which is centered along the country's southwestern border with Iraq, would support Saddam Hussein. Heightening Iran's concern was the fact that this region also holds the largest reserves of the country's oil and gas resources. The majority of Iran's Arab population remained loyal to Tehran, perhaps because, as Shia, they resented Saddam's suppression of their Shia brethren in Iraq. Nevertheless, a shadowy Arab insurgent movement exists and has conducted a number of bombings against government targets.

The two most potent and significant ethnic insurgencies are those of the Kurds and the Baluchs.

The Kurdish PJAK

Around 7 percent of Iran's population is Kurdish, with principal population concentrations in the western area of the country along the borders with Iraq and Turkey.[8]

Although there is a long history of Kurdish separatism in Iran—just as there is in Iraq and Turkey—Kurdish society is tribal in structure, and the competing tribes have had a difficult time unifying. Neither the shah's government nor the current Islamic Republic has been willing to grant the Kurds autonomy, and both have viewed the Kurds as potential sources of rebellion. The fact that the majority of Kurds are Sunni has further inhibited their integration into Iran's Shia-dominated society and government. During the Iran-Iraq War, both countries sought to stoke rebellions by the other country's Kurdish community, but this only led to greater repression of both communities.

An armed Iranian Kurdish resistance group, the Free Life Party (known by its Kurdish language acronym PJAK) is based in Iraq and is believed to be closely associated with the major Turkish Kurdish opposition group, the PKK. As a result, PJAK also is on the U.S. State Department's list of terrorist organizations, along with the PKK. PJAK has conducted a number of guerilla attacks inside Iran, mostly targeted at Iranian security forces. Iranian forces have responded by arresting, and usually executing, PJAK leaders and by staging attacks of their own against Kurdish towns in the western part of the country.

PJAK has demonstrated the ability to inflict damage on the Iranian regime, but primarily limited to the areas where the Kurdish population is concentrated. It is not conceivable that the PJAK could pose an actual threat to the regime, except in the context of a broader regime collapse in the face of intense opposition pressure, in which case PJAK would be able to contribute to the opposition effort. However, PJAK's fundamental goal is independence for Iran's Kurds, and no Iranian government—whether secular and liberal or religious and conservative—is likely to support this.

Independence, or even greatly enhanced autonomy, by Iraqi Kurds could serve to inspire PJAK and Iranian Kurds, and possibly create a source of external support.

Jundullah: The Baluchi Insurgency

The seminomadic Baluchi people inhabit an area that includes Iran, Pakistan, and Afghanistan. The majority of the 8 million Baluchis live in Pakistan, but Iran is home to around 2 million of the predominantly Sunni Baluchis.[9] Many Baluchis in all three of the countries they inhabit have sought independence—or, at a minimum, greater autonomy—in a new Baluchi nation. The Iranian Baluchis have not fared well under the Islamic Republic, which has been suspicious of both their secessionist tendencies as well as their Sunni religion. As a result, Iran's largely Baluchi province of Sistan va Baluchistan has suffered under the Islamic Republic: it is Iran's most economically backward province and its people have been subject to discrimination and periodic crackdowns. Under President Ahmadinejad, the repression grew worse, as the regime in Tehran closed a number of Sunni mosques and religious institutions in Sistan va Baluchistan.[10]

Not surprisingly, Tehran's repression has been met with resistance by the Baluchis—including armed resistance in the form of a guerilla organization called Jundullah. Beginning in 2009, Jundullah launched a series of high-profile attacks, including against Revolutionary Guard units in Sistan va Baluchistan, local police forces, and the suicide bombing of a Shia mosque in the capital city of Sistan va Baluchistan.[11]

The government in Tehran has accused the United States and Saudi Arabia of providing aid and support to Jundullah, despite the fact that the United States in 2010 declared Jundullah a terrorist group. More likely, Jundullah receives support from al-Qaeda and the Taliban, both of which are Sunni based and have incentives to undermine Iran's Shia regime. In February 2010, Iran captured and executed Jundullah's leader, but the resistance movement has continued its attacks.

Jundullah's reach is limited, as are its goals. It is capable of launching guerilla and terrorist actions in Sistan va Baluchistan but probably not much farther afield. The greatest risk Jundullah poses to the Iranian regime would be in the event of significant political turmoil in Iran that required the regime to center its security forces on Tehran or other major cities. In this event, Jundullah (as well as Kurdish and other separatist groups) would very likely take advantage of the opportunity to intensify its guerilla activities.

EXTERNAL SOURCES OF CONFLICT

Iran does not lack for enemies. Since the Islamic Republic was established in 1979, Iran has found itself in direct or indirect conflict with Saddam Hussein's Iraq; the Taliban government in Afghanistan; Israel; the United States and other Western powers; and Saudi Arabia and the GCC states. Some of these conflicts predated the establishment of the Islamic Republic and have ancient roots, such as the Persian-Arab competition for supremacy, the Sunni-Shia doctrinal rift, and the various tribal and ethnic conflicts that transcend regional state borders. But there is no doubt that the Islamic Republic has faced a generally hostile external environment and in turn has conducted regional and international policies that have exacerbated rather than ameliorated this hostility.

Theories abound about the goals and objectives of Iranian foreign policy. Some interpret Iranian actions as essentially defensive and designed to ensure that the Islamic Republic is respected in the region and regarded as a prominent actor in the Gulf. Others view Iran's policies as essentially revolutionary, a concerted program to undermine pro-Western governments throughout the Middle East and to secure greater control over energy policy and other issues in the Gulf region.[12]

The United States

The Islamic Republic and the United States have been enemies for over 30 years; the two countries do not have diplomatic relations and have made diplomatic contact only infrequently over the past three decades. The conditions under which the Islamic Republic was founded—by the overthrow of a U.S. ally, the shah—and the ensuing hostage crisis created an environment of animosity that has proven difficult to improve. The fact that the Iranian regime has relied on external enemies to enhance its domestic political control has further inhibited an improvement in relations between the United States and Iran.

But the U.S.-Iranian relationship has not been determined only by mutual resentment and mistrust. Rather, there are fundamental ideological and strategic differences between the two countries that have been exacerbated by emotional factors. The Iranian Revolution was motivated in large part by a desire to return Iran to its Shia Islamic roots and reverse the westernizing policies of the shah. The United States, in particular, epitomized what Iran's revolutionaries viewed as the corrupting influence of the West as well as the Western powers' desire to dominate and control Iran through puppet rulers such as the shah. Even if the two nations established an ongoing diplomatic dialogue, the fundamental differences in perspective and objectives would continue to limit the extent of any reconciliation. Moreover, many of Iran's regional objectives and ambitions are nationalistic in nature and thus would likely remain even if there were a change of regime.

The fundamental sources of conflict in the U.S.-Iran relationship are:

- Iran's regional political activism, which in almost all cases runs counter to U.S. objectives or threatens U.S. allies. These ideologically driven actions include Iran's support for Syria, the Hezbollah organization in Lebanon, extremist Shia organizations in Iraq, Hamas in Palestine, and antiregime elements in Saudi Arabia and the GCC states. From the Iranian perspective, U.S. support for Israel and conservative Arab regimes, such as Saudi Arabia and Jordan, are direct challenges to Iran's goals of regional influence. One exception to the situation is the mutual animosity Iran and the United States share for the Afghan Taliban.
- Iran's desire to be recognized as the dominant power in the Gulf region. This nationalistic goal—one that was shared and pursued as much by the shah as by the Islamic Republic—is opposed by the United States primarily because the Islamic Republic is not a U.S. ally and seeks to advance an ideological agenda that is incompatible with U.S. goals. By contrast, the United States was the shah's principal arms supplier, as he was seen to be an anti-Soviet bulwark and a supporter of U.S. objectives (under the shah, for example, Iran maintained diplomatic relations with Israel).
- The U.S. objective of preserving Western access to oil and gas resources in the Gulf region and Central Asia, preferably via the active involvement of Western energy and exploration firms, and the maintenance of steady and reliable energy prices. This objective runs counter to the Islamic Republic's goal of minimizing Western, and especially U.S., influence in the region as well as Iran's desire for greater influence within the Organization of the Petroleum Exporting Countries (OPEC) cartel.

Most of the issues of contention in the U.S.-Iranian relationship relate to one or more of these fundamental sources of conflict. The tensions in the bilateral relationship are compounded by elements of historic mistrust, mutual recriminations, and extremist rhetoric—the latter principally from Iran, such as Ahmadinejad's denial of the Holocaust and threats against Israel, but also have been evident in U.S. policy, such as President George W. Bush's labeling Iran as an "axis of evil."

U.S. concerns about Iran's nuclear energy program and its strong opposition to Iran developing nuclear weapons is a function of these underlying sources of conflict. Few believe that Iran would ever use a nuclear weapon, especially given that the most likely target (Israel) possesses a massive retaliatory capability of its own. Rather, the cause of concern is the existence of an Iranian nuclear retaliatory capability, which would allow Iran to more brazenly interfere in the affairs of other states in the region and more convincingly claim that it must be accepted as the region's dominant power.

The key issue to consider when analyzing Iran's nuclear objectives is Iranian national interests, as perceived in Tehran. If Iran's leaders determine that the acquisition of nuclear weapons capability will enhance Iran's security, status, and leverage, then Iran is likely to continue down the path to nuclear weapons regardless of the sanctions or threats it receives from the United States or Israel. In fact, these sanctions and threats may only reinforce the security arguments of those in Iran who favor developing a nuclear weapons capability.[13]

The U.S.-Iranian cold war is likely to continue into the foreseeable future. Even a more reformist Iranian regime will continue to pursue the regional policies that are of concern to the United States, and the chances of any Iranian government—even one not dominated by clerics—entering into a partnership or alliance with the United States is remote. Nevertheless, any changes that bring about greater trust and less rhetorical hostility would lessen the chances of the cold war becoming a hot war. Such changes, however, would have to be mutual: President Obama's initial outreach to Iran and his rejection of the more hostile posture that had been adopted by President Bush was not reciprocated in Tehran, perhaps demonstrating that the U.S. role as "Great Satan" is still an important binding agent in Iranian politics.

After three decades, the U.S.-Iranian cold war has developed into a relatively stable confrontation, in which each side seems to understand the boundaries of the interaction and the other side's red lines—the lines that, if crossed, might lead to direct armed conflict. This understanding is especially important for Iran, which has more to lose in a direct military confrontation. Thus, although U.S. military forces spent much of the first decade of the 21st century in combat operations in neighboring Iraq and Afghanistan, Iran maintained a cautious policy that did not provoke the United States (of course, this was facilitated by the fact that the United States and Iran both desired the ouster of Saddam Hussein and the Taliban; in effect, the U.S. military helped to advance Iranian foreign policy goals).

Iranian students rally in Isfahan in support of their country's nuclear energy program, which is widely popular in Iran even among regime opponents. (AP Photo/Vahid Salemi)

Although a direct military confrontation between the United States and Iran must be rated as highly unlikely, there certainly exist scenarios in which such a confrontation could occur:

Israel-Iran conflict: An Israeli-Iranian conflict, either direct or indirect through proxies such as Hezbollah, could easily draw the United States into a military confrontation with the Islamic Republic. For example, if Israel were to launch a preemptive military strike against Iran's nuclear facilities, as it has threatened to do, Iran could very well respond by attempting to close off the strategic Strait of Hormuz, through which much of the Gulf's oil ships. In this scenario, the United Sates and other Western powers would likely take military action to keep the waterway open. A direct Iranian military attack on Israel would also lead to calls for U.S. action, even though Israel is more than capable of defending itself from Iran.

Iran crosses the nuclear threshold: If Iran were to become a military nuclear power, the United States would be obliged to respond in some manner—if for no other reason than to maintain credibility, given that U.S. presidents from Clinton through Obama have declared that an Iranian nuclear weapons capability is unacceptable. The possible U.S. responses to an imminent Iranian nuclear capability range from a preemptive military strike—either unilaterally or in alliance with Israel and other allies—to subversive actions against Iranian facilities to a severe tightening of international sanctions against Iran, up to and including a complete international ban on the purchase of Iranian oil. Even as a preemptive action, a military strike against Iran would be wrought with potential complications, and several statements by U.S. military leaders in 2010 and 2011 suggested that a such a strike was not the preferred U.S. response to the Iranian nuclear program.[14] If Iran were to achieve the ability to manufacture and deliver nuclear weapons, U.S. options for a military response would diminish substantially, and U.S. options would be limited to sanctions.[15]

Iranian attack on Gulf Arab states: Iran does not possess the military capability of launching a sustained military operation against the much better armed members of the GCC, so a direct war is not likely. In the event, however (perhaps in response to Iranian actions against the Strait of Hormuz), the United States would certainly come to the assistance of its GCC allies, most likely through supportive measures such as additional arms sales and logistical help. More problematic would be Iranian subversive actions against one or more of the Arab states—such as Bahrain (this, in fact, already has occurred). Here again, U.S. support for its allies probably would be indirect, although a direct threat to U.S. interests—such as the U.S. Navy's Bahrain-based 5th Fleet or Gulf oil supplies—could provoke a direct U.S. military response.

Civil unrest in Iran: Based on the U.S. response to events in the Middle East in the spring of 2011 (and, in particular, the U.S. response to the unrest in Syria, an Iranian ally), it is highly improbable that the United States would become directly involved in political unrest in Iran. While the United States would offer rhetorical support to groups that wish to replace the Islamic Republic with a more liberal form of government (as well as behind-the-scenes financial support), direct U.S. involvement would risk reinforcing support for the regime and would involve U.S. forces coming into direct confrontation with well-armed Iranian forces, such as the Revolutionary Guards, who would remain loyal to the regime. If, however, a future regime crackdown against liberal forces (such as the Green Movement) took an extremely violent form, political pressure from publics in the United States and the West might force the United States to respond with indirect but coercive military actions, such as a naval blockade or no-fly zone.

Iranian intervention in Iraq: As the United States completes its withdrawal from Iraq, concerns about the country's future stability, and how to maintain it, are mounting (see chapter 4, on Iraq), and Iran's role in its neighbor's future is a cause of concern. Iran's exact goals in Iraq are subject to debate: Those who see Iran as an essentially aggressive power fear that the Islamic Republic seeks to secure Shia dominance in Iraq to use it as a base for expanding Iran's influence throughout the Arab world. Those who hold a more defensive view of Iran's regional policy consider that Iran's primary objective is to ensure that Iraq never again becomes a threat to Iran and to protect the rights of the Shia majority in Iraq.

There is no doubt that the U.S. invasion of Iraq and overthrow of Saddam Hussein greatly benefited Iran, because it removed from power Tehran's arch enemy and the ensuing election process brought to power an Iraqi government dominated by Shia political parties. But during 2004–2008—the period of greatest instability in Iraq that many regard as a civil war—the United States and Iran found themselves in indirect conflict, as Iran armed and funded Shia militia organizations that in turn attacked U.S. forces. But by 2010, both the United States and Iran had agreed to support a second term for Nuri al-Maliki as prime minister (Iran had for several years supported Maliki's Shia-dominated party), and the violence subsided along with the beginning of the U.S. withdrawal. As long as Iraq is governed by a Shia majority who regard the Islamic Republic as an ally, Iran will be satisfied with the outcome.

The danger of renewed conflict in Iraq, or even renewed civil war, after the U.S. withdrawal is significant, and Iran would act to ensure that such a conflict did not harm its interests or that of its Iraqi allies. This could lead to more direct Iranian involvement in conflict, specifically through Tehran's support of Shia militias and armed groups such as the Mahdi Army of Shia cleric Moqtada al-Sadr. Such Iranian interference would pose a dilemma for the United States but would be highly unlikely to lead to the redeployment of U.S. troops; more likely, the United States would limit its activity to supporting and arming anti-Iranian elements, perhaps in conjunction with Saudi Arabia and other GCC states.

Iraq

The future of Iranian-Iraqi relations will, to a large degree, determine the state of stability or instability in the Gulf region.[16] As noted, Tehran benefited from the ouster of Saddam Hussein and the political empowerment of the Iraqi Shia community. His-torical ties connect Iran to Iraq's Shia, most of Iraq's major Shia political parties re-ceived support from Tehran in their formative stages, and many of Iraq's Shia leaders lived in exile in Iran during the Saddam era. With the U.S. withdrawal, one might posit that Iraq will soon become a de facto Iranian satellite, a situation that would be of grave concern to the United States and the Sunni-dominated regimes of the GCC. But this is not likely to happen.

First, both Sunni and Shia Iraqis view their identity as Arab (Kurdish identity is a different issue). The traditional Persian-Arab competition would inhibit too great an Iranian role in Iraq. During the Iran-Iraq war of 1980–1989, the vast majority of Iraqi Shia remained loyal to Iraq and did not rise up in support of the Islamic Republic, as some (including some in Tehran) might have expected.

Second, if democracy takes root in Iraq and internal conflicts are dealt with through the political process, the sense of Iraqi identity and nationality will continue to grow, making it further unlikely that Iraq would willingly accept the role of an Iranian satel-lite. Moreover, the potential stability of democratic Iraq will serve as a model to Ira-nian reformists, such as members of the Green Movement, and a model that will not necessarily be to Tehran's liking. In the event of renewed civil unrest in Iran along the lines of the June 2009 demonstrations, Iraqi politicians may feel inclined to support the reformists.

Finally, Iraq's leaders will be careful to weigh the concerns of Saudi Arabia and the GCC states and are well aware that becoming too close to Tehran could provoke subversive actions by the Arab states of the Gulf to defend Iraq's Sunnis and contain Iranian influence.

Israel

Israel and Iran have a complicated relationship. Under the former shah, the two countries enjoyed diplomatic relations and were regarded as two of the pillars of U.S. strategic policy in the region. With the advent of the Islamic Republic, the relationship became one of intense animosity and hostility, as Iran's clerical leaders declared Israel to be but an outpost of the "Great Satan" United States, and one that, as a Jewish state, represented a defilement of the Muslim world. Nevertheless, the two nations found themselves uncomfortably in alliance on certain issues, such as the need to remove Iraq's Saddam Hussein from power, and rumors abounded of secret Israeli-Iranian co-operation and even arms shipments.

The election of Mahmoud Ahmadinejad further exacerbated Iranian-Israeli rela-tions, at both the rhetorical level (such as Ahmadinejad's bombastic threats to destroy Israel and his blatant anti-Semitism, and Israel's vows to attack Iran if it came close to developing nuclear weapons) as well as at the level of policy (Iran's nuclear program accelerated, to the great consternation of Israel). Ahmadinejad also pursued a proxy war against Israel by strengthening Iran's ties to Syria and to Lebanon's Hezbollah party as well as the Palestinian Hamas organization, which controlled the Gaza Strip.

Because of the intensity of the animosity, the lack of direct communication, and the fact that domestic political dynamics in both states promotes confrontation, the

Israeli-Iranian cold war will continue as long as the clerical regime controls Iran. Moreover, it could very easily become a hot war, in the form of either a direct military confrontation or, more likely, a proxy war. Several scenarios are possible:

Israeli military strike against Iranian nuclear facilities: Israeli officials on numerous occasions have stated that the development of nuclear weapons by Iran would be an existential threat to Israel and a development that the Jewish state would not allow to take place. Israeli concerns reached a fever pitch in 2009 and 2010, when many commentators argued that an Israeli military strike had become inevitable, despite the fact that U.S. leaders were opposed to an Israeli action.[17] But in late 2010, U.S. intelligence agencies began leaking analyses that concluded Iran was farther from nuclear weapons capability than once thought, which lessened the urgency for a preemptive attack. Moreover, in mid-2009, the United States and Israel began deploying a computer worm—known as Stuxnet—with the goal of undermining Iran's nuclear facilities from the inside. Stuxnet, described as "the most sophisticated cyberweapon ever deployed,"[18] wreaked havoc on Iran's nuclear facilities and is believed to have substantially delayed the program's progress. In addition, Israeli strategists increasingly concluded that the risks of a military strike outweigh the benefits. Israel does not have the capability to destroy all Iranian nuclear-related targets in one blow, so the best that could be accomplished is a further delay in the program. Iran's likely retaliation for an Israeli strike also is a source of concern to Israeli (and U.S.) leaders: Such retaliation could range from stoking another war with Hezbollah along the Israeli-Lebanese border, terrorist strikes against Israeli or Jewish targets across the globe, or attacks against energy-related targets in the Gulf. After the Green Movement's rise in 2009, Israeli and U.S. officials also began to consider the consequences of an Israeli strike for domestic politics in Iran: by arousing nationalist sentiment, an Israeli attack could bolster the clerical regime at the expense of budding liberal activists. By mid-2011, the odds of an Israeli military strike against Iran had diminished substantially, but the threat remains, and a sudden advance in Iranian nuclear capabilities could place the option back on the table.

Israeli-Hezbollah confrontation or war: Hezbollah, although an indigenous Lebanese political movement, is in many ways a proxy military force for Iran, from whom it receives most of its arms and military training. Thus, a renewal of open hostilities between Israel and Hezbollah automatically becomes a proxy war between Israel and Iran, with the risk of spreading to other fronts. As Hezbollah becomes an increasingly legitimized actor in Lebanese politics, however, its ties to Iran may loosen; at a minimum, Hezbollah will calculate the costs and benefits of a conflict with Israel based on its own objectives, not those of Iran.

Political instability in Syria: The Baath regime in Syria is Iran's closest ally in the Arab world and an important conduit for Iranian arms to Hezbollah and Iranian influence over the Palestinian issue. Syria also is Israel's only well-armed Arab foe and a country with which Israel has fought several wars. Israel's occupation and subsequent annexation of Syria's Golan Heights ensures that the two countries will remain enemies for the foreseeable future. An Israeli-Iranian confrontation could arise in the context of civil war or extended political turmoil in Syria. In such an event, Iran would likely come to the aid of its allies—essentially, the ruling Assad family and senior Alawite leaders. The shipment of Iranian arms to Syria would be seen as a threat by Israel, as would the presence of Iranian military advisors. While Israel would not be likely to become directly involved in a Syrian civil war, it would undoubtedly regard certain outcomes as unacceptable (such as a government that was even more beholden to Iran) and would take steps to prevent these outcomes from occurring. It should be noted, however, that, due to geographic constraints, Iran would have a very limited ability to send military forces to Syria. This fact lessens the chances of a direct Israeli-Iranian confrontation.

Saudi Arabia and the GCC

Yet another cold war Iran finds itself in is with the majority Sunni Arab monarchical states of the Gulf region that are united in a collective security pact—the Gulf Cooperation Council—that was founded largely due to fears aroused by the Islamic revolution in Iran in 1979. This cold war is based on several core incompatibilities: ideological differences (conservative monarchies as opposed to Iran's republican form of government); religious differences (Shia versus Sunni Islam); and historical competition between Persians and Arabs. It is compounded by strategic competition over influence in the Gulf region and control within the decision-making process of OPEC. These core conflicts are more enduring than any particular regime in power and would continue to exist even under conditions of dramatic political change in Iran or one of the GCC states.

These core conflicts are manifest in multiple ways: For example, Iran's nuclear power program, and its potential to generate nuclear weapons, is of serious concern to the Gulf states—perhaps even more so than it is to Israel, because Israel at least enjoys a nuclear retaliatory capability. But the GCC states have been reluctant to publicly demonstrate support for a U.S. (or even less so, an Israeli) preemptive strike on Iran. The GCC leaders know that oil facilities in their nations, as well as the strategic Strait of Hormuz, would be possible targets of Iranian retaliation in the event of an Israeli or U.S. military action. The GCC's concerns about Iran are reflected in the arms sale agreements signed with the United States, which together will provide the GCC states with over $120 billion in weapons systems by 2015.[19]

In the early days of the Iranian Revolution, Iran actively sponsored Shia extremist groups in the Gulf Arab states, especially those with large Shia populations such as Bahrain, and also appeared to be behind disruptive protests at the annual Muslim hajj pilgrimage to Mecca, Saudi Arabia. Under the more moderate President Khatami, Iran ended much of this political activism, and Ahmadinejad continued the new policy during his term in office. But when the Shia community in Bahrain rose up in protest against the Sunni monarchy in 2011, accusations of Iranian involvement and meddling quickly were made, suggesting that the GCC states still have concerns about Iran's ability to influence their domestic politics. Several Gulf states—Qatar and the UAE, in particular—have territorial disputes with Iran related to islands and offshore gas fields.

A fighting war between Iran and the GCC states is not likely. Unless Iran were to cross the nuclear weapons threshold, the GCC states would hold a large military advantage due to their purchase of advanced U.S. and other Western weaponry. Iran's capabilities would be limited to the power of disruption (of oil shipping) and support for insurgents within the GCC states, and the ability to launch medium-range missiles against economic targets. These are very serious capabilities but probably would not be worth the damage that GCC air forces could inflict on Iran and the strong possibility of U.S. involvement in the conflict.

NOTES

1. *CIA World Fact Book*, https://www.cia.gov/library/publications/the-world-factbook/.

2. See, for example, Ali Ansari, ed., *Preliminary Analysis of the Voting Figures in Iran's 2009 Presidential Election* (London: Chatham House and the Institute of Iranian Studies, University of St. Andrews, June 2009).

3. "Tehran's Rallying Cry: 'We Are the People of Iran,'" *Time* (June 15, 2009).

4. For an excellent analysis of the 2009 elections and their immediate aftermath, see Ali M. Ansari, *Crisis of Authority: Iran's 2009 Presidential Elections* (London: Chatham House, 2010).

5. Demographic data from *CIA World Fact Book 2011*.

6. Barbara Slavin, "The Incredible Shrinking Ahmadinejad," *Foreign Policy* (May 25, 2011), http://www.foreignpolicy.com/articles/2011/05/25/the_incredible_shrinking_ahmadinejad?page=0,0.

7. See, for example, John Bradley, "Iran's Ethnic Tinderbox," *Washington Quarterly* 30, no. 1 (2006–2007), 181–90.

8. *CIA World Fact Book 2011*.

9. Ibid.

10. Alireza Nader and Joya Laha, *Iran's Balancing Act in Afghanistan* (Santa Monica, CA: RAND Corporation, National Defense Research Institute, 2011), 11.

11. Ibid.

12. See Kenneth Katzman, *Iran: U.S. Concerns and Policy Responses*, Congressional Research Service Report RL32048 (2011), 38–50.

13. For an excellent and timely overview of the Iranian nuclear issue and an assessment of U.S. policy options, see Lynn E. Davis et al., *Iran's Nuclear Future: Critical U.S. Policy Choices* (Santa Monica, CA: RAND Corporation, 2011).

14. See David Sanger and Thom Shanker, "Gates Says U.S. Lacks Policy to Curb Iranian Nuclear Drive," *New York Times* (April 18, 2010).

15. For a thorough overview of U.S. sanction options, see Kenneth Katzman, *Iran Sanctions,* Congressional Research Service Report RS20871 (February 2, 2010).

16. The best overview of Iran-Iraq relations are the periodically updated reports by Kenneth Katzman, *Iran-Iraq Relations*, Congressional Research Service Report RS22323 (August 13, 2010), www.opencrs.com.

17. See Jeffrey Goldberg, "Point of no Return," *Atlantic Monthly* (September 2010).

18. William J. Broad et al., "Israeli Test on Worm Called Crucial in Iran Nuclear Delay," *New York Times* (January 15, 2011).

19. See Katzman, *Iran: U.S. Concerns and Policy Responses*, 39.

4 IRAQ

Mina Al-Oraibi

It is impossible to look at any part of the Middle East without recognizing the importance of Iraq to the region. Iraq forms an integral part of the Arab world, along with being a strategic neighbor of Turkey and Iran. On the border with Saudi Arabia and Kuwait, Iraq has historical ties and important tribal connections with the Gulf states. At the same time, Iraq has a strong historic political bond with neighbouring Jordan and Syria due to Baghdad's respective monarchical and Baathist past. To understand the hot spots and sources of potential instability in Iraq, a quick overview of its history is needed to set the context in which the country finds itself today.

Iraq, historically known as Mesopotamia, the land between two rivers, has been inhabited for centuries, and the trajectory of its development stretches with that of mankind itself. Its development is rich from the rise and fall of the ancient civilization of Sumer dating back to 3500 BCE, to the Islamic caliphate under the Abbasids, from 750 to 930 CE, when for nearly two centuries Iraq was home to the dynasty that "was by far the greatest political power in the Islamic world."[1] While its boundaries, laws, and politics have been evolving for centuries, Iraq as it is known today took the modern nation-state form with the collapse of the Ottoman Empire after World War I. It was established by uniting the three provinces of Basra, Baghdad, and Mosul, which remain the three main cities of Iraq to this day.

Once the Ottomans were defeated by the Allies in 1920, new nation states were born out of the previous provinces of the empire. Britain was given the mandate over Iraq, and its modern-day borders were set in 1920 until its independence in 1932. During that time, Britain ruled the country through alliances with key players, most importantly the newly appointed monarch, King Faisal I. It was during this time and under the leadership of key figures like prime ministers Nuri Al-Sa'id and Yassin Al-Hashimi that Iraq undertook major developmental projects that were later overseen by the Iraq Construction Council established in 1951. Although there were significant improvements to the infrastructure of the country, there was simmering discontent due to Iraq's close ties with Britain, twinned with a general wave in the Arab world of a move away from monarchist sentiments to republican ambitions. This sentiment was strengthened following the Free Officer revolution in Egypt in 1952 that overthrew the monarchy and made Egypt a republic.

Iraq's relationship with Britain was scrutinized by many nationalists, and during World War II, some, like Rashid 'Ali Al-Gailani and army colonels Salah-ud-Din As-Sabbagh, Kamel Shabib, Mahmud Salman, and Fahmi Sa'id, chose to side with Germany in the hope of undermining British control of the country. While the attempted coup by Al-Gailani and the four colonels in 1941 failed, nationalist stirrings had erupted and would be hard to control.[2] The Baath and Communist parties began to grow at this time, with the influence of the Free Officer gaining momentum, to reach a climax in 1958.

Iraq's history changed dramatically on July 14, 1958, when a coup d'etat led by General Abdul Kareem Qasim ended the monarchy and created the Republic of Iraq. This bloody coup, which led to the killing of King Faisal II, his family, and Prime Minister Nuri Al-Sa'id, began a string of successful and botched revolutions and coups between rival groups in Iraq. Just as the Cold War gripped political developments around the world, the postwar generation in Iraq was torn between communism and nationalism. Youth movements, students, professionals, and the general population faced a struggle between Communists and Baathists. Arab nationalists who aligned with Egypt's president, Gamal Abdel Nasser, were less influential than Communists and Baathists, yet were part of the political groups battling over control of Iraqi streets in the aftermath of the 1958 coup.

Throughout Qasim's rule, Baathists were preparing for their time in office. Their plans succeeded in February 1963, which led to Qasim's execution but only brief Baathist control over Iraq. Abdul Salam 'Arif ousted the Baathists in November of the same year and ruled until 1966, when a helicopter crash led to his death. His brother, Abdel Rahman 'Arif, took over but only for a brief period, which ended with the July 1968 coup that led to Baathist rule over Iraq that was to last until 2003. Ahmed Hasan Al-Bakr was Iraq's president from 1968 until 1979, yet Iraq's fate under the Baathists was eventually determined largely by one man: Saddam Hussein. Hussein became president on July 16, 1979, having been vice president to Al-Bakr for a decade. As president, Saddam's first move was to eliminate his rivals in a public meeting, where key members of the Baath party were called out and summarily executed, being accused of a plot to overthrow Saddam. Having eliminated his rivals internally, Saddam turned to consolidate his position in the region and dragged the country into a costly and lengthy war with Iran.

The 1979 revolution in Iran, leading to the birth of the Islamic Revolution and the end of the pro-Western Mohammad Reza Shah Pahlavi's reign, led to fears of the spread of the revolution. Gulf Arab countries and the United States backed Iraq politically and militarily in the bloody war that stunted the growth of both Baghdad and Tehran. Iraq became known as the protector of the eastern border—that is the protector of the eastern border of the Arab world in what was perceived as a Persian resurgence.

The Iraq-Iran War, from 1980 to 1988, cost both countries over 1 million lives and hundreds of millions of dollars. It drained Iraq's resources and held it back from advancing, while making Saddam Hussein a stronger dictator within his country. It was during the war that Saddam Hussein's regime started its campaign against the Kurds, culminating in the Anfal, a systematic attack using biological and chemical weapons in March 1988, which went generally unnoticed internationally. Moreover, it was during this time that Saddam's regime used increasingly violent and oppressive methods to suppress any internal discontent.

Iraq and Iran finally agreed to a cease-fire in 1988, and there were high hopes for Iraq to start economic development and use its vast oil wealth to improve its infrastructure rather than wage war. However, Saddam Hussein's invasion of Kuwait on August 2, 1990, made Iraq a pariah state and cost it its place in the international arena. The Gulf War of 1991 to liberate Kuwait was followed by over a decade of international sanctions that crippled Iraq's economy and society. While Iraq was isolated internationally, Saddam Hussein's brutality internally was exacerbated, which was met with little international pressure to change his behavior or hold him accountable for the suffering of his people. An internal uprising in 1991 included 14 of Iraq's 18 provinces moving against the regime, but it was quickly put down by the Iraqi air force, which went into international no-fly zones and supposed safe havens without international intervention. "The Iraqi intifada was allowed to be crushed."[3] The brutality used in quashing the uprising led to most internal opposition being eliminated or exiled; those who remained became too terrified or weakened to mount successful attacks on the regime, although there were a few attempts.

From 1991 to 2003, Iraq continued to be isolated in the region and internationally. Corruption in the Oil for Food program administered by the United Nations left the population suffering, while the regime grew stronger. Sanctions undermined the country's infrastructure and ate away at its middle classes with a dramatic rise in inflation, the effects of which will be felt in Iraq for years to come. It has been described as "the worst corruption scandal in United Nations history."[4]

Iraq's history changed dramatically starting with the war on March 19, 2003, and culminating to the fall of the Saddam Hussein regime on April 9, 2003. The reasons behind the 2003 war continue to be contentious both in and outside Iraq. While the official U.S. and coalition reasoning was related to the claim that Iraq had weapons of mass destruction, no such weapons were discovered after the 2003 invasion by a coalition led by the United States. Moreover, the presumed links between Saddam Hussein and the al-Qaeda organization were also not corroborated.

Regardless of the divisions over the decision of going into war, the overthrow of the Saddam Hussein regime began a new chapter in Iraq's history. A new constitution, system of government, and flag were introduced along with elections and increased freedom of expression. With support from the international community administered by the International Compact with Iraq, signed between the Iraqi government and the United Nations in 2007, Iraq began the long road toward stabilization. However, this road to recovery has been and will be for some time paved with obstacles.

In getting recognition from the international community that was demonstrated in the first conference for the International Compact in Sharm Al Sheikh in May 2007,

Iraq overcame a key stumbling block toward its reintegration into the international fold. Yet there are many potential hot spots in Iraq—due to its internal instability and the upheaval following years of war as well as to the troubled neighborhood in which it exists. When discussing any of the potential sources of conflict—be it water resources or sectarian tensions—both internal and external dynamics come into play in varying degrees. It is for this reason that predicting the outcome of existing or potential conflicts can be testing, as the actors and variables are both inside and outside Iraq.

There are issues that affect internal stability such as returning refugees and the need for equal distribution of wealth, which, if unaddressed, can lead to major problems for the government and stability of the country in the long term. The flaws within the system of government and the lack of institutionalized rule of law will prove challenging for years to come. Moreover, cross-border challenges—including relations with and the amount of autonomy granted to the Kurds—and water resources could lead to diplomatic and military troubles for Iraq.

ARMED STRUGGLE

Internal violence and factional fighting has become one of the most lethal threats to Iraq's stability since 2003. Whether fighters are referred to as terrorists, insurgents, or patriots wanting to eject foreign troops from the country, the different parties carrying arms and bringing blood and violence to the streets of Iraq are perhaps the greatest danger to Iraq's security, undermining the nation's political and economic stability. Even when armed clashes on the ground subside, the proliferation of weapons means the danger of armed struggle is never far away. Weapons caches continue to be found in Iraq on a near-daily basis, with 2,660 weapons caches found in 2006, 6,969 caches in 2007, and over 6,300 in the first half of 2008.[5] The problem of weapon flows through porous borders in the region means it will be some time before this threat subsides.

The use of arms as a way to settle political differences is a key potential danger for the country. Political maturity among Iraq's various parties has been progressing, albeit slowly, since 2003, with the end of one-party rule characterized by Saddam Hussein's regime. While the first elections held in January 2005 were based to a great extent on sectarian divisions, the parties involved have continued to strengthen, and alliances between cross-confessional groups have emerged, if only briefly, on key issues such as the future of the disputed province of Kirkuk. The elections of March 2010 witnessed two nationalist blocs, Al-Iraqiyaa and State of Law, getting the majority of the votes, indicating a move away from sectarian division. However, much of this political course has the use of force or arms as a backdrop that makes it all the more fragile. The manipulation of sectarian differences within the country means that any political disagreement can spill over onto the streets if framed in a religious or ethnic context. The issue of sectarian conflict will be raised later in this chapter, yet it is important to keep in mind while studying the other contentious issues in the country, because it is the one element that could push Iraq to oblivion.

Key actors on Iraq's political stage have armed groups answering to them and outside the ranks of the national army and police. Several prominent militias have grown within Iraq, sometimes with outside assistance. The Mahdi Army, known often by its

Arabic name Jaish Al-Mahdi or the U.S. military's acronym JAM, is foremost among these militias. The leader of the group, a young Shia cleric named Moqtada al-Sadr from the revered family of al-Sadr, emerged after 2003 and has fiercely opposed the U.S. invasion and military presence in Iraq, repeatedly vowing to fight U.S. troops and those working with them. He formed Jaish Al-Mahdi in 2003 and first clashed with U.S. troops and later with Iraqi security forces. Moreover, elements from Jaish Al-Mahdi have been involved in sectarian killings and assassinations in Iraq in a wave of violence following the bombing of holy shrines of Al-Hadi and Al-'Askary in Samarra in 2006. While there is no accurate figure agreed upon, the Mahdi Army's size has been estimated to amount to 60,000, heavily concentrated in Sadr City in Baghdad and the holy city of Najaf.[6] One of the challenges to reining in the Mahdi Army that Sadr himself has admitted to is that the militia is not a cohesive whole, and controlling armed, disgruntled, and often unemployed members is not always possible. Sadr's previous declarations that some of the elements who commit crimes of kidnappings, murder, and theft are not acting according to his orders make it even more difficult to stop their actions and hold their leadership accountable.

Recognizing the rejection of most civilians to the indiscriminate use of force, in August 2008, the Sadrist movement announced changing the Mahdi Army into a social movement called the Mumahidoon, those who follow the revered Twelfth Hidden Imam Mahdi. The crossing over between militants and civilian social movements

Mahdi Army militiamen hold a picture of radical Shiite cleric Muqtada al-Sadr as they celebrate the withdrawal of British troops from Basra in 2007. The Mahdi Army remains a powerful force in Iraqi politics. (AP Photo/Nabil al-Jurani)

makes this group more difficult to track and contain, especially because there has not been a formal demilitarization program or collection of weapons from those who claim to have given up arms. While Sadr announced a long-term truce, he has also said that he will keep a group of special forces to carry out operations he directs, meaning that the threat of the use of arms has not subsided. The possibility of the reemergence of the Mahdi Army poses a threat to Iraq, especially because this is an urban, trained, and armed group working in some of the most heavily populated parts of Iraq.

Smaller units of outlawed armed groups, using names like Thar Allah (meaning revenge of God) and Jund Al-Sama (Soldiers of the Sky), which appear in various locations in Iraq but remain concentrated in the south, also pose a threat to the country's security. Putting a religious spin on their operations often gives these militias more scope to be present within the local community. Moreover, both the Iraqi and U.S. armies have spoken of the danger of special groups who have been trained by Iranian special forces—the Iranian Revolutionary Guard Corps (IRGC)—and carry out attacks and assassinations in Iraq. These groups have emerged as having the most advanced equipment and sophisticated plans of attack. Their ability to slip through the border into Iran makes them a harder target for Iraqi forces. These special groups will be discussed later in regard to Iraq's relations with Iran.

Groups backed by Shia political parties and leaders are not the only ones with arms. Sunni insurgents, especially those from the former Iraqi army and remnants of militias like Fiday'een Saddam, have brought much blood to Iraqi streets. They are harder to identify as specific groupings, because they work underground without a known political arm, and most do not have clear leadership lines and have fragmented over time. The characteristics of these groups have changed since the 2003 war. After an initial alliance with al-Qaeda in Iraq, many Sunni insurgents turned their guns toward al-Qaeda fighters who began attacking their people. However, some continue to commit crimes of kidnap and murder under different names such as the Revolution of 1920 Brigades' Kata'ib Thawrat Al-'Ishrin and Mujahideen Brigades' Kata'ib Al-Mujahidin.

Although many elements of former fighters have stopped targeting Iraqi and U.S. forces, another problem can emerge from those who have stopped fighting against the government but have yet to integrate into their armed forces. Stemming from the Awakening Movement, also known by its Arabic name Sahwat, Sons of Iraq is a scheme that the U.S. Army found instrumental in stabilizing Iraq, paying out a monthly salary of approximately $25 million to a force of 100,000 armed men. Although this was meant to be a temporary group, to be integrated into Iraqi national armed forces, the integration has thus far failed, with the Iraqi government hesitant to take them on board. Until these men are integrated into the Iraqi army and police, or given civilian jobs, having a separate command structure and weapons can end up being as much a destabilizing factor as it was previously stabilizing. The Iraqi government showed unease at the growth and strength of these movements without establishing a viable program to deal with them. However, during 2010, the Iraqi government did implement some measures to bring in small numbers of Sahwat members.

Along with outlawed militias, there is the threat of groups that participate in government. For example, the Badr Brigade is the Iranian-trained wing of the Supreme

Islamic Iraqi Council (SIIC), a key party in the coalition running Iraq. While the Badr Brigade was formally disbanded in 2005 to become the Badr Organisation, a political entity represented in parliament, it continues to carry arms. Today, it operates mainly in the southern part of Iraq and has clashed repeatedly with Jaish Al-Mahdi elements in competition over control of the southern part of the country.[7]

Other militias aligned with political parties that could be used to settle political differences are the Kurdish controlled *peshmerga*. While elements of the peshmerga played a stabilizing role, potential conflicts between the federal and local governments could become violent with the proliferation of arms. The presence of peshmerga forces in volatile areas of Ninevah and Diyala Provinces have agitated situations of friction between Arabs and Kurds in the past and may do so in the future.

An example of the potential problems that can occur with different leaderships for the armed forces is the confrontation between the Iraqi federal government and the Kurdish Regional Government (KRG) in the summer of 2008, when the Iraqi Ministry of Defence requested that the peshmerga unit—the 34th division approximately 4,000 strong—withdraw from Diyala Province, where it was stationed in Khanaqin and Qara Tepe, two areas with heavy Kurdish population concentration. The peshmerga's initial rejection of this request had serious political consequences in Baghdad. An armed standoff was avoided as the KRG agreed to withdraw its forces, but this incident highlighted the potential problems of having armed units not answering to one command structure. Many in Baghdad have called for the peshmerga to be merged with Iraq's national forces to avoid ethnic conflicts; however, the Kurdish leadership reject this idea, counting on their forces for power and influence.

To face those groups carrying arms and to take away their professed raison d'être—that is, to protect their people—Iraq's own national armed forces are crucial, whether army or police. Iraq's army has been a crucial symbol of its unity and modern-day status from the days of the Arab Revolt in 1920 and securing its independence to its participation in the Arab-Israeli wars and the war with Iran. The Coalition Provisional Authority's (CPA's) decision to dismantle the Iraqi army, according to CPA order 22 on August 18, 2003, was perhaps one of the most detrimental orders because it led to 450,000 armed men being suddenly unemployed with no means of earning a living.

The CPA order 22, titled "Creation of a New Iraqi Army," was based on excluding members of the old army, with no immediate replacement. Years of training and investment have been required to maintain the new Iraqi army, which has undergone significant improvements, yet its unity and ability to function as an independent body for the service of the people remains vulnerable due to political pressure and militia infiltration. The government has recruited some militia elements, especially from the Badr Brigade, into the national armed forces, yet still lacks a cohesive program to ensure that the allegiance of these new soldiers and police officers is to the national army rather than their previous militia leadership. This is a greater difficulty within police ranks, as the Iraqi Ministry of Interior has suffered from sectarian policies, and members of armed militias were recruited in police ranks without a proper demilitarization and initiation program.

Along with the problems of the official armed forces of Iraq is the related issue of weapon proliferation throughout the country. This is a problem that flares up at intervals and will continue to be a problem until Iraq's government is able to enforce its will and authority on all those carrying guns outside of the country's jurisdiction.

Civilians in Iraq are generally armed, with the current law allowing for each household to have one weapon, usually a small pistol, due to the security situation in the country. However, many households have more than one weapon, and there is no licensing program to keep track of these arms. There is also a much wider arms problem, with most army depots in 2003 left unguarded, leading to vast looting of heavy weaponry. As militias and civilians armed themselves, a strong weapons black market has emerged in Iraq, and demilitarization programs have failed to produce exact numbers of weapons collected by the government and off the streets.

CONSTITUTIONAL FLAWS

Building trust in Iraq's armed forces is part of the greater task of building confidence in the government and rule of law. The 2003 war and the fall of the Saddam Hussein regime gave Iraqis the opportunity to establish a system of government and constitutional reform anew, a chance that is rarely granted to a modern nation-state. However, the need for swift action in installing a new constitution meant that it was hastily drafted and in need of revision even before it was ratified in October 2005.

Iraq faces potential crises stemming from the constitution that was adopted after a nationwide referendum resulted in 78 percent approval for it. Although the text of the constitution was accepted by parliament and the people, it contains a key article that has left it open to criticism and at times is undermined by politicians and parliamentarians. Article 142 of the Iraqi constitution states that the Iraqi Council of Representatives should create a committee to look into the text of the constitution and suggest amendments within four months of ratifying the constitution. The committee was formed under the leadership of Humam Hamoudi, then minister of parliament from the Supreme Islamic Iraqi Council, but six years after ratification, there was no amendment to the text that should be the key reference of Iraq's advancement. Not only has the constitution been breached by not settling amendments in the beginning of 2006 as was dictated by Article 142 to start with, this is a matter that should have been passed as a law that should be a foundation for the country and should remain valid for generations to come rather than a constitutional article. The issue of constitutional flaws continues to resurface as a way of undermining the rule of law, while crucial constitutional matters are often solved by unorthodox political settlements that secure the position of those in power. The decisions of the federal court—the institution mandated to solve constitutional differences—are often politicized.

Possible points of dispute surrounding the constitution are not limited to the document itself but to the actual system of government and development of the federal republic. The Iraqi constitution clearly declared Iraq a federal republic, with Article 115 of the constitution stating that every province has the right to establish a region based on a local referendum. There are two ways to go about this: the request of one-third of the members of the provincial council or the demand of one-tenth of the province population to conduct such a referendum. While the basic outline of establishing the regions has been drawn, internal rivalries mean that the implementation is much more contentious.

There is much interest in the potential of establishing a federal region in the southern part of Iraq, encompassing the all-important southern province of Basra. Basra has huge oil resources (estimated to be 20 percent of the Middle East's oil reserves), has fertile lands, and is home to Iraq's only ports. There are divisions between different Iraqi political parties over the type of region to be established in Basra. While the SIIC calls for a federal region of nine provinces, the Al-Fadhila Party calls for a region made up of only Basra. The reasoning behind the two different types of regions extends to the motivation of each party—hegemony over the whole country or control of the key province.

The issue of the southern region is not only focused on Basra. The power of Sh'i 'ulama (that is, religious clergy) stems from three major interlinked sources: knowledge of the sacred text, monopoly over its interpretation, and control over religious taxes.[8] All three combine in southern Iraq. The all-important holy cities of Najaf and Karbala are also part of the debate over having a southern region with equal powers and semiautonomy similar to the Kurdistan region in the north of the country. Najaf and Karbala are significant primarily due to their religious importance, not only for half of Iraq's population who are Shia, but also for Shia the world over. This religious importance gives significant weight to political parties who can control the cities or potential region. Rivalry among Shia parties over Najaf have previously led to armed clashes, with the followers of Moqtada al-Sadr attacking government forces in 2007, leading to a downturn of support for his movement.

There is also a financial element related to the control of Najaf and Karbala. Pious Shia give *khums*, a fifth of their wealth, to the *marja'ia*, religious authority, who are often based in one of the two cities. The khums should in theory go to the imam and descendents of the Prophet; as the imam is not present, the *majaia* or *'ulema*, take the imam's share and deposit it in mosques or the shrines. Wealthy Shiites donate money, carpets, and jewelry to pay for the upkeep of the shrines in the two cities. Added to this are visitors from around the world, but predominantly from Iran, whose pilgrimages generate wealth for those who are in control of the two cities. Pilgrims also donate to the upkeep of the shrines.

The importance of the potential southern region cannot be understated, and the different parties and groups who have a stake in its development are many. The rivalries among these groups make this a potentially serious issue for Iraq; yet the rivalries also serve to hold back implementation of any one party's plans, because none are dominant enough to impose their will.

Along with the constitution and federalism, there are key areas of potential conflict in Iraq due to the system of government that is based on allotting key positions of power depending on sect or ethnicity. While some believe this is crucial to ensure power sharing, others warn that this sectarian division stands contrary to the idea of a national identity. The Lebanese example is used to mark both the advantages and disadvantages of such an arrangement, where wrangling over allotting positions depending on sects has led to holding up the formation of governments for months on end. Moreover, candidates for key government positions are not necessarily the most competent but rather represent a certain faction.

While not officially in the Iraq constitution, the de facto system of rule is to have a Shiite prime minister and a Sunni president and head of parliament, one of which is to be a Kurd. The presidency council is to include one Shia, one Sunni, and one Kurdish representative, divided between the president and his two deputies. There had been efforts to end the system of the presidency council, which gives the right of veto to the president and his two deputies, but political mistrust and the need for more senior positions to distribute to the rival parties means the council is probably going to remain in Iraq for some time.

Other issues related to preserving the national identity of Iraq is its national flag. The divisions and problems surrounding introducing a new flag are representative of the divisions within the country and the need for consensus on forging a way forward to maintain the unity of the country. The attempt to change the Iraqi flag the first time in 2003 failed greatly. The colors blue and white were suggested, which caused a national outcry, because green, white, red, and black are used by most Arab nations. Although the blue-and-white model was abandoned, the flag was changed in February 2008, removing the three stars of the former Iraqi flag. However, this is not to be the final design; the parliament is committed to introducing a new flag, while many Iraqis continue to associate with the old one.

The need to finalize the constitution and flag is pressing for a country that needs to build its inner confidence and national identity after years of war and occupation. Moreover, a common ground needs to be achieved by the different political and social groups to consolidate the new federal order in Iraq, without leading to clashes over the control of the newly formed regions.

CORRUPTION'S WOES

Corruption is a key problem that faces many postwar countries, and Iraq is no exception. The misuse of national funds leads to not only problems of maladministration but organized crime and violence as well. Transparency International, the international organization monitoring corruption, has warned that Iraq is in danger of becoming "the biggest corruption scandal in history."[9]

Although it is difficult to measure exact figures of corruption due to the nature of the problem and the lack of methods of monitoring, corruption figures are estimated in the billions of dollars. The Office of the Special Inspector General for Iraq Reconstruction, a temporary U.S. federal agency set up to monitor fraud and abuse of funds intended for reconstruction, has repeatedly spoken of the threat of corruption. In a report issued in July 2008, the inspector general, Stuart Bowen, reported that $50 billion had been allotted from the United States for reconstruction, with Iraq allotting a similar amount.[10] There is little evidence of the advancement of basic services to warrant these figures. Bowen warned in 2006 that "Iraqi government corruption could amount up to $4bn a year, over 10 percent of the national income, with some money going to the insurgency."[11] This continued to be a problem, as Bowen reported in October 2010 that "public corruption pervades all levels of the government."[12]

Corruption affects a spectrum of activities in Iraq, from the lack of transparency regarding granting tenders and the lack of accountability for unfinished reconstruction projects to the smuggling of Iraqi oil. It means that monies allotted to developing Iraq's infrastructure, a key to its future stability, are instead diverted to the bank accounts of corrupt politicians and contractors.

The consequences of corruption are that vast amounts of money are stolen, under different guises of commissions or inflated pricing of tenders, and also that money allotted in the budget for public spending often does not get spent. Although this is sometimes due to maladministration, incompetence, and sometimes security conditions, corruption is also a key factor. In the first post-Saddam years, only one-third of the budget was being spent; the rest was held up due to corruption. Capacity building and training means that an average of two-thirds of the budget has been spent since 2007, but it is still not close to the full spending that the recovering nation needs. The establishment of an anticorruption academy and Commission of Integrity often do not have real powers of implementation; the head of the former institution was not confirmed two years into being named to that position.

Although Iraq signed the United Nations Convention against Corruption in 2008, implementation of this treaty and other anticorruption measures is complicated. While it is hoped that this treaty will hold those responsible accountable, there is little being done to practice that accountability.

There is real danger of internal discontent festering, with politicians becoming increasingly wealthy while general services remain rudimentary. Years of neglect during the Saddam Hussein reign, coupled with corruption in recent years, has meant that services such as electricity and water supply remain below basic standards. Unemployment figures are difficult to access in Iraq, with figures varying from 19 percent to 40 percent, depending on the source. Lack of opportunities and the need for finances can lead to internal strife, especially if young men are not employed and turning to organized crime as a way to make a living. In addition to official unemployment figures, there are figures relating to disguised unemployment. Iraq's vast wealth and the five-year national economic programs developed since 2007 should mean that Iraq overcomes these obstacles in the medium term, yet corruption could further undermine these efforts.

KIRKUK IS KEY

If one geographical location was to be termed a hot spot in Iraq, it would have to be Kirkuk. With riches that spread from ethnic diversity to oil fields, many parties and politicians have ambitions there. This has sparked political and armed clashes in the past and most likely will in the future.

While all Kurdish officials insist upon the Kurdish identity of the province and its capital, also called Kirkuk, native Arabs and Turkmen insist that they have an equal a stake in it. Kirkuk is a microcosm of Iraq; if the problems in this province can be solved, similar problems throughout the country can be. However, if problems in this province escalate, this can lead to a chain reaction in the country.

It was hoped that Article 140 of the Iraqi constitution would settle this problem, but it has already proven inadequate, with deadline after deadline passing without a resolution. Article 140 called upon the central government in Baghdad to normalize relations in Kirkuk, conduct a census, and have a referendum in Kirkuk and other disputed areas in Iraq by December 31, 2007. This deadline passed without any of the stated targets being met. While the resolution has been postponed, the United Nations took on a more active role in trying to resolve the dispute. Thus, Kirkuk has also become a test for the United Nations in Iraq and its capability to resolve key conflicts in this country.

All three targets stated in Article 140 pose problems in implementation. Normalizing relations refers to reversing Saddam Hussein's policy of Arabizing Kirkuk, a campaign that he launched during the 1980s to move Kurds out of Kirkuk while moving Arabs from other parts of the country to replace them. However, a reverse policy of driving out Arabs from Kirkuk since 2003 is in danger of repeating the tragedy of mass forced movement of populations. Kurdish officials insist that Arabs in Kirkuk cannot remain there, and a system of monetary compensation for those who voluntarily want to leave has been implemented. Yet no official policy has been stated for those who do not voluntarily leave, with widely circulated reports of intimidation of Arabs and Kurds causing agitation on both sides. One of the key problems is the lack of accurate and neutral data on the number of Iraqis who were forcefully moved into or out of Kirkuk.

Kurdish officials have insisted that it is not possible to carry out a census of the province until the normalization of relations is complete—that is, removing Arab settlers from Kirkuk. However, it is difficult to assess which Arabs are originally from the province and which ones are settlers from other parts of the country. There are those who have been there just a few decades but feel that this is now their home. On the other hand, forcefully removed Kurds long to return to their original homes. A census would mean that exact numbers and proportions of Kurds, Arabs, Turkmen, Assyrians, and other minorities would be known, yet this process is held up for political reasons. One suggestion has been to use the census of 1957, before any policies of forced removals, as the basis for the ethnic makeup of the city. According to the 1957 census, Kurds constituted 33.26 percent of the Kirkuk population, Turkmen made up 37.62 percent, and Arabs comprised the rest with 33.53 percent. However, the 1947 census shows that Kurds make up only 25 percent of the Kirkuk the city and 53 percent of the province.[13]

The struggle over Kirkuk has both symbolic and financial motivations—which means that there are two potential types of conflicts over it. While the Kurdistan region has oil and gas riches, they are not enough to ensure self-efficiency for the region. Kirkuk would be a vital addition for the region and its natural wealth; its oil reserves are estimated to be between 11 billion and 15 billion barrels, the sixth-largest proven reserve. However, Kurdish nationalists resent claims that portray the conflict over Kirkuk as being purely related to oil. They insist that this is a historic and integral part of Kurdistan, yet their insistence sparks fears of Kurdish plans to break from Iraq.

The basic principle of whether to include Kirkuk as part of the Kurdistan region—and under the authority of the KRG or not—remains in question. Kirkuk is a critical region for Iraq that can make or break power-sharing agreements in Iraq. There have been proposals to keep Kirkuk as a separate province, without attaching it to any one region in Iraq. Kurdish politicians flatly reject any such suggestions, especially because Kirkuk's status as part of the Kurdistan region is enshrined in the region's 1992 constitution and all official documents in the region.

Although Kirkuk is the most high-profile part of Iraq with possible conflict status, Article 140 covers various other disputed territories whose control could lead to internal stability. Tal 'Afar, with its Turkmen majority population in Nineveh Province, and Khaniqeen are some of these areas, while some ultranationalist Kurds have even called for the important city of Mosul, capital of Nineveh, to be included in the Kurdistan region. Mosul has a majority of Arabs but has Kurdish residents, while some surrounding villages have an overwhelming Kurdish majority. Standoffs between the national Iraqi army and peshmerga elements over Khaniqeen following disagreements over the UN proposals for implementing Article 140 in the summer of 2008 are telling of the possibility of a flare-up in one disputed region affecting others.

The future of Kirkuk is a key fixture in deciding the future of the Kurdistan region and its relations with the federal government of Iraq.

KURDISTAN

The Kurdistan region of Iraq has emerged as an oasis of calm in post-2003 Iraq. Having effectively secured its semiautonomy since 1991, with international forces helping local forces, peshmerga, keep Saddam Hussein's army at bay, Kurdistan had a 12-year head start to rebuild itself as compared to the rest of the country. After a brutal civil war between the two leading parties—the Kurdish Democratic Party and the Patriotic Union of Kurdistan—the region has emerged with a relatively secure political and security situation, resulting in an economic boom that is unrivaled in the rest of the country. Named by the KRG as "the Other Iraq" in an international media campaign, its leadership likes to boast of the difference between Kurdish regional stability compared with the rest of the often volatile areas of Iraq. However, this clear separation between the two parts of Iraq can have long-term detrimental effects for the country, with the fears of a break-up of Iraq surfacing occasionally.

Kurdish leaders and their people make no secret of their wish for an independent Kurdistan, a country in its own right for a minority that has its own distinct language and history. However, since 2003, Iraqi president Jalal Talabani and Kurdish regional president Masoud Barazani have both expressed their dedication to keeping Kurdistan a part of a united and federal Iraq. Both politicians have upheld the right of the Kurdish people to self-determination and have repeatedly said that the desire for an independent Kurdistan is common among many Kurds. The possibility of pursuing that desire would lead to an eruption of conflicts in Iraq and potentially in neighboring countries. Covering a land space of almost 16,000 square miles, with a population of approximately 3.7 million, Kurdistan has some of the most fertile lands of Iraq and would constitute an important loss of land, population, and resources for Iraq. Moreover, the implications for the region are many.

Apart from the possibility of declaring independence, Kurdistan faces a series of threats that can undermine it. Internally, Kurdish security is maintained by the Kurdish forces, peshmerga, along with the intelligence service *asayish*, and there have been few security problems in the region. However, there are militant groups, such as Jund Al-Islam and Ansar Al-Islam, within the region that continue to pose a threat to its stability. They have conducted bomb attacks that included the attack on the Kurdistan Democratic Party offices on the first day of Eid Al-Adha, the Muslim festival celebrating the end of pilgrimage season, on February 1, 2004, that killed more than 60 people and injured dozens. Kurdish officials have been targets of assassination attempts, and security is tightly monitored in the region. However, Kurdistan has not been subjected to the frequent mass attacks on civilians witnessed in other parts of the country, and there is little to indicate a change in the near future.

Politically, the Kurdish region has two dominant parties: the Patriotic Union of Kurdistan (PUK) and the Kurdistan Democratic Party (KDP) hold the reins of power. There are few political freedoms in forming independent parties with real influence within the region, and there is much room for improvement regarding freedom of expression. Furthermore, there are internal stirrings of unrest and anxiety due to a growing feeling among Iraqi Kurds that they suffered greatly under Saddam Hussein's regime, and their own leaders have not worked hard enough to compensate them for their sacrifices. While new buildings for the parliament and gated compounds are built for officials, basic infrastructure and services such as water and electricity are still below standards. There are also widespread reports of corruption. A rare glimpse of internal discontent surfaced with a riot in Halabja in 2006 that was swiftly subdued.[14] In what was meant to be a ceremony to mark the tragic events of March 1988 and the Anfal campaign, demonstrators attacked the museum and memorial site for the victims. They complained that although they suffered in the past and the issue of the Anfal has been widely publicized by local politicians, they had yet to receive fair treatment or compensation from the local rulers. This was the strongest public demonstration and criticism of the two parties that have ruled the Kurdistan region since 1991. It was an indication of what could happen if simmering discontent were to spill over.

Anger about the lack of services and resources is not taking place just in Halabja. Smaller demonstrations have come out in Arbil, the capital of the region, Suleimania, and other towns and cities. However, they are quickly controlled. Unless these serious concerns are addressed, the stability of the region can be undermined.

Resentment led to unexpected support for a new and third political party in Kurdistan's July 2009 elections. Goran, meaning change, received close to a quarter of the seats in the Kurdish local parliament in a development that shook the Kurdish political establishment.

A more immediate threat to the stability of the Kurdistan region is external. Turkey, Iran, and Syria all have sizeable Kurdish populations, and they are carefully watching the developments in Iraq. All three countries are weary of the example of Iraq and the development of a semiautonomous Kurdish region, fearing similar developments in their own territories. With an estimated 20 million Kurds, Turkey has the most to lose, and it has not held back in pursuing ways to undermine the Kurdish region in Iraq. Regular bombing campaigns are carried out on the borders between the two countries, and military incursions, although brief, have been used to keep Iraqi Kurdish aspirations in check. While the Turkish authorities insist that these military actions are to target the PKK—the Kurdistan Workers' Party, which is listed as a terrorist organization in Iraq, Turkey, and the United States—the bombing campaigns have been a clear indicator of Turkey's willingness to use force against the Kurds.

Iran has also taken part in military operations targeting the Kurdistan region of Iraq, saying that it is targeting PIJAK, the PKK wing for Kurdish separatists in Iran. This is a worrying trend, because the attacks have drawn little international criticism,

although organizations such as the United Nations High Commission for Refugees have warned of the humanitarian impact of such campaigns, especially in regard o displacement among civilians.[15] The PUK and KDP keep the armed Kurdish groups at bay but face the problem of their constituency's local pressures to support Kurds across the border. Moreover, the Kurdistan region in Iraq hosts various Kurdish political parties, such as the KDP-Iran, that cannot operate in Turkey, Syria, and Iran. This is a further source of agitation with neighboring countries.

The local autonomy promised to "the predominately Kurdish areas lying east of the Euphrates, south of the southern border of Armenia . . . , and north of the frontier of Turkey with Syria and Mesopotamia" in the Treaty of Sevres in August 1920 continues to be a dream for most Kurds, and one that may be beginning to become a reality with the local

Iraqi Kurds fly the Kurdish flag in the northern city of Kirkuk, a potential flashpoint for conflict between Iraqi Kurds and Iraqi Arabs. (Marwan Ibrahim/AFP/ Getty Images)

autonomy of the KRG. For the short term, this does not appear to be a likely development; however, it is a possibility that is always invoked when relations between Arbil and Baghdad are strained.

OIL—BLACK GOLD

While vast oil reserves make Iraq potentially one of the richest countries of the world, oil also contributes to current conflicts and possible future troubles for the country. The struggle between various political factions in Iraq over oil is not merely about wealth and control of resources; it is indicative of the conflicting viewpoints emerging in Iraq—one that believes in centralization and nationalist handling of the economy and another advocating decentralization and privatization.

The exact amount of Iraq's oil reserves is not known, because full exploration of the country was halted for many years. Iraq has 115 billion barrels of proven old reserves, meaning it enjoys one of the largest endowments of reserves in the world.[16] In October 2010, Iraq's oil minister, Hussein Al-Shahristani, announced that Iraq's reserves were revised and raised to 143.1 billion barrels. While this is a source of wealth for Iraq, it has yet to be exploited as such.

To understand Iraq's current status regarding oil, it is important to understand the country's oil policy in past decades. From 1963, Iraqi governments pursued policies under socialist slogans. The Iraqi Petroleum Company was nationalized in June 1972 with orders from Saddam Hussein, who was vice president at the time. National control of the country's oil resources became a key part of Iraqi policy until 2003, unlike neighboring countries such as Saudi Arabia, which entered an agreement with the United State to set up the national oil company Aramco in a process that began as early as 1933. National control has meant that oil resources have not been exploited in the best possible manner, but Iraq has been free to decide its oil policy.

Iraqi oil minister Shahristani in Prime Minister Nuri al-Maliki's government was a believer in national control over oil fields and exploration, while others, such as Kurdish regional prime minister Barham Salih, firmly believes in privatization to maximize efficiency in oil production

There are potential problems of controlling oil within Iraq, from production to revenues, with an unclear situation regarding central and regional control of oil fields and contracting rights. The Kurdistan regional government has signed oil exploration and production contracts with foreign companies like DNO and Hunt Oil; however, the Iraqi Ministry of Oil refuses to grant legitimacy to these contracts. Problems between Iraq's Ministry of Oil and the Kurdistan regional government over these oil contracts erupted in 2006, without a clear resolution. Both sides insist that they are upholding the Iraqi constitution in their arguments; the federal court is the ultimate party to resolve this issue but has not been consulted.

The example of the Kurdistan region is monitored closely, because it can mean that future regions, once established, take similar actions. Southern Iraq has much larger proven reserves, and should a southern region be established, control of the oil fields will be a major source of competition and potential conflict. Between 2006 and 2009, Basra's oil was the source of 90 percent of the Iraqi budget wealth.

Oil is crucial to Iraq's growth, but without national agreement on how to go forward in developing this sector, this vital resource is being held up. One positive dimension is that the Iraqi constitution states in Article 108 that "Oil and Gas are the property of all the Iraqi population in all regions and provinces." All politicians publicly agree with this statement; however, the mechanism for the distribution of this wealth remains a sticking point.

RELATIONS WITH THE NEIGHBORS

Iraq's future is linked to its neighbors in many ways. Iraq shares long borders with Iran (906 miles), Jordan (112 miles), Kuwait (149 miles), Saudi Arabia (506 miles), Syria (376 miles), and Turkey (219 miles). Each of these countries has interests in Iraq and presents possible points of contention.

To say that Iraq's relations with its eastern neighbor, Iran, are complicated is an understatement. Sharing the longest border with Iraq, stretching over 900 miles, the two countries are intricately linked in terms of territory, history, and populations. Rivalries between the two countries have made them clash at different points throughout history, peaking with the eight-year war that has left many scars.

One point of disagreement between the two countries is linked to rivalry between the two holy cities of Shia Islam: Najaf in Iraq and Qom in Iran. While Najaf has traditionally been the place of scholarship for Shia clerics, Mahdi Haeri Yazdi established

Qom "as a center of learning to rival Najaf" in the 1920s.[17] To this day, rivalries exist not only between the two cities but between the established clerics teaching there and new clerics being taught. There is also competition over the control of religious decrees, and issues and overall loyalty of Shia believers in Iraq, Iran, and beyond.

The rivalry between the Iraqi Shia political parties often spills into the rivalry of who is more authentic as a religious figure based on the teachings one has received. Rivalry between Shia political parties has been affected by their relationship with Iran. While the Supreme Islamic Iraqi Council continues to be closely allied with Iran, the al-Fadhila party clearly highlights its Arab roots and endeavors to remain independent from Iran's influence. Iran wields power in Iraq due to its influence over its key parties—most notably SIIC but also the Sadr movement led by Moqtada al-Sadr who resided in Qom from 2008. However, to assume that all Shia parties and politicians are somehow affiliated with Iran is a grave mistake, one that often U.S. policy makers and Arab rulers have committed, leading to the alienation of important Shia leaders and parties in Iraq. This is a key destabilizing factor, as Iraqi national politics becomes influenced by other countries' interests. Moreover, various Iraqi politicians and movements are opposed to this influence, which could lead to a conflict between the two sides.

Another point of possible conflict between Iraq and Iran is the presence of the Mujahedine-e-khalq in Camp Ashraf in Iraq's Diyala Province. While Iran continues to call for the closure of the camp and for the expulsion of the group, Iraq is faced with a difficult choice. The multinational forces in Iraq granted the inhabitants of Camp Ashraf protected status since 2004, and under the Geneva Conventions, they cannot be deported or returned to their country where they would face persecution. However, the Iraqi government announced in 2008 that the group, which was protected during Saddam Hussein's rule, is a terrorist organization. This decision was in great part due to much pressure from Iran. Moreover, the Iraqi government has announced that it wants to control the camp and clear it of weapons. Moving to implement the expulsion of the armed group could lead to clashes, though many residents of the camp have chosen to leave since 2003.

Relations between Iraq and Iran are determined by a tangled web of political, religious, and military issues. The most immediate issue between the countries is related to special forces that Iraqi and U.S. officials have said play a significant role in the escalation of violence in Iraq. Weapon caches and members of the IRGC have been found in Iraq, with links to militias and unlawful armed groups causing disruption there.[18] The use of the special forces to disrupt stability in Iraq has been effective in several parts of the country, especially the south, and poses a significant problem for Iraqi security forces as they are usually small units crossing back and forth between the porous border between Iran and Iraq.

Iran's tense relations with the United States, which have been officially cut since 1980, are often at the center of Iraqi-Iranian relations. Iran has been vocal in its rejection of a close relationship between Iraq and the United States and has frequently made public statements calling for the expulsion of U.S. forces from Iraq. Iran's parliamentary speaker, Ali Larijani, has said on several occasions that the "US proposed security agreement is in fact aimed at humiliating the dignity of the Iraqi nation."[19] Iran's weariness about this agreement resulted in pressuring Iraqi politicians into rejecting the agreement; yet Iran failed in the end to impose its will.

Iraq's other non-Arab neighbor, Turkey, is vital to Iraq's interests on many levels. Although Turkey refused to give the United States and its allies approval to use Turkish territory and air space to attack Iraq during the 2003 war, it was quick to support the new Iraqi government and, along with Iran, began to take steps early on to secure its influence in Iraq in the long term. Turkey kept its embassy operating in Baghdad from the time of Saddam Hussein's regime and continued operating in Iraq afterward, even though the embassy was targeted by a suicide bomber in October 2003. Moreover, Turkey opened a consulate in Basra to ensure a role in the south of the country.

However, relations between the two countries are not always stable. The main source of contention is the status of Kurds in Iraq. Now that the Kurds have a secure autonomous region and enjoy political power within their own region through the KRG and through politicians with key positions in the Iraqi central government (such as President Jalal Talabani), Kurds in Turkey, Iran, and Syria are looking to bolster their positions in their respective countries. The issue of the PKK in particular has been a problem between Iraq and Turkey, and, although Turkey has not held back in the past from using military might to fight the PKK, this can be a serious source of instability for Iraq in the future.

Kirkuk also can lead to Turkish intervention in Iraq, with Turkish politicians openly warning that they would step in to protect the Turkmen minority in the province. Turkish air strikes or military incursions to do so could have devastating effects on Iraq's struggle for stability.

On the other hand, Turkey is the gateway to Europe for Iraq, and the bridge it provides is crucial, especially in terms of gas exports from Iraq to Europe. This provides both opportunities and long-term challenges to Europe, especially if Turkey eventually joints the European Union. A volatile neighbor on its borders is not something Europeans can afford.

Iraq's relations with its Arab neighbors are vital for its long-term stability. At first, most Arab countries kept a wary distance from Iraq after the 2003 war, with apprehension over what the United States claimed would be the start of a flourishing democracy to influence the region. With time, this reluctance has been replaced in countries such as the United Arab Emirates and Jordan with a desire to improve relations.

Kuwait's relations with Iraq were a source of major conflict in the past but are unlikely to be so in the near future. There have been sporadic claims in Iraq in the past over Kuwait, culminating in Saddam Hussein's invasion of Kuwait in 1990. While Iraq is unlikely to make any such claims in the future, there has yet to be an agreement on the border dispute between the two countries, which includes questions over the shared Rumaila oil field. Furthermore, the issue of compensation claims and war reparations stemming from the 1990 invasion remains problematic. Although there are no official figures given of the amount of money at stake, the claims are estimated to reach $30 billion and another $17 billion of loans. This is a problem that drains Iraqi resources, with 5 percent of Iraqi oil revenues being diverted to pay off the claims since 1991, and could continue to be problematic for some time. The claim of Kuwaiti Airlines on two Bombardier Canadian airplanes that Iraq purchased in the summer of

2008, which Canadian courts granted, are an example of how this problem can affect Iraq's long-term growth. Indeed, in May 2010, the Iraqi government dissolved the national airline due to Kuwait's consistent claims over any flights the airline makes.

In 2011, a new problem emerged between Iraq and Kuwait over Kuwait's decision to build Port Mubarak Al-Kabeer. Building of the port started in April 2011 and it is expected to be completed by 2016 to become the largest port in the Middle East at an estimated cost of $1.1 billion. Politicians, parliamentarians, and environmental experts in Iraq have cautioned that the Kuwaiti port not only can threaten Iraq's access to the Khor Abdullah waterway, but that it can also lead to serious environmental impact to the area between the two nations. Moreover, Iraq itself has ambitions to build its own mega-port, the Al-Faw port, at an estimated cost of $6 billion. However, the Iraqi port remains at a planning stage while internal disagreements and rivalries hold it up. Meanwhile, the tensions between Iraq and Kuwait could escalate closer to the time of completing the port.

Relations with Saudi Arabia are contentious; Saudi diplomacy has been slow, to say the least, to catch up with Iraq's other neighbors in supporting the post-Saddam governments. While the Saudis were not on good terms with Saddam after the Kuwait invasion, the new Shia-dominated governments in Baghdad have caused concern in Riyadh. The growing role of Iranian influence in Iraq and in other parts of the Middle East has sparked fears among Saudis who have opted for a policy of containing Shia politicians in Iraq as their way to counterbalance Iran's influence.

Diplomacy is not the only stumbling block between the two nations. Saudi nationals made up the highest proportion of foreign fighters coming into Iraq, and anger at U.S. troops being present in the region focusing there; 45 percent of foreign fighters in Iraq in 2007 were from Saudi Arabia.[20] Unless Saudi Arabia can impose more stringent controls on its borders in order to stop the flow of militants to Iraq, this will remain a serious cause for concern in Iraq.

Syria is another country that has played a role in Iraq's instability, with most foreign fighters crossing Syria's border to enter Iraq. However, this problem was in decline during 2011 as Syria had to deal with its own domestic instability and calls for reforms. Attacks from fighters accused of coming from Syria were in sharp decline during 2011.

Syria is also home to many former Baath regime officials who support the insurgency in Iraq. This is a trait common also to Jordan, which is hosting Saddam Hussein's daughter Raghad, who makes no effort to hide her support of violence in Iraq. The space permitted to such figures to destabilize Iraq is a cause of concern in the medium term for the country. Moreover, both Syria and Jordan host the majority of Iraqi refugees; Syria is estimated to have over 1.05 million Iraqi refugees (after a peak of 1.4 million), while Jordan is home to about 450,000 Iraqis.[21] Syria and Jordan continue to wield pressure on Iraq to resolve the issue of the refugees.

The twice-annual meetings of the foreign ministers of Iraq's neighboring countries that were taking place between 2007and 2009 helped ease tensions between Iraq and its neighbors. It was especially important to host the April 2008 meeting in Kuwait, which was seen as a watershed in the relations between Kuwait and Iraq. However, these meetings were held under the pressure and coaxing of the Untied States during the Bush administration, and the Obama administration chose not to continue them. Trust has yet to be fully built between these countries to continue the mechanism of regular ministerial meetings without American intervention.

RELATIONS WITH THE UNITED STATES

Relations between Iraq and the United States can be compared to Iraq's relations with Britain during the years of the mandate. Although both the United States and Iraq have endeavored to highlight Iraq's sovereign rule since the handover of power from the Coalition Provisional Authority to the Iraqi government in June 2004, the presence and support of the United States, both militarily and politically, in Iraq was instrumental to upholding the current system of government and the constitution. Just as the British were faced with the responsibility of "working out the details of disengagement" with the ending of the mandate in 1932,[22] U.S. officials have to wrangle with how to disengage militarily from Iraq while maintaining influence in the country and securing key strategic and economic interests.

The presence of U.S. forces in Iraq is an important source of stability while Iraqi armed forces are built up and, more importantly, trust between the Iraqi people and government is established. However, the U.S. presence in Iraq continues to be an excuse used by extremists to strike in Iraq under the guise of fighting an "occupation." After much debate and political manoeuvring, the United States and Iraq came to an agreement that a Status of Forces agreement would have to have a time horizon for the withdrawal of U.S. troops from the country—the end of 2011. After intense debate about setting a time frame, President Obama confirmed in February 2009 in a speech at Camp Lejeune (North Carolina) that the United States will pull its troops out of Iraq. Although 2011 witnessed several months of negotiations over the possibility of extending U.S. troop presence in Iraq, the effort was ended in October 2011. President Obama confirmed on October 21, 2011, that all U.S. forces would be leaving Iraq by the end of 2011. The presence of foreign troops, their immunity, and conduct can lead to troubles between the two countries in cases relating to troop misconduct; the Iraqi government insisted on limiting troop immunity to those in combat operations and on bases only, but the United States refused to accept this condition. Moreover, both Iraqi prime minister Maliki and American president Obama made electoral pledges to work on ending the U.S. military presence in Iraq—both leaders could not afford the political capital of extending troop presence. The decision to withdraw American forces from Iraq raises two potential threats. One is increased security threats in Iraq that need U.S. logistical and intelligence support that Iraqi forces do not yet have. The second is the threat of U.S. political disengagement from Iraq and playing less of a role in influencing stability in the country as American leaders try to deal with the great changes in the Middle East.

Different Iraqi and U.S. points of view emerging on key issues can lead to tensions flaring between the two countries. One of these issues is related to the future of the Sons of Iraq program. The United States Army gave this group support and a promise to be integrated into Iraqi forces, yet this promise has not been fulfilled due to an Iraqi government reluctance to trust these fighters, who, in the not-too-distant past, were fighting this same government. The Iraqi government's insistence in taking over control of all security affairs in the country would mean taking over control of the fate of this armed group, which trusts the United States more than its own government.

In addition to the different viewpoints in Iraq and the United States regarding military and security issues, relations between Iraq and the United States are increasingly affected by Iran. Both the United States and Iran see Iraq as a strategic place of influence and struggle to maintain the greater clout there, which does not contribute to the stability of Iraq. Iraqi politicians often find themselves wanting to appease one side or the other, which distracts them from the important efforts of stabilizing their own country.

While relations with the United States are less likely to cause problems for Iraq compared to relations with other countries in the region, internal complaints of U.S. interference can lead to undermining the government and can cause violence to spread.

SECTARIAN TENSIONS

One of the hot spots that has exploded in Iraq since the 2003 war is the issue of sectarianism. For most outsiders, and especially U.S. decision makers, sectarian identities became a way to understand Iraq and the complex dynamics of the country; however, this led to a superficial and often flawed perspective. Iraq's mosaic of various sects and ethnicities was clumsy divided as Sunni, Shia, and Kurd—a false categorization that mixed race and sect. Kurds are majority Sunni but have a minority Shia also; while Arabs in Iraq are Muslims (Shia and Sunni) and Christian and a very small minority of Jews. Moreover, there are small groups of Yezidis, Turkmen, Mandaeans, Assyrians, and others who are often ignored by invoking this crude division of the three main groups. Because politics in Iraq has been dictated to a great extent by outside forces since 2003, these divisions became de facto power bases.

Regardless of the recent causes for focusing on these divisions, it cannot be ignored that the main two religious groups are Sunni and Shia Muslims. Key Iraqi tribes, including the Jibbur and Tameem, are both Sunni and Shia and have not had problems of sectarian conflicts in the past. However, the sectarian division of power that was administered by the CPA in 2003 led those who wanted to come to power in Iraq to position themselves within the sectarian and ethnic spectrum. Through sectarian politics, an environment of division has developed in Iraq, where politics is often based on sectarian and ethnic divides rather than on political programs suited to the needs of the electorate.

Sectarian divisions plague Iraq's new system of government. For example, while 78 percent of voters accepted the constitution in the October 15, 2005, referendum, two major Sunni-dominated provinces voted against it with huge majorities. According to the Iraqi Electoral Commission, 96 percent of voters in Anbar and 81 percent in Salahuddin rejected it. The sectarian disagreement on the constitution is a source of concern, because the constitution should be a unifying rather than divisive document. When constitutional crises have arisen in the past, Sunni politicians have referred to their rejection of the constitution as being the binding document to resolve disputes.

Sectarian-based politics led to political parties and alliances being built wholly on superficial prejudices based on race or sect. The use of religious figures—most importantly, the revered Shia cleric Ayatollah Sistani—to garner support for political parties led to the majority of Shia Arab voters in past elections to dedicate their votes to the United Iraqi Alliance bloc. Similarly, Kurdish voters look to the Kurdistan Alliance to represent them, while Sunni Arabs turn to the Tawafuq (Accordance) Front. The trouble with this system is that it constrains political maturity among these blocs working together due to ethnic and sectarian prejudices, which has led to the stumbling of key legislation such as the hydrocarbon law to regulate the oil and gas resources of Iraq. These divisions do not reflect the will of the Iraqi people, who, if given the chance, are likely to vote for secular or nationalist groups. The elections of March 2010 proved this, as former prime minister Ayad Allawi—a secular Shia who has both Shia and Sunni leaders in his coalition—was able to get the most votes, with 91 of Iraq's 325 parliamentary seats going to him. Next in terms of popularity was Prime Minister Maliki, who ran on a platform of "State of Law" and also had nationalist nonsectarian allies. He was able to secure 89 seats in parliament. Although the two have personal and political differences, which meant they did not agree on government formation for more than eight months, their popularity among Iraqis indicated that voters did not want sectarian blocks. Yet this process is still nascent.

Sectarian divisions are dangerous because they can easily spill over to armed confrontation. The sectarian violence that dogged Iraq in 2006 to 2007 was the worst in Iraq's modern history. Sectarian tensions are particularly worrisome when they are exploited by extremist groups in the region. The threat of the al-Qaeda network, extremism, and the use of indiscriminate violence are not limited to a particular country or boundary. However, Iraq has been a particularly fragile victim of the violence promoted by al-Qaeda, through the actions of the al-Qaeda in Mesopotamia group. While its lethal attacks peaked in the first years after the 2003 war, levels of violence have come down as more and more Iraqis rejected the al-Qaeda doctrine. However, problems of security vacuums arising in certain areas, porous borders, and high rates of unemployment among young Iraqi men mean that al-Qaeda has been able to continue its work in Iraq and recruit new followers and suicide bombers. The Central Intelligence Agency has warned that Iraq is in danger of becoming the breeding ground for terrorists around the world. In its National Intelligence Estimate for 2007, the National Intelligence Council stated the "Al-Qaeda will probably seek to leverage the contacts and capabilities of Al-Qaeda in Iraq (AQI), its most visible and capable affiliate and the only one known to have expressed a desire to attack the home land." Moreover, the estimate warned that "its association with AQI helps al-Qa'ida to energize the broader Sunni extremist community, raise resources, and to recruit and indoctrinate operatives, including for Homeland attacks."[23]

The role of al-Qaeda in Iraq within the larger al-Qaeda network is directly related to the United States. There are different views regarding the role of the United States in Iraq in fighting terrorism. While the Bush administration maintained that U.S. troops in Iraq are vital, key opponents of maintaining troops in Iraq, like then Senator—later Vice President—Joe Biden and Ike Skelton have argued that U.S. presence in Iraq has meant deviation from the larger struggle against al-Qaeda in Afghanistan.[24] While the threat of terrorism has reduced in Iraq, it has not gone away, and the possibility of its re-emergence is very real. Al-Qaeda leaders such as Ayman Al-Zwahiri (and formerly Osama bin Laden) have made it clear in various video recordings and letters to their followers that Iraq continues to be a key battleground for the organization. The spate of attacks that al-Qaeda launched on Iraq's Christian community in November 2010 were another example of al-Qaeda's ability to resurface.

One of the results of sectarian strife since 2003 has been the internal displacement of over 2.5 million Iraqis, with another 2 million spilling across the border to neighboring countries.[25] The exact numbers of internally displaced Iraqis and refugees is not known due to several reasons, one being that most have left to live in rented accommodations or at the houses of friends or family rather than in the camps, where it is possible to count the residents. While many organizations have not been able to estimate the numbers, the United Nations High Commission for Refugees estimated that, until 2008, 4.7 million Iraqis had left their homes to go to other, less violent parts of the country or to cross the borders into neighboring countries.

In addition to the human suffering of those who had to leave their homes and neighborhoods, the mass movement of people has strained Iraq internally and externally. Pressure is put on scarce resources in a country where the government still struggles to provide basic services. Areas receiving refugees have not been given extra support to maintain the level of basic services for those already living there. Also, the future return of internally displaced Iraqis and refugees could lead to problems regarding land ownership and long-term education deficiencies for children and youths. The failure to deal with this situation could lead to internal upheavals as dissatisfaction increases. Moreover, as the years pass, many refugees may choose not to return to Iraq, depriving the country of vital human resources.

The issue of the provision of poor public services for Iraqis is one that threatens the proper governing of Iraq and has led to shadow economies. Groups like the Mahdi movement have made strides at gaining public support by providing public services that the government failed to provide. This was a key tactic used by Hezbollah throughout the previous two decades in Lebanon, and there are fears it will be repeated in Iraq, creating a parallel shadow state to the official state.

The threat of sectarian or civil war breaking out in Iraq had devastating consequences for millions in Iraq and could again have detrimental consequences. Close proximity between Sunnis and Shiites and the extent of intrasectarian marriage means that families, tribes, and towns would have to be broken up to avoid attacks. National unity is the only way out of this situation; however, the last few years in Iraq have demonstrated the difficulty of maintaining unity in the face of political and regional manipulation.

WATER

Water security is a potential source of tension for Iraq and its northern neighbors. Previously, the vulnerability of water resources was considered a potential problem in the distant future, but in recent years it has become a much more immediate concern. In a region with heightened climate change risks, long periods of droughts, and sand storms, water shortages increasingly represent a problem that must be dealt with. Having two rivers, the Euphrates and Tigris, Iraq should be safe from water worries. However, a combination of natural and political causes has made water a serious point of concern for the country.

Water politics is a key factor in Iraq's relations with its neighbors, as 90 percent of the Euphrates and 50 percent of the Tigris water flows come from outside the country. Turkey is the source of both rivers. The Euphrates flows through Syria, but the Tigris flows straight into Iraq. Turkey has the advantage of controlling these waters, regulating its flow into Iraq as it wishes. There is no international agreement on how to distribute and control the water.

Turkey has built major dams that allow it to benefit from hydraulic power, but its neighbors have lagged behind in building similar projects. Furthermore, Turkey's utilization of the rivers means that less water is available to Iraq. While this has been a problem in the past, Turkey's future ambitions have the potential of creating major problems in one of the most politically wrought basins in the world. Ankara has in its sights on developing the Southeastern Anatolia Development Project—known as GAP, the acronym of its Turkish name. Turkey has been planning the project for over three decades, but it is only in the last few years that Iraq has realized the full extent of the project (which is estimated to cost $32 billion) and the effects it will have on Iraq's access to the Euphrates and Tigris Rivers. Upon completion, the GAP will include 22 dams and 19 hydroelectric power plants using most of the waters from the two rivers. Moreover, plans have been drawn up by Turkey to use waters of the basin to irrigate hundreds of thousands of fields in the underdeveloped area of southeastern Turkey.

Although a trilateral body of government officials representing Iraq, Turkey, and Syria has been convened periodically since 2007, this committee has failed to come to an agreement on the future of the water distribution. In March 2008, the three countries announced the creation of an institute of 18 water experts from each country to discuss the issues related to water. However, this is a long distance away from reaching an international agreement on water flows. While there is acknowledgement by all sides on the need to reach an agreement, if this is not achieved, potential conflicts will arise with the progression of the GAP. Syria has also announced irrigation projects that will further reduce Iraq's water supply, while Iraq continues to have problems in developing its irrigation networks.

Reduction of rainfall and droughts exacerbate the problem posed by the struggle over water, with increasingly hot summers and dust storms straining Iraq's agriculture. Water shortage, coupled with reduction in rainfall, affects Iraq's crop production, which can have a detrimental effect on Iraq's economy. Agriculture is the second-largest contributor to Iraq's gross domestic product behind oil. Agricultural employs an estimated 20 percent to 35 percent of the nation's workforce. It is estimated that 26 percent of Iraq's lands are cultivable, yet the water shortage and basic farming practices mean that less than half of these lands are cultivated annually. Farming in areas like the province of Diyala is a vital source of income for farmers and provides Iraq with some of its basic needs for wheat and vegetables. Iraq's wheat production in 2011 was expected to be 15 percent lower than the year before.[26]

In addition to the importance of water as a resource, the lack of clean water poses a threat to sanitation and the health of Iraqis. The outbreak of cholera in Iraq in 2007 was a worrying reminder. Lack of functioning sewage systems in many parts of the country is another problem that poses a dangerous time bomb for the country.

Along with the potential struggle for sustainable water resources is the potential of conflict over the Shatt AlArab waterway. Shatt AlArab is vital to Iraq because it is the only river basin in Iraq into which the Euphrates and Tigris flow. A key reason behind the Iraq-Iran war was control of the Shatt AlArab, Iraq's only water route. Control over the waterway has yet to be determined, because the border was set on the Tathooq point, the deepest point in the waterway. The point continues to move naturally closer to Iraq's border, giving more water to Iran. It is feared in the long term that this might become a source of contention.

CONCLUSION

Iraq's recent past has been troubled by armed conflict, political discord, and social breakdown. Heightened tensions in the years following the 2003 war led to various naysayers speaking of "the end of Iraq."[27] However, the country was able to pull itself from the brink of collapse—or away from the "abyss," as the former commander of the multinational forces in Iraq, General David Petraeus, has said. A voter turnout of 62 percent endorsed the political process in the March 2010 elections. However, the situation in Iraq remains fragile in an increasingly insecure region. An upsurge in violence, a security vacuum, or a breakdown in political dialogue can all lead to huge upheaval, but the idea of breaking up the country has been discredited for the time being.

A mix of consensual politics, economic reform, sustained development of internal security forces, and better relations and more stringent border control with neighboring countries is necessary to manage the potential hot spots in Iraq.

It is important to keep in mind that while Iraq has many sources of concern in its immediate and near future, unlike several other countries in the region, it also has a multitude of sources of optimism ranging from natural wealth to strategic positioning in the region.

NOTES

1. Hugh Kennedy, *The Court of the Caliphs: The Rise and Fall of Islam's Greatest Dynasty* (London: Weidenfeld & Nicolson 2004), ix.

2. Hanna Batatu, *The Old Social Classes and the Revolutionary Movements of Iraq* (London: Saqi, 2004), 205.

3. George Packer, *The Assassins' Gate: American in Iraq* (New York: Farrar, Straus and Giroux, 2006), 27.

4. Barbara Slavin, "Scope of Oil for Food Fraud 'Overwhelming,'" *USA Today* (November 17, 2005), http://www.usatoday.com/news/world/2005–11–17-oil-for-food_x.htm.

5. Michael E. O'Hanlon and Ian Livingston, *Iraq Index: Tracking Variables of Reconstruction and Security in Post-Saddam Iraq* (Washington, DC: Brookings, August 2008), http://www.brookings.edu/saban/~/media/Files/Centers/Saban/Iraq%20Index/index.pdf.

6. Iraq Study Group in 2006 estimated the militia to be 60,000 strong. James A. Baker III and Lee H. Hamilton, *The Iraq Study Group Report* (Washington, DC: USIP, December 6, 2006), 11.

7. Lionel Beeher, *Iraq's Militia Groups* (Washington DC: Council on Foreign Relations, October 26, 2006).

8. Falah Jabar, *The Shiite Movement in Iraq* (London: Saqi, 2003), 146.

9. Transparency International, *Global Corruption Report 2005*, http://www.transparency. org/news_room/in_focus/2005/gcr_2005.

10. Stuart Bowen, *Quarterly Report and Semiannual Report to the United States Congress,* Office of the Special Inspector for Iraq Reconstruction (July 30, 2008), http://www.sigir. mil/publications/quarterlyreports/July2008.html.

11. "Iraq Corruption 'Costs Billions,'" *BBC News* (November 9, 2006), http://news.bbc. co.uk/2/hi/middle_east/6131290.stm.

12. Special Inspector General for Iraq Reconstruction, *Quarterly Report to the United States Congress* (October 30, 2010), http://www.sigir.mil/publications/quarterlyreports/Octo-ber2010.html.

13. David McDowall, *A Modern History of the Kurds* (London: I. B. Tauris, 2004), 314.

14. Robert F. Worth, "Kurds Destroy Monument in Rage at Leadership," *New York Times* (March 17, 2006), http://www.nytimes.com/2006/03/17/international/middleeast/17kurds.html.

15. "Northern Iraq: Turkish Shelling Causing Displacement," UN Refugee Agency (December 18, 2007), http://www.unhcr.org/news/NEWS/4767a6f94.html.

16. Lawrence Kumins, *Iraq Oil: Reserves, Production, and Potential Revenue,* CRS Report for Congress (April 13, 2005), http://www.fas.org/sgp/crs/mideast/RS21626.pdf.

17. Vali Nasr, *The Shia Revival: How Conflicts within Islam Will Shape the Future* (New York: Norton, 2007), 119.

18. Sara Moore, "Iran Threatens Iraq's Stability, Officials Say," U.S. Department of Defense (April 8, 2008), http://www.defenselink.mil/news/newsarticle.aspx?id=49502.

19. Iran National News Agency (February 9, 2008), http://www1.irna.ir/en/news/view/line-17/0809018327144053.htm.

20. According to figures presented by the U.S. Army and printed in various newspapers, including Ned Parker, "Iraq Insurgency Said to Include Many Saudis," *Los Angeles Times* (July 15, 2007), http://articles.latimes.com/2007/jul/15/world/fg-saudi15.

21. United Nations High Commissioner for Refugees, *Iraq Situation: UNHCR Global Report 2009* (June 2010), http://www.unhcr.org/4c08f25e9.html.

22. Peter Sluglett, *Britain in Iraq: Contriving King and Country* (London: I. B. Tauris, 2007), 120.

23. National Intelligence Council, "The Terrorist Threat to the US Homeland," *National Intelligence Estimate* (July 2007), http://www.dni.gov/press_releases/20070717_release.pdf.

24. Richard Willing, "Report on al-Qaeda Threat Inflames Debate," *USA Today* (July 18 2007), http://www.usatoday.com/news/washington/2007-07-17-intelligence-estimate_N. htm?csp=34.

25. UN Refugee Agency, http://www.unhcr.org/iraq.html for all information on Iraqi refugees.

26. Michael Shean, *Middle East: Wheat Production Forecast to Decline in 2011,* U.S. Department of Agriculture Aquastat Water Report no. 34 (Washington, May 2011), http://www. fao.org/nr/water/aquastat/countries/iraq/index.stm.

27. Peter Galbraith, *The End of Iraq: How American Incompetence Created a War without End* (New York: Simon & Schuster, 2006).

5   ISRAEL

Rafael D. Frankel

HISTORICAL BACKGROUND

For nearly 2,000 years, following the conquest of the Roman Empire of Jerusalem in 70 CE, the Jewish people were scattered around the world, mostly in Europe, Russia, and Arabia. Though persecution of the Jews occurred throughout that time, the idea of returning to the biblical land of Israel and establishing a Jewish state, Zionism, did not grab hold of a significant portion of Jews until the late 19th century. Following a series of pogroms in Russia, the first *Aliyah* (meaning "ascension" in Hebrew) of between 25,000 and 35,000 Jews moved to Palestine, then under Ottoman rule. Additional pogroms and anti-Semitic laws throughout mainly eastern Europe then galvanized the First Zionist Congress in 1897, which set as its goal the reestablishment of a Jewish state on the biblical land of Israel and led to a second wave of Jewish immigration.

After World War I, the League of Nations gave Britain mandatory control over Palestine. During the interwar years, Britain pursued an ambiguous policy toward Jewish immigration, sometimes supporting it but often seeking to stifle it as tensions grew between the native Arabs (mostly Muslim and some Christian) and the Jews, even those who came from families who had inhabited Palestine for generations. (Indeed, Jerusalem is said to have had a majority Jewish population since the 1600s.) During a series of race riots in the 1920s and 1930s, including the Arab Revolt of 1936 to 1939, British policy steadily moved closer toward Arab demands, and by the end of the interwar years, Britain had placed tight restrictions on Jewish immigration.

Following the Holocaust, in which 6 million Jews were killed by the Nazis, pressure mounted on Britain to allow surviving European Jews to immigrate to Palestine. When Britain did not amend its policy on Jewish immigration, and anti-Jewish violence perpetrated by Arabs mounted, the Jews of Palestine formed their own militias, and a revolt against British rule began. After two years of violence in Palestine between the Jews, Arabs, and British army, the British decided in 1947 to allow the newly formed United Nations (UN) to decide what to do with the territory.

Approval for a Jewish state, broken up into three noncontiguous cantons on 56 percent of mandatory Palestine, was given by a United Nations General Assembly vote on November 29, 1947. According to the Partition Plan, the remainder of the territory was designated to the native Arabs in order to realize their own dreams of statehood. Though the Jewish Agency, which represented the Palestinian Jews, agreed to the terms of the Partition Plan, the native Arabs and neighboring Arab governments rejected it. After declaring independence on May 14, 1948, Israel was attacked the following day by the surrounding Arab states—Egypt, Trans-Jordan, Syria, Lebanon, Iraq, and Saudi Arabia. The armies of those countries were joined by Palestinian irregular forces who were not content with the share of Palestine designated to them by the UN. Despite overwhelming enemy numbers, Israel managed to win the war but at a pyrrhic cost of 1 percent of its total population killed only three years following the end of the Holocaust, which murdered one-third of all Jews worldwide. Though a cease-fire was called, ending hostilities, the Arab states maintained their rejection of Israel and refused to sign peace treaties with the Jewish state. As a result, Israel has yet to exist for a single day in true peace, 63 years after its birth.

In the 1950s, the unremitting violence Israel has been subject to mostly came from Palestinian *fedayeen* who would cross one of Israel's borders and attack civilians. Israel's first prime minister, David Ben-Gurion, responded to these attacks by ordering reprisal raids inside Arab territory, during which civilians were also killed. In 1956, Israel fought its second war against Egypt, when it allied with France and Britain to retake control of the Suez Canal, which was nationalized by Egyptian president Gamal Abdel Nasser. Though Israeli troops took the Sinai Peninsula during the war, they were forced back to the 1949 border in exchange for shipping rights in the Red Sea under heavy pressure from the United States and the Soviet Union.

The unilateral denial by Egypt of those shipping rights, and the unilateral removal by Egypt of UN peacekeepers from the Israel-Egypt border were major factors in prompting the Six-Day War in June 1967. Due to Nasser's decision to mass troops on the border, constant terror and rocket attacks from Syria, and a stir of propaganda in the Arab world predicting the imminent destruction of the Jewish state, Israel felt obliged to launch a preemptive attack on Egypt. That attack obliterated nearly the entire Egyptian air force in a matter of hours.

In the subsequent days, the war expanded to the Jordanian and Syrian fronts with the result being that, after six days, Israel had captured the Sinai Peninsula and Gaza Strip from Egypt, East Jerusalem and the West Bank of the Jordan River from Jordan, and the Golan Heights from Syria. While originally hailed as a miraculous triumph for the Jewish people and Israel, 44 years later, it is hotly debated inside Israel whether the resulting occupation of what is now 3.76 million Palestinians was worth the territorial gains.

In the lead up to the Six-Day War, there was real fear that Israel would not survive another combined assault by the Arab armies. After the rapid and massive victory, the consensus of historians is that the political and social structure of the state grew arrogant and hubristic. The Yom Kippur War of 1973 (called the October War by the

Arabs), when Egypt and Syria launched a surprise attack against Israel on Judaism's most holy day of the year, changed that.

Following the four-year War of Attrition (1967–1970), consisting of attacks and counterattacks by Israel and Egypt across the 1967 cease-fire lines, Egyptian president Anwar Sadat, who assumed control following the death of Nasser, openly stated his intention to attack Israel multiple times in 1973. Over the course of that year, Egypt and Syria conducted large-scale battle simulations close to the border, causing Israel to mobilize its reserves multiple times—a very costly maneuver for the tiny state whose army was dependent on its reserves. Though there were warnings that an attack by Egypt and Syria was planned, Israel's prime minister this time around, Golda Meir, decided not to initiate a preemptive strike both due to intelligence failures and her desire not to harm Israel's relationship with the United States, which, after 1967, had become Israel's strongest ally.

That decision proved costly, as 2,656 Israeli soldiers were killed and 7,250 wounded in the 1973 conflict. The staggering losses of the Yom Kippur War and the fact that Israel was taken by surprise led to massive protests around the country, which eventually caused Meir to resign as prime minister. While the result of the Yom Kippur War put an end to the feeling of invincibility in Israeli society, it restored a measure of honor in Egypt and Jordan. Despite the fact that the countries suffered their forth and third lost wars respectively to Israel, they managed to inflict heavy damage on the Jewish state following their humiliation in 1967.

This relative victory, some historians say, paved the way for Sadat to be able to sue for peace with Israel from a position of perceived strength. In November 1977, Sadat, at the invitation of Israeli prime minister Menachem Begin, became the first Arab leader to visit Israel, addressing the Israeli Knesset (parliament) in Jerusalem on the topic of how the two countries, and the region, could achieve peace. The historic visit led to the Camp David Accords of 1978, mediated by President Jimmy Carter, in which Egypt, in exchange for a return of the entire Sinai Peninsula, became the first Arab country to sign a peace treaty with Israel. (Egypt did not want the Gaza Strip.)

Though it was believed at the time that the Israel-Egypt accords would provide momentum for broader Arab-Israeli peace, it was not to be. Instead, in 1982, Begin, with prodding from then Defense Minister Ariel Sharon, decided to throw Israel into the ongoing Lebanese Civil War, invading Lebanon from the south and moving up to Beirut with the stated goal of eliminating the Palestine Liberation Organization (PLO) terrorist network that had continually struck Israel from Lebanese territory. During the war, in which Syria was also engaged, Israel sided with factions of the Lebanese Christians. Though the PLO was eventually routed from Lebanon, Israel would not extricate itself from the security zone it established in the south of that country for 18 years. During that time, it lost dozens of soldiers every year, mostly to Hezbollah— the Iranian-backed Shiite resistance militia that did not exist prior to Israel's invasion of its northern neighbor. It was only in 2000 that Prime Minister Ehud Barak decided to initiate a unilateral withdrawal from Lebanon, setting the stage for the 2006 Second Lebanon War.

In the intervening years, however, the security situation shifted from a focus on the surrounding Arab armies to the Palestinians. After 19 years of occupation by Jordan (in the West Bank) and Egypt (in Gaza) and another 20 years of occupation and land confiscation by Israel, Palestinian society reached a boiling point in 1987. The first intifada (uprising in Arabic) was largely characterized by Palestinian youths throwing stones at Israeli soldiers. But there were also waves of stabbings of Israeli civilians and other violent incidents. Over 1,100 Palestinians were killed by Israeli forces during the uprising, which lasted six years, and 160 Israelis were killed by Palestinians.[1] Additionally, it is believed that more than 1,000 Palestinians were killed by their own people—summarily executed after being accused of collaborating with Israeli intelligence services.

The first intifada concluded with the signing of the Oslo Accords between Israel and the PLO in November 1993, an agreement for which Israeli prime minister Yitzhak Rabin, defense minister Shimon Peres, and PLO chairman Yasser Arafat shared the Nobel Peace Prize. The talks, conducted in secret, provided a framework for the creation of a Palestinian state in the West Bank and Gaza, including the withdrawal of Israeli forces from those territories, along with economic and security agreements between the two peoples. However, despite initial success, including the withdrawal of Israeli forces from Palestinian cities, and the establishment of the Palestinian Authority, the Oslo process ultimately failed. Why it failed is the subject of endless debate and will probably never be agreed upon by the various parties in the conflict. It is, however, fair to say that the following five factors all played a major role in derailing the peace process: (1) numerous suicide bombings from the militant, Islamist group Hamas and others; (2) the assassination of Rabin by an extremist right-wing Israeli Jew; (3) Israel's continued settlement construction in the West Bank; (4) corruption in the Palestinian Authority; (5) and the failure of Arafat to transform himself from a guerrilla fighter into a statesman.

In July 2000, in a last-gasp effort to save the foundering Oslo process, President Bill Clinton called a second Camp David summit, this time between Israeli prime minister Barak and Arafat. Two months after the summit failed, the second intifada broke out following a visit to the Temple Mount by then Israeli opposition leader Ariel Sharon. The second Palestinian uprising was far more deadly than the first, with various Palestinian militant groups employing all means of deadly attacks against Israeli soldiers and civilians, the most gruesome of which were the suicide bombings, which, at the height of the intifada, occurred with near daily frequency. With the election of Ariel Sharon as prime minister in the beginning of 2001, Israel took a harder line against the Palestinians and in 2002, during Operation Defensive Shield, reoccupied nearly all of the cities and territory Israeli Defense Forces (IDF) vacated during Oslo. At that time, Israel also began building a separation barrier around and in the West Bank. Israel's stated purpose for building the fence was to stem the flow of suicide bombers penetrating into Israel proper, though critics charged that its route was also designed to confiscate more Palestinian land. (A fence was built around Gaza in the mid-1990s.) Additionally, in the summer of 2002, President George W. Bush, in the aftermath of the September 11, 2001, attacks on the United States, made the strategic decision to cease talking with Arafat, who the United States and Israel had returned to viewing as a terrorist rather than a peace partner.

At the same time, Bush, with input from the UN, Russia, and the European Union, also published the Road Map for Peace—a three-phase series of steps that

Israel and the Palestinians were supposed to take to get them back on track toward a peace agreement. The Road Map, however, was never adhered to by either side, was never pushed hard by the United States, and ultimately went nowhere. In the meantime, Israel's reestablishment of its security presence in the West Bank had a dramatic effect, and the bombings hitting Israel steadily declined in number. Then, on November 11, 2004, Arafat died from a mysterious illness, which he had begun displaying symptoms of only a few weeks earlier. His death paved the way for the election of Mahmoud Abbas, his long-time aid, to the presidency of the Palestinian Authority. Abbas, a critic of Palestinian violence in the second intifada, soon hammered out a cease-fire agreement with the various Palestinian militant factions, including Hamas, bringing an unofficial end of sorts to the second intifada in which more than 1,000 Israeli soldiers and civilians and more than 5,000 Palestinian militants and civilians were killed.

With a cease-fire secured, Prime Minister Sharon decided it was time to implement the unilateral withdrawal from the Gaza Strip that he had first proposed in early 2004. Under the plan, Israel would remove, forcibly if necessary, the 8,500 Jewish settlers living in the Gaza Strip, and all of the IDF's infrastructure and equipment. Control of every last inch of Gaza would be handed over to the Palestinian Authority for nothing in return. Despite widespread protest from the right wing in Israel, and a revolt among his own Likud party, the Sharon government and the IDF implemented the disengagement plan from the entire Gaza Strip in August and September 2005, ending a 38-year Israeli civil and military presence in the 139-square-mile, destitute territory, teeming with over 1.4 million Palestinians. (Four small settlements in the West Bank were also evacuated.)

Following the political upheaval that beset Israel in the aftermath of the Gaza withdrawal, Sharon formed a new political party, which he was to head in early elections called for March 2006. However, in January of that year, he suffered two strokes, the second of which left him brain dead and on artificial life support. Presumably, Sharon's plan was to follow the Gaza model in the West Bank, removing Israeli settlements that were east of the security barrier Israel built. That mantle was taken up by Ehud Olmert, who took Sharon's place on top of the Kadima party list, and was elected prime minister. However, prior to the Israeli elections, Hamas—which totally rejects Israel's right to exist, was responsible for more attacks than any other Palestinian faction during the second intifada, and is listed by the United States and Europe as a terrorist organization—won the Palestinian Legislative Council (PLC) elections.

With a terrorist group now heading the PLC (Abbas was still president of the Palestinian Authority), Israel's withdrawal options from the West Bank, and its relations with the Gaza Strip, were drastically complicated. Together, the Western states of the international community and Israel placed three demands on Hamas that they said must be met before any diplomatic recognition and financial support of the Palestinian Authority—which is heavily dependent on foreign aid for its budget—would resume. The conditions were recognition of Israel's right to exist, adherence to all previously signed agreements between Israel and the Palestinian Authority, and a cessation of all violent activities directed at Israel. Hamas immediately refused those conditions and, until the present time, has not relented on a single one.

Just three months after Olmert assumed control as prime minister, Hamas, in co-ordination with other Palestinian factions in Gaza, breached the Gaza security fence, killing one Israeli soldier and kidnapping another, Corp. Gilad Shalit. This led to a massive IDF operation in the Gaza strip aimed at securing Shalit's release and dealing a heavy blow to Hamas's military infrastructure. Just three weeks later, in July 2006, Hezbollah launched a cross-border raid from Lebanon, killing six soldiers and kidnapping two more, reservists Ehud Goldwasser and Eldad Regev.

That raid sparked the month-long Second Lebanon War, during which Hezbollah launched over 4,000 rockets into northern Israel, pummeling Israeli cities, including Haifa, Israel's third-largest metropolitan area, for weeks on end. For the most part, the IDF was powerless to stop the Ketusha rocket attacks, which Hezbollah launched from small mobile platforms in southern Lebanon. Israeli ground forces, though dealing significant blows to Hezbollah guerrillas, also suffered significant casualties in operations inside Lebanon.

Though the math of the war was lopsided—with Israel having killed around 1,600 Lebanese civilians and Hezbollah fighters as opposed to 163 Israeli civilians and soldiers dead—and vast tracks of Beirut and southern Lebanon bombed out, the political settlement embodied in UN Security Council Resolution 1701 was widely interpreted as having favored Hezbollah. Despite requirements in the resolution that the two kidnapped soldiers be returned and that Hezbollah disarm itself, neither of those conditions was implemented following the cease-fire. In Israel, outrage over the war's failures led to

An Israeli soldier holds his weapon at an artillery position in northern Israel along the tense Lebanon border. (AP Photo/Oded Balilty)

calls for Olmert, Defense Minister Amir Peretz, and Army Chief of Staff Dan Halutz to resign. While Halutz resigned, and Peretz was voted out of office after losing the Labor Party leadership vote, Olmert remained prime minister despite record-low approval ratings and an independent investigatory commission which laid much of the blame for the war's failures squarely on his lap.

Olmert's popularity was further eroded when next summer, Hamas initiated a violent takeover of the Gaza Strip, control of which had been fought over between it and Fatah (the long-dominant Palestinian political party of Arafat and Abbas) since Hamas won the PLC elections in January 2006. The five-day Palestinian civil war showed just how inept Fatah forces under the command of Abbas were. Despite Fatah's overwhelming numerical and firearms advantage in Gaza, Hamas easily took control of the territory.

With Hamas in control of Gaza, Abbas officially dismissed the Hamas-controlled government and appointed his own cabinet of mostly political independents and technocrats to control the West Bank, effectively severing joint operation of the two Palestinian territories, with Fatah controlling the West Bank and Hamas ruling Gaza. Whereas the flow of foreign aid from Europe and the United States (in addition to customs revenues held in escrow by Israel) now resumed in the West Bank, the economic and physical blockade of Gaza was tightened as a result. Supplies of only basic necessities were now allowed into Gaza, which Israel declared a "hostile entity," and the Raffah border between Gaza and Egypt was closed down.

From that point on, the conditions and fates of the West Bank and Gaza diverged, as did their respective relations with Israel. In Gaza, living conditions plummeted dramatically as the legitimate economy was vanquished and the sporadic violence between Israel and Hamas continued. Daily Hamas rocket attacks were met with frequent Israeli air raids on suspected terrorists. Israel also targeted the tunnels Gazans dug under the Egyptian border, where goods of all kinds, including gasoline, food, vehicles, and animals were smuggled through with increasing quantity as the siege of Gaza was tightened. Numerous attempts were made by Hamas fighters to break the siege and were almost always repelled by Israel with deadly force.

After one year of deadly stalemate, a cease-fire was brokered by Egypt in June 2008. Under the terms of the agreement, Hamas was to cease all attacks against Israel, including the launching of Qassam rockets, and Israel was to steadily ease the embargo imposed on the 1.4 million people of Gaza. However, the cease-fire was never observed to its fullest by either side, and by November it lay in ruins after Israel killed what it said was a group of Hamas fighters attempting to tunnel under its border. When the six-month armistice was nearing its conclusion in December, Hamas decided not to renew the terms and, in the first two days following its termination, bombarded southern Israel with more than 100 rockets.

Israel's response was crushing. On December 27, 2008, Israel initiated Operation Cast Lead, which began with a devastating week-long air bombardment of Gaza followed by a two-week ground campaign. In the first day of air strikes alone, around 200 Palestinians were killed, mostly police graduates in Gaza City. Unlike the resistance the IDF encountered from Hezbollah in 2006, the Hamas fighters did not prove to be particularly adept combatants. Moreover, though Hamas did succeed in launching hundreds of rockets during the war, the damage caused by the Qassams was far less than Hezbollah's Ketushas. By the end of the war, which was concluded by dual unilateral cease-fires from Israel and Hamas, between 1,166 and 1,417 Palestinians were killed (the numbers are disputed) including between 295 and 926 civilians. Meanwhile, 13 Israelis were dead, 10 of whom were soldiers. According to the United Nations, more than 250,000 Gazans were materially and negatively impacted by the war, either through death, injury, or destruction or damage to their property.[2]

But much like Lebanon, the IDF's victory on the battlefield brought with it significant international political damage. Condemnation was heaped upon Israel from all corners of the globe for the number of civilians who were killed in the fighting and the vast destruction that was laid upon the already dilapidated Gaza Strip. The rules of engagement for IDF forces, which included targeting mosques, homes, and most

structures utilized by fighters or for storing weapons, were also criticized amid a bar-
rage of photos and videos the international media sent from Gaza toward the end and
after the war. (Israel had imposed a ban on foreign journalists in Gaza from November
2008 onward, which was only lifted in the last days of the conflict.)

Ostensibly to set the record straight about what took place in Gaza during the war,
the United Nations appointed South African judge Richard Goldstone to head an investigatory committee. However, the right-wing Israeli government elected following
the war, led by Prime Minister Benjamin Netanyahu, made the strategic decision not to
cooperate with the committee. The end result, known as the Goldstone Report, found
that both Israel and Hamas committed war crimes and possibly crimes against human-
ity during the course of the war. But both the report itself and most of the international
attention after its publication, focused mostly on the Jewish state. While the majority
of Israelis saw Operation Cast Lead as a legitimate, defensive campaign against a terrorist organization that had unceasingly targeted Israeli civilians, most of the rest of the
world saw it as a merciless aggression against an already victimized population. Nearly
two years later, in a *Washington Post* op-ed piece, Goldstone retracted the charge that
Israel intentionally harmed civilians and claimed that the UN Human Rights Council
was biased against Israel. Nevertheless, the UN did not retract the report's findings.

And yet, with the steadfast, if now somewhat conditional support of the United
States behind it, Israel maintained its blockade of Gaza in the face of loud and growing
international condemnation. Following the war, numerous attempts by various human
rights organizations were made to break the blockade on Gaza, with Israel sometimes
allowing ships into the Gaza port and sometimes rejecting them. Then, on May 31,
2010, a clash occurred in international waters aboard the *Mavi Maramara,* the lead
ship in a Turkish-backed flotilla on course for Gaza. The confrontation on that ship between an elite IDF naval force and an assortment of Islamist agitators and human rights
activists left nine of the passengers dead and two IDF soldiers seriously wounded.
After yet another international uproar over charges of disproportionate force used by
Israel, the Netanyahu government finally conceded to ease the Gaza blockade. Yet despite more than five years in captivity, Israeli soldier Gilad Shalit remains the prisoner
of Hamas in Gaza, denied by his captors even of the right to meet representatives of
the Red Cross.

The 2007 Hamas takeover of Gaza also provided a wake-up call to officials in Jerusalem and Washington, who, after seven years of zero progress on Israeli-Palestinian
peace talks, concluded that it was time to restart negotiations with Abbas. This second
round of official Israeli-Palestinian peace talks officially started at Annapolis, Maryland, in November 2007, at a conference organized by the United States and attended
by countries throughout the world, including influential Middle East nations like Saudi
Arabia, Syria, Jordan, and Egypt.

As a result of those talks, then Prime Minister Olmert offered Abbas a final status
agreement just before his term in office ended, following his resignation in July 2008
under the veil of corruption charges. Though the terms of the agreement were more
generous than those offered to Arafat at Camp David in 2000, Abbas never gave an official reply, and the offer died when Olmert was replaced in office by Benjamin Netanyahu in March 2009.

Since the assumption of power by Netanyahu and U.S. president Barack Obama, conditions on the ground in the West Bank have improved in some respects. With successful U.S.-Jordanian training of Palestinian security forces and the tenure of internationally respected Palestinian prime minister Salam Fayyad, hundreds of IDF checkpoints in the West Bank were removed. U.S. pressure also led the Netanyahu government to impose a 10-month settlement construction freeze in the West Bank. Together with the improved conditions on the ground, an influx of billions of dollars in foreign aid initiated an economic renaissance in the West Bank.

However, to date, progress on the economic front has not been matched by advances at the negotiating table. Direct Israeli-Palestinian negotiations, briefly resumed after much U.S. prodding, were scuttled again when Israel refused to extend its West Bank settlement moratorium, and the Palestinians refused to negotiate while Jewish settlement construction continued. Indirect negotiations, meanwhile, conducted by U.S. Special Envoy George Mitchell, bore no significant fruit. With both sides firmly entrenched in their positions, at the time of this writing, the Obama administration has more or less acknowledged that its efforts to date have failed and that it is searching for new ideas on how to revive the moribund peace process.

Further doubt was thrown on prospects for a negotiated settlement when Fatah and Hamas announced in April 2011 that the two had reached an agreement on establishing a coalition government that would prepare for a fresh round of Palestinian national elections. This announcement prompted Netanyahu to state that the Palestinian Authority "must choose either peace with Israel or peace with Hamas. There is no possibility for peace with both."[3] Eighteen years after starting what was supposed to be a six-year process, Israelis and Palestinians appear to be no closer to a peace agreement than they were at the beginning.

SECURITY THREATS

The Palestinians

During the 1948 War of Independence, around 700,000 Arabs fled or were forced from their homes within the 1949 armistice lines that delineated Israel's border until 1967. They and their decedents make up the Palestinian refugees who live in the West Bank, Gaza Strip, and surrounding Arab countries—their ultimate national fate still undetermined 63 years following the war. While the return of these Palestinian refugees to their homes was an issue in the immediate aftermath of the first war, as was the lack of a Palestinian state, these issues were exacerbated following the Six-Day War, when Israel took control of Gaza and the West Bank. Thus began the now 44-year occupation by Israel of the Palestinians in the West Bank and the since terminated occupation of the Gaza Strip, collectively home to 3.76 million Palestinian refugees and nondisplaced Palestinians.

Unlike the Arabs who remained in Israel following the 1948 war, the Palestinians brought under Israeli control in the 1967 war were never granted citizenship or civil rights. Further complicating matters, in the 1970s, Israel began constructing Jewish settlements inside the West Bank and Gaza Strip, often in extremely close proximity to

Arab cities and villages. While all of the Gaza settlers were evacuated in 2005, the settlements in the West Bank have undergone a drastic expansion, and the number of Israelis living there is now around 300,000, excluding around 200,000 who live in areas of Jerusalem annexed since 1967.[4] Though the majority of the population is grouped in three main settlement blocks and in the Jerusalem metropolitan area, hundreds of other Jewish settlements are positioned all over the West Bank. It is these settlements, with an estimated population of 80,000 to 100,000, that would likely be evacuated as part of a still theoretical peace agreement between Israel and the Palestinians.

The settlements and the final borders of Israel and a Palestinian state are only one of the major issues that separate the two sides in their negotiations. The fate of the refugees, and where they will have a right to return to—Israel or the Palestinian state—is another major issue, as are security arrangements, the status of Jerusalem, and water rights. Until these outstanding issues are settled, and even possibly after an agreement, Israel will face a continuing threat from the Palestinians. The nature of this threat is multifaceted and involves violence, demographics, and international political maneuvering.

The violent aspect is the easiest to understand. Though the attacks of the second intifada eventually subsided, no official end to violent resistance against Israel was ever called by the Palestinian militant groups. The most famous and powerful of these groups is Hamas, which means "zeal" in Arabic and also represents the acronym of its full name: the Islamic Resistance Movement. Founded in 1987 in Gaza, Hamas was born out of the Egyptian Muslim Brotherhood and, as such, is an Islamist movement dedicated to bringing Islam into the daily and civic lives of Palestinians. However, Hamas is also a militant organization bent on Israel's destruction.

During the second intifada, West Bank cells of Hamas took the gruesome lead among Palestinian militant groups in their deadly campaign of suicide bombings, nearly always targeting Israeli civilians on buses and in restaurants. Hamas irregular forces also engaged in shooting and stabbing attacks over the years. Its most deadly attack came on March 27, 2002, when a suicide bomber killed 30 Israelis who were celebrating Passover at a hotel in the coastal city of Netanya. That attack was the proverbial last straw for the Israeli government headed by Ariel Sharon. In the days following, Israel engaged in Operation Defensive Shield, retaking control of the West Bank and dealing a severe blow to Hamas's military infrastructure there, which remains under check until this day.

As Israel reasserted security control in the West Bank, Hamas's military operations shifted. Following Israel's withdrawal from Gaza in 2005, the group focused on building its military infrastructure in the coastal territory, which had always been its home base. Hamas quickly became adept at manufacturing and launching Qassam rockets, which until a tentative cease-fire was called in June 2008, bombarded the Israeli towns surrounding the Gaza Strip on a daily basis. Though the Qassams are highly inaccurate and the majority of them do not cause damage, from 2005 to 2008, they killed 14 Israelis. They also caused deep psychological trauma to the town of Sderot and other Israeli communities located in close proximity to Gaza that were forced to live under a constant state of fear. Recent improvements in Hamas's rocket technology seem now to have expanded the range to include areas as far north as Tel Aviv.

Hamas also carried out numerous operations intending to breach the Gaza security fence, including the one in 2006 in which Corp. Shalit was captured. Another border operation was directed against Egypt in January 2008, when Hamas blew a hole in the southern border wall, allowing Palestinians unfettered access to Egypt for a week before Egyptian authorities sealed the breach. Its most successful military operation, however, was the aforementioned summer 2007 take over of Gaza, when heavily outnumbered Hamas fighters assumed total control of the territory from Fatah forces in five days.

How did Hamas in Gaza build up such a military capability? For years, Hamas had managed to smuggle in small arms and bomb-making material via tunnels that were dug under the Egyptian border. Egyptian authorities were either inept at halting this smuggling or, more likely, made only halfhearted attempts at stopping it. Following the Israeli withdrawal, the tunnel infrastructure was greatly expanded as Israel no longer patrolled the Philadelphi corridor, a narrow strip of land between Gaza and Egypt. Since then, Hamas has managed to smuggle into Gaza both more and better weapons, including antitank missiles and rocket-propelled grenades. Some smuggling is also accomplished at sea, despite the Israeli navy's efforts to blunt such activity.

Hamas's main supplier of weapons, military training, and financing is Iran. While the Hamas-Iran relationship runs back to 1991, it was in 2006 that the connection between Hamas and Iran blossomed into a more genuine strategic partnership as the twin events of Hamas's electoral victory in January and the Israel-Hezbollah war in July–August pushed the two closer together. With the international community boycotting the Palestinian Authority after the elections, Hamas turned to Arab and Muslim countries to finance the Palestinian Authority budget. Iran agreed to supply Hamas with $250 million to finance its operations. Militarily speaking, the coordination was enhanced greatly following the Hezbollah war later that year, which both Hamas and Iran viewed as a template (rocket attacks and guerilla operations) for how to successfully engage Israel despite inferior numbers and fire power. Iran has at times taken Hamas fighters out of Gaza and paid for their training in Iran, Lebanon, or other fields. Iranian-made rockets have also made their way into Hamas's hands in Gaza, and Iranian technical instruction has allowed Hamas to upgrade its weapons, specifically rockets and other explosives. Through this military buildup (particularly its rocket capabilities), its alliances with Iran and Syria, and its completely rejectionist stance toward Israel, Hamas, firmly entrenched on Israel's doorstep, constitutes a major security concern to Israel.

Although Hamas is the best known militant Palestinian group, others such as Islamic Jihad and the al-Aqsa Martyrs Brigade also pose threats to Israel. Indeed, at times when Hamas has observed periods of calm with Israel, it is mainly these two groups that were responsible for rocket attacks from Gaza and other terror activities in Gaza and the West Bank. Like Hamas, Islamic Jihad is completely rejectionist toward Israel and is committed to its destruction. It is also financed by Iran, but to a much lesser degree—around $10 million per year in weapons and cash. It is not a large organization, but it has carried out deadly attacks against Israel at crucial moments that have aggravated already tense situations. Though not a major player, it has the potential to act as a spoiler to any positive movement made toward calm or peace by Israel and the Palestinians. The al-Aqsa Martyrs Brigade, meanwhile, is nominally affiliated with the Fatah party of Palestinian Authority president Abbas, even though he denounces their tactics. Although the brigade has engaged in terror attacks against Israel, its political ideology does allow for the possibility of the two-state solution. Its violence, therefore, is viewed by its leaders as a means toward ending the Israeli occupation of the West Bank and blockade of the Gaza Strip rather than the outright destruction of the Jewish state.

The other main player in Palestinian political life is Fatah, and the threat that it poses to Israel is not so much a violent one but a political one. Fatah leaders such as Abbas, who accept Israel's right to exist and at least the principle of a two-state solution, and those who oppose violence against Israel have lost local legitimacy with the failure of the peace process. As evidenced by the putative national unity agreement with Hamas, Fatah is now considering alternative political avenues to its alliance with the United States and its dedication to peace talks. Among other avenues, this has manifested itself in the September 2011 bid by the Palestinian Authority to gain United Nations recognition for a Palestinian state while bypassing negotiations with Israel. Moreover, Abbas has previously indicated that he will not stand for reelection during a future vote for the presidency of the Palestinian Authority.

Who leadership of the Palestinian people would fall to in that case is uncertain. While trends as late as 2008 indicated steady gains by Hamas, views since then have done an about-face as conditions in Gaza and the West Bank, respectively, have so drastically diverged. According to polls at the time of this writing, support for Fatah is up to 45 percent, while support for Hamas is down to 26 percent.[5] But even if the lack of political progress eventually leads that trend to reverse, what is most threatening about the possible change in political direction of Fattah is not that it may lead to a third intifada. (Given Israel's current military posture in the West Bank and the cordon around Gaza, the Palestinians are simply not in a position to engage in another large-scale uprising.)

Rather, the greatest threat to Israel from the Palestinians (including the moderates) might be their ability to reject the two-state solution. In so doing, the Palestinians would be playing a demographic and geopolitical game. If current birth rates remain static, the number of Arabs living in Israel and the Palestinian territories will soon eclipse the number of Jews. At that point, counting on the postcolonial liberal attitudes of the Western nations, the Palestinians may simply demand equal voting representation in a single state shared between Israelis and Palestinians. A one-state solution, in that context, would likely mean an end to the Jewish state. While that scenario seems highly implausible given the current political support Israel has in the United States and Europe, it is, nevertheless, a long-term security threat to Israel that Israeli politicians and security personnel take very seriously.

Hezbollah

For the first 40 years of Israel's existence, the main threat to its security was the combined Arab armies with which Israel engaged in five full-scale wars. While terrorist attacks were frequent since the founding of the state, they did not become the focus of Israel's security establishment until the first intifada. But today, the asymmetric threat to Israel from nonstate actors such as Hamas and Hezbollah is a formidable one.

The 2006 war with Hezbollah, a Lebanese Shiite organization with political, social, and military wings, showed just how difficult fighting such enemies can be. Despite overwhelmingly superior firepower, Israel basically fought Hezbollah to a draw in the month-long war that was triggered on July 12, 2006, by the kidnapping of Israeli soldiers Ehud Goldwasser and Eldad Regev in a Hezbollah cross-border raid. During the conflict, Israel inflicted heavy damage on the southern section of Beirut, where Hezbollah is headquartered, as well as many of the Shiite towns in southern Lebanon, where Hezbollah fighters fought Israeli soldiers in pitch battles.

With training and financing from Iran to the tune of $250 million per year, it is helpful to think of the Hezbollah military wing not so much as a terrorist group but more as a division of the Iranian army. Hezbollah fighters operate with a true command structure, extensive training, and equipment. They are also divided into full-time fighters, reservists, and citizen sympathizers. This sophistication, coupled with six years of preparation (from the time Israel pulled out of southern Lebanon in 2000), helped Hezbollah deal severe blows to the invading Israeli army, especially the tank corps, leading to 151 Israeli soldiers killed as opposed to an estimate of around 400 to 500 Hezbollah fighters. Israeli army operations during the war were also severely complicated by Hezbollah's frequent use of civilian infrastructure—homes, mosques, schools, and so on—from which Hezbollah launched rockets and fired at invading Israeli forces. Throughout the war, the IDF faced a dilemma it never managed to fully solve, as it weighed the consequences of firing on Hezbollah forces in areas populated by civilians.

Perhaps Hezbollah's most impressive accomplishment in the war was its launching of more than 4,000 rockets into Israeli cities—mostly Iranian-made Ketushas. Despite Israel's best efforts, the IDF was unable to prevent the rockets from landing on northern Israeli cities for the duration of the war. Indeed, in the war's final weeks and days, the number of rockets falling on Israel only increased, to the order of more than 200 per day by war's end.

A cease-fire called for in United Nations Security Council Resolution 1701 brought an end to the war and also called for Hezbollah to disarm, move its forces north of the Litani River, and return the two kidnapped soldiers. However, six years later, Hezbollah's military and political strength has only increased. Before the 2006 war, intelligence estimates said that Hezbollah possessed around 10,000 to 12,000 Ketusha rockets capable of striking at least as far south as Haifa, 20 miles from the Lebanese border. Today, the IDF estimates that Hezbollah possess upward of 40,000 rockets, many of which are capable of striking as far as Dimona, in southern Israel, putting nearly the entire Israeli population within Hezbollah firing range. Israeli officials additionally fear that a recent transfer of Scud missiles was made from Syria to Hezbollah—a charge Syria denies.

Though United Nations Interim Force In Lebanon (UNIFIL) and Lebanese army forces now patrol southern Lebanon, there is no doubt that Hezbollah remains the strongest force in the region—even if its fighters no longer openly man positions as they did from 2000 to 2006. Moreover, the kidnapped soldiers were only returned on

July 16, 2008, after Israel agreed to the original Hezbollah demands to release con-
victed Lebanese terrorist Samir Kuntar from jail and return four Hezbollah prisoners
taken during the war as well as 199 bodies of slain Hezbollah fighters and Palestinian
terrorists Israel still possessed. The prisoner swap was largely interpreted by regional
and Lebanese political analysts as a significant victory for Hezbollah, both over Israel
and in terms of its political support in Lebanon and the Arab world at large.

As a result of the May 21, 2008, Doha Agreement between the vying Lebanese
political factions, Hezbollah gained a veto power over any Lebanese government decisions. More recently, Hezbollah managed to replace the Lebanese prime minister with
a candidate of its own choosing in yet another sign of its ascendant political power.
Crucial in that regard is Hezbollah's strong support from most Lebanese Shiites in
southern Lebanon as well as many in Beirut and other parts of the country. The Party
of God's increased domestic power compounds the threat to Israel as it grants Hezbollah a modicum of legitimacy as a political actor and by increasing the chances that a
future war would be an interstate war between Israel and Lebanon rather than between
Israel and Hezbollah. And, as always, it strongly benefits from its alliance with Iran
and its support from Syria. As such, Hezbollah's military capabilities represent at least
a partial deterrent to Israel attacking Iran.

The deterrence works both ways, however. Having ignited a war that saw vast
tracks of Lebanon pulverized by the Israeli Air Force and over 1,100 Lebanese killed,
Hezbollah leader Hassan Nasrallah admitted afterward that had he known of the consequences, he would not have ordered the kidnapping that started the fighting.[6] The
assurance that the death and destruction would be even more severe during a second
conflict was interpreted by many regional analysts as the reason that Hezbollah did not
attack Israel during the 2008–2009 Gaza war with Hamas, demonstrating that, if anything, Israel did reestablish significant deterrence against Hezbollah in 2006.

Iran

Whether Iran is developing a nuclear weapon or not depends on who you believe.
But the assumption in Israel, the United States, and the majority of Arab and Western
capitals, backed up by both open source and secret evidence, is that it is. A nuclear
weapon in the hands of a country who's president has called for Israel's destruction numerous times presents what the Israeli security establishment refers to as an existential
threat; in other words, a threat that has the possibility to destroy Israel entirely.

The top leaders of both Israel and the United States have said numerous times that
they will not allow Iran to obtain nuclear weapons. However, the diplomacy attempted
to date to convince Iran to give up its nuclear program—led mainly by Britain, France,
and Germany during the Bush years and more recently by the Obama administration—
has proven unsuccessful, with Iran vowing to continue the work. Four sets of United
Nations sanctions have not affected a suspension of Iran's nuclear work, and different
intelligence agencies now estimate that Iran already may have produced enough fissile
material to build at least one nuclear weapon. Mounted on a Shihab-3 missile, whose
range may stretch as far as 1,200 miles, such a weapon presents a possible doomsday
scenario for Israel.

As that time draws near, the prospect of an Israeli preemptive strike on Iran's nuclear facilities becomes more probable. However, while an Israeli surprise attack successfully destroyed Iraq's nuclear program in 1981, and what was believed to be a Syrian program in 2007, the Iranian program is much more sophisticated. Media reports that cite intelligence experts say the nuclear program is scattered around dozens of sites in Iran, the most sensitive of which are buried deep underground, where they may be impervious to all but other nuclear weapons.

Previously, Israel had hoped that if a military option became the only way of preventing Iran from obtaining a nuclear weapon, the United States would lead the attack. However, with U.S. forces bogged down in Afghanistan and still present in Iraq and a U.S. public increasingly weary and opposed to war, that scenario does not appear likely. If Israel attacks Iran, presumably on a green light from the United States, the counterattack will likely be severe. Not only might Iran launch hundreds of its missiles at Israel, Hezbollah would likely resume its rocket bombardments of Israel as well. Hamas and Syria could also join in the attack against the Jewish state under such a scenario, resulting in what some estimates say would be severe destruction to the main Israeli population centers.

The debate in Israel about whether to attack Iran thus centers mainly over what is worse: the enormous but probably reversible destruction that would almost certainly occur as a result of a preemptive war or the improbable but total annihilation of the country if Iran does indeed become a nuclear weapons country and uses the weapon against Israel. Containing Iran in a similar fashion as the Soviet Union was contained in the Cold War seems the preferred choice of Israel's Western allies.

To have any hope of succeeding in such an attack, Israel would likely need to acquire the rights to use Iraqi or Saudi air space—a particularly challenging diplomatic maneuver. Recent speculation in Washington, D.C., has also questioned whether Israel would ultimately obtain approval from the Obama administration for such an attack. Indeed, initiating such an action without U.S. consent might seriously jeopardize Israel's relations with its one staunch ally and cause severe damage to Israel's long-term security.

At least in the near future, though, an Israeli attack on Iran appears remote, as recently retired Mossad chief Meir Dagan estimated in January 2011 that the Islamic Republic could not build a nuclear weapon before 2015.[7] Covert measures undertaken by Israel and other countries are believed to be responsible for the delay in Iran's progress. Those measures are speculated to include cyber attacks on Iranian nuclear facilities and assassinations of key Iranian nuclear scientists.

Syria

Though Syria and Israel remain in a technical state of war, the border is quiet. Israel continues to occupy the Golan Heights, which it conquered from Syria in 1967, but there are no battles or even skirmishes between Israeli and Syrian troops. Over the years, talks between the two countries on a peace agreement have taken place, the most serious of which were in 2000, when the two sides met directly in the United States. During 2008, at least four rounds of indirect talks, facilitated by Turkey, aimed at restarting those negotiations. The general terms of a peace deal between Israel and Syria are already known: Israel gives back the Golan Heights, and Syria agrees to a full peace treaty and normalization of relations and ceases its support of Hezbollah, Hamas, and Islamic Jihad.

Until then, however, it is through those groups—which Damascus hosts—that Syria continues to bleed Israel. It is in the Syrian capital that both Hamas and Islamic Jihad have their main political headquarters. Hezbollah also enjoys significant support from Syria both politically and militarily, as Syria facilitates weapons transfers from Iran to Hezbollah across the Syria-Lebanon border.

In the political mix that is the contemporary Middle East, most analysts point to an extremist alliance with Iran at its head and including Syria, Hezbollah, and Hamas. (This is now in flux, given the protests that have gripped Syria and other parts of the Middle East since the Tunisia Revolution began in January 2011.) The extremist camp is in contrast to a moderate camp including most of the Sunni Arab states and the Palestinian Authority headed by Fatah. During the George W. Bush years, it was hypothesized among Middle East experts that with the correct carrot-and-stick approach, Syria could be broken off from the extremist camp and moved to the moderate camp. Such diplomacy would require the extensive involvement of the United States and, of course, an eventual deal with Israel. Unfortunately for Israel, direct engagement with Syria by the United States under the Obama administration has not borne any significant fruit, and Syria remains close allies with Iran. Therefore, rather than as an individual military threat, it is in the context of a larger, regional conflagration involving Iran, Hezbollah, and Hamas that Syria's missiles and soldiers become a true problem for an IDF forced to fight on four fronts.

That is not to say that the Syrian army alone could not inflict significant damage on Israel. With hundreds of surface-to-surface missiles capable of hitting the major Israeli population centers, an advanced chemical weapons program, and an army of over 400,000 men, including reservists, Syria is a formidable military threat. Moreover, on September 6, 2007, Israel bombed what anonymous U.S. and Israeli officials have told media sources was a nuclear weapons program facility inside of Syria. Since then, speculation is rife about whether Syria possesses a nuclear weapons program and, if so, how far along in development it is; or, at least, how far along in development it *was* before the bombing.

Iraq

Previous to the 2003 U.S. invasion, Iraq was a dangerous enemy to Israel. Having participated in the 1948 war against the newly created Jewish state, Iraq, later under the rule of Saddam Hussein, also launched Scud missiles at Israel during the first Gulf War in 1991. Saddam also made it a policy to pay thousands of dollars to the families of Palestinian suicide bombers. The Iraqi threat was once so acute to Israel that the IAF took the dramatic step in 1981 of bombing the Iraqi Osirak nuclear facility, where Iraq was developing nuclear weapons.

While the Iraqi threat appeared to be wiped out after the United States took control of Iraq in 2003 in a war championed by the Israeli government at the time, eight years later it is unclear what Iraq's eventual posture will be vis-à-vis the Jewish state. If the nascent, democratic Iraqi government comes to favorable terms with the United States on a long-term strategic alliance, the threat Iraq poses to Israel is likely minimal. However, if Iraq, a country with a Shiite majority whose Shiite-led government has cultivated ever-closer ties with Iran, eventually leans toward an alliance with the Islamic Republic, its threat to Israel could return. In this case, Iraq could be added to the extremist axis of Iran, Syria, Hamas, and Hezbollah, significantly strengthening that alliance against Israel with another oil-rich state.

Internal Political Conflict

The Israeli political landscape is one of the most confusing and dynamic in the democratic world. Due to a low threshold for political representation (2 percent of the popular vote), 12 political parties are represented in the Knesset, Israel's parliament. The largest party, Kadima, holds only 28 of 120 seats and sits in opposition to the government led by right-wing Likud. Though power in this government is particularly diffuse even by Israeli standards, it is indicative of the general manner in which Israeli governments have operated for at least the last two decades. Under this formula, the strongest political party must cobble together a ruling coalition by granting political concessions to a host of smaller, issue-oriented parties.

The main results of this system are twofold. First, the governments rarely finish their full four-year terms, as events on the ground in always-tumultuous Israel invariably fracture the coalition, leading to a no-confidence motion or the resignation of the government and the calling of early elections. Even before governments fall, it is common that cabinet shuffles will take place as a result of minor coalition partners leaving and joining the government. Replacing the leaders of the various ministries on a regular basis has made it difficult for any minister or ministry to execute a long-term plan. Therefore, long-term projects and strategic vision is often in short supply in the Israeli government.

Second, the smaller parties with enough votes to matter wield a disproportionate amount of political power given what their minority support in Israeli society would tend to indicate. Because many of these smaller parties are religious parties, religious Israeli Jews, who are outnumbered by their secular counterparts, wind up not necessarily making government policy but in many sensitive and important areas are the deciding factor in government decisions.

The most obvious example of this outsized influence is poured into the Jewish settlements in the West Bank. Though a significant number of settlers moved there due to economic reasons (the government subsidizes homes there), others were ideologically compelled, as they seek to maintain a perpetual Israeli hold on what is the biblical Jewish land of Judaea and Samaria. For that, they receive the aforementioned government subsidies and protection from the IDF. Probably even more frustrating to the average Israeli, Orthodox Jews are not required to serve the mandatory army service of all other non-Arab Israeli men and women; they receive special tax breaks, and, due to their large family sizes, they receive the majority of welfare payments dolled out by the state.

These issues, along with others, have created a schism in Israel between the Orthodox and secular Jews that produces significant political strife. Furthermore, the vast majority of religious Israelis oppose returning any land taken in 1967 in return for a peace deal with the Palestinians. That is not to say that right-wing, secular Israelis do not also possess those views, but it is one major fault line pitting secular and religious Israelis against each other in the political context.

As a whole, the Israeli body politic has moved dramatically toward the center since the beginning of the second intifada as left-wing Israelis largely gave up on the prospect of peaceful coexistence with the Palestinians and right-wing Israelis largely came to view the continued occupation of the West Bank and Gaza strip not as an asset but a liability. Opinion polls thus consistently show that around 75 percent of Israelis favor a peace agreement with the Palestinians that would involve relinquishing control over most of the West Bank and the Gaza Strip, but a majority also thinks that they have no peace partner on the other side.

More important in the context of threats to the state, however, is the conception within Israel of what would happen if a deal was signed with the Palestinians and an Israeli government attempted to evacuate, forcibly, Jewish settlements within the West Bank that sat on land that would become part of a Palestinian state. Though the eviction of the Gaza Strip settlers in 2005 went off without any major violence being perpetrated by the settlers, there is a real fear that the same peaceful withdrawal could not be replicated in the West Bank, where the settlers are, by and large, more religious and ideological.

An Israeli policeman stands guard as Jewish settlers celebrate the annual Purim parade in the predominantly Palestinian West Bank city of Hebron. (Menahem Kahana/Getty Images)

When Israeli police, backed up by the army, evacuated the illegal outpost Amona on February 1, 2006, it took thousands of officers to accomplish the job, during which more than 200 of at least 5,000 protestors and security officers were injured. In the days following the incident, the country exploded in hateful rhetoric between the left- and right-wing political camps. Other violent incidents directed at the army and police by settlers have occurred in the historic city of Hebron, where Jewish residents rioted on August 7, 2007. Protesting against the eviction of two families who were occupying Palestinian homes, the settlers wore masks and threw stones at the army and police. At least 11 police officers and 26 protestors were injured in the clashes as the settlers pelted police with rocks, chunks of metal, soda bottles, slippers, shoes, and pots of cooking oil.[8] Since the partial settlement freeze announced by Prime Minister Netan-yahu in November 2009, tension has mounted further between religious West Bank settlers and the IDF. Numerous confrontations ensued during the settlement freeze in which IDF soldiers and officers were injured at the hands of Jewish settlers, who also have taken to attacking Palestinian civilians in retaliation for moves by the Israeli government to curb illegal construction by the settlers.

Exacerbating the problem is the serious question of whether the religious soldiers who serve in the army would follow orders to forcibly evacuate settlements in which many of them live. While the problem of soldiers disobeying orders was a minor one during the Gaza disengagement, prominent rabbis have already said that they will instruct their followers to disobey such orders if they were issued in regard to the West Bank. Such a scenario poses a nightmare dilemma for the army, which has long been the one institution that brought together Israelis of all social and political walks of life (save the ultra-Orthodox Jews and the Israeli Arabs). The problem within the army brought on by a possible evacuation of the West Bank grows more acute with each passing day due to the fact that, over the years, the religious Jews who do serve in the army have slowly become more prominent in the officer's corps and the prestigious, and dangerous, combat units that were once predominantly populated by left-wing, secular Israelis from the kibbutzim (collective communities).

It is, therefore, impossible to know what will happen if an Israeli government (assuming it could muster together a coalition) attempted to evacuate a significant portion of the Jewish settlements in the West Bank. The range of possibilities flows from a withdrawal (albeit on a much more massive scale) a bit less orderly than the one from Gaza to a civil war.

Even leaving aside the fight that an increasingly unlikely withdrawal from the West Bank would produce, the secular versus religious political battles in Israel seem destined to gain intensity rather than subside as the religious continue to grow as a percentage of the population. When the state was formed in 1948, the vast majority of Israelis were secular. In 2006, the number of Israeli Jews 20 years and older defining themselves as ultra-Orthodox (7 percent), religious (10 percent), and religious-traditionalist (14 percent) approached the 44 percent who describe themselves as secular.[9] Since religious Jews see having children as a duty commanded by God, their portion of the population will continue to rise, and political battles over what kind of state Israel is supposed to be could become increasingly intense.

Because Israel lacks both a constitution and official borders, its citizens have never formally decided how to balance issues of land, religion, and democracy. In other words, who deserves to be a citizen of Israel with full civic rights? How much should religion—in this case Judaism—figure into the running of the state? And what exactly are the boundaries of the state? All these questions are profoundly important to the future of Israel, and all of them are also fought over in increasingly bitter tones between its citizens.

Israeli Arabs

Discussing Israeli Arabs as a threat to the state is offensive to many Israeli Arabs. And yet the evidence cannot be ignored that, increasingly, this demographic group, once thought of as a possible bridge between Israel and the Arab world, might one day become as hostile toward the Jewish state in which they live as the citizens of the neighboring Arab states.

Israeli citizens with full voting rights, the Israeli Arabs, mostly Muslim but some Christian, remained in their homes and villages during the fighting in 1948 and remain there to this day. After 17 years, they were released from military rule in 1966, but following 43 years of living freely in Israel, as a whole they have not fully integrated into Israeli society despite numbering 1,250,000, and accounting for 16.5 percent of Israel's population.[10]

While instances of Israeli Arabs participating in terror attacks against Jews are rare, a number of incidents have recently taken place in which Israeli Arabs have aided terror groups or been arrested while working for one. In May and June of 2008, two Israeli Arabs and four Palestinians living in East Jerusalem were arrested for attempting to establish an al-Qaeda cell in Israel and plotting to down the helicopter of President Bush during his visit. Later in June 2008, two Israeli Arabs were arrested for, and confessed to, being operatives for al-Qaeda. Other instances of Israeli Arabs assisting Hezbollah have occurred over the years, as has aid given to Palestinian terrorists, usually in the form of transportation into Israel.

Despite these high-profile cases, the number of Israeli Arabs acting with terror groups against Israel accounts for the smallest minority of the population. Nevertheless, what is a significant long-term threat to Israel are the increasingly hostile attitudes toward the Jewish state by its own citizens. Arab Israelis point to inferior economic conditions compared to Jewish Israelis and unequal rights under the law—particularly where land rights are concerned—as sources of their increasing frustration and feelings of being second-class citizens in Israel.

These feelings came to a boil during the 2006 war with Lebanon, when some Israeli Arabs whose family members were killed by Hezbollah rockets blamed not Hezbollah for the deaths but Israel. The language of Arab Israeli youth, particularly in their music, is also indicative of the general antipathy the younger generation feels toward Israel and the sympathy and identification they possess for the Palestinians. Indeed, when asked what nationality they are, more say Palestinian than Israeli.[11]

The resentment is real and growing. According to the 2009 Arab-Jewish Relations Index published by University of Haifa professor Sami Smooha, only 51.6 percent of

Arab Israelis recognize Israel's right to exist as a Jewish, democratic state, and only 59.4 percent believe it has the right to exist as an independent country within the 1949 borders. These baseline measures of support for Israel have fallen precipitously in polls Smooha conducted since 2003, indicating a dramatic shift in views about Israel among the younger generation of Israeli Arabs. And the proportion of Israeli Arabs who believe violence against their own state is justified to achieve their political goals has risen—from 5.6 percent in 2003 to 13.9 percent in 2009. The 2010 poll also indicated that 32.3 percent of Israeli Arabs had participated in protests in honor of the *nakba* ("disaster" in Arabic), the Palestinian commemoration of their displacement in the 1948 war. In 2003, only 12.6 percent of Israeli Arabs participated in such events.

In recent years, even Arab Israeli Knesset members have pushed the boundaries of actively working against the state they officially represent, if the accusations of Israel's internal security agency, the Shin Bet, are to be believed. Currently exiled in Jordan, former parliamentarian Azmi Bashara is accused of treason for aiding Hezbollah during the 2006 war. According to the Shin Bet, he passed along information to Hezbollah agents and advised the group on targets to strike in Israel. Both are charges he denies.

Delegitimization

What weaves together the nonmaterial threats Israel faces today—whether from the Palestinians, Hezbollah, or its own people—is the phenomenon of delegitimization. This strategy is inherently a political one that seeks to undermine the legitimacy of Israel's actions and, in its more extreme form, the right of Israel to exist as a Jewish state. For some years now, the anti-Israel movement pioneered by Arab nationalists and expanded by Islamic extremists, has been joined by an assortment of human rights organizations and other liberal movements and institutions. This has spawned the Boycott, Divest, and Sanctions movement and other anti-Israel campaigns now gaining strength not just in the Arab and Muslim world but in Europe as well. Their goal, as many leaders of the movement claim, is to turn Israel into a pariah state similar to white-ruled South Africa.

The British boycott of Israeli academicians and an import ban on items produced in Israeli West Bank settlements; the Spanish expulsion of an Israeli team from a solar energy science competition;[12] pressure campaigns mounted on top musicians to forgo performances in Israel;[13] the boycott movement against the 2009 Toronto Film Festival simply for screening movies about Tel Aviv (some of the movies were quite self-critical);[14] and many other examples all represent recent manifestations of the effort to delegitimize the Jewish state. Indeed, if the momentum of the delegitimization movement is not halted, then the Goldstone Report and the international uproar following the Gaza flotilla incident are only the initial examples of the international isolation and castigation Israel will be subject to in the future. The commission of inquiry into Israel's next war might produce an environment where its defense minister is indeed arrested during a vacation in Europe, as Ehud Barak nearly was during his September 2009 visit to London.

More importantly, as a small country in the heart of a hostile region, Israel is dependent on international trade and political and military support. Any movement that threatens those pillars of the Israeli economy and foreign policy is a threat to national security. As the efforts to delegitimize Israel gain steam, especially in Europe, Israeli security officials have become more attuned to this postmodern threat to the state.[15]

The Arab Spring

Massive waves of protest swept across the Arab world in early 2011, dramatically altering the political and security landscapes of the Middle East. In Tunisia and Egypt, peaceful protests resulted in the ousting of long-time authoritarian regimes. At the time of this writing, the Assad regime was brutally suppressing a revolt in parts of Syria, and it appeared that Yemeni president Ali Abdullah Saleh would soon succumb to the massive opposition demonstrating against his rule. For Israel, the spring of 2011 brought both hope and peril, as the security and political establishment attempted to reorient themselves to new challenges and new opportunities.

In positive terms, Israelis were encouraged that the wave of discontent that led to the protests had little to do with Israel. Rather, Arab youth in particular demonstrated about lack of opportunity, stagnant economies, lack of political freedoms, and perceived corruption in their own governments. Some Israeli voices also believed that more representative governments in the region might create political opportunities that were previously denied, since the authoritarian regimes often used the Israeli-Palestinian conflict as an excuse for maintaining their vast security apparatuses.

However, the potential dangers are equally real. Already, the new Egyptian government has engaged in some rapprochement with Iran. It has also helped to broker the Hamas-Fattah reconciliation and indicated that it will no longer maintain the siege on Gaza with Israel. Loss of control over the Sinai Peninsula by the military government was probably at least partially responsible for a terror attack that emanated from Sinai against Israel in August 2011, killing eight people. The Egyptian government was also unwilling or unable to stop rioters in Cairo from sacking the Israeli embassy one month later. These moves are linked to Egyptian public opinion, which, though probably not pining for war with Israel, is also more hostile toward the Jewish state than the Mubarak regime was. A Pew Research Center poll conducted following the ouster of Mubarak found that a majority of Egyptians favor abdicating the peace agreement with Israel.[16] As such, it is clear that the Egypt-Israel relationship, which laid the foundation for Israeli security doctrine for three decades, is now tenuous at best.

The people power demonstrated throughout the region has not been lost on Fatah either. Many analysts read the reconciliation with Hamas as directly related to public calls for Palestinian unity and widespread anger at the United States for failing to take a harder line against continued Israeli settlement construction in the West Bank. If there is a silver lining to Israel, it is that Hamas has felt such pressure as well. This is true both in Gaza and in Syria, where the challenge to the Assad regime has thrown into doubt the viability of Hamas's external base remaining in Damascus.

But the turmoil in Syria has Jerusalem equally concerned. Though Bashar Assad, like his father before him, has proven an implacable foe, the Syrian border has been the most quiet of Israel's frontiers ever since the 1973 war. The possibility of a larger civil conflict breaking out in Syria represents a possible change in that regard and would likely affect Israel's relationships with Iran, Lebanon, Hezbollah, and Hamas in unforeseen ways. As a result of the Arab spring of 2011, Israel is therefore confronting what could be a series of strategic shifts in its security calculations, only the first wave of which has yet been felt.

NOTES

1. Statistics taken from B'Tselem, the Israeli Information Center for Human Rights in the Occupied Territories, *Statistics: Fatalities in the First Intifada,* http://www.btselem.org/english/statistics/first_Intifada_Tables.asp.

2. Rafael D. Frankel, "Why Gaza's Moderates Are Losing Hope," *Christian Science Monitor* (September 2, 2009).

3. "Abbas Must Choose between Israel, Hamas—Netanyahu," *Reuters* (April 27, 2011).

4. Statistics obtained from B'Tselem, the Israeli Information Center for Human Rights in the Occupied Territories, *Statistics: Settlements and Land,* http://www.btselem.org/Download/settlement_population_eng.xls.

5. Palestinian Center for Policy and Survey Research, *Palestinian Public Opinion Poll,* no. 36 (June 10–13, 2006), http://www.pcpsr.org/survey/polls/2010/p36e.html#main.

6. "Nasrallah Sorry for Scale of War," *BBC News* (August 27, 2006), http://news.bbc.co.uk/2/hi/middle_east/5291420.stm.

7. Matti Friedman, "Mossad Chief: Iran Won't Go Nuclear before 2015," *Associated Press* (January 7, 2011).

8. Steven Erlanger, "Police Fight to Remove West Bank Settlers," *New York Times* (August 8, 2007).

9. The 2006 Social Survey conducted by Israel's Central Bureau of Statistics, general Web page, http://www.cbs.gov.il/reader/?MIval=cw_usr_view_SHTML&ID=576; specific report, http://www.cbs.gov.il/webpub/pub/text_page.html?publ=6&CYear=2006&CMonth=1.

10. Sammy Smooha, "Arab-Jewish Relations in Israel: Alienation and Rapprochement," *United States Institute of Peace* (December 2010), http://www.usip.org/publications/arab-jewish-relations-in-israel.

11. Ibid. Statistics in this paragraph come from Tables 2, 3, and 4 of the report.

12. Giles Tremlett, "Spain Expels Israeli Scientists from Solar Energy Competition," *The Guardian* (September 24, 2009), http://www.guardian.co.uk/world/2009/sep/24/spain-solar-competition-israelis.

13. Freemuse: Freedom of Musical Expression, "England/Israel/Palestine: Pink Floyd Star Rejects Cultural Boycott" (March 13, 2006), http://www.freemuse.org/sw12575.asp.

14. Haaretz Service and Associated Press, "Palestinians: Boycott Toronto Film Festival over Tel Aviv Spotlight" (October 9, 2009), http://www.haaretz.com/hasen/spages/1113780.html.

15. Even Prime Minister Netanyahu has recognized the threat delegitimization represents to Israel, saying on October 16, 2009: "The delegitimization of Israel must be delegitimized." News Agencies and Barak Ravid Haaretz Service, "'Delegitimization of Israel Must Be Delegitimized" (October 16, 2009), http://www.haaretz.com/news/delegitimization-of-israel-must-be-delegitimized-1.5970.

16. Lahav Harkov, "Poll: Most Egyptians Favor Annulling Peace with Israel," *Jerusalem Post* (April 26, 2011).

6 JORDAN

Jordan epitomizes the "artificial state," a political entity created by a colonial power to meet that power's perceived strategic needs. The British carved Jordan out of its Middle Eastern mandated territory in 1922, providing a throne for the powerful Hashemite family of Mecca, who had lost out to the Saud family in their struggle for control of the Arabian Peninsula. The Hashemites had led the Arab nationalist cause against the Ottoman Empire during World War I, with the help and assistance of the British. The Hashemite army, known as the Arab Legion, was British led and commanded and was known as the most effective fighting force in the Middle East.

Jordan in 1922 was sparsely populated by mostly Bedouin tribes, and, over the course of the next few decades, Jordan's first ruler and eventual king, Abdullah, secured tribal loyalty through a mix of negotiation and military might, usually firmly reinforced by British authorities. Yet while Abdullah sought to achieve stability within Jordan's borders, he was also eager to expand these borders. When war broke out in 1948 between Arab states and the newly independent Jewish state of Israel, Abdullah's Arab Legion moved quickly to seize the West Bank of the Jordan River and the eastern part of Jerusalem, the location of the al-Aqsa Mosque, one of Islam's holiest sites. This territory had been designated for the Palestinian state that was supposed to be created simultaneously with Israel. Although Abdullah captured it to prevent Israeli forces from taking over, he absorbed the new territory into Jordan and formally annexed it in 1950.

Adding the West Bank to pre-1948 Jordan changed the country dramatically, from a nation of approximately 500,000 Bedouin tribespeople to one of 1.5 million people, a majority of whom were Palestinian residents of the West Bank and Palestinian refugees who fled (or were expelled from) the area that had become the state of Israel. The Hashemite Kingdom thus became overnight a frontline country in the Arabs' conflict with Israel, as well as a state whose majority population was Palestinian. King

Abdullah was assassinated in Jerusalem in 1951 and was succeeded by his grandson, King Hussein, when he came of age in 1953. King Hussein ruled Jordan for the next 46 years, a period of turbulence and conflict that at several times threatened the kingdom's existence.

For most of King Hussein's long rule, he kept the country allied with the United States and the West, a policy that often put him at odds with more radical regimes and forces in the Arab World.[1] One exception was in 1967, when he united with Egypt and Syria in war with Israel (Israel actually launched the war against Syria and Egypt preemptively, but Jordan chose to join the battle). When the dust settled after a mere six days of fighting, Jordan had lost control of the entire West Bank to Israel, and tens of thousands of new Palestinian refugees had flooded into the kingdom.

The Palestinian resistance movement, led by Yasser Arafat's Palestine Liberation Organization (PLO), subsequently based its operations in Jordan, tapping the large Palestinian refugee community for guerilla fighters. The PLO and associated organizations launched insurgent attacks against Israel from Jordanian territory, often prompting harsh Israeli retaliation. In 1970, the Popular Front for the Liberation of Palestine, a Marxist faction in the PLO, hijacked three international commercial airline flights, landed the planes in the Jordanian desert, and destroyed them with explosives (after freeing the passengers and crews)—a scene that was televised and shown around the world. This deed, combined with the growing freedom of action that PLO fighters were exhibiting, convinced King Hussein that the Palestinian resistance movement had become a "state within a state."

UN-run refugee camps remain home to many of Jordan's majority Palestinian population. (AFP/Getty Images)

The king ordered the Jordanian army to disarm the PLO fighters, which resulted in an extremely bloody conflict that risked drawing in Syria (a supporter of the PLO fighters). The bloodshed peaked in Black September of 1970, when the Jordanian military inflicted heavy casualties among both PLO forces and Palestinian civilians in Jordan. However, the imminent threat to Jordan's stability as a state persisted throughout much of 1970 and 1971. Jordan's highly trained armed forces, who were strongly loyal to the monarchy, eventually prevailed and drove the bulk of the PLO fighters into Lebanon. King Hussein had dodged a bullet; the Palestinian majority in Jordan did not rise up in support of the PLO, as some feared, and his kingdom remained intact. Yet the conflict exposed cracks at the core of Jordan between the Hashemite monarchy and the majority Palestinian population; the future remained uncertain, and relations with Israel remained in an official state of war.

In 1988, King Hussein took a bold step designed to disengage Jordan from direct conflict with Israel as well as address the country's demographic concerns, when he publicly renounced claims to the West Bank. By taking this step, the king redefined Jordan's borders to what they had been initially—the East Bank of the Jordan River—and simultaneously signaled that the future of the West Bank would have to be determined by Israel and the Palestinian liberation movement. Although the king had thus renounced rule over the large Palestinian population in the West Bank, his country still was fragile. For one thing, many Israelis—especially those on the political right wing—insisted on describing Jordan as the "Palestinian state." For some Israelis, the long-term goal was to have the Palestinians of the West Bank migrate to Jordan—voluntarily or forcefully—leaving the historic lands of Judea and Samaria for Jewish settlement. Were this to occur, it most likely would spell the end of Hashemite rule in Jordan and move the front line of the Israeli-Arab conflict to the Jordan River. Thus, in order to guarantee stability for his country, King Hussein still needed a negotiated peace between Israel and the Palestinians.

The other significant exception to King Hussein's generally pro-Western stance was his support for Saddam Hussein after the Iraqi dictator launched an invasion of Kuwait in 1990. The king's decision to support Saddam Hussein was complex. Iraq and Jordan had enjoyed a close economic relationship for many years, with Jordan's port of Aqaba serving as a major transshipment point for goods destined for Iraq. Jordan also had supported Iraq during its long war (1980–1988) with Iran; King Hussein saw secular Iraq as a bulwark against the revolutionary Islamic regime in Iran. In addition, Jordan received substantial economic aid from Iraq's oil-rich government. A final factor may have been Yasser Arafat, who had thrown the PLO's support behind Iraq. With Jordan's large population of Palestinian refugees and the history of tension between them and the Hashemite monarchy, Hussein may not have wished to risk alienating them further.

The consequences of Jordan's support for Iraq were largely detrimental, however. The Arab Gulf states immediately halted their economic aid to Jordan and expelled more than 300,000 workers with Jordanian passports, most of them Palestinian; Jordan also was flooded with tens of thousands of refugees who were fleeing the fighting. The economic sanctions that the world imposed on the Saddam Hussein regime effectively dried up the lucrative trade between Jordan and Iraq. And, finally, the decision to support Iraq drove a wedge between the United States and Jordan that was not to be removed for several years. The shift proved costly for Jordan: the United States was not only a source of financial aid, it also was the principal supplier of weapons and equipment to the Jordanian armed forces.

By the early 1990s, Jordan was "rehabilitated" in the United States' eyes, although the Arab Gulf states harbored resentment over King Hussein's support for Saddam for considerably longer. King Hussein was a vocal supporter of the 1993 Oslo Accords between Israel and the PLO, and he used this historic agreement to initiate an Israeli-Jordanian peace agreement that was signed in 1994. Perhaps feeling that his fragile state was more secure once Israel and the PLO were negotiating, King Hussein launched a gradual democratization process in the 1990s. But political opening and parliamentary elections in 1993 and 1997 revealed a strong undercurrent of support for Islamist groups, in particular the political wing of the Jordanian branch of the Muslim Brotherhood, known as the Islamic Action Front. Implicit in this support for Islamist groups was opposition to Jordan's peace treaty with Israel, strong sympathy for the Palestinian cause, and a certain degree of anti-Western sentiment.

King Hussein's death in 1999 after a long battle with cancer again raised concerns about Jordan's stability and cohesiveness. His son and designated heir, King Abdullah II, received the allegiance of the armed forces and carried out a smooth transition. He promised to open the political system further but took only modest steps in this regard. However, Jordan continued to be affected by developments in its neighborhood. The second intifada between Israel and the Palestinians that broke out in 2000 had serious implications in Jordan, intensifying anti-Israeli sentiment among the majority Palestinian population and resurrecting fears of Israel's designs to transform Jordan into the Palestinian homeland. Both concerns have persisted with the plight of Gaza and the rift between Fatah and Hamas. In 2010, a group of retired Jordanian army officers even went to the length of sending an open letter to the king, expressing deep misgivings about the Jordanian regime's willingness to bend to Israeli and U.S. pressure. The officers believed this tendency might result in Jordan becoming a de facto Palestinian state.[2] As the volume of these rumblings of dissatisfaction has increased, the Jordanian-Israeli peace treaty remained in force, although relations between the two nations cooled significantly under a succession of right-wing Israeli governments.

Jordan was concerned about the U.S. invasion of Iraq in 2003 and publicly was opposed to a military attack against Saddam Hussein's regime. But King Abdullah made sure not to position his country as being overtly anti-U.S., as his father had done in 1990. Once the war began, Jordan discreetly supported the United States. Once again, Jordan became the destination for refugees, this time Iraqi civilians who fled across the border seeking safety from both the U.S. attack and the subsequent civil war in Iraq. Jordan's economy was ill prepared to deal with a large influx of refugees. Even worse, the factional violence that characterized postinvasion Iraq spilled into Jordan. In November 2005, Iraqi suicide bombers launched a coordinated attack on three hotels in Amman, killing 60 and wounding scores more; most of the victims were Jordanian, but by attacking hotels, the intention was clearly to send a message to foreigners as well. Abu Musab al-Zarqawi, the Jordanian-born militant who founded the organization al-Qaeda in Iraq, claimed responsibility for the attack and said it was in retaliation for Jordan's support for U.S policy. Al-Zarqawi had been previously implicated in the attack on the Jordanian embassy in Iraq, which left 18 dead, and the murder of a U.S. diplomat in Amman in 2002. Al-Zarqawi was killed in 2006 by U.S. forces in Iraq.

King Abdullah expressed concern that the Iraq conflict would exacerbate the historical division between Shiite and Sunni Muslims. In 2004 he warned that if Iraq descended into chaos, it would benefit only Iran's revolutionary regime and would threaten to create a "Shiite crescent" in the Middle East.[3] Jordan's fate was increasingly seen as tied to that of Saudi Arabia, Egypt, and the other Sunni-dominated regimes in the region.

In January 2011, reflecting the regional trend and the events in Tunisia and Egypt, Jordan experienced demonstrations and public demands for greater freedoms. The king made some visible reforms, and he retained the loyal support of the Jordanian army. The king's overriding goal in any reform process is to ensure that the political balance of power in Jordan remains skewed in favor of the East Bank tribal and clan leaders; a true liberal democracy would empower the country's majority Palestinian population and risk the monarchy's survival. The still unanswered question is whether a reform process can create enough representative power to assuage the protestors while maintaining a balance of power that favors East Bankers over Palestinians and that preserves the monarchy's centrality.

Each of the potential conflicts Jordan confronts reflects one or more aspects of the country's underlying sources of fragility: a weak sense of national identity that renders Jordanian society especially vulnerable to transnational trends and movements; a Palestinian majority whose ultimate relationship to the state depends in large part upon how (and if) the Israeli-Palestinian conflict is resolved; and pressures on the state from various sources to further democratize the political process. On top of this, Jordan is a small developing state with few natural resources and no economic clout that is powerfully influenced by developments outside of its control. Finally, its geographic location—bordering Israel/Palestine to the west, Iraq to the east, Syria to the north, and Saudi Arabia to the south—makes it inevitable that Jordan will be affected by virtually any major conflict or destabilizing event in the broader Middle East.

TERRORISM

Jordan is tragically familiar with terrorism. King Abdullah I, the country's first ruler, was assassinated in Jerusalem by Palestinian militants, and two of the country's prime ministers were killed in terrorist attacks. In its first decades, the principal terrorist threat to Jordan derived from radical left-wing groups—most of which were part of the Palestinian liberation struggle—who were opposed to the country's close ties to the West as well as to its monarchical form of government.

In more recent years, especially after the U.S. invasion of Iraq in 2003, Jordan has been the target of the terrorist groups that have flourished in Iraq's anarchic and chaotic political environment—the November 2005 attacks in Amman were the most dramatic example. Ironically, in light of King Abdullah's concerns about a Shiite crescent, the greatest terrorist threat to Jordan from Iraq so far has emanated from Sunni groups, such as al-Qaeda. Their opposition to the Jordanian regime derives from its peace with

Israel and its close relationship with the West (in particular, the United States). While Jordan will likely remain a target due to these conditions, concerns about home-grown terror are perhaps less prevalent, due in part to the popular revulsion at the high death toll of Jordanian civilians in the 2005 attacks.

The degree to which Jordan is victimized by terrorism in future years will depend to a large extent on Iraq's success in achieving internal unity and cohesion. As long as Iraq is unstable, its instability and violence are more likely to infect Jordan, if for no other reason than the fact that several hundred thousand Iraqi refugees live in Jordan and the two countries share a border. Since the fall of Saddam Hussein's regime in 2003, Jordanian security officials have discovered dozens of terrorist cells in Jordan— almost all of which originated in, or were supported by, terrorist elements in Iraq.[4]

Jordan also faces potential terrorist threats in the event that the Palestinian question remains unresolved into the distant future. The Palestinian Hamas Party, which seized power in the Gaza Strip in large part because of the failure of Israel and the Palestinian Authority to make serious progress in negotiating a peace accord, has links with the Jordanian Muslim Brotherhood. A severe deterioration in or total collapse of the Israeli-Palestinian peace process would likely further strengthen Hamas and even raise the possibility of its coming to power in the West Bank. Such a situation would be a cause of great alarm in Jordan for a host of reasons, not the least of which is the prospect of collaboration between Hamas and indigenous Islamist groups in Jordan.

Jordan also is vulnerable to Iranian-inspired and Iranian-supported terrorism. As an Arab country that has made peace with Israel and is close to the United States, and as a majority Sunni country that has warned against the regional dangers posed by Iran's revolutionary Shia regime, Jordan could become an Iranian target in the event that relations between Iran and the Sunni Arab states deteriorate. Iran does not have the military capability to directly attack Jordan, except perhaps with medium-range missiles. The United States, however, would almost certainly respond to a direct Iranian attack on Jordan. Thus, terrorism becomes the weapon of choice if Iran were to seek to inflict damage on the Hashemite kingdom.

INTERNAL CONFLICT WITH ISLAMIST OPPOSITION

Jordan is officially a constitutional monarchy, but the king in fact possesses immense powers, including the power to appoint and dismiss the prime minister. The king also has the final say in cabinet appointments. Jordan's highly effective intelligence service answers to the palace, as does its small but well-trained military. In 2001, King Abdullah suspended parliament and delayed scheduled elections because of regional tensions caused by the Palestinian uprising and Israel's harsh response. During this period, Abdullah passed scores of temporary laws without parliamentary oversight while also cracking down on demonstrations and curtailing press freedoms. In November 2009, Abdullah once again dismissed parliament, scheduling elections for late 2010 and renewing activists' fears of a raft of temporary laws passed with a vacant parliament, as had occurred earlier in the decade.[5]

Nevertheless, Jordan also exhibits certain elements of democratic culture— certainly more so than most states in the region. The lower house of parliament is

Jordan's King Abdullah II waves to crowds who line the streets of Mazar Shamali, 80 miles north of Amman. The young king has proposed political reforms to preempt the kind of uprising that has occurred in other Arab states. (AP Photo/Yousef Allan)

directly elected by popular vote, and its members can (and often do) voice opposition to government programs. Political parties are legal and reflect a broad range of views, but many Jordanians identify more with tribal families and tend to vote for individuals based on tribal affiliations, not parties. As a result, election campaigns have sometimes provided an arena for airing xenophobic sentiments toward Palestinians, widening the historic rift between Palestinian Jordanians and East Bank natives and prompting government sloganeering in an attempt to sew the frayed national fabric.[6] In this context, Jordanian Islamists have discovered success. The Muslim Brotherhood's political wing—the Islamic Action Front (IAF)—won 17 seats in the 2003 parliamentary elections (out of 110), but only 6 seats in the November 2007 elections. The IAF boycotted the November 2010 legislative elections in protest against what it claimed were unfair electoral laws. The IAF remains, however, Jordan's principal opposition party, although it walks a careful line and is periodically subject to government harassment. The IAF is opposed to Jordan's peace treaty with Israel and is supportive of the Palestinian Hamas Party; its leaders also have criticized Jordan's military cooperation with the United States.

Although the king has been able to remain securely in control, the IAF could gain increased popularity depending upon developments in the region. For example, when Israel behaves particularly harshly toward the Palestinians in the occupied West Bank and Gaza, popular opinion in Jordan tends to be affected, usually to the benefit of parties (such as the IAF) that are opposed to the country's peace with Israel and are sympathetic to the Palestinians' plight. Similarly, rising anti-American sentiment tends to favor the IAF. Any significant reform program that increased the representativeness of parliament would also likely benefit the IAF.

Because Jordan has allowed opposition parties to function and compete in elections, it is unlikely that the IAF or other opposition parties would resort to violence. The IAF and the Muslim Brotherhood describe themselves as the "loyal opposition" and over the years have often supported the monarchy.[7] They were quick to condemn the November 2005 al-Qaeda attack in Amman and have voiced support for the government's efforts to combat terrorism.

Nevertheless, the complete collapse of the Israeli-Palestinian peace process, and the various repercussions this would cause, could change the internal dynamics in Jordan relatively quickly. A Palestinian movement under the leadership of Hamas and in a state of open conflict with Israel would receive both sympathy and support from Jordanians—especially the majority Palestinian population—and such a situation could embolden the Muslim Brotherhood and the IAF to more aggressively oppose the Jordanian government.

CONFLICT WITH ISRAEL

Although Jordan ended 47 years of war with Israel in 1994, when the two nations signed a peace treaty, the possibility of conflict remains. Despite the 1994 treaty, Israel remains extremely unpopular among the Jordanian population, and animosity toward the Jewish state rose considerably in the wake of Israel's harsh response to the second Palestinian intifada that began in 2000. Outcry over the Israeli assault on Gaza during Operation Cast Lead in late 2008 only heightened these sentiments. Thus, although King Abdullah, like his father, has maintained official diplomatic relations with Israel, there remains a persistent undercurrent of hostility among the Jordanian public.

Jordan would never seek a conflict with Israel, and indeed would try its best to avoid conflict due to the disparity in military capability between the two countries (it should be recalled that Jordan lost control of the West Bank to Israel in 1967 in a matter of days). There are several scenarios, however, under which Israeli actions might create a situation in which Jordanian and Israeli forces would find themselves in confrontation.

The most conceivable such scenario would be the coming to power in Israel of a right-wing extremist government under a leader such as Avigdor Lieberman. The Israeli right (including some members of the mainstream Likud Party) has for decades argued that Jordan is the Palestinian state. An extremist right-wing government might try to actualize this ideology by attempting to forcefully transfer West Bank Palestinians across the Jordan River into the Hashemite kingdom. Faced with what would be an existential threat, the Jordanian government would certainly resist, which would likely bring it into conflict with Israeli forces.

Another situation that could bring Jordanian and Israeli forces into confrontation would be an intensive Israeli military operation in the West Bank. Even if this did not involve an attempt to forcefully transfer Palestinians, Israeli military actions could still lead to a flow of Palestinians across the Jordan; during the 2000–2005 al-Aqsa intifada, it is estimated that 200,000 West Bank Palestinians fled to Jordan.[8] Jordan's efforts to restrict immigration could bring its forces into confrontation with Israel's. Moreover, a particularly violent or harsh Israeli operation in the West Bank could lead to anti-Israel terror attacks or guerilla operations by Palestinians living in Jordan. If Israel responded by attacking guerilla bases in Jordan, the Jordanian army might feel obliged to defend the country.

In sum, any potential conflict between the Hashemite kingdom of Jordan and Israel would be derivative of Israeli actions against Palestinians in the West Bank and not the result of a direct confrontation between Jordan and Israel. If, however, a change of regime were to take place in Jordan—for example, if the IAF/Muslim Brotherhood were to assume control at the expense of the Hashemite monarchy—direct confrontation with Israel would be a renewed possibility.

CONFLICT WITH WEST BANK PALESTINIANS

Just as potential Jordanian-Israeli conflict emanates from developments in the Israeli-occupied West Bank, that area also holds the possibility for Jordanian-Palestinian conflict. Jordan's symbiotic relationship with the West Bank has been a source of tension since the 1948 war, when the area was absorbed into the Hashemite kingdom. Although Jordan lost the West Bank to Israel in 1967, close family ties between West Bank Palestinians and the Palestinian population in Jordan remain strong, as every Palestinian in Jordan can trace his or her roots to the lands west of the Jordan River. Jordan's long-term stability and identity are inextricably bound to developments in the West Bank.

Several scenarios could lead to conflict between Jordan and West Bank Palestinians (in addition to the scenarios involving Israel). As frustration with the stalled peace process and Israeli restrictions grows among West Bank Palestinians, so does the popularity of the militant Hamas Party. The secular Fatah Party, which lost control of the Gaza Strip to Hamas in 2007, would resist Hamas's efforts to seize control in the West Bank through force, likely leading (as happened in Gaza in 2007) to violent conflict between the two parties.

Such instability and conflict in the West Bank would be a direct threat to Jordan's stability. It likely would create another refugee flow into Jordan, further burdening the Jordanian economy (this refugee flow would be tacitly—and perhaps openly—encouraged by Israel). The prospect of a Hamas victory would also pose a threat to the Hashemite kingdom, which favors a secular authority in the West Bank. Hamas and Jordan's Muslim Brotherhood share the same lineage—both parties were inspired by Egypt's Muslim Brotherhood—and Hamas's victory in the West Bank could embolden Jordan's Muslim Brotherhood to become more politically assertive. Much like the Egyptian government's anxieties about Gaza, the last thing Jordan's Hashemite rulers want to see is a radical Islamist regime on its border.

Because of these threats posed by a Fatah-Hamas civil war in the West Bank, Jordan might feel impelled to intervene militarily on the side of Fatah. But such intervention would pose serious dangers. First, it would risk a Jordanian-Israeli confrontation, because Israel views the West Bank as a region critical to its national security. It is unlikely, in fact, that Jordan would intervene in West Bank violence without Israeli approval. Second, Jordanian intervention in Palestinian internal affairs would risk alienating Jordan's own majority Palestinian population, all of whom, as noted, have family ties with Palestinians in the West Bank. Finally, if Jordan were to intervene on the side of the secular Fatah Party (the most probable scenario), it would do so at the risk of angering Islamist forces both within Jordan and across the region. In sum, open civil war between Palestinian factions in the West Bank would create a series of nightmare scenarios for Jordan. Almost as threatening would be a peaceful Hamas takeover of the West Bank—something that could conceivably be the outcome of the April 2011 Fatah-Hamas reconciliation agreement. It thus is no surprise that King Abdullah has been at the forefront in pushing for a comprehensive Israeli-Palestinian peace agreement: His kingdom's survival depends on it.

IRAQ

Jordan's relationship with Iraq has been simultaneously close and complicated since both countries were created in the 1920s by the British mandatory power. Iraq, like Jordan, was ruled by the Hashemite family. Unlike the Jordanian regime, the Iraqi monarchy was overthrown in a military coup in 1958. When the secular, revolutionary Baath Party seized power in Iraq in 1968, the two countries found themselves on different sides of the Middle East's ideological divide—Jordan was pro-West and close to the United States, while Iraq was opposed to the region's conservative regimes and relied on the Soviet Union for weapons and support. Nevertheless, Jordan and Iraq continued to share many mutual interests, including close commercial relationships, a deep hostility toward Syria, and, after the Iranian Revolution of 1979, concern about growing Iranian influence in the region.

From a security perspective, developments in Iraq are destined to have an effect on Jordan and could draw Jordan into conflict. Although King Abdullah quietly supported and assisted the 2003 U.S. invasion of Iraq that overthrew Jordan's former ally, Saddam Hussein, he also was concerned about the fate of postwar Iraq. The only outcome in Iraq that would ensure a stable relationship with Jordan is one that creates a peaceful, multisectarian government in Baghdad that is generally (if not overtly) pro-Western and relatively free of Iranian influence. In light of the 2005 Amman bombings, Jordan additionally desires an Iraqi state that can effectively clamp down on cross-border terror. Any outcome short of these dynamics will be a source of concern in Amman and could lead to conflict.

Two possible outcomes of Iraq's political restructuring would be particularly worrisome for Jordan. The first would be a strong Iraqi government—dominated by the majority Shiite community—that is aligned with Iran. This situation could arise only in the context of the further diminution of Sunni power in Iraq, in which case tens of thousands more Iraqis would seek exile, many in Jordan. Jordan already hosts between 750,000 and 1 million Iraqi refugees who have fled the violence; the Jordanian economy and society would be strained by a further influx of Iraqis. Although Jordan could respond to this situation by strengthening its border forces and preventing immigration, many Jordanians would sympathize with the Iraqi Sunnis and may insist on aiding them. Moreover, the Sunni Jordanian Muslim Brotherhood would feel a religious impulse to come to the aid of fellow Iraqi Sunnis and not only would demand action by Amman but might also support Sunni terrorist attacks against a Shiite-dominated Iraqi government.

Iranian influence over a Shiite-dominated Iraqi government would also arouse considerable alarm in Amman. King Abdullah has publicly warned of a Shiite crescent developing in the Middle East in the event of Iranian domination of Iraq and claimed that Iran's goal is "to have an Islamic republic of Iraq; if that happened, we've opened ourselves to a whole set of new problems that won't be limited to the borders of Iraq."[9]

Relations between an Iranian-dominated Iraq and Jordan would be tense, if not hostile. It is not hard to envision border incidents or acts of terrorism leading to a direct military confrontation between the two countries, which easily could devolve into a broader regional conflict. At a minimum, a pro-Iranian government in Iraq would oblige the Jordanian government to spend more money on defense and military hardware (although such burdens would likely be eased by U.S. aid), further straining Jordan's weak economy. Moreover, Jordan would no longer be able to count on Iraq as a reliable source of oil.

Perhaps equally disturbing to Jordan's leaders is the very real prospect that Iraq will descend into an extended period of sectarian conflict and insensate violence—a civil war that could last for many years. This scenario would increase the refugee flow (and prevent current Iraqi refugees in Jordan from returning home) as well as create an environment in Iraq in which terrorism continues to flourish. Any signs that the minority Sunni community in Iraq was losing or under siege would increase pressure from the Muslim Brotherhood and the Jordanian populace for government intervention.

Whatever the ultimate outcome in Iraq, it will profoundly affect Jordan's security and stability. Jordan's ability to affect that outcome, however, is severely limited. Jordan has been training members of the Iraqi police on anti-insurgency methods and has welcomed Iraqi refugees, the majority of whom are Sunni, but otherwise has virtually no ability to influence the internal dynamics of Iraq.

IRAN

Jordan has regarded Iran as a potential regional threat since the Iranian Revolution of 1979, which created the Islamic Republic in Iran. The new government in Tehran was hostile to the United States—Jordan's principal foreign patron—as well as to traditional monarchies. Iran also sought to spread Islamist government throughout the Middle East and thus was fundamentally opposed to all secular regimes that did not govern by sharia, or Islamic law (in Jordan, sharia is only applied in personal status law). In addition, as a predominantly Shiite Muslim nation, the rise of an Islamist government in Iran threatened to exacerbate the Shiite-Sunni schism in the region.

In 1980, Iraq's new leader—Saddam Hussein—launched a war with Iran. Saddam was a member of the secular Baath Party and a Sunni, although Iraq was majority Shiite. His goal was to bring an end to the revolutionary Shiite government in Iran before it was able to solidify power and start to export its revolution. Jordan strongly backed Saddam's war and became a major conduit of weapons and supplies to Iraq. King Hussein took the lead in forming the Arab Cooperation Council, a military alliance among

Jordan, Egypt, and Iraq that was designed to create a bulwark against Iran. Jordan's support for Iraq essentially confirmed its hostility to the Islamic Republic.

The ideological and policy differences between Jordan and Iran are so great that it is hard to imagine a relationship based on anything other than mistrust and hostility, barring a dramatic change of regime in one of the countries. Geographic distance rules out most forms of direct confrontation—although Iran does possess missiles with a range that could reach Jordan. The Jordanian-Iranian conflict is more likely to be conducted indirectly—through terrorism, espionage, and support for allies. More specifically, the conflict is likely to play out in Iraq, where both Jordan and Iran exert influence and where each supports different sectarian groups (for Jordan, the Sunnis; for Iran, the Shia).

The degree to which Iraq becomes an indirect battleground for Jordan and Iran, however, depends upon how internal developments in Iraq proceed. If Iraq descends into civil war and widespread sectarian violence, both Jordan and Iran will actively support their respective sectarian allies. Iran's extensive global terrorist network would give it the ability to strike at Jordanian targets—both in Iraq and possibly in Jordan as well. Jordan also shares a long desert border with Syria, Iran's principal Arab ally.

Even if Iraq evolves into a peaceful and stable society, Jordan and Iran will remain fundamentally opposed to one another for ideological and religious reasons. In addition, as long as Jordan is seen in the region as an ally of the United States—and is one of the few Arab states having relations with Israel—Jordan is subject to being targeted by Iranian-inspired terrorism. If, for example, Israel or the United States were to engage in a direct military confrontation with Iran, the outcome could be a broader regional conflagration that Jordan would be hard-pressed to avoid.

SYRIA

Jordan has a history of strained relations with Syria, based largely on ideological differences and on Syria's ambition to play a dominant role in the Levant. After achieving full independence from France in 1946, Syria turned in a leftist and republican direction, the exact opposite of Jordan's pro-Western monarchy. With the encouragement and support of the Soviet Union, Syria joined Nasser's Egypt in 1958 in a short-lived union (known as the United Arab Republic), which was directed against Israel and U.S. allies in the area, such as Jordan.

Jordan and Syria were on the same side during the 1967 Six-Day War, but several years later, during Jordan's brief but bloody battle against Palestinian guerillas, Syria threatened to come to the aid of the guerillas and massed troops along the Jordanian border. Warnings from the United States, as well as the reputation of Jordan's armed forces, prevented Syria from becoming involved in the fighting. Jordan did not join Syria and Egypt's 1973 war against Israel, but publicly King Hussein supported his Arab allies and sent token forces to the Syrian front.

The two countries continued to eye each other warily and pursue different policies throughout the 1980s and 1990s, but they never came to blows. Syria was hostile to Saddam Hussein's regime in Iraq and supported the U.S.-led 1991 Gulf War; Jordan had aligned with Saddam and opposed the war. Syria also forged close ties with the Islamic Republic of Iran, in part to balance U.S. influence in the region and in part due to religious affinity: Syria's ruling al-Asad family is a member of the country's minority Alawite community, which is doctrinally and historically linked to the Shia. In 2004, Jordan's King Abdullah warned of a growing Shiite crescent in the region, which included Iran, Iraq's Shiite community, Lebanon's Hezbollah, and the Alawites of Syria.

The roots of animosity between Syria and Jordan are deep, but the two countries have avoided direct confrontation despite sharing a long border. Several regional developments could, however, bring the two states into a military confrontation. The current Syrian regime, for example, likely would support Iran in any regionwide conflict, and the Syrians could open a new front in the event Jordanian forces became involved in a civil war in Iraq. Syria's long border with Jordan also could serve as an entry point for Iranian-backed terrorist groups.

Another possible scenario that could lead to conflict between Syria and Jordan would be civil war in Syria aimed at overthrowing or replacing the Alawite-dominated regime, and signs of such a scenario were growing in early 2012. In such an event, Jordan might be inclined to lend at least material support to anti-Alawite forces in order to bring about a government that is more in line with Jordanian priorities. Iran would most likely lend support to Syrian factions that wanted to maintain the Syrian-Iranian alliance. In any event, political turmoil in Syria could result in conflict involving Jordan, including the possibility of a flow of refugees across the border. Despite the history of animosity between the two countries, most Jordanian leaders probably would prefer that Syria remain internally at peace, even if under the Assad regime.

NOTES

1. For a fascinating inside account of the U.S.-Jordanian partnership, see the memoir by Jack O'Connell, the CIA station chief in Amman from 1963 to 1971. Jack O'Connell, *King's Counsel* (New York: W. W. Norton, 2011).

2. Robert Fisk, "Why Jordan Is Occupied by Palestinians," *The Independent* (July 22, 2010), http://www.independent.co.uk/opinion/commentators/fisk/robert-fisk-why-jordan-is-occupied-by-palestinians-2032173.html.

3. Robin Wright and Peter Baker, "Iraq, Jordan See Threat to Election from Iran," *Washington Post* (December 8, 2004), http://www.washingtonpost.com/wp-dyn/articles/A43980–2004Dec7.html.

4. Oraib Al Rantawi, "Post-Saddam Iraq and the Threats facing Jordan," *Bitterlemons* 3, no. 45 (December 15, 2005), http://www.bitterlemons-international.org.

5. Jillian Schwedler, "Jordan's Risky Business As Usual," *Middle East Report Online* (June 30, 2010), http://www.merip.org/mero/mero063010.html.

6. Curtis Ryan, "'We Are All Jordan' . . . But Who Is We?" *Middle East Report Online* (July 13, 2010), http://merip.org/mero/mero071310.html.

7. W. Andrew Terrill, *Jordanian National Security and the Future of Middle East Stability* (Carlisle, PA: Strategic Studies Institute, U.S. Army War College, 2008), 14.

8. Ibid., 61.

9. David Hirst, "Arab Leaders Watch in Fear as Shia Emancipation Draws Near," *The Guardian* (January 27, 2005).

7 KUWAIT

Kuwaitis date the origin of their country to 1756, when the Sabah family secured control over land along the Persian Gulf roughly equating to the country's modern borders; the Sabahs remain Kuwait's ruling family to this day. The Sabahs adeptly maintained considerable independence under Ottoman rule, and as the Ottoman Empire began its inexorable decline, the ruling family reached out to Britain, signing a treaty in 1899 that gave Britain control over Kuwait's foreign policy.

Oil was discovered in Kuwait just before the outbreak of World War II, and the resource began to be extensively exploited in the war's aftermath. With a small population base, the ruling family was able to spread the proceeds fairly widely, modernize infrastructure, and build schools and hospitals (as a result of these initiatives, Kuwait today has one of the highest literacy rates in the Middle East and a highly regarded health care system). Kuwait also established the world's first sovereign wealth fund in 1953, the Kuwait Investment Board, with the specific objective of diversifying the country's sources of income. In 1965, the Kuwait Investment Board was replaced by the Kuwait Investment Office, which established its main office in London, from which it began to make strategic investments in mostly European equities and real estate. Kuwait's economy was thus connected to Western economies from an early stage, well before those of the other oil-rich Arab states.

Kuwait achieved full independence in 1961, and the ruling Sabah was declared the country's first emir. Neighboring Iraq, which had been independent since 1932, expressed opposition to Kuwait's independence. Iraqis had long argued that Kuwait was in fact a part of their country, making the argument that the boundaries were drawn randomly by Britain in 1923. The argument had historical merit: during the era of Ottoman rule, Kuwait was included in a *vilayet* (an Ottoman administrative area) with its capital at Basra, a city that fell within Iraq's borders. The Iraqis resented in particular the fact that independent Kuwait enjoyed a long Gulf coastline, allowing it to develop ports, while Iraq was stuck with a very short coastline and the port of Basra, whose shallow waters made a deep-water port unfeasible. But Britain made clear that it would defend Kuwait's independence and even sent troops in 1961 to ensure that Iraq did not attempt a forceful takeover.

Kuwait's wealth grew dramatically in the 1970s as international oil prices soared; in 1975, Kuwait nationalized its oil resources. In 1976, the emir established the Reserve Fund for Future Generations, which was allocated 10 percent of Kuwait's annual state revenue and mandated with seeking long-term investments that would generate stable income for generations to come, even after the depletion of the nation's oil resources. It also further connected Kuwait to Western nations as Kuwaitis began to take significant stakes in prominent European and U.S. companies as well as make large real estate investments in Western countries.

Given its small population base, Kuwait welcomed thousands of immigrants to perform work that Kuwaitis did not want to do—and with the country's cradle-to-grave welfare program, that included many jobs. Kuwaitis before long became a minority in their own country, as Palestinians (many of whom were refugees from the 1948 and 1967 Arab-Israeli wars), Lebanese, and South Asians moved in.

The 1979 Iranian Revolution and the subsequent establishment of the Shiite-dominated Islamic Republic in Iran was a cause of great concern to Kuwait's leaders. Kuwait's population is estimated to be between 20 and 25 percent Shia.[1] Since the early 20th century, Kuwait also has been home to a number of Iranians—estimates of the Iranian population of Kuwait range as high as 75,000[2]—virtually all of whom are Shia. Kuwaiti authorities responded to the events in Iran by increasing surveillance over the Shiite community and effectively barring Kuwaiti Shia from sensitive government and military positions. Sunni-Shiite tensions were at an all-time high in the immediate postrevolution period.

When war broke out between Iraq and Iran in 1980, the Kuwaitis unhesitatingly supported Saddam Hussein's regime, despite the ongoing tension with Iraq over Kuwait's borders. For Kuwaitis, it was simply a question of the lesser of two evils; Saddam, they believed, posed less of a threat than did an Iranian victory over Iraq, which could lead to Iranian control of the heavily Shiite southern parts of Iraq that border Kuwait. It was not only the Shiite Islam of Iran that frightened the Kuwaitis. The revolution in Tehran was in large part targeted against monarchical governments, like Kuwait's, as well as countries that were close to the West, and to the United States in particular. While Kuwait was not as close to the United States as Saudi Arabia was—in fact, during the Cold War, Kuwait was the first Arabian Peninsula state to establish relations with the Soviet Union—its close business and commercial ties to the West rendered it an enemy in the eyes of Iran's revolutionaries.

Saddam Hussein's decision to invade Kuwait in August 1990 was most likely motivated by several factors. Although Iraq had just completed a long and extremely costly war with Iran (the two countries had signed a truce in 1988), Saddam believed (correctly) that capturing Kuwait would be a relatively quick operation. It is also likely that he was under the impression that the United States would not oppose an invasion, or at least would not respond militarily. Moreover, although wars are costly and Iraq was carrying a huge ($82 billion) debt burden after eight years of war with Iran,

Saddam may have seen the capture of Kuwait as a long-term net financial gain. Control of Kuwait would vastly increase Iraq's oil reserves and thus increase the country's income—as well as its influence within the Organization of the Petroleum Exporting Countries—for decades (Saddam had complained during the months prior to the invasion that Kuwait and other Gulf states were colluding to keep oil prices low, which was not in debt-ridden Iraq's interests).

Having just fought Iran to what was essentially a draw, Saddam may have relished the thought of a quick military victory that would enhance his power and prestige throughout the Gulf and the broader Middle East. Finally, Iraq's decades-long claims to Kuwait undoubtedly played an important role in Saddam's calculations by serving as a unifying factor among Iraqis, even those who were opposed to the Baathist regime. It is no surprise that Saddam declared Kuwait to be Iraq's newest province as soon as his troops had secured control.

Whatever Saddam's motivations may have been, the consequences of the invasion were devastating for Kuwait. Almost half the Kuwaiti population fled the country as Iraqi troops marched in. Incessant Iraqi bombing inflicted extensive damage on Kuwait's infrastructure and oil facilities and created an environmental disaster. Further damage was caused by the Coalition Forces, led by the United States, in the process of driving Iraqi troops out of Kuwait.

The country's reconstruction cost billions of dollars, in addition to the $16 billion Kuwait spent to fund the Coalition Forces, which in turn required the Kuwaiti government to sell many of its overseas assets and investments. And with Saddam Hussein still in power in Iraq—albeit substantially weakened by military losses and international sanctions—Kuwaitis remained traumatized and anxious for most of the 1990s. A defense pact signed with the United States in September 1991 eased fears substantially, but at the expense of reducing Kuwait's long-cherished foreign policy independence. Under the terms of the pact, the U.S. military was provided access to Kuwaiti port facilities and air bases, and ground-based U.S. troops conducted training exercises on Kuwaiti soil. The United States also was allowed to pre-position military supplies in Kuwait in the event of a regional conflict. Kuwait became the center of U.S. military operations in the Gulf for the ensuing decade, and in 2001 the defense pact was extended for another 10 years.[3]

Kuwait's relationships with other Arab states generally were strengthened by the war with Iraq. All of the Gulf Arab states—with the exception of Yemen—provided troops to the Coalition Forces, as did Syria, Egypt, and Morocco. Saudi Arabia was second only to the United States in the number of troops provided, and Saudi Arabia also underwrote a substantial portion of the war's costs. While the motives of Saudi Arabia and the other Gulf Arab states were not purely altruistic by any means—they all, and especially Saudi Arabia, feared the consequences of Iraqi control over Kuwait— the Kuwaitis nevertheless were heartened by the support.

Kuwait's relationships with Jordan and the Palestine Liberation Organization (PLO), however, were damaged by the war. Both King Hussein and Yasser Arafat supported Saddam Hussein's position, if not the actual invasion, and refused to lend support to the Coalition Forces. Kuwait's bitterness over the positions of Jordan and the PLO led to the expulsion from Kuwait of hundreds of thousands of Palestinian and

Jordanian workers, many of whom held important middle management jobs. While the expulsions caused a refugee crisis in Jordan—the destination of most of those who were expelled—it also hindered Kuwait's reconstruction by removing an important contingent of the workforce.

Kuwait's reconstruction—both physical as well as social—took the better part of the 1990s, and with Saddam Hussein still in power in Iraq during that period, Kuwaitis remained vigilant. The new defense ties with the United States, however, increased confidence to the point that foreign investment, particularly in the country's energy sector, resumed.

Kuwait strongly backed the strict U.S. and Western sanctions against Iraq in the years following the war—both diplomatically and financially—and Kuwait's government was one of the few in the Arab world to support the U.S. invasion of Iraq in 2003. It provided the United States with virtually unlimited use of its air bases, international airport, and seaports. Kuwait also gave extensive logistical support in conjunction with the invasion, providing supplies of food and fuel and serving as the staging point for U.S. troops moving into and out of Iraq.[4]

INTERNAL CONFLICTS

Kuwait's domestic politics are unique to the region. Although the country's leaders are always members of the ruling Sabah family, Kuwait enjoys a feisty parliament that has not been reluctant to challenge the ruling family on policy issues. It would be a stretch to call Kuwait a democracy: suffrage is severely limited, although slowly expanding (women were given the right to vote in 2005, and the first women were elected to parliament in 2009), and the emir can dissolve the parliament and call new elections at will, which has been done frequently when the parliament has become too aggressive. But the 50-seat parliament's independence nevertheless has served as a check on total dominance by the Sabah family and has injected a level of debate in Kuwaiti society that exists in few other Arab states.

As a result, some of the opposition that exists in many parts of the Arab world has an official outlet in Kuwait. Even though political parties as such are not allowed, the members of parliament are aligned by "tendencies," including Islamists. The parliament elected in 2009 included 16 Sunni Islamists (mostly members of the Kuwaiti Muslim Brotherhood); 5 Shiite Islamists; and 4 women. The inclusion of Islamists in parliament has helped to reduce the chances that Islamist groups will act in a violent way or attempt to otherwise undermine the government.

As long as Kuwait's parliament is allowed to express opposition to government policies, and as long as the country enjoys a relatively free press (official press censorship ended in 1992), it is not likely that Kuwait will witness the kind of internal challenges to the regime experienced by many other Arab states. Indeed, the events that shook the region in early 2011 did not spread to Kuwait. Even the tensions between Shia and Sunnis, which periodically arise over issues of access to employment and other rights, are likely to take place on a formal political level. Kuwaiti Shia staged demonstrations in March 2011, but their ire was directed at the government of Bahrain, whose Sunni-dominated leadership was cracking down

Women serve in Kuwait's parliament and senior government posts, an exception among Gulf countries. (AP Photo/Gustavo Ferrari)

harshly against its Shia majority. Future relations between Shia and Sunnis in Kuwait will be determined to a certain extent by the nature of Kuwait's relations with Iraq and Iran, its neighbors and the most populous Shiite majority countries in the world.

IRAQ

Despite the fact that the Baathist regime of Saddam Hussein has been overthrown in Iraq and replaced with a democratic—if shaky—coalition government, Iraq remains Kuwait's primary security concern. The long history of Iraqi claims against Kuwait (which well predated Saddam), the unstable political situation in Iraq and a political culture there that is prone to violence, and the links between Iraq's majority Shiite community and Kuwait's minority Shiite community guarantee that Iraq will be a cause of anxiety for Kuwaitis for years to come. Kuwaiti vigilance toward developments in Iraq will increase substantially after the United States withdraws most of its combat forces from Iraq.

Kuwait has attempted to build ties with the most significant political factions in Iraq, and especially with the governing Shiite parties. This has not always been easy for Kuwaitis to stomach. For example, the Da'wa Party of Iraqi prime minister Nuri al-Maliki staged a number of terrorist incidents in Kuwait and against Kuwaiti targets in the 1980s in support of the Kuwaiti Shiite community. Kuwait did not appoint an ambassador to the al-Maliki government until July 2008. The ambassador, however, was a

Kuwaiti Shia, which signaled that Kuwait was coming to terms with the fact that Shiite parties would most likely dominate Iraqi politics for the foreseeable future.

In addition to Kuwait's historical concerns about Iraqi power in the region, there are tangible issues that separate the two countries. Kuwait has not dropped its claims to reparations for Iraq's 1990 invasion—a total of approximately $25 billion, which Kuwait argues is owed to its citizens for the destruction of their property and businesses. As a result, the United Nations has mandated that 5 percent of Iraq's annual oil revenue be transferred to Kuwait. The Iraqi government has denied responsibility for the actions of the Saddam regime and, in any event, argues that its own reconstruction will be made more difficult without full access to its oil revenues. Further complicating matters is the fact that Iraq owes Kuwait an additional $25 billion in debt incurred by Saddam (most of this debt originated as Kuwaiti loans to Saddam during Iraq's war with Iran). Kuwait has at times pledged to write off this debt, or a substantial portion of it, but has not yet done so.

It is hard to envision another Iraqi military attack on Kuwait as occurred under Saddam. Kuwait has largely rebuilt and modernized its armed forces, thanks to massive U.S. arms sales, while Iraq's armed forces were devastated by the U.S. invasion

Iraqi artillery and vehicles destroyed during the 1991 Gulf War still litter the Kuwaiti desert. Iraq's efforts to avoid paying Kuwait some $25 billion in UN-mandated reparations for Saddam Hussein's 1990 invasion have alarmed Kuwaitis and strained relations that have slowly improved since the fall of the Iraqi dictator. (Michael Wood)

and, although rebuilt, are focused more on maintaining domestic stability and resisting any attempts at aggression by Iran. It is easy, however, to imagine the Kuwaiti-Iraqi relationship continuing to be characterized by deep mistrust (on the part of the Kuwaitis) and resentment (on the part of the Iraqis). In the past, one of the few factors that united the two countries was fear of Iranian power; but with Iraq now dominated by Shiite parties and personalities, Kuwait is understandably nervous about possible Iraqi-Iranian collusion. Indeed, developments in the Iraqi-Iranian relationship will in large part determine the course of Kuwaiti-Iraqi relations.

Another threat to Kuwait would derive from a return to civil war in Iraq—only in a future scenario without the presence of U.S. troops. Such a situation would be especially dangerous for Kuwait if it took the form of a Sunni-Shiite contest for power, as this could radicalize Kuwait's Shiite community and create conditions favorable for the development and expansion of terrorist groups in the region. A return to civil war in Iraq could also produce a refugee crisis, with Iraqis attempting to flee across the 120-mile border into Kuwait.

The ideal situation for Kuwait would be an Iraq that is strong enough not to descend into civil war, which could lead to intervention by Iran and heightened activism by Kuwaiti Shia, but weak enough that it does not pose a military threat to Kuwait. Although Kuwait's official position is that Iraq should be a unified country, many Kuwaitis believe that an Iraq divided among Shiite, Sunni, and Kurdish states also would be in Kuwait's interest, for the three entities would be focused on countering each other's power and none would have the ability to launch an attack against Kuwait.[5] A stable but nonthreatening Iraq also is in Kuwait's economic interests, as the emirate is well positioned to serve as a transshipment hub for Iraq's large southern oil fields.

IRAN

Kuwait's relationship with Iran has traditionally been complex. On the one hand, the Iranian Revolution in 1979 caused concern among many Kuwaitis who feared that their country's Shiite community would become a target for Iranian leaders' pledge to export their revolution throughout the region. In response to the revolution, Kuwait joined Saudi Arabia, Qatar, the United Arab Emirates, Bahrain, and Oman in forming the Gulf Cooperation Council (GCC), a mutual defense pact, in 1980. On the other hand, Iranian animosity toward the Saddam Hussein regime in Iraq paralleled Kuwait's own concerns about Iraqi aggression. When war broke out between Iran and Iraq in 1980, Kuwait initially took a neutral position; seeing the two countries it most feared fight each other was in line with the interest of the Kuwaiti government, which hoped that the two would exhaust themselves and that both would emerge weakened and unable to pose a regional threat.[6]

Kuwait's policies changed around 1982, when it appeared that Iran was winning a decisive victory on the battlefield. Kuwait reluctantly joined other GCC states in providing support for Saddam's war effort in the form of grants, loans, and logistical support. The Kuwaiti press and diplomats also began to openly side with Iraq. In response to this change in policy, Iran started providing active support for antigovernment Shiite groups inside Kuwait and was believed to be behind some terrorist attacks in Kuwait, including bombings of the U.S. and French embassies, an assassination attempt on the emir, and bombings of oil pipelines. This response, of course, further raised Kuwaitis' fears of Iran.

Even after Iran and Iraq signed a cease-fire in August 1988, Iranian provocations continued. In 1984, Iran attacked two Kuwaiti oil tankers, leading the Kuwaiti government to request that the United States reflag its tankers as U.S.-registered vessels and provide the requisite military protection for them.

Iran was officially neutral during the 1990–1991 Gulf War, although its leaders suggested indirectly that they were not opposed to the U.S.-led military effort to oust Saddam's forces from Kuwait. In the wake of the war, as Kuwait began the arduous task of rebuilding, Iran took on a more moderate position toward exporting revolution and appeared willing to establish good working relationships with its Arab neighbors. Moreover, the presence of U.S. forces and facilities in the region served to calm Kuwaiti fears of both another attack from Saddam or Iranian aggression.

There is a limit, however, as to how close Kuwait and Iran ever can become under the current leadership in Tehran. The Iranians have campaigned for a permanent end to U.S. presence in the Gulf region and the establishment instead of a Gulf-wide security structure—which, of course, would be dominated by Iran, the region's largest power. Kuwait still favors a U.S. presence in the region—including in Kuwait—and sees this as a guarantor against both Iranian adventurism as well as an Iraqi resurgence. The election in 2005 and reelection in 2009 of the more radical Mahmoud Ahmadinejad as president of Iran further hardened Iran's position and further alarmed the Kuwaitis.

Unrest in 2011 among the Shia community in Bahrain, which many accused of being stoked by Iran, caused alarm among Kuwaitis, who saw it as confirmation of their fear that Iran seeks to destabilize the Gulf's Sunni-led monarchies. In the midst of the Bahraini unrest, Kuwait expelled several Iranian diplomats who it accused of spying for Iran.

Kuwait is concerned about Iranian nuclear plans and certainly does not wish for Iran to acquire nuclear weapons. It is not that Kuwait fears a nuclear attack; rather, the acquisition of nuclear weapons by Iran would alter the balance of power in the Gulf region substantially in Iran's favor and render the U.S. security guarantee less effective. Nevertheless, Kuwait's leaders have been cautious about openly opposing Iran's plans, and the emir in November 2009 declared that Iran has the right to pursue peaceful nuclear development. At the same time, Kuwait has opposed the option of a U.S. military strike (and, without doubt, an Israeli strike) on Iran as a way of stalling the Islamic Republic's nuclear program. Kuwaitis correctly fear that such an attack would risk a counterattack by Iran aimed at pro-U.S. countries in the region and would also inflame the host of extremist elements in the Arab and Islamic worlds. Thus, Kuwait's leaders are stuck in a position of opposing the introduction of nuclear weapons into the region but not favoring any military actions to prevent such a development.

TERRORISM

Kuwait has not suffered from a major terrorism problem, although the nature of the terrorist threat is such that this situation could change with little or no warning.

In the 1980s, Iranian-inspired terrorist groups launched several attacks, as described above. More recently, the U.S. military presence in Kuwait has provoked several attacks against U.S. facilities, most of which have been minor and notably unprofessional in nature.

Al-Qaeda has attracted Kuwaiti recruits, mostly from among the several hundred Kuwaiti volunteers who fought in Afghanistan, Chechnya, and Bosnia, but the terror organization is not believed to have a cell operating inside the country. In August 2009, Kuwaiti intelligence and counterterrorism forces foiled a planned attack against Kuwaiti and foreign targets inside the country. Kuwaiti authorities claimed that the attackers were members of an al-Qaeda–affiliated group but not of al-Qaeda itself. If carried out successfully, the attack would have been one of the most dramatic ever in the Gulf region: intended targets included U.S. military facilities and oil refineries.

The fact that the planned attack was exposed and thwarted by Kuwaiti officials is an indication of the capabilities of the country's counterterrorism infrastructure. Because Kuwait is a small country—both geographically and in population—with one international airport, it is easier for intelligence forces to keep tabs on potential terrorist operations. A bigger concern for Kuwaiti officials is the funding by private Kuwaiti citizens of terrorist groups and operations outside of Kuwaiti. After the September 11, 2001, attacks on the United States, Kuwaiti officials enacted new rules concerning financial transfers and transactions and froze the accounts of a number of suspected terrorist sympathizers.[7] Kuwaiti education officials also launched a review of school curricula to ensure that extremist ideology was not being taught, and Kuwaiti officials started to more closely monitor imams (and the content of their sermons) and Islamic charities.[8]

In January 2005, Kuwaiti security police engaged in a clash against a group calling itself the Peninsula Lions. Eight terrorists were killed, and police raided a bomb-making facility operated by the group. The group is believed to have been loosely connected to al-Qaeda but appears to have been quite small, and some have speculated that security forces may have eliminated all of its members.[9] Later that year, Osama bin Laden called on al-Qaeda supporters to target oil installations throughout the Gulf, which caused considerable concern among Kuwaitis. In August 2009, Kuwaiti authorities uncovered a plot by six Kuwaiti nationals—all believed to be affiliated with al-Qaeda—to bomb the main U.S. military base in Kuwait, along with an oil refinery and several government buildings.

A number of factors will render Kuwait an attractive target for regional terrorist groups, including the presence of U.S. troops and facilities in Kuwait as well as the emirate's close ties to the United States; the presence at any given time of over 20,000 Western expatriates; many attractive potential economic targets, such as oil refineries and tankers; the desert border with Iraq, which could allow for infiltration of terrorist operatives (especially in the event that Iraq descends into civil war); and the prospect of terrorist groups crossing the border from Saudi Arabia. The latter has become less of a concern ever since the Saudis' crackdown on terrorist groups inside the kingdom, which led many of them to flee to Yemen, which is geographically much farther from Kuwait. In February 2010, Kuwait announced that it would construct a security belt along the country's border with Iraq to prevent the infiltration of terrorists.[10]

RADICAL CHANGE IN SAUDI ARABIA

Kuwait and Saudi Arabia have had generally positive relations since Kuwait's independence. The two countries have shared conservative, monarchical forms of government (although Kuwait is a substantially more open society); energy-based economies; and concerns about Iraqi and Iranian aggression. Since the 1990 Iraqi invasion of Kuwait, both countries also have shared close ties with the United States. Kuwait and Saudi Arabia solved a potential border problem in 1992 by creating a 62,000-square-mile neutral zone between them in which the two countries equally share oil production.

The greatest threat posed to Kuwait by Saudi Arabia is the potential for some type of extremist takeover of the kingdom—a development that is out of Kuwait's hands to control or affect. In this eventuality, Kuwait would find itself bordering an oil-rich radical state and would have very little ability to defend against it. Short of a full takeover of the Saudi government by extremists, there is also the possibility of a resurgence of extremism in Saudi Arabia—in the form of al-Qaeda cells or other extremist groups—which could spill over into Kuwait.

NOTES

1. Tracy Miller, ed., *Mapping the Global Muslim Population: A Report on the Size and Distribution of the World's Muslim Population* (Washington, DC: Pew Research Center, October 2009).

2. "Iranians in Kuwait," *Kuwait Times* (June 21, 2009).

3. Kenneth Katzman, "Kuwait: Security, Reform and U.S. Policy," *Congressional Research Service* (December 9, 2009), 9.

4. Ibid., 10.

5. See W. Andrew Terrill, *Kuwaiti National Security and U.S.-Kuwaiti Strategic Relationship after Saddam* (Carlisle, PA: Strategic Studies Institute, U.S. Army War College, 2007), 55.

6. Ibid., 59.

7. Ibid., 70.

8. Anthony H. Cordesman and Khalid R. al-Rodhan, *The Gulf Military Forces in an Era of Asymmetric War: Kuwait* (Washington, DC: Center for Strategic and International Studies, 2006), 25.

9. Andrew Hammond, "Kuwait: Tensions Bursts," *Middle East International* (February 18, 2005), 24.

10. "Kuwait Eyes 'Security Belt' on Iraq Border," *Kuwait Times* (February 13, 2010).

8 LEBANON

Lebanon has in many ways mirrored every other Middle Eastern conflict since its creation as an independent state in 1943. A small, mountainous country with only 4 million people, Lebanon's role in the region has been far greater than its size would suggest. Composed of a diversity of religious sects as well as a sizable population of Palestinian refugees, Lebanon often has been used as a vicarious battlefield for its warring neighbors and the venue in which the region's ideological and religious conflicts are played out. The fact that the Lebanese have never succeeded in creating a strong sense of national identity has made the country particularly susceptible to outside interference, as various Lebanese sects have sought allies and defenders abroad.

The area now known as Lebanon was under the rule of the Ottoman Empire from the 16th century until 1918, but Ottoman rule was weak and local leaders enjoyed significant power. Several important communities live within Lebanon's borders: Maronite Christians, who mostly inhabit the mountainous central and northern regions as well as East Beirut; Sunni Muslims, who are prominent in West Beirut; the Druze, a secretive sect of Islam whose power center is in the Chouf Mountains south of Beirut; and the Shia, who are dominant in the south of the country. (These geographical concentrations are based mainly on tradition and are not rigidly defined subregions; in fact, Lebanese of all sects are represented throughout the country.) Other large communities include Greek Orthodox (based in the far north) and Greek Catholics. In many ways, Beirut is the glue that holds Lebanon together. All of the country's sects regard Beirut as the heart of Lebanon, and as a major port, most trade is centered in Beirut.

By the late 19th century, foreign powers also had gained a presence in Lebanon. France saw itself as the protector of the country's Maronite Christian community that lived mostly in the mountainous areas of the north. U.S. missionaries, mostly Protestant, also operated freely in the country and established a number of schools and hospitals. When a civil war broke out in 1860, France's emperor Napoleon III sent military forces to defend the Maronites.

When the Ottoman Empire fell following World War I, France was granted a mandate over Lebanon under the terms of the Sykes-Picot Agreement. The French created local governmental arrangements that ensured Maronite dominance. After France fell to Germany in World War II, Lebanon came briefly under the control of the Nazi-supported Vichy government but in 1941 was occupied by British and Free French forces. The Lebanese declared independence on March 22, 1943.

The new state was based on an agreement that had been reached between the Maronites and the Sunnis, who together composed a majority of the population. Known as the National Pact, this agreement was based on the Maronites' acceptance of Lebanon's independence from France and its position as an Arab country (Lebanon became a charter member of the Arab League) and the Sunnis' agreement not to pursue a merger with Syria or any other Arab state. Moreover, the National Pact designated a strict division of governmental positions according to religious affiliation: the president of the republic was to be a Maronite Christian, the prime minister a Sunni Muslim, and the speaker of parliament a Shia Muslim. While this appeared at the time as a clever way to balance sectarian power, over time the National Pact served to make sectarian divisions more rigid by institutionalizing them. Moreover, the various sectarian groups in Lebanon continued to look to outside powers—both regional and global—for support. As a result, Lebanon's attempts to maintain its identity as a unified state have constantly been challenged.

In 1958, Lebanese Christians felt threatened by the creation of the United Arab Republic, a federation formed by Egypt and Syria under the leadership of Egypt's charismatic, pan-Arabist president Nasser. Muslims and leftist forces in Lebanon were attracted to Nasser's message and sought to orient Lebanon closer to the Arab world. Clashes broke out between sects. Lebanese president Camille Chamoun, a Maronite (as per the national pact), requested U.S. intervention to save his government, which President Eisenhower provided in the form of a U.S. marine landing in Beirut. After several more weeks of fighting, a truce was declared, and the national pact was reconfirmed by all sides.

Fifteen years of relative quiet followed the events of 1958, a period in which Lebanon prospered economically and developed as the financial, banking, and tourism center of the Middle East. This brief golden age was further boosted by the surge in Arab oil wealth—Lebanese banks led the way in financing development projects in the oil-rich states of the Arabian Peninsula, and wealthy Arabs throughout the Middle East enjoyed Lebanon's relatively liberal and open lifestyle. But Lebanon's newfound prosperity was not shared equally: Maronite Christian and Sunni Muslim families controlled much of the banking and financial services sector, and many Lebanese continued to live in poverty. The Shia community, in particular, received few benefits of Lebanon's economic growth.

The Arab-Israeli war of 1967 created a new challenge for Lebanon. Although the Lebanese army wisely stayed out of the war, Israel's occupation of the West Bank created a new surge of Palestinian refugees, many of whom moved to refugee camps in Lebanon that already housed several hundred thousand Palestinian refugees from the

1948 war. When Jordan's King Hussein drove the Palestine Liberation Organization (PLO) out of Jordan in 1971, most of the PLO's fighters, as well as its political leadership, moved to Lebanon. The introduction of heavily armed guerilla fighters into a state that, by its very nature, was politically fragile was a recipe for disaster. Moreover, by hosting the PLO fighters, Lebanon for the first time found itself in Israel's crosshairs.

Tensions rose steadily, and in April 1975 full-scale fighting broke out between a loose coalition of Maronite Christian forces led by the Phalangist Party, long controlled by the Gemayal family, and an equally loose coalition of leftist Muslim, Shia, Druze, and Palestinian forces led by the Druze and their Jumblatt family (because of the loose nature of these coalitions, they cannot be accurately described as two cohesive blocs). In very simple terms, the Maronite coalition sought to drive out the PLO and secure Maronite dominance in Lebanese politics; the leftist coalition sought to create a more secular and Arab-aligned state in alliance with the Palestinian cause.

The most intense period of fighting lasted for 18 months, although insensate violence continued for years; over 30,000 people were killed during this period, a devastating loss for a country of only around 4 million at the time. In June 1976, Syrian troops invaded Lebanon to bring an end to the war. The Syrians were motivated by the fact that the tide had begun to turn in favor of the leftist PLO forces. Despite the Syrian Baath Party's usual position in support of the PLO and leftist, pan-Arab movements, Damascus did not want to see a radicalized Lebanon on its border. The United States and other major Western powers tacitly supported Syria's intervention.

But Syrian forces avoided the far south of the country out of a desire not to confront Israeli troops. As a result, PLO guerilla attacks against Israel continued, leading to fierce Israeli retaliation. In 1982, Israel launched a full-scale invasion of Lebanon in an attempt to drive the PLO out for good (this followed a smaller-scale Israeli invasion in 1978). While Israel partially achieved its goal (the PLO leadership and fighters were escorted to Tunisia by Western forces), Lebanon was left in disarray; Israel's indiscriminate attacks against Lebanese targets left the country in a state of physical ruin matched only by its state of political ruin.

Israel attempted to establish a puppet government in Beirut under the Phalangists but failed miserably. In the south of the country, a coalition of Shia and other leftist forces began to strike at Israeli troops, who eventually withdrew to a narrow strip along the border. An intra-Maronite civil war broke out that caused extensive deaths in Beirut and in the mountain towns to its north; political assassinations became routine. Only the 60 percent of the country that was under Syrian control enjoyed relative tranquility.

After almost 15 years of conflict, nearly 150,000 are believed to have died, tens of thousands more injured, and as many as 1 million Lebanese were either internally displaced or emigrated abroad. The country's economy was in shambles and many of the formerly most dynamic sectors—such as banking and financial services—had migrated to other regional centers, such as Dubai.

In October 1989, the Arab League sponsored a conference in Taif, Saudi Arabia, to which the entire Lebanese parliament was invited. The resulting agreement, known as the Taif Accords, produced a period of relative calm, despite the fact that several Lebanese groups refused to endorse the agreement. Syria further solidified its control over the Lebanese political process, and elections were held in 1992 for the first time in 20 years. Rafik Hariri, a Sunni Lebanese billionaire (whose fortune was made in Saudi Arabia) assumed the position of prime minister and launched a massive reconstruction project centering on Beirut and attracting substantial investment capital from Lebanese citizens who had moved overseas.

The south of Lebanon remained out of the sphere of the Lebanese government's influence. Israel's repeated attacks against Shia forces in the south—most notably in 1996—helped to fuel the rise of Hezbollah, a Shia political movement with ties to Iran. But after 22 years and growing weariness with battle, Israel finally withdrew unilaterally from southern Lebanon in 2000.

In February 2005, Prime Minister Hariri was assassinated by a massive car bomb in Beirut. Hariri had been at odds with Syria over efforts by Syrian allies in the parliament to extend the term of office of the president, who also was a Syrian ally. Fingers immediately pointed to Syria as the culprit for Hariri's murder, and a surge of anti-Syrian sentiment spread over the country. A major protest rally was held in Beirut to demand the withdrawal of Syrian forces and an investigation into the murder of Hariri; this protest, and subsequent ones, were dubbed the Cedar Revolution and led to a the creation of an anti-Syrian political coalition known as the March 14 Alliance, headed by Hariri's son, Saad. A competing pro-Syrian political coalition known as the March 8 Alliance formed soon afterward; its leading members were the Shia Hezbollah and Amal Parties. International pressure grew on Syria to withdraw its forces, and an interim report by the United Nations Special Tribunal for Lebanon indicated Syria was indeed behind the Harriri assassination further squeezed Damascus. Syria began withdrawing its troops, a process that was completed by April 2005 (Syrian agents and a network of Lebanese supporters remained behind). Parliamentary elections were held a few months later and resulted in a victory for the anti-Syrian March 14 Alliance coalition; Saad Hariri became prime minister.

Hezbollah, which remained in control of the south—where Lebanese army forces were not allowed to deploy—continued to carry out provocations against Israel. In July 2006, Hezbollah fighters attacked an Israeli patrol along the border, killing several people and taking two hostages. Israel retaliated with massive force directed not just at Hezbollah but at the entire Lebanese state. Israel's purpose was to force the Lebanese government to rein in Hezbollah, although virtually every Middle East specialist knew that this was impossible. Nevertheless, Israel destroyed much of Lebanon's infrastructure and killed nearly 3,000 Lebanese, most of whom were civilians. But Hezbollah fighters put up a surprisingly tough battle and rained rocket fire on towns in northern Israel. After 160 Israeli soldiers had been killed, Israel began to look for a way out and accepted a United Nations–brokered cease-fire.

Even after the withdrawal of Syrian troops in 2005, Lebanon remained politically fragile. Hezbollah's militia moved into West Beirut and fought battles with the Lebanese army. The fighting was quelled only by the intervention of the Arab League, which called an emergency meeting in Qatar that produced a new power-sharing agreement between the March 14 and March 8 Alliances and a new Lebanese president; under the new agreement, Hezbollah and other members of the March 8 Alliance have an effective veto over major cabinet decisions, which often has created political and

A supporter of assassinated Lebanese prime minister Rafik Hariri holds an anti-Syria sign during Hariri's funeral procession in Beirut in 2005. (AP Photo/ Mahmoud Tawil)

governmental gridlock. The fragile coalition government reflects the role of outside powers, as well: The United States, France, and Saudi Arabia openly support the March 14 Alliance, while Iran and Syria are major supporters of the March 8 Alliance.

In late 2010, rumors began circulating that the United Nations Special Tribunal for Lebanon would issue a final report—expected in 2011—that would implicate Hezbollah operatives in the assassination of Rafik Hariri. In response, Hezbollah's leadership claimed that Israel was responsible for the assassination and questioned the credibility of the most important tribunal witness. A report that accuses Hezbollah of involvement in Hariri's assassination would have dangerous implications for the country's stability and could very well produce a new round of fighting. In January 2011, Hezbollah withdrew its support for the Hariri government, causing it to fall and putting even more pressure on the government to reject the Special Tribunal's findings.

After five months of political brinkmanship and bargaining, Najib Mikati was appointed prime minister. A Sunni (as the prime minister is required to be), Mikati was the choice of Hezbollah, and he proceeded to appoint a cabinet dominated by members of the pro-Hezbollah, pro-Syria March 8 Alliance. None of former prime minister Hariri's supporters were appointed to the cabinet. Lebanon was left with a rigidly stratified political system that was incapable of undertaking any serious political or economic measures.

Lebanon's political situation remained in deadlock as the forces of change erupted in the Arab world, including in Syria. Lebanon was not directly affected by the people power movement in large part because it already enjoyed a considerable degree of freedom of speech and political organization and did not suffer under an authoritarian leader. Unrest in neighboring Syria, however, could limit the ability of Damascus to assist its allies in Lebanon, especially Hezbollah and the other members of the March 8 Alliance.

INTERNAL CONFLICTS

Most of the conflicts that could potentially lead to violence in Lebanon are related to internal conflicts among the Lebanese, reflecting the fact that the underlying causes of the country's traumatic civil war have never been resolved. It is important to recognize, however, that virtually every contentious internal issue in Lebanese politics is connected to external, regional issues, and the issues are often heavily influenced—or even directed—by external actors. In particular, Syria, Lebanon, Iran, and Saudi Arabia all have wielded considerable power over Lebanon, and each country has its own formal or informal allies within Lebanon.

Conflict between the March 8 and March 14 Alliances

Hezbollah, the dominant party in the March 8 Alliance, operates a military force separate from—and by most accounts, stronger than—the Lebanese Armed Forces. In April 2010, the U.S. Department of Defense reported that Hezbollah had "successfully exceeded" the amount of weaponry it possessed prior to the 2006 war with Israel and may have even acquired more advanced weaponry from Syria and Iran.[1] Hezbollah's weapons caches, while principally designed for use against Israel or Israeli forces, could also be used in any conflict with the government of Lebanon and its less well-armed military.

Despite calls from the United Nations, Western states, and its political opponents in Lebanon, Hezbollah has steadfastly refused to disband its military wing and commit itself to becoming a purely political movement (United Nations Security Council Resolution 1701 explicitly called on Hezbollah to disarm and allow the Lebanese armed forces to maintain security in southern Lebanon). Hezbollah's leaders argue that the Lebanese armed forces are inadequate to defend the country against Israel and point to the 2006 war—in which the effectiveness of Hezbollah's militia shocked Israel—as proof that its militia still is needed. Hezbollah's leaders also have refused calls to merge their militia forces into the Lebanese army and place them under army command.[2] By maintaining its militia, providing a wide array of social services in southern Lebanon, and operating a regional satellite television channel (al-Manar), Hezbollah effectively has become a state within a state. It is hard to imagine how this situation can be maintained in the long, or even medium, term without leading to either a fracturing of Lebanon or a return to civil war or both.

In addition, the fact that Hezbollah refuses to acknowledge Israel's right to exist—and in fact, declares its right to wage war against Israel—makes it virtually impossible for any Lebanese government to negotiate any agreements with Israel. It is thus conceivable that the Palestinian Authority and even Syria could reach peace agreements with Israel, leaving Lebanon as the sole rejectionist state.

At the end of 2011, the biggest threat to Lebanese stability centered on the yet-to-be-released report of the Special Tribunal for Lebanon. If the tribunal indicts Hezbollah in the former prime minister's assassination, the odds of renewed violence are high. Even if the tribunal does not indict Hezbollah members, or delays indefinitely the release of its report, it is difficult to imagine a scenario in which the March 8 and March 14 Alliances develop a peaceful modus operandi.

Conflict between the Shia and Sunni Communities

The tensions between the two alliances reflect broader tensions between Lebanon's Shia and Sunni communities, which in turn reflect regional divisions between

Shia and Sunni that are evident in Iraq and the Gulf countries—a stark example of how Lebanon's internal conflicts mirror regional ones.

The Hariri family is seen among Lebanese as the leader of the Sunni community, making it difficult for Sunni leaders to dissociate from an effort to identify those responsible for the former president's assassination. The Sunni community is supported by Saudi Arabia, a country with concerns of its own over the rising power of Shia Iran, as well as of Hezbollah, an organization with close ties to Iran. In July 2010, a Saudi-Syrian summit attempted to resolve the Lebanese impasse, but with little success. Afterward, the Saudis seemed to back away from the issue but could very well be drawn back in if the Sunni community appears to be under threat. Syria's minority Alawite government, under siege at home due to popular unrest, is the principal external backer of Hezbollah and the main conduit through which Iranian support to Hezbollah is provided. If the Syrian regime falls, Hezbollah will be weakened, although it likely will still enjoy the support of a plurality of Lebanese.

The likelihood of open conflict between Shia forces (led by Hezbollah but possibly joined by fellow members of the March 8 Alliance) and Sunni forces (possibly joined by certain Maronite Christian militias) remains very high regardless of how the tribunal issue is resolved (even if this issue is resolved through a negotiated compromise, it likely will be replaced by any of a host of other issues of disagreement). It is thus all too easy to envision Lebanon falling into another widespread civil war and "a meltdown of the post-Taif state."[3]

Palestinian Refugee Camps

Lebanon is home to around 400,000 Palestinian refugees and their descendents who fled from or were driven out of their homes by Israeli forces during Israel's 1948 war of independence. Roughly half of the Palestinian refugees in Lebanon still live in refugee camps run by the United Nations, and they suffer from extreme poverty. Lebanon has a policy of not granting citizenship to Palestinian refugees, who are left as effectively stateless persons. The vast majority of the Palestinians in Lebanon are Sunni Muslims, and, because of Lebanon's delicate and unstable sectarian balance, Christian as well as Shia leaders have not wanted to increase the number of Sunni citizens. But the discrimination against Palestinian refugees in Lebanon has gone far beyond merely denying them citizenship. In the 1950s and 1960s, they were not even allowed to leave the camps without explicit permission and were denied most forms of employment. Today, Palestinians still are denied access to Lebanon's health care system and may not attend Lebanese schools (the United Nations provides medical services and runs schools in the camps).

The Palestinian presence in Lebanon has been a contributing factor to the political turmoil that has plagued Lebanon since the early 1970s. When the PLO was based in Lebanon between 1972 and 1982, residents of the refugee camps were recruited to become fighters against Israel, thus making the camps, as well as the rest of Lebanon, the target of Israeli attacks. Moreover, PLO fighters joined in the Lebanese civil war in support of the leftist, mostly Sunni forces against the conservative, mostly Christian forces. A number of horrific massacres—perpetrated by both sides—took place during this fighting, culminating in the organized and Israeli-assisted massacres at the

Sabra and Shatila refugee camps by Christian militia, in which over 800 Palestinian civilians died.

Although the PLO departed Lebanon in 1982 and later signed an accord with Israel, the Palestinian refugee camps in Lebanon remain heavily armed and the base of a number of extremist organizations. In the spring and summer of 2007, the Nahr al-Bared camp near the northern city of Tripoli, home to around 30,000 Palestinians, was the scene of fierce fighting between Lebanese army troops and members of an armed organization called Fatah al-Islam (not related to the Palestinian liberation group known as Fatah). Fatah al-Islam is a radical Sunni group with loose connections to al-Qaeda formed when its leader, Shaker al-Abssi, spent time in Iraq fighting against U.S. forces. Al-Abssi returned to Lebanon via Syria and moved into the Nahr al-Bared camp.[4]

The 2007 fighting broke out when Lebanese government security forces staged an assault against a camp building that contained several Fatah al-Islam members who allegedly had been involved in a bank robbery. The ensuing firefight escalated rapidly into a battle between Fatah al-Islam's militia and the Lebanese army. Heavy shelling of the camp by the army caused extensive damage and loss of life, including many civilian casualties in the densely populated camp. After several months of fighting, the Lebanese army took control of the Nahr al-Bared camp. Shaker al-Abssi, however, escaped unharmed and later vowed that Fatah al-Islam would continue its fight against the Lebanese government. Reports in 2008 that al-Abssi was killed by Syrian security forces have never been confirmed.

Regardless of al-Abssi's fate, Fatah al-Islam—and other jihadist groups—remain a potential source of instability in Lebanon. And the Palestinian refugee camps remain a prime source of recruitment for extremist groups. The existence of the camps—and the fact that their eldest inhabitants are among the hundreds of thousands of Palestinians who fled their homes in 1948—exemplify the degree to which Lebanon's internal problems and sources of conflict reflect regional conflicts over which the Lebanese have virtually no control. While the Lebanese have been rightly criticized for the institutionalized discrimination against and lack of rights offered to Palestinians, the ultimate fate of the Palestinians in Lebanon will be decided by forces outside of Lebanon.

EXTERNAL CONFLICTS

Just as Lebanon's internal hot spots are closely linked to the interests and actions of outside actors, so too are the country's external hot spots linked to developments inside the country. Many of the Middle East's conflicts are played out in Lebanon via the interaction of Lebanese actors, either with each other or directly with an outside power. The fact that the Lebanese government has minimal control over powerful internal forces—such as Hezbollah—means that Lebanon will continue to be a proxy battlefield for regional powers.

War with Israel

The risk of an Israeli operation against Lebanon—which could range from a full-scale invasion to a targeted aerial bombing mission to a special forces action—is a

Hassan Nasrallah's Hezbollah Party is the most dominant force in Lebanese politics and the only sectarian party with its own armed forces. (AP Photo/Mahmoud Tawil)

constant factor in recent Lebanese history. Although Israeli operations usually are not against the Lebanese state, Israel's often indiscriminate use of firepower has meant that every Israeli incursion has led to extensive damage to Lebanon's infrastructure and considerable loss of civilian life. At times, Israeli operations have explicitly targeted Lebanese infrastructure in an attempt to pressure the Lebanese government to do what it is fundamentally unable to do: control the behavior of powerful armed groups such as Hezbollah or, in the period between 1972 and 1982, the PLO.

The greatest risk for a conflict with Israel relates to Hezbollah. The Shia organization's ongoing acquisition of weaponry will at some point reach a level that poses an unacceptable threat to Israeli security. Alternatively, either side could provoke the other to divert attention from other issues—Hezbollah, for example, might provoke a conflict with Israel to detract from the report of the Special Tribunal for Lebanon, while Israel might provoke a conflict in Lebanon to avoid making concessions to the Palestinians in peace talks. Hezbollah, as a leader of the rejectionist forces in the region that do not acknowledge Israel's right to exist, might be induced to provoke a conflict if it appeared that Israeli-Palestinian negotiations were moving forward productively. In addition, as a strong supporter of Iranian interests in the region, Hezbollah might be persuaded by Iran to launch an attack against Israel in retaliation for an Israeli attack on Iranian nuclear facilities (in expectation of this, Israel might launch a preemptive strike against Hezbollah prior to, or in coordination with, an attack on Iran). Finally, with tensions as high as they are, there is a constant risk that a conflict will break out even if neither side is seeking it.

The risk of a conflict in Lebanon between Hezbollah and Israel will remain high for the foreseeable and probably distant future. The nature of any such conflict will depend upon a number of factors, including how it started and by whom it was provoked. In addition, Israel's strategic objectives in any conflict with Hezbollah will determine the type of war Israel fights. If the goal is the destruction of Hezbollah as a military force—as it was, unsuccessfully, in 2006—Israel would likely stage a massive invasion accompanied by aerial bombardment of Hezbollah targets as well as of Hezbollah's supply lines into Syria. A more limited goal would translate into more limited military operations.[5]

Lebanon also has been a battleground for conflicts between Israel and Syria, although tensions eased substantially after Syrian troops withdrew from Lebanon in

2005. Even when both countries militarily occupied parts of Lebanon, they were very careful to avoid a direct confrontation, and that seems even less likely after 2005. Nevertheless, Syria's close ties to Hezbollah, and the fact that Hezbollah's weapon supply mostly arrives overland via Syrian territory, mean that a future conflict between Israel and Hezbollah could escalate into a wider Israeli-Syrian confrontation, with the field of battle likely being Lebanon.

Confrontation with Syria

Lebanon's relationship with Syria has been a source of discord and conflict from the beginning of each country's independence. Syrian nationalists have long argued that Lebanon never should have been separated from greater Syria by the French, and Syria never recognized Lebanon as an independent nation. The two countries maintained a tense relationship throughout their first decades of independence, with Syria attempting to affect events in Lebanon by working through allied parties and political figures and operating an extensive intelligence network in the country. While a Syrian takeover of Lebanon was not a realistic option, Syria's secondary goals—maintaining some degree of control over Lebanon's political process and preventing Lebanon from becoming a pro-Western or pro-Israeli outpost were easier to achieve. A vast network of economic ties—both formal and informal, legal and corrupt—also developed between the two countries.

When Syrian troops entered Lebanon during the height of Lebanon's civil war, many Lebanese were fearful that Damascus would exploit the opportunity to seize full control of the country. But the Syrian intervention came with the approval of the Arab League, and even of the United States, and was limited to specific regions of Lebanon. (Meanwhile, Israel began a series of interventions in southern Lebanon, culminating in its massive invasion of 1982, so that Lebanon found substantial parts of its territory under the control of foreign troops.) Although Syrian troops tried to maintain a low profile in Lebanon, their presence allowed Damascus to greatly expand its intelligence operations in Lebanon and conduct operations (including assassinations) against Lebanese politicians who it did not deem were sufficiently supportive of Syrian goals. Black market economic activity also thrived, as Syrian troops took advantage of Lebanon's more vibrant economy to smuggle goods back home.

In the face of heavy international pressure, accusations that Syria was behind the assassination of Lebanese prime minister Rafik Hariri, and coordinated Lebanese political opposition, Syria agreed to withdraw its troops from Lebanon in 2005. In 2009, Syria and Lebanon exchanged ambassadors for the first time in their history (Syria had never before officially recognized Lebanese sovereignty). But due to its close ties with Hezbollah—a function of Syria's close ties with Iran—Syria was able to maintain significant influence in Lebanon. In late 2010, Syria attempted to broker an agreement between Prime Minister Saad Hariri and Hezbollah over the issue of the Special Tribunal for Lebanon in an effort to maintain its central role in Lebanese politics. Without troops on the ground, Syria has been forced to use diplomacy and covert operations to achieve its objectives in Lebanon.

Syria will continue to play a major role in Lebanon as long as Syria remains a unified state with the ability to project power, a situation that is in doubt (see chapter 11 on Syria). Although Syria has recognized Lebanon's sovereignty, this in no way has diminished Syria's desire to ensure that the Lebanese state remain in its sphere of influence. At any given time, Syria will likely have allies in Lebanon, such as Hezbollah, as well as enemies, such as the more conservative and pro-Western members of the March 14 coalition. The possibility of Syrian troops returning to Lebanon, however, is remote. Syria has found it far easier (and less controversial) to achieve its goals through the control and manipulation of Lebanese actors. This may involve targeted violence—such as assassinations—but not military conflict. The political unrest that broke out in Syria in 2011 makes an armed intervention in Lebanon, or even the threat of such an intervention, far less likely.

A major Israeli intervention in Lebanon, however, could provoke the use of force by Syria if the country felt that its interests, or its allies, were being threatened to an unacceptable degree. But given the extreme asymmetry in military power between Syria and Israel, such a step would be taken very cautiously and only after all the alternatives had proven unsuccessful.

Another scenario that could lead to a military intervention by Syria would be the total collapse of the Lebanese state and a return to the kind of civil war that devastated the country in the 1970s; in that event, Syria may intervene to protect its allies, prevent its opponents from securing control, or merely to maintain a certain degree of order. Given the precarious politics of Lebanon, this possibility can never be ruled out.

A new scenario that arose in 2011 is the possible collapse of Syria into civil war. If this were to happen, Syria's allies in Lebanon would no longer be able to count on support from their patrons in Damascus, and Syria's collapse might embolden the March 14 Alliance to move against Hezbollah and its allies. Moreover, refugees fleeing turmoil in Syria would likely cross the border into Lebanon with potentially destabilizing consequences.

Iranian Intervention

Iran's influence and ability to interfere in Lebanese politics has grown substantially since 2005; in some ways, it was Iran that most aggressively filled the vacuum left by Syria's troop withdrawal. Iran's influence derives from its close relationship with Hezbollah at all levels—including weapons supplies, training, and financial support. This does not mean that Hezbollah is completely or permanently under the control of Iran, however; although they share the Shia religious denomination with Iran, Hezbollah's members are nevertheless Lebanese Arabs, not Persians. Moreover, Iran is not contiguous to Lebanon, so its direct support of Hezbollah requires cooperation from Syria, which has its own interests in Lebanon.

But as long as Hezbollah and Iran see eye to eye and their relationship is mutually beneficial, and as long as Syria is willing to provide a conduit for Iranian arms, Iran must be seen as a major player in Lebanese politics. This was evident in October

2010, when Iranian president Mahmoud Ahmadinejad visited southern Lebanon to a hero's welcome.

While Iran would not become directly involved in a conflagration in Lebanon, it has the influence with Hezbollah to persuade to the Lebanese group to act on its behalf, especially in the event of an Israeli or U.S. attack on Iran's nuclear facilities. Once again, Lebanon could end up being the battlefield for a conflict that is ostensibly between Iran and Israel. The consequences, however, would reverberate throughout the Lebanese polity and put the country's stability at serious risk.

NOTES

1. Casey Addis, "Lebanon: Background and U.S. Relations," *Congressional Research Service* (August 3, 2010), 1.

2. Paul Salem, "Tensions over Tribunal Threaten Country's Delicate Sectarian Balance," *Los Angeles Times* (October 1, 2010).

3. Ibid.

4. See Rebecca Bloom, *Backgrounder: Fatah al-Islam* (New York: Council on Foreign Relations, June 8, 2007).

5. See Daniel C. Kurtzer, *A Third Lebanon War* (New York: Council on Foreign Relations, July 12, 2010).

9   THE MAGHREB

The region known as the Maghreb—Arabic for "the West"—comprises the nations of Algeria, Libya, Morocco, and Tunisia, and has a total population of around 85 million.[1] Although the Maghreb is physically in Africa, it usually is considered part of the broader Middle East due to its majority Arab population and the predominance of Islam; all of the states of the Maghreb are members of the Arab League. Nevertheless, the Maghreb enjoys a distinct identity and history, and its location along the southern Mediterranean has led to more interaction with Europe than with the rest of the Middle East. Millions of Maghrebi immigrants work and live in Europe, and the region enjoys beneficial trade and commercial relationships with the European Union. France, in particular, maintains a special relationship with its former colonies of Algeria, Morocco, and Tunisia.

The Maghreb has not been the scene of such major conflicts as the eastern Arab world, but it has not been free of conflict by any means. Algeria suffered through a long and bloody war of independence from France, culminating in independence in 1962 but not before an estimated 1 million Algerians had been killed (Algeria's independence struggle was immortalized in the 1966 film *Battle of Algiers*). Between 1992 and 1998, Algeria witnessed a violent civil war between government forces and Islamist insurgents that left over 100,000 dead. Algeria still is not free of the insurgent threat.

Algeria also fought a short border war with Morocco in 1963 (popularly known as the Sand War) over disputed territory in the Sahara Desert. The war ended in a stalemate but served to solidify ongoing hostility between the two countries that survives to this day. The hostility was deepened in subsequent years by the fact that Morocco was ruled by a conservative pro-Western monarchy, while Algeria was under the control of a revolutionary pro-Soviet regime that viewed itself as part of the pan-Arab revolutionary nationalist movement. The Algerian-Moroccan conflict found a new front in 1975, when Morocco took over the former Spanish colony of Western Sahara.

The Western Sahara conflict has defined Moroccan foreign policy for over 30 years. The Moroccan monarchy had always claimed the Western Sahara as part of greater Morocco, and when Spain withdrew in 1975, Morocco took control of the northern part of the territory; in 1979, it assumed control of the entire region when Mauritania gave up its claims to the southern part of the Western Sahara. Thus began a protracted war between Moroccan troops and guerilla fighters of the Polisario Front, an organization of indigenous Saharawis who demanded independence for the territory. Algeria became the major supporter and arms supplier to the Polisario forces.[2] While the conflict has been subject to diplomatic efforts in recent years, it remains unresolved.

Both Morocco and Algeria have substantial Berber minority populations.[3] Berbers were the indigenous peoples of North Africa prior to the Arab invasion in the seventh century, and they have maintained many of their cultural and linguistic traditions. While some Berbers have assimilated into Algerian and Moroccan society, others have fought to preserve their culture and have been at odds with the national governments. Smaller Berber populations live in Tunisia and Libya.

Libya has had a checkered history since its independence in 1952. The former Italian colony initially was ruled by a conservative monarchy that hosted a major U.S. naval base. In 1969, the monarchy was overthrown in a coup by Col. Mu'ammar Gadhafi, a mercurial leader who espoused his own unique revolutionary political ideology that was opposed to both Marxism and capitalism. He used Libya's growing oil wealth to support a diverse range of international revolutionary groups, from radical Palestinian forces to the Irish Republican Army. He fought brief border skirmishes with Egypt after Cairo signed a peace treaty with Israel in 1979.

Growing hostility from the West—and the United States in particular—reached a peak in 1992, after Libya was accused of abetting the terrorist attack on Pan Am flight 103 over Lockerbie, Scotland. Faced with heavy economic and political sanctions, Gadhafi became increasingly isolated. In 2003, following the U.S. invasion of Iraq and newly declared war on terrorism, Libya suddenly agreed to settle outstanding legal claims related to the Pan Am 103 attack. Later that year, Libya announced it was ending its programs of develop weapons of mass destruction. The West gradually lifted sanctions, and in 2006 the United States reopened diplomatic relations with Libya that had been broken for over 20 years.

Tunisia is the only Maghrebi state that enjoyed a relatively peaceful history since independence under two authoritarian regimes and a dominant political party. France granted independence in 1956 after mostly nonviolent political agitation by Tunisian nationalists, and ties between the two countries remain close. Tunisia also managed to remain unaffected by civil war in neighboring Algeria and Mu'ammar Gadhafi's political radicalism in neighboring Libya. An Islamist extremist group known as al-Nahda staged some isolated terrorist attacks in Tunisia in the 1980s and 1990s, but the group was largely dismantled by Tunisian security forces, and its leader sent was into exile in London.

In January 2011, Tunisia's authoritarian government was overthrown by an unexpected and apparently unplanned massive popular uprising that was fueled by unemployment (especially among youth), inflation, and growing awareness (thanks in part to social networking technology) of extensive corruption by the Ben Ali family. The uprising was not led by any particular political movement or leader and left a political void amid random violence. The overthrow of Ben Ali is credited with sparking the demonstrations in Egypt that ultimately led to President Mubarak's ouster and a subsequent political chain reaction throughout the Arab world.

The most violent uprising occurred in Libya, where a full-fledged civil war broke out against the regime of Col. Mu'ammar Gadhafi, who had been in power since 1969. The opposition was led by a host of political interests, including tribal opponents of Gadhafi, Islamists, secular liberals, and disgruntled members of the armed forces. NATO forces joined in the fight in support of the anti-Gadhafi forces. Despite the victory of the anti-Gadhafi forces in late 2011—and the death of Gadhafi at the hands of armed rebels—the Libyan civil war is not likely to be resolved quickly. Gadhafi may still have supporters in the country who could cause trouble, but more important is the fact that Libya is a tribal and clan-based society, and, while various forces were unified in their struggle against Gadhafi, there is no guarantee that they will remain so in a post-Gadhafi era.

Algeria, still reeling from years of civil war and terrorism, has been governed unsteadily since 1999 by a coalition of political forces—including the army and security services—who support President Abdelaziz Bouteflika, whose third term as president is due to end in 2014. Given the region's now widespread opposition to long-serving leaders, it is likely that he will either step down in 2014 or his candidacy will provoke popular unrest. He has met calls for political change by reshuffling his cabinet, but serious political reform has not been enacted.

Morocco's King Mohammed VI enjoys a level of political legitimacy matched by few other Arab leaders. Protests broke out in the country in 2011 but were targeted more at the government rather than the monarchy, which remains the ultimate political authority despite the existence of a popularly elected parliament with over 20 political parties. The second largest party in parliament, the Islamist Party of Justice and Development (PJD), is not part of the governing coalition. The country's largest Islamist movement, the Justice and Charity Party, is opposed to the monarchy and thus is not a legally sanctioned party. In April 2011, the king announced the formation of an Advisory Committee for the Revision of the Constitution, but some of the youth-led protest organizations declared that they would not cooperate with it. In June 2011, the king went further and announced a series of reforms that, if taken to their logical conclusion, could lead to the Arab world's first true constitutional monarchy; but the process will be long and arduous.

As the Tunisian uprising and Libyan civil war demonstrate, the greatest threat to peace and stability throughout the Maghreb derives more from internal political dynamics than from external threats. Islamist extremist groups still conduct terrorist attacks in Algeria, and Morocco and Tunisia also have been the target of terrorist attacks. Until recently, Libya was too closed to the outside world to assess the presence of extremist groups, but the extensive opposition to the Gadhafi regime may ultimately take on an Islamist character. The organization known as al-Qaeda in the Islamic Maghreb (AQIM)—which began in Algeria but reportedly has cells throughout the region—could prove to be a disruptive force in coming years.

The threat of Islamist extremism in all four Maghreb countries is closely linked to another phenomenon: democratization. None of the four could be classified as a true democracy, although Algeria, Morocco, and Tunisia have held multiparty elections with varying degrees of freedom, and Tunisia appears to be on the road to genuine democracy. True democracy would not only risk depriving elites of their power, it also raises the risk of bringing Islamist parties into office. Denying these parties a voice in the democratic process, however, leaves them no alternative but insurgency. This, in a nutshell, is the dilemma facing each of the Maghreb states: how to bring about greater democracy and political participation without handing victory to extremist elements. One answer is to cultivate the development of opposition secular parties, but the region's history of closed political systems will make this a long and difficult process. In the meantime, the public clamoring for greater political participation will lead to conflict and possibly to greater influence by extremist movements. As the events in 2011 in Tunisia revealed, an uprising against authoritarian regimes in which there is no clear alternative is a recipe for prolonged unrest, political vacuums, and uncertain outcomes.

The challenge is compounded by the fact that all four Maghreb states suffer from demographic pressures—in particular, growing populations of young citizens who face a future with limited opportunities. The demographic problem is most acute in Algeria and Morocco and is least acute in Tunisia, but it affects all four societies and, ironically, was first translated into widespread political unrest in Tunisia. One traditional response to these demographic pressures has been migration to Europe—France, Spain, the Netherlands, and Italy all have large populations of North African migrants. In recent years, however, European states have begun to express concern about the rising tide of immigration, and there are worrying signs that this demographic safety valve may be closing in the face of resistance from xenophobic and ultranationalist parties in Europe. If emigration to Europe becomes more difficult, unemployment in the Maghreb states will rise, as will frustration and, potentially, political radicalization.

ALGERIA

Al-Qaeda in the Islamic Maghreb

Algeria's civil war started in 1991, when the military intervened to invalidate national elections that had been won, in a surprise vote, by the Islamic Salvation Front (FIS). The FIS responded by launching an insurgency campaign that raged for most of the decade, leaving more than 100,000 Algerians dead. The government eventually prevailed, and the FIS's armed wing, the Islamic Salvation Army, disbanded in 2000. The government also offered amnesty to any insurgents who turned in their weapons. Since then, the threat of a major uprising or insurgency has declined dramatically, but small groups of Islamist extremists—who refused to accept the FIS's defeat or participate in the amnesty offer—have staged terrorist attacks and car bombings throughout the country, and especially in the capital, Algiers.

The most worrisome of these groups is known as al-Qaeda in the Islamic Maghreb (AQIM), which claims an affiliation with the al-Qaeda organization, although an actual operational linkage has never been proven. Most likely, it is an independent organization that shares al-Qaeda's ideology of Islamist extremism and has adopted al-Qaeda's brand for purposes of recruitment and prestige.[4] Its first terrorist attacks were in 2002, and its stated goal is to overthrow the Algerian government and establish an Islamist state from which it would spread its activities to other Maghreb nations. European experts have expressed fears that AQIM could exploit large Maghrebi migrant communities in Europe to export their acts of violence even further afield.[5] These concerns about AQIM's global reach notwithstanding, Algeria has bore the brunt of the group's violence, perhaps most notably in the lethal attacks on the prime minister's office and United Nations (UN) buildings in Algiers in 2007. The Algerian government has responded aggressively, however, and analysts believe that AQIM's power has receded since the bloody events of 2007.[6] Nevertheless, officials still worry that the large population of unemployed youth in Algeria's urban areas will provide a steady recruiting pool for AQIM's activities. Moreover, there are concerns that AQIM is extending its networks into the Sahara Desert across Algeria and into Mauritania, where it might operate with a measure of impunity far from the gaze of central governments.[7]

Another problem posed by AQIM is that the uptick in domestic terror attacks appears to have slowed the advancement of Algerian democracy by providing government leaders with ample justification for curtailing political rights and further entrenching authoritarian forms of rule. Hopes for democratization that accompanied

Twin truck bombings by an affiliate of al-Qaeda targeted United Nations offices and a government building in Algiers in 2007. (AP Photo)

multiparty elections in May 2007 have largely dissipated. In 2008, parliament abolished the two-term limit on the presidency without any debate. The measure paved the way for President Abdelaziz Bouteflika, who came to power with strong military support in questionable elections of 1999, to secure a third term in 2009 with 90 percent of the vote. Several political parties boycotted the vote, complaining of insufficient transparency. Further extremist attacks will likely boost Bouteflika's efforts to solidify his position in power, which may contribute to political stability in the short term but will not help to promote democratic change.

Berber Opposition

Algeria's large Berber communities contributed to the struggle for independence against France but then felt marginalized when the newly independent Algerian government adopted a strong Arab identity and sought to suppress Berber culture and languages. During the Algerian civil war, the Berbers generally supported the government against the extremist Islamist forces, which they viewed as a greater threat to their culture and identity, but they also accused the government of failure to provide adequate protection of Berber villages against extremist attacks.

The 1980s witnessed several violent clashes between Berber activists and government forces, but in recent years, Berber opposition to the Algerian government normally has taken nonviolent forms—such as protests, demonstrations, and appeals to international human rights organizations. Berbers have not made demands for independence or separation from the Algerian state. Rather, their demands traditionally have focused more on respect for their cultural and linguistic rights. Some progress has been made in this regard, such as in 2004 when President Bouteflika responded to threats of a Berber boycott of elections by announcing that the Berber language of Tamazight would be recognized as a national language. Nevertheless, many grievances against the government remain, and advances in democratization in Algeria would provide a legitimate political outlet for Berber demands.[8]

Tensions with Morocco

Algeria and Morocco have a long history of tense relations, originating in part from postindependence border disagreements and in part due to the different natures of the two regimes: Algeria was a revolutionary, nonaligned republic, while Morocco was a conservative, pro-Western monarchy. The fact that Algeria and Morocco are the two largest nations in the Maghreb creates a certain degree of built-in competitiveness in their relationship as both vie to be leader of the region.

While many of the underlying causes of tension have receded in recent years (such as the ideological competition), the long history of mistrust continues to sour bilateral ties between the two countries. Nevertheless, the fact that the Western Sahara is no longer a shooting war has helped to ease tensions substantially (although Algeria and Morocco still maintain opposing positions on the conflict). Algeria's gradual move away from its socialist revolutionary past and toward a democratic, multiparty future also has eased some of the ideological conflict that characterized relations with Morocco in the early years of independence. Finally, changes in political leadership have affected relations in a positive way: the death of Morocco's King Hassan II in 1999 and the assumption of power by his son, King Mohammed VI, led Morocco to reassess its traditional hostility to Algeria. President Bouteflika's election in Algeria in 1999 started a similar process in Algeria. It also is significant that Bouteflika spent his youth in Morocco, where he trained for the independence struggle against France.

LIBYA

Libya came out of the international cold in 2003 and had resumed normal diplomatic ties with most Western nations by 2006. This successful process of reintegration into the world removed one of the greatest threats to the Libyan government: that of an attack by the United States—similar to the U.S. invasion of Iraq in 2003—designed to overthrow what had been characterized for years as a terrorist state. Indeed, twice in the 1980s, U.S. warplanes did attack Libya, and virtually every Western country imposed harsh economic sanctions on the regime of Mu'ammar Gadhafi. But by 2007, Libya was more of a target for Western business interests keen on access to the country's energy resources.[9]

This acceptance of Gadhafi by the international community after years of isolation shifted the threat to his regime to internal opposition forces. Without the specter of foreign attack, which served to unify Libyans, Gadhafi lost one of the main sources of his power. Moreover, the parade of Western businesspeople and tourists who visited Libya after its reopening exposed Libyans to the outside world. And when neighboring Tunisians and Egyptians rose up in protest against their long-ruling autocrats in early 2011, there was no way Libyans could avoid the revolutionary fever, despite Gadhafi's strong control over the media and the security forces.

But unlike Ben Ali and Mubarak, Gadhafi made it clear from the beginning that he would hold on to the end, as the violent response to protesters by his security forces demonstrated. Libya soon descended into civil war, with pro- and anti-Gadhafi forces holding various regions of the country (anti-Gadhafi forces were strongest in the east, and pro-Gadhafi forces were strongest in the west) and fighting for control of the major cities, Tripoli and Benghazi. Gadhafi's violent response to civilian protesters provoked international outrage, and in March 2011 the United Nations imposed a no-fly zone over Libya that was endorsed by the Arab League (Gadhafi was not helped by the fact that in his long and erratic rule he had alienated most of the Arab world's leaders and still was looked upon with disdain by the West). NATO forces, including the United States, launched air strikes against Gadhafi's forces as Western leaders demanded his ouster.

Prospects for post-Gadhafi Libya range from a protracted, and possibly very bloody, civil war among the various forces that brought down Gadhafi to a de facto division of the country along east-west lines to a shattered country under the control of regional warlords to a successful installation of a government of national unity and the creation of a democratic system. But despite the hopeful establishment of a National Transitional Council (NTC) in August 2011, the lack of a strong leader and of a clearly defined agenda for the nation's future—renders the situation fraught with uncertainty.

The challenge for the NTC is to maintain legitimacy with the Libyan people until democratic elections can be held—although elections in and of themselves will not guarantee political stability. Even with Gadhafi's ouster and death, Libya could remain in a state of civil strife for years to come as various forces vie for control.

Libyan Islamic Fighting Group

In the 1990s, Islamist extremists groups—perhaps inspired by the civil war in Algeria—staged a number of violent attacks across Libya, including an attempt to assassinate Colonel Gadhafi. The principal extremist organization is known as the Libyan Islamic Fighting Group (LIFG) and is composed of Libyans who, after fighting in Afghanistan against the Soviet Union in the 1980s, returned home with the goal of establishing an Islamist state in Libya. The LIFG was never believed to be larger than a few hundred activists.[10] Libyan security forces reacted aggressively, killing or arresting many members of the LIFG, and for several years, the Islamists appeared to be effectively under control. But in 2006 they staged a public demonstration against the government in the city of Benghazi. Although that event may have reflected some degree of power possessed by the movement, recent developments suggest that the government does not consider the Islamists to be a real threat. In 2010, the Libyan government, in a move spearheaded by Mu'ammar Gadhafi's son Saif al-Islam, released several hundred imprisoned Islamists—some from the LIFG—after they had completed a much-publicized rehabilitation program similar to Saudi and Yemeni initiatives.

It is unclear what role Islamist groups will play in the post-Gadhafi future.

Chad Conflict

Soon after Mu'ammar Gadhafi came to power in Libya in 1969, he aggressively renewed Libya's claim to the northern part of Chad, known as the Aouzou Strip (Libya had made claims to the strip as early as 1954). Gadhafi took advantage of an ongoing civil war in Chad between Muslim guerillas (known as the FROLINAT) and the central government, which was led by a Christian president. Libya provided arms to the FROLINAT and engineered a failed coup against the Chadian president, who eventually relented and agreed in 1972 to Libyan control of the Aouzou Strip. But Chadian opposition to the agreement grew, leading to the overthrow of the government and renewed resistance against Libya.

It soon became clear to most observers that Gadhafi was interested in more than just the Aouzou Strip: he really wanted to create a client state in Chad that would help expand his influence into sub-Saharan Africa.[11] Eventually, even the FROLINAT split into pro- and anti-Libyan factions. Meanwhile, Chad slipped further into civil war and chaos, and Libyan forces intervened several times between 1978 and 1987 in support of one or another faction, but always with the purpose of holding on to the Aouzou Strip. By 1987, however, virtually every faction in Chad had united behind the goal of ousting Libya from the strip. Libyan troops began to retreat in the face of this unified counterattack, and in late 1987 Gadhafi agreed to a cease-fire brokered by the Organization of African Unity.

In 1990, Libya and Chad agreed to submit the dispute over the Aouzou Strip to the International Court of Justice for resolution, which in 1994 ruled by a vote of 16 to 1 that the territory belonged to Chad. Libya accepted this outcome. Relations between the two countries have been peaceful ever since, and the Libya-Chad conflict no longer is an active issue for either country. Libya's preoccupation with civil war and the internal struggle for control makes it highly unlikely that any foreign issues will be on the agenda.

MOROCCO

Al-Sirrat Al-Moustakim

In May 2003, Islamist extremists conducted five simultaneous suicide attacks against Western and Jewish targets in Casablanca that killed 45 people. The attack came as a surprise to many Moroccans, who always had thought that their country was free of the kind of extremism that had plagued neighboring Algeria. Moroccan Islam had traditionally been characterized by moderation and tolerance; the country has one of the largest Jewish communities in the Arab world. Moreover, Morocco's ruling monarchy is widely regarded as a spiritual as well as secular force—one of the king's titles is Commander of the Faithful, and the popular belief is that the ruling family is descended from the Prophet Muhammad.

The perpetrators of the 2003 attack were believed to have been an indigenous radical Islamist group known as al-Sirrat al-Moustakim (the Straight Path), a small but radical organization that, like so many Islamist extremist groups in the Middle East, was founded by veterans of the Afghan war against the Soviet Union. Al-Sirrat al-Moustakim is not known to be officially connected to al-Qaeda, but al-Qaeda's former leader, Osama bin Laden, publicly called for attacks against Morocco due to the country's historically close ties with the United States and the West. It also is known that Moroccan radical Islamists, perhaps affiliated with al-Sirrat al-Moustakim, were involved in the deadly Madrid train bombings of 2004.

The Moroccan government responded to the attacks by launching a massive crackdown on Islamist activists, arresting thousands and confiscating weapons and explosives. New antiterrorism laws were pushed through the Moroccan parliament, and closer cooperation with Western antiterrorism efforts was established. Government authorities also began to scrutinize the teachings in Islamist schools and mosques to ensure that radical ideologies were not being expounded. Perhaps most significantly, the government launched a major economic reform campaign to address the issues of poverty and unemployment, and thus to remove some of the principal incentives that may drive young men to radical groups. But this campaign will take time and faces a daunting task—many Moroccan cities are characterized by teeming slums, and the country's economy has not grown sufficiently fast to make a large dent in unemployment and underemployment rates.

The threat of further Islamist extremist attacks remains significant. In September 2006, government security forces uncovered a plot to attack major tourist sites, and minor suicide attacks were carried out in March and August of 2007. Despite the government's roundup of many activists, it takes only a handful of committed people to carry out a dramatic terrorist attack. In addition, Morocco is a major tourist destination for Europeans and is open to considerable foreign influences, which then often become targets for the extremists. It is unlikely, however, that Islamist extremist forces would become strong enough to seriously threaten the state or provoke a mass uprising. Unlike most other Middle Eastern states, Morocco allows moderate Islamist political parties to participate in elections and hold seats in parliament, thus providing a legitimate outlet for those who support Islamist values.

Berber Opposition

Around 30 to 40 percent of Morocco's population is Berber, and an even larger number of Moroccans has some Berber ancestry. Berber opposition to the government centers on cultural issues, particularly language. Parents are not allowed to give their children traditional Berber names and instead must register them at birth with Arabic names. Berber activists claim that, as a result of restrictions on their language, Berber children—many of whom speak Tamazight at home—struggle in school and thus do not have the same opportunities as Arabic-speaking children do.

A large number of Berbers, however, are well assimilated into Moroccan life and even serve in government posts and the military. While the Moroccan government refuses to acknowledge Tamazight as an official language, King Mohammed VI has made several efforts to integrate Berber language and culture more fully into national institutions. In 2001, the king established a Royal Institute for Amazigh Studies to promote scholarly attention to Berber culture. Additionally, some schools offer Amazigh language classes to all students, though activists complain that most schools fail to provide the amount of instruction stipulated by the ministry of education. As intense as these cultural struggles may be, Morocco—unlike Algeria—does not have a history of violence between the government and Berbers, and future conflicts are most likely to remain peaceful. Berber political parties are represented in parliament, giving the community at least a platform for expressing its views.

Ceuta and Melilla

Ceuta (Sabta, in Arabic) and Melilla, two small port cities on the northern coast of Morocco, and a few small islands in the Mediterranean Sea have been Spanish-controlled territories for nearly five centuries. To the irritation of Moroccans, Spain retained control of the cities and islands after Morocco gained independence from France in 1956 and maintains a military base in Ceuta.

Morocco always has insisted that the Spanish territories are rightfully part of Morocco and should be returned, but Spain claims that the two cities and islands are an integral part of Spain and, thus, of the European Union (they are the only parts of European territory located in Africa). Spain has granted citizenship to all 150,000 residents of the territories, 40 percent of whom are Muslim (mostly Berbers), with the rest being Christian. By all accounts, a majority of the residents favor continued association with Spain.

Periodically, disagreement over the Spanish territories has led to serious tensions between Morocco and Spain. In July 2002, a small group of Moroccan forces occupied the tiny, uninhabited island of Perejil (a Spanish-claimed territory) and established a base there. Spain immediately protested and received the support of the European Union. Morocco's actions were endorsed by every member of the Arab League except for Algeria. Following a tense week, Spain dispatched naval and air force commandos to reoccupy the island, which occurred without incident. The Moroccan troops were flown to Ceuta and escorted to the Moroccan border. Spanish troops remained on the island until U.S. secretary of state Colin Powell was able to mediate an agreement by both sides to accept the status quo, at which time Perejil returned to its deserted and peaceful existence.[12]

In November 2007, Spain's king Juan Carlos paid an official visit to Ceuta and Melilla—the first such royal visit in 80 years. The visit sparked a loud protest from the Moroccan government, which temporarily withdrew its ambassador from Spain. Many Moroccans viewed the king's visit as a provocative act by Spain.

The biggest issue concerning the Spanish territories is that of illegal immigration. Every day, illegal immigrants from sub-Saharan Africa attempt to cross into Ceuta and Melilla (and thus into Europe) from Morocco. Spain has constructed fences along the borders of both Ceuta and Melilla to prevent the flow of immigrants, but with only limited success. The human rights organization Amnesty International has accused Spain and Morocco of using excessive force and violating the human rights of African immigrants trying to cross over the fences; scores of immigrants have died or been killed attempting to make the crossing.[13] Given the heightened concerns in Europe about immigration—and especially about the possible immigration of Islamist terrorists—this issue may become a greater source of tension between the two countries than the issue of territorial sovereignty.

Western Sahara

In 1991, Morocco and the forces of the Polisario Front agreed to a UN-supervised truce that ended their conflict, at least on the battlefield. The UN also proposed a political solution based on a referendum among the Western Sahara's population to allow them to choose either independence or unification with Morocco. But the two sides could never agree on precisely who should be allowed to vote in the referendum (Morocco has moved thousands of settlers into the territory since taking it over in 1975, and the Polisario wanted to disallow their participation in the referendum). Former U.S. secretary of state James Baker served as special UN envoy from 2000 to 2004 but was unable to break the deadlock. Morocco's firm position is that the question of its sovereignty over the territory is nonnegotiable, suggesting that it would not accept a referendum outcome that it does not win. Baker attempted to find a "third way"—official Moroccan sovereignty combined with extensive local autonomy—but did not receive enough support from either side to bring this about. A subsequent UN-led mediation effort collapsed in November 2010.

In the meantime, Morocco has continued to solidify its hold over the Western Sahara and constructed a sand wall along the desert border of the Western Sahara and

Algeria, the home base of the Polisario fighters. Morocco has also channeled significant financial resources into the region to build infrastructure and homes for Moroccan immigrants who continue to move into the region, which is rich in phosphates and offshore fishing resources.

The Polisario is weak and probably does not have the resources to wage a meaningful conflict against Morocco's well-armed military, although it probably could relaunch a limited guerilla war. The Polisario leadership, headquartered in the Algerian city of Tindouf just across the border from Western Sahara, has suffered from disagreements and defections, including several by former officials who have fled to Morocco and now advocate for Morocco's position in the conflict. Algeria continues to provide a haven for the Polisario but is no longer actively promoting or encouraging armed incursions into the Western Sahara. Algeria's continued support, however—even if just political in nature—has continued to hamper an improvement in relations between Morocco and Algeria. It also has hindered the development of the Arab Maghreb Union, an organization established with the goal of bringing about greater economic and political integration among the nations of the region. The Union has not convened a meeting since 1994, partially due to the persistent rancor between its two largest members over the Western Sahara. The possibility of a shooting war between the two Maghreb powers, however, is remote.

Domestic Political and Social Unrest

Morocco experienced a peaceful transfer of power in 1999, when King Hassan II died and his son, King Mohammed VI, assumed the crown. Morocco's monarchy enjoys widespread legitimacy and respect among the populace. The new king gained even greater popularity after assuming power and announcing plans to open the political system to greater participation; he also freed a number of political prisoners and dissidents who had been jailed by his father and loosened controls on the press. Demonstrations are not uncommon in Morocco, but they usually are focused on one or two issues and are not aimed at an overthrow of the regime (for example, several demonstrations in 2003 protested the U.S. invasion of Iraq and, indirectly, Morocco's close relationship with the United States).

Morocco has a multiparty parliament, which includes moderate Islamist parties (such as the Party of Justice and Development, which supports the monarchy), socialist parties, and a Berber party, as well as the dominant (and progovernment) Istiqlal Party. In September 2007 parliamentary elections, Istiqlal captured the largest number of seats, with the moderate Islamist PJD coming in second. But the voter turnout was extremely low, indicating to some observers that the Moroccan populace does not yet have faith in the democratic process.[14] The municipal elections of 2009 witnessed the rise of a new centrist party—known as Authenticity and Modernity—headed by a former royal insider; the party appears poised for success in the 2012 general elections. However, the party's origins in the palace coupled with the general political impotency of the legislature in comparison to the king appear to confirm the fact that significant progress toward a more open political system will occur only at the discretion of the king.

The greatest potential source of political unrest comes from al-Adl wal-Ihsane ("Justice and Charity"), an Islamist political organization that has not legally been recognized as an official political party. Al-Adl wal-Ihsane has called for the abolishment of the monarchy and the establishment of a republic, and, while it disavows violence, some fear that the organization could become radicalized if denied a voice in the political process.

Greater than the threat of political unrest is that of social unrest. Despite government efforts at economic reform, unemployment remains over 10 percent—perhaps as high as 20 percent in some urban slums—and much of the population lives in poverty. The country must maintain a fairly steady growth rate to ensure that enough jobs are available. Morocco's security forces are well trained and loyal to the king and historically have been able to control incidents of unrest, but the rising threat from terrorist groups (such as al-Sirrat al-Moustakim) means that future unrest could be more violent. To a large degree, the government is in competition with Islamist elements—both radical and moderate—to see who can best provide for the disaffected and marginalized among Morocco's population. In this kind of environment, social unrest against the government could very quickly assume an Islamist cast.

TUNISIA

Until the 2011 uprising that overthrew the government of Zine el-Abidine Ben Ali, Tunisia had been the most politically stable of all the Maghreb nations since achieving independence from France in 1956, and the country has not been involved in any conflicts with neighboring states. Perhaps not surprisingly, Tunisia also is the most economically advanced state in the Maghreb, with low poverty rates, a large middle class, and a relatively diverse economy. It was cracks in this economic success—especially high levels of youth unemployment—that led to the 2011 uprising.

Traditionally, Tunisia featured one of the Arab world's most secular societies, thanks in large part to the enlightened policies of its first president, Habib Bourguiba. But as Bourguiba's tenure in office extended indefinitely through the 1960s, 1970s, and 1980s, he became increasingly intolerant of political opposition. By the mid-1980s, the only significant outlet for political opposition to Bourguiba's government was through membership in the Mouvement de la tendance islamique (MTI), or Islamic Tendency Movement.

Bourguiba cracked down on the MTI aggressively, arresting hundreds of its members, including its founder and leader, Rached Ghannouchi. Bourguiba's harsh response to the MTI concerned many Tunisians, who, while not sympathetic to the group, generally favored a more peaceful and tolerant approach to politics. Ultimately, Bourguiba's response to the MTI led to his ouster in 1987, when his prime minister, Zine el-Abidine Ben Ali, assumed the presidency after a team of doctors declared the elderly Bourguiba unfit.

Throughout its history, Tunisia has been aligned with the West and was a close ally of the United States during the Cold War. This policy helped to assure Tunisia's security at a time when its neighbors, Algeria and Libya, were pursuing more radical policies. After the Cold War, Tunisia became a bit more circumspect in its approach to the United States and did not, for example, support either the 1991 or 2003 U.S. wars against Iraq. Nevertheless, Tunisia remained open to Western businesses and was a strong supporter of the U.S.-led war against international terrorism.

Ben Ali initially attempted to open up the political system, releasing a number of political prisoners (including some Islamists) and allowing opposition parties. He even attempted to reach out to the Islamists, although his government banned political parties based on religion. Tunisia's Islamist movement responded by changing the name of the MTI to the Hizb al-Nahda (Renaissance Party), and began staging public demonstrations and a violent attack against an office of Ben Ali's ruling party. Ben Ali responded quickly and severely to this renewed Islamist activism, which was especially disturbing in light of the violent civil war then under way in neighboring Algeria. The Tunisian government's tactics were strongly criticized in the West and among human rights organizations, but this did not deter Ben Ali from effectively eradicating the most extremist Islamist elements in Tunisian society. In the process, however, Ben Ali also clamped down on political discourse in general, and even secular opponents of the government found themselves suppressed. Along with the economic pressures mentioned above, these factors contributed to the 2011 uprising that forced Ben Ali out of office.

Islamist extremists still have a presence in Tunisia and periodically carry out attacks, but the government has not been under serious threat from Islamists since the 1980s and early 1990s. The stagnant political system, in which opposition parties have

Protestors burn a photo of former Tunisian president Zine El Abidine Ben Ali during a demonstration in Tunis. Ben Ali fled the country January 2011 after 23 years in power, pushed out by weeks of deadly protests driven by anger over joblessness, corruption, and repression. (AP Photo/Christophe Ena)

not been able to develop significant followings, would be a source of concern only if it were combined with popular opposition or a more powerful Islamist movement. In fact, Tunisians enjoy a very high standard of living, with low rates of poverty, good health care, and widespread educational opportunities. Women's rights are more advanced in Tunisia than anywhere else in the Arab world. As long as the country's economy offered opportunities, Islamist radicals had little human fodder from which to recruit. This does not mean, however, that a small number of extremists could not conduct acts of terrorism and violence, as indeed they have. The more uncertain situation Tunisia entered at the beginning of 2011 raised anew the specter of Islamic extremism, although Tunisia remained one of the most secular societies in the Arab world.

Ultimately, the combination of economic stagnation, poor job opportunities for the young, and political frustration (i.e., the inability to bring about a change in government through peaceful means) led to the uprisings that overthrew President Ben Ali in January 2011. In 2009, President Ben Ali was reelected to his fifth presidential term. He had amended the constitution twice to extend his rule beyond previously established term limits. Moreover, the ruling party of President Ben Ali—the Constitutional Democratic Rally (RCD)—dominated political life in Tunisia since before independence (the RCD was a direct descendent of the Destour Party, Tunisia's original independence movement). Other parties were allowed to compete in elections (except parties based on religion, which were banned), but no other political organizations were able to match the resources and political reach of the RCD. Until 2011, the RCD was able to meet the political aspirations of Tunisians by offering broad opportunities for participation and harsh suppression of dissent. Demands for greater political freedom and openness were frequently made by the intelligentsia, Tunisians living outside the country, and by prodemocracy organizations in the West. These demands—combined with economic crisis—eventually led to a level of political unrest that the government would not be able to control or suppress.

Tunisia entered a period of political instability following the ouster of Ben Ali. Several interim governments were appointed but then forced to resign when faced with accusations that they contained people associated with the Ben Ali regime or his formerly dominant political party, the RCD, which was banned. By May 2011, more than 50 new political parties had been established, and al-Nahda, the Islamist party that had been banned by Ben Ali, was reconstituted and legalized and garnered the most votes in the country's first national elections in October 2011.

Al-Nahda (and Other Islamist Extremists)

The formerly banned Islamist party al-Nahda is now the dominant political force in Tunisia, although it played virtually no role in the 2011 popular uprising. Under Ben Ali, most of its members were arrested, and its leader—Rached Ghannouchi—fled into in exile in London; he returned soon after the overthrow of Ben Ali. Tunisia is an overwhelmingly Muslim society, but its decades of religious tolerance and openness to the West mean that al-Nahda's best route to success will be to follow the path of more moderate Islamist parties, such as in Turkey. Al-Nahda's leadership has claimed for many years that it has renounced violence, and there is no serious evidence to refute this.

Groups loosely affiliated with al-Qaeda and other regional Islamist terrorist organizations, however, have made their presence known in Tunisia. In April 2002, a suicide truck-bomber attacked an ancient Jewish synagogue on the Tunisian resort island of Jerba (which has been home to a Jewish community for centuries). The attack left 21 dead, including a number of German and French tourists, and was the worst terrorist attack in Tunisian history. Al-Qaeda claimed responsibility for the bombing, which, significantly, targeted a Jewish site as well as Western tourists.

In December 2006 and January 2007, Tunisian security forces engaged in several gun battles with people who the government claimed were plotting terrorist attacks; over a dozen plotters were killed, and more were arrested. Such incidents will likely continue sporadically, especially if the AQIM organization is capable of expanding its influence and capabilities in the region. It is highly unlikely, however, that an Islamist insurgency—whether domestic in origin or a component of al-Qaeda—will seriously threaten the stability of the Tunisian government and state. Tunisia's security forces are well trained and have proven effective in suppressing armed opposition. Tunisia's economic success created little sympathy among Tunisians for extremist groups.

Domestic Unrest

Like most Middle Eastern states, Tunisia has experienced periods of domestic unrest related to economic distress or reactions to events occurring elsewhere in the Middle East (such as the U.S. wars against Iraq and the Israeli-Palestinian conflict). Given Tunisia's relative economic success, economic unrest was rare until late 2010 and early 2011. Unemployment is a chronic problem, but an extensive social welfare system (including free medical care and education) ensures that few Tunisians live in abject poverty. The bigger problem is underemployment—especially among young university graduates who cannot find employment suitable to their qualifications.

Even prior to 2011, there were some conflagrations fueled by economic grievances. In 2008, for example, the province of Gafsa in the south convulsed with broad protests against unemployment and unfair hiring practices on the part of a local phosphate extraction company. The government response was swift and harsh, imprisoning and allegedly torturing both participants in the protests and members of the press who covered the events.[15]

Whatever the nature of the new government that emerges in Tunisia, it will have to address economic expectations and potential social discontent. An open political process will facilitate debate over these issues but does not rule out the possibility of further political unrest.

NOTES

1. Central Intelligence Agency, *The World Fact Book 2011* https://www.cia.gov/library/publications/the-world-factbook/index.html.

2. An excellent account of the Morocco-Polisario war is Tony Hodges, *Western Sahara: The Roots of a Desert War* (Westport, CT: Lawrence Hill Books, 1983).

3. The Berbers are a minority in each country only in terms of self-identification. In fact, most scholars believe that the majority of people in Morocco and Algeria are at least partially of Berber descent, even if they identify as Arab.

4. For an excellent analysis of al-Qaeda in the Maghreb, see Noureddine Jebnoun, *Is the Maghreb the Next Afghanistan?* Center for Contemporary Arab Studies Monograph (January 2008).

5. See Guida Steinberg and Isabelle Werenfels, *Al-Qaida in the Maghreb: Just a New Name or Indeed a New Threat?* (German Institute for International and Security Affairs, March 2007).

6. See Jean-Pierre Filliu, *Al-Qaeda in the Islamic Maghreb: Algerian Challenge or Global Threat?* Carnegie Endowment for International Peace, Middle East Program, no. 104 (October 2009), http://www.carnegieendowment.org/files/al-qaeda_islamic_maghreb.pdf.

7. David Lewis, "Analysis—Raid Shows Resolve, Trouble in Fight vs. Sahara's Qaeda," *Reuters Africa* (July 27, 2010), http://af.reuters.com/article/mauritaniaNews/idAFLDE66P1OA20100727.

8. See "Assessment for Berbers in Algeria," *Minorities at Risk*, Center for International Development and Conflict Management, University of Maryland, http://www.cidcm.umd.edu/mar.

9. For an overview of U.S.-Libyan relations, see Christopher M. Blanchard, "Libya: Background and U.S. Relations," Congressional Research Service, *CRS Report for Congress* (June 19, 2007), http://www.fas.org/sgp/crs/mideast/RL33142.pdf.

10. Michael Clark, *In the Spotlight: The Libyan-Islamic Fighting Group,* Center for Defense Information (January 18, 2005).

11. See Mario J. Azevedo, *Roots of Violence: A History of War in Chad* (London: Taylor & Francis, 2007).

12. Tracy Wilkinson, "Spain's Little Piece of Africa," *Los Angeles Times* (January 11, 2006).

13. Amnesty International, *Spain and Morocco: Failure to Protect the Rights of Migrants* (October 26, 2006).

14. See Asmae Otmani, "Morocco: The Elections Are Over; Let Voter Education Begin," *Arab Reform Bulletin* (September 18, 2007), http://carnegieendowment.org/arb/?fa=show&article=20837.

15. Human Rights Watch, *Tunisia: Quash Unfair Convictions* (April 26, 2010), http://www.hrw.org/en/news/2010/04/26/tunisia-quash-unfair-convictions.

10   SAUDI ARABIA

The Saudi state is the creation of Abdul Aziz Ibn Saud, the leader of a powerful family composed of several related clans originally from the Nejd area of the Arabian Peninsula. The Saud family had attempted to create a political entity independent of the Ottoman Empire (which ruled the region) as early as 1744, when Mohammed Ibn Saud forged an alliance with Mohammed Ibn Abdul Wahhab, a religious reformer, to spread Wahhab's pure form of Sunni Islam throughout the region. This effort, along with another attempt in 1884, failed.

But by the early 20th century, the Ottomans had become sufficiently weakened that they were unable to resist the Saud's power, which was based on family unity and the passionate devotion of the Wahhabist religious reformers. In 1901, Abdul Aziz Ibn Saud conquered Riyadh, an oasis town in the middle of the Arabian Peninsula. From here his desert forces conquered the entire Nejd region and then marched eastward to capture the lands along the Persian Gulf. Following World War I and the final collapse of the Ottoman Empire, Ibn Saud directed his ambitions westward. By securing control of Mecca and Medina, Islam's two holiest cities located in what was then the region of Hejaz, Ibn Saud could solidify his family's position as the protectors of the Islamic faith, and in the process provide religious legitimacy to the Wahhabist belief system.

The only one who stood in his way was Hussein, the sherif of Mecca, who controlled Hejaz and who had been a British ally during the war. Ibn Saud's desert warriors succeeded in capturing Mecca in 1924 and Medina in 1926, driving Hussein's forces out of the Arabian Peninsula, where his descendents (with British assistance) established the Hashemite dynasty in Jordan. Ibn Saud declared the establishment of the Kingdom of Saudi Arabia.

The Saud family has ruled the country ever since, and every Saudi king has been a son of Ibn Saud, who had three wives. The family is loosely divided among three clans, who, for the most part, have been sufficiently unified to keep the state together for over 80 years. All together, the Saud family includes thousands of princes, each of whom holds a position of power at the national or local levels. Despite the royal trappings, the Saud family's deep reach and broad-based hierarchy in many ways more resembles a political machine than a traditional European-style monarchy.

While the Saud family has been the foundation of the Saudi state since its inception, two other factors have helped to define Saudi Arabia: Islam and oil. The Saud-Wahhabi alliance has remained strong, largely because they legitimize each other. Wahhabism is a strictly conservative interpretation of Islam, which rejects all non-Sunni sects (including Shiism). Wahhabism's literal interpretation of the Qu'ran has made Saudi Arabia a somewhat austere state, in which women's rights are curtailed, alcohol is forbidden, and other religions are forbidden to practice.

The Wahhabist clerics are the guardians of religious law, and as a country that officially is ruled by sharia (the system of Islamic law), the clerics are in effect the country's legal system. Even political decisions must past muster with the religious authorities. For example, after Iraq's invasion of Kuwait in 1990—which posed a direct security threat to Saudi Arabia—the Saudi king did not ask for U.S. military aid until the religious authorities issued a fatwa (a religious edict) that declared such assistance from "infidels" to be consistent with Islam. The clerics also control the religious police, who act independently to enforce Islamic strictures.

Wahhabism has also served as the ideological framework for Islamic extremists, including Osama bin Laden's al-Qaeda movement. This connection to extremist forces has often placed the Saudi state in an uncomfortable position, especially after the al-Qaeda terrorist attacks of September 11, 2001, in which 15 of the 18 hijackers were Saudi nationals. It has also made it difficult for those in the kingdom (including members of the Saud family) who wish to enact reforms or allow more personal freedoms. Despite its conservative nature and its alliance with the Wahhabist clerics, the Saudi state has been the target of Islamic extremist groups, including al-Qaeda. Nevertheless, the Saud family and the Wahhabist clerics need each other, and their mutually beneficial alliance shows no signs of weakening.

The other factor that has helped to define Saudi Arabia is oil, first discovered in the 1930s by U.S. oil companies. The United States immediately understood the importance that Saudi Arabia would play in the world, and in 1945 President Franklin Roosevelt met with King Ibn Saud to negotiate what was to become a de facto alliance between the two countries. The benefits of Saudi Arabia's oil wealth first became apparent in the 1970s, when soaring international oil prices delivered a financial boon to the kingdom. The Saud family launched a massive modernization program that led to the building of entire new cities as well as universities, airports, and all the other trappings of modernity. Thousands of U.S. and other Western businessmen flooded the kingdom in search of business deals and sales opportunities.

Saudi Arabia is believed to contain up to 25 percent of the world's known oil reserves and has been the leading force in the Organization for the Petroleum Exporting Countries (OPEC). Its oil wealth also has rendered Saudi Arabia of great strategic importance to the West. Successive U.S. administrations have sought to defend the conservative Saudi state through arms sales and an implicit defense pact, which was most evident in 1991, when the United States and a coalition of allies took military action to drive Saddam Hussein's Iraqi forces out of neighboring Kuwait.

Saudi policy has thus focused on maintaining a delicate balancing act: remaining true to its conservative religious principles, which in many fundamental ways is incompatible with (and even hostile to) Western influence and Western values, while simultaneously forging a strong de facto alliance with the United States to preserve the kingdom's security. This balancing act has not always been easy for Saudi rulers.

Saudi Arabia's security is further complicated by demographic trends. Of the kingdom's population of around 24 million (not counting more than 5 million foreign guest workers), over 60 percent are under the age of 25.[1] While the official unemployment rate among Saudi men is around 8 percent (employment figures are not kept for women, most of who do not work), some sources estimate that the true unemployment rate is closer to 25 percent, especially for young men.[2] Because of its oil wealth, the Saudi state is capable of providing an extensive safety net for the unemployed, thus masking to a large degree the social impacts of unemployment. The psychological impacts, however, can be serious, and the attraction of many young Saudi men to extremist religious movements may in part be a result of their unemployment and uncertain futures.

Saudi Arabia was largely spared unrest during the events in the Arab world of the spring of 2011. Although opposition elements made several attempts to inspire protests, the demonstrations that did occur were disorganized and poorly attended. Saudi

Saudi men salute as they carry a national flag during street celebrations and support for Saudi king Abdullah. The Saudi king promised a multi-billion-dollar package of reforms, raises, cash, loans, and apartments in what appeared to be an attempt to prevent the kind of unrest that spread throughout the region in 2011. (AP Photo)

security forces were mobilized to forestall any serious disruptions. Moreover, the nature of Saudi Arabia's political system is such that members of the large royal family each have their own patronage networks and thus are able to ensure that basic needs are met and that people enjoy a sense of access to power. Moreover, King Abdullah was genuinely popular with most elements of Saudi society and was regarded by many as being in favor of carefully controlled but significant political reform. The economic distress and hopelessness behind the uprisings in Egypt, Tunisia, and elsewhere in the Middle East did not exist in Saudi Arabia, which continues to provide cradle-to-grave social services to its people.

Nevertheless, Saudi Arabia is not forever invulnerable to popular protests against a monarchy that is in essence all-powerful. The large youth population, the growing exposure by Saudis to outside influences, and the regional trend toward more representative government will continue to influence Saudi society. The defining moment may be when the next succession occurs.

Saudi Arabia faces a number of conflicts and potential conflicts, the most serious of which emanate from domestic sources and a possible confrontation with Iran.

INTERNAL OPPOSITION: SUNNI (WAHABBIST) EXTREMISTS

The Saud family's alliance with the Wahhabist religious authorities first started to show signs of strain in the middle 1970s, after a global rise in oil process produced windfall profits for the kingdom, leading to a massive investment spree that brought thousands of Western businesspeople to the kingdom. The more conservative elements of the religious establishment were outraged by the presence of infidels in the kingdom and feared that the Saudi government was becoming too close to Western powers, both economically and militarily.

In 1979, hundreds of armed religious radicals seized control of Mecca's Grand Mosque, taking thousands of hostages. The radicals' demands, broadcast over the Mosque's loudspeakers, included a cessation of oil sales to the United States and the expulsion of all Westerners from Saudi Arabia. Saudi security forces besieged the mosque, and a two-week-long battle ensued. The insurgents finally surrendered, but not before over 250 hostages, radicals, and Saudi troops had been killed.[3]

After this incident, Saudi leaders made significant concessions to the religious authorities, including plowing billions of dollars into religious schools and institutions to appease radical elements.[4] The kingdom also encouraged—and helped to finance—the Afghan resistance to the Soviet invasion, including the participation of thousands of Saudi extremists who might otherwise have been sowing dissent within the kingdom.

But the Iraqi invasion of Kuwait in 1990 generated new challenges. Although Islamist groups were by and large opposed to Saddam Hussein's secular Baath government in Iraq, many devout Muslims were horrified by the stationing of U.S. and other Western troops on Saudi soil. Although Saudi officials were careful to secure approval from clerics before allowing foreign troops into the country, many more radical Islamic groups (such as Osama bin Laden's al-Qaeda organization) viewed their presence as blasphemous. Tensions between the Saudi government and extremist groups rose following the war, when U.S. troops remained in Saudi Arabia even after Saddam's ouster from Kuwait. Moreover, hundreds of Saudi extremists who had been dispatched to Afghanistan to fight Soviet forces in the 1980s had now returned home with a new appreciation for the methods of insurgency.

In June 1996, a U.S. military housing complex in eastern Saudi Arabia was attacked by terrorists who exploded a truck bomb laden with thousands of pounds of explosives next to the eight-story Khobar Towers Building. The attack killed 19 U.S. Air Force servicemen. Responsibility for the attack was blamed variously on Saudi extremist groups, Lebanese extremist groups, and the government of Iran. After extensive investigation over several years, the consensus grew that that al-Qaeda was the culprit (this conclusion was reached by both William Perry, who was U.S. secretary of defense at the time, and later by the National Commission on Terrorist Attacks Upon the United States—known as the 9/11 Commission).[5]

The September 2001 al-Qaeda terrorist attacks on the United States, in which 15 of the 19 hijackers were proven to be Saudis, sent shudders throughout the Saudi ruling family and led to a serious rift between the United States and Saudi Arabia. The Saudis scrambled to both deny that the kingdom itself was threatened by extremists groups while simultaneously launching an internal investigation to identify and detain al-Qaeda activists and sympathizers. The country also created an impressive antiterrorism training center (which itself was attacked by terrorists in 2004) and began rooting out al-Qaeda cells and killing or detaining hundreds of al-Qaeda operatives and choking off the extremists groups' financing. The Saudi military also conducted an internal investigation to identify any members of the armed forces who were sympathetic to the extremists. Between 2003 and 2005, 57 Saudi troops and an untold number of insurgents were killed in antiterrorism operations in Saudi Arabia. By 2009, Saudi leaders were claiming that all al-Qaeda insurgents in the kingdom had either been killed or had fled to Afghanistan or Yemen (the fact that Yemen borders Saudi Arabia, however, means that the threat has been merely pushed across the border—the threat emanating from Yemen is discussed below).[6]

Along with harsh tactics of suppression, the Saudi government also instituted soft tactics against extremist elements, including rehabilitation of prisoners and the provision of jobs and financial assistance to former jihadists. Progovernment clerics have been sent to schools and community centers to advocate against violence and in favor of the state. The Saudis claim that these unconventional programs have been successful, and they were praised by U.S. defense secretary Robert Gates during a 2009 visit to the kingdom.[7]

There is no doubt that the extremist threat in and to Saudi Arabia had lessened by the end of the decade, and the death of al-Qaeda leader Osama bin Laden dealt a further blow to the jihadist movement. But the underlying sources of Wahhabist extremism remain, principally anger toward the government for its close ties to the United States and opposition to voices within the kingdom that advocate for modernization and social reforms. Moreover, the level of extremist activism in the kingdom is to a significant degree determined by broader developments within the Islamic world, including the plight of the Palestinians and the conflicts in Afghanistan and Pakistan. A sudden and violent resurgence of Wahhabist extremism thus cannot be ruled out and may be especially evident during a future succession period.

INTERNAL OPPOSITION: THE SHIA AND ISMAILI MINORITIES

Shia Muslims are believed to account for about 15 percent of Saudi Arabia's population of 28 million, although the kingdom publishes no official tally of the Shia population. Saudi Shia are concentrated principally in the eastern part of the kingdom and are heavily represented—perhaps even a majority—in the cities of Dammam, Qatif, and al Hasa, important centers of oil production and refining.

Abdul Aziz Ibn Saud promised to protect the Shia minority when he founded the Saudi kingdom, but over the years the Shia have been treated with distrust and discrimination. The predominant Wahhabi religious movement views the Shia as heretical, and Wahhabi imams frequently have incited against the Shia, placing the Saudi government in the uncomfortable position of defending the Shia minority against the religious leadership with whom it is in alliance.

Many Saudi Shia were inspired by the 1979 Islamic revolution in predominantly Shia Iran that led to civil disobedience, protests, and acts of violence by Saudi Shia for much of the 1980s. The Saudi government responded forcefully and was never seriously threatened, even in areas where the Shia population was large. Nevertheless, the kingdom was sufficiently unsettled by the disturbances that in 1993, King Fahd negotiated an understanding with Shia leaders whereby the state would act to remove aspects of discrimination and the Shia community would agree to cease accepting assistance from abroad (principally Iran). Both sides seemed to acknowledge that violence was in the interests of neither.

The al-Qaeda attacks against the United States in 2001, and the subsequent crackdown on al-Qaeda activities in the kingdom, served to further ease relations with the Shia minority, for it was clear that the greatest threat from religious extremism in Saudi Arabia derived from extremist Sunnis, not Shia. Moreover, the more secular or progressive elements of both Sunni and Shia society found a new logic in working together to prevent the rise of extremism.

The 2003 U.S. invasion of Iraq, which led to the overthrow of Saddam Hussein's regime, created a new challenge in relations between Sunni and Shia in Saudi Arabia. Saddam's regime had been Sunni dominated, even though Iraq's population is majority Shia. Within months of his overthrow, it became increasingly clear to most observers in the region that either Iraq's Shia would become the dominant force in a unified Iraq or the country would disintegrate along sectarian lines and a majority Shia state would be created in southern Iraq, along the Saudi border. Either prospect was worrying to Saudi Sunnis, explaining why many young Saudi Wahhabists have volunteered to fight for Sunni extremist groups in Iraq. The Saudi government also has expressed concern about the Shia domination of Iraq and about the threat of Iranian influence over Iraq's political development.

But for Saudi Arabia's Shia population, the rise of a Shia-dominated government in neighboring Iraq was seen as a positive development and raised the possibility of the first Shia-ruled Arab state (Iran, although Shia ruled, is not Arab). In part to prevent a new round of unrest, Saudi king Abdullah met with Shia leaders soon after assuming the throne in 2005. Abdullah promised to undertake new efforts to counter both official and unofficial discrimination against the Shia and also used the occasion to release several Shia clerics who had been arrested during earlier crackdowns. The biggest challenge for the kingdom, however, will be to ensure that Wahhabist clerics follow the king's lead and support a more fully integrated Saudi society.

The unrest that broke out among the Shia community in Bahrain in early 2011 was worrying for the kingdom because of Bahrain's proximity to the eastern areas of the kingdom, which also are heavily populated by Shia. The kingdom's support for the Sunni minority monarchy in Bahrain—in the form of a contingent of Saudi troops who were sent to help quell the uprising—is indicative of the kingdom's concerns. An intensification of the Shia-Sunni conflict in Bahrain, which appears inevitable in light of the harsh response against Shia protesters by the Bahraini government, will have serious reverberations in Saudi Arabia.

In addition, general dissent could, over time, lead to more demonstrative actions by the Saudi Shia community. In addition to events in Bahrain, developments in Iraq and the overall evolution of Saudi-Iranian relations will affect the relationship between Sunni and Shia in Saudi Arabia. Of particular concern would be marginalization or oppression of the Sunni community in Iraq by the majority Shia government. In that event, Sunni extremists in Saudi Arabia might seek revenge by attacking the local Shia population, and many of these potential Sunni extremists will have had experience conducting insurgency because of their service in Iraq.

A further danger would derive from efforts by some Sunni leaders in the region—such as Jordan's King Abdullah—to portray the region as drifting into a Shia-Sunni confrontation. Saudi Arabia has understandably discouraged such a perspective, but the kingdom's relations with Shia Iran and developments in Iraq (and to a lesser degree in Lebanon, where the single largest segment of the population is Shia) could encourage more people in the region to align more with their religious identities than their national identities. Such a development could only bode ill for Sunni-Shia relations in Saudi Arabia.

Saudi Arabia also is home to several hundred thousand Ismailis, an Islamic sect that is more closely connected to Shiism than to Sunnism. The Ismailis live primarily in the southwestern part of the kingdom in the province of Najran, bordering Yemen. The Ismailis—who, like the Shia, are regarded as a heretical sect by Wahhabist Sunnis—have suffered from discrimination and lack of access to government jobs and other opportunities.[8] In early 2000, the Saudi government closed several Ismaili mosques and arrested several Ismaili clerics just prior to a religious holiday, sparking protests and demonstrations in Najran city. Resulting demonstrations by Ismailis led to a shoot-out at a Najran hotel in which several Ismailis were killed and hundreds arrested. The government crackdown lasted for several months.

The Ismailis do not pose as a great a threat to the kingdom's stability as do their fellow Shia in the Eastern Province, in large part due to their remoteness from other parts of the kingdom and their distance from the Shia centers of Iraq and Iran. Nevertheless, Ismailis could take advantage of generalized dissent within Saudi Arabia to press harder for their rights, and, given the history of the government's response to such protestations, open conflict is not out of the question. Moreover, Najan's proximity to Yemen means that the region could become entangled in any conflict scenario involving Saudi Arabia and Yemen.

STRATEGIC COMPETITION WITH IRAN

There are several fundamental reasons why Saudi Arabia and Iran are almost destined to be competitors, if not necessarily enemies, regardless of the nature of each country's government: They are the two most powerful states in the Persian Gulf region; they vie for leadership within OPEC; Saudi Arabia is predominantly Sunni, while Iran is predominantly Shia; and the Saudis are Arabs, while Iranians are Persians. Thus, even during the period of the shah's rule in Iran, when both countries were monarchies and close allies of the United States (indeed, the United States viewed the two states as the pillars of stability in the Gulf region), tensions often arose over issues such as the sovereignty of small Gulf islands and oil production levels, and each country watched suspiciously as the other sought to modernize and expand its military (although both countries were armed primarily by the United States). Fundamentally, each sought to be recognized as the leading power in the Gulf region, a competition rendered more complex by the disparities in size (Iran is more than twice as populous as Saudi Arabia) and oil wealth (Saudi Arabia's petroleum reserves are substantially greater than Iran's).

The underlying competition between Saudi Arabia and Iran became outright confrontation in 1979, when the revolution led by Ayatollah Khomeini overthrew the shah and established the Islamic Republic. Overnight, the Saudis' former strategic friend—if not ally—had become their arch enemy. The new regime in Tehran called openly for the overthrow of the Saudi royal family and questioned the legitimacy of Wahhabi theology. Under the shah, who had attempted to rule Iran in a secular manner, the Shia-Sunni rift was downplayed; but under the ayatollahs, Iran declared itself a Shia Islamic republic and strictly enforced the practice of Shia theology. Saudi leaders openly feared that the Shia population in the kingdom would become a "fifth column" and that Iran would use the Saudi Shia to undermine the Saud monarchy.[9] The sectarian division now became the defining feature of the Saudi-Iranian relationship, along with the fiercely anti-U.S. position of the new Iranian government.

The outbreak of war between Iran and Iraq in 1980 further strained relations between Saudi Arabia and Iran (even though the war was instigated by Iraq). Although Saudi leaders were never close to the secular Baathist Iraqi regime of Saddam Hussein, they clearly viewed Iran as a greater threat—and Saddam, despite his flaws, was a Sunni; if his regime were to fall at the hands of Iran, the Shia revolution in Tehran would win a critical victory, one that the Saudis could not accept.

The Saudis provided aid to Iraq in two critical and direct ways: First, they provided tens of billions of dollars in direct financial assistance and encouraged their oil-rich Arab neighbors, such as Kuwait and the United Arab Emirates, to do the same. Second, they dramatically increased their production of oil, causing oil process to plummet by nearly 50 percent. The fall in oil prices made it much more difficult for Iran to fund its war effort. Iran deeply resented the Saudi support for Saddam and threatened retaliation. The two states were in a virtual cold war, although each was careful to avoid a direct military confrontation.

A major crisis in the Saudi-Iranian relationship occurred in 1987, when Iranian pilgrims conducting the hajj in Mecca staged a demonstration in support of the Islamic Revolution. The resulting battle with Saudi security forces led to the deaths of nearly

500 Iranians and to the severing of diplomatic relations between the two countries. The demonstration confirmed Saudi fears that Iran was intent upon undermining the Saudi regime; this incident marked the lowest point in Saudi-Iranian relations, and possibly the most dangerous as well.

But by the early 1990s, several factors served to moderate the animosity between the two countries. Iran and Iraq agreed to a cease-fire in 1988, which ended the most dangerous element in Saudi-Iranian relations and also left Iran militarily drained and much less of an overt threat to Saudi Arabia. The death in 1989 of Iran's ultimate leader, Ayatollah Khomeini, created an internal power struggle that prevented Iran from being as aggressive in exporting its revolution as it had been in the previous decade. More-over, Saddam Hussein's invasion of Kuwait in 1990 dramatically shifted regional dynamics: the Saudis now viewed their erstwhile ally Iraq as their greatest threat, a view shared by Iran. The two nations restored diplomatic relations in late 1991.

By the late 1990s, relations had improved even further. Iran was led by a succession of moderate leaders—at least compared with the original postrevolution leadership—who sought a more peaceful and pragmatic relationship with Saudi Arabia.[10] The presence of U.S. forces in the kingdom during and following the Iraqi invasion of Kuwait was a cause of concern to Iran but also made the Saudis feel more secure, thus allowing them to explore a modus vivendi with Iran. In 1990, Iranian president Khatami paid a state visit to Jeddah, an event that would have been almost impossible to imagine a few years earlier.

The thaw in Saudi-Iranian relations did not remove the underlying competitive factors, but it did create an environment in which disagreements could be discussed at high levels and be less subject to misunderstanding. The September 11, 2001, terrorist attacks on the United States further strengthened the growing rapprochement between Saudi Arabia and Iran, because both countries feared al-Qaeda's influence in the region, albeit for different reasons. Both Iran and Saudi Arabia cooperated with the United States in the search for Osama bin Laden and in opposition to the Taliban regime in Afghanistan, al-Qaeda's patron and host. A new era in Saudi-Iranian relations may have been solidified at this time were it not for two factors.

First was the U.S. invasion of Iraq and the overthrow of the Baathist regime. Both Saudi Arabia and Iran had warned the United States against invading Iraq—the Saudis because they feared an unstable and chaotic Iraq and the Iranians because they disliked the idea of U.S. troops on Iran's western border (U.S. troops already were in Afghanistan, along Iran's eastern border). After Saddam's overthrow, Iraq did indeed descend into chaos, as the Saudis had predicted. But of even greater concern to the Saudis—and something that they also had predicted—Iraq's majority Shia community asserted its power after the removal of the Sunni-led Baathists. This phenomenon renewed Saudi fears of Iraq becoming an Iranian-dominated Shia state, which could in turn lend support to Saudi Arabia's own disaffected Shia community. The fact that Iraqi Shia are Arabs, not Persians, would make a Shia-dominated Iraq even more influential among Arab Shia in Saudi Arabia and elsewhere in the Gulf.

The second factor that derailed the budding Saudi-Iranian détente was the election in Iran in 2005 of an arch-nationalist president, Mahmoud Ahmadinejad, to replace the more moderate Khatami. Not only did Ahmadinejad's election herald a new era in

Iranian regional assertiveness, it also ushered in a new style of international politics for the Islamic Republic. Although Ahmadinejad was of course a Shia, he sought to increase Iran's influence throughout the Sunni Arab world by taking strong stands on such issues as the Israeli-Palestinian and Israeli-Lebanese conflicts and by his strident anti-Americanism. He extended aid and support to the Lebanese Shia group Hezbollah, as well as to Hamas, a Sunni Palestinian resistance group based in the Gaza Strip. The Saudis and other conservative Sunni leaders—such as Jordan's King Abdullah—began to fear that Ahmadinejad's popularity with the Arab street would be used by Iran as leverage against Arab governments.

When Hezbollah fought Israel to what many perceived to be a draw in the summer of 2006, Iran's apparent popularity in the Arab world grew. Hezbollah—and, by extension, Iran—were seen as the only actors willing to take on Israel directly, unlike the conservative Sunni Arab states, which still officially supported a negotiated agreement with the Jewish state. Hezbollah's resistance against Israel stood in stark contrast to the comprehensive peace proposal put forward in 2002 by Saudi Arabia's then crown prince Abdullah, a proposal that Israel immediately rejected and the Bush administration essentially ignored.

Ahmadinejad's advancement of Iran's nuclear energy program, which many observers believe is also designed to develop a nuclear weapons capability, further unsettled the Saudis. The prospect of a nuclear-armed Iran would dramatically alter the strategic balance of power in the Gulf region, if not the entire Middle East. Saudi leaders feared that a nuclear-armed Iran would substantially increase its political leverage in the region as well as become an element of pride among Shia communities in Arab states. The mere fact that Iran has defied the West—and the United States specifically—over its nuclear ambitions has generated pride among Shia throughout the region and has helped Ahmadinejad increase his popularity even among non-Shia Arabs.[11]

While conflict between Saudi Arabia and Iran is not a certainty, competition and suspicion between the two regional powers is—at least for the foreseeable future. The following arenas of competition and scenarios are the ones most likely to lead to direct conflict, or conflict by proxy forces.

Developments in Iraq

In the words of an important RAND Corporation study, "each state [Iran and Saudi Arabia] sees the struggle for Iraq as a zero-sum game."[12] Any zero-sum game is dangerous, and this one is all the more so in that it involves Saudi and Iranian support for antagonistic Iraqi militant groups, geographical proximity that makes subversion and arms transfers relatively easy, and the fact that the venue is at the center of global petroleum supplies.

For Saudi Arabia, a Shia-controlled Iraqi government that is closely aligned with—or even a proxy for—the Iranian government is an unacceptable outcome. The Saudis will continue to insist that Iraqi Sunnis be well represented in the Iraqi national government and Sunni economic interests—specifically, a share of Iraq's oil wealth—be guaranteed. Equally unacceptable to Saudi Arabia would be the creation of a separate

Shia Arab state in southern Iraq, under Iranian influence, that would serve as a beacon and source of support for Shia communities in eastern Saudi Arabia and elsewhere in the Gulf.

The critical moment in this zero-sum game will come now that U.S. forces have withdrawn from Iraq. If Iraq descends into sectarian warfare or appears headed toward dismemberment along sectarian lines, both Iran and Saudi Arabia will intervene—most likely through proxy forces—to try and ensure a favorable outcome. Even intervention through proxy forces will seriously exacerbate the Saudi-Iranian bilateral relationship, with possible repercussions in other issue areas.

Conflict by Proxy in Lebanon

Saudi Arabia and Iran have been involved in a proxy conflict in Lebanon since at least 2006, when the Iranian-backed Lebanese Shiite group Hezbollah provoked a short war with Israel that left much of Lebanon's infrastructure in tatters and further destabilized that country's fragile political system. Saudi Arabia strongly supported the Lebanese government, led by Saad Hariri, and the country's Sunni community. For the Saudis, Iranian influence in Lebanon not only poses a threat to that country's Sunni community, it also creates an environment in which conflict or war with Israel is a constant risk.

In the summer of 2010, Saudi Arabia attempted to negotiate with Syria to bring about a more lasting agreement in Lebanon between the government and Hezbollah. Although Saudi leaders always have been wary of Syria due to Syria's radical ideology, anti-Islamic policies, and close ties with Shia Iran, they also believed that a deal involving Syrian guarantees would be a way of extracting Iranian influence from Lebanon. The Saudi mediation attempt failed, however, and within six months Syria was in the throes of popular unrest, which weakened the country's ability to direct events in Lebanon. But the situation in Lebanon remains volatile, and Saudi Arabia's leaders will continue to be concerned over the prospects of an Iranian-backed government in Lebanon.

Conflict by Proxy in Yemen

Since 2004, Shia rebels in northern Yemen have staged several uprisings against the Sunni-dominated Yemeni central government. In August 2009, fighting intensified, with reports of over 100 rebels killed and 100,000 civilians rendered refugees.[13] Because Yemen and Saudi Arabia share a porous border—and Saudi Arabia has concerns about its own Shia population—the unrest in Yemen has been a cause of serious concern to Saudi Arabia. The Yemeni government has accused the Iranian government of sending money and arms to the Shia rebels; Iran, in turn, has suggested that Saudi Arabia is providing assistance to the Yemeni government.[14]

Unlike the Saudi-Iranian proxy wars in Lebanon and Gaza, the conflict in Yemen poses a direct threat to the kingdom. While it is unlikely that Iran would send troops to Yemen—the logistics would be extremely difficult—it is quite possible that the Saudis could intervene militarily if they came to believe that the Yemeni government was threatened with overthrow or if the fighting risked spreading across the Yemeni-Saudi border.

Saudi soldiers look out from Mount Doud, a high strategic position in the southern Saudi province of Jizan. Yemen is one of Saudi Arabia's principal security concerns. (AP Photo/Hassan Ammar)

Nuclear-Armed Iran

If Iran succeeds in developing a nuclear weapons capability, the strategic balance of power in the Gulf region will be altered dramatically. In this event, Saudi Arabia would have three options, none of which are particularly appealing: (1) accept Iranian regional hegemony and work to appease Tehran; (2) pursue a costly nuclear arms program of its own, at the risk of sparking a regional nuclear arms race; or (3) invite the United States to deploy nuclear weapons on or near Saudi territory, thus relying on an unpopular external power to be the guarantor of Gulf security.

Although Saudi Arabia is a signatory to the Treaty on the Non-Proliferation of Nuclear Weapons, the country would have to consider the nuclear option in the event that Iran was confirmed to possess nuclear weapons. In the meantime, Saudi Arabia has tried to position itself as the leading advocate for a nuclear weapons–free Middle East, a position that involves a focus on Israeli as well as Iranian nuclear intentions. But in a sign that Riyadh is keeping its options open, the Saudi government announced in August 2009 that it would pursue construction of the kingdom's first nuclear power plant.[15]

U.S. or Israeli Preemptive Strike on Iran

Perhaps the most dangerous scenario for Saudi-Iranian relations would be a U.S. or Israeli military attack on Iran. Iran's leaders have strongly suggested that such an attack would be met with retaliation, including the possibility of attacks on U.S. allies in the region (such as Saudi Arabia) as well as attacks on commercial tanker traffic in the Gulf and at the strategic Strait of Hormuz. A military attack on Iran could also arouse the anger of Shia communities in Saudi Arabia and neighboring Bahrain.

Diplomatic Tensions

As long as Iran pursues the aggressive, regionwide policy as it has under President Ahmadinejad, Saudi Arabia and Iran will find themselves in opposition over a host of diplomatic issues, including Iran's support for the Palestinian Hamas Party and the Lebanese Hezbollah Party, as well as Iran's influence with the Syrian regime of Bashar al-Assad. One of the primary objectives of Saudi Arabia's push for Israeli-Palestinian peace is to bring an end to a conflict that, left unresolved, leaves an open door for Iranian influence in the Middle East.

Another diplomatic issue that causes friction between Saudi Arabia and Iran is their differing policies and objectives within OPEC. As a rule, Iran prefers higher oil prices and greater production, reflecting the needs of a populous country with ongoing economic development needs. By contrast, Saudi Arabia prefers moderate oil prices designed to protect OPEC's market share and provide a stream of income for decades to come. It is hard to envision the two countries developing a unified approach when it comes to oil production and prices.

While none of these diplomatic tensions would, in themselves, be likely to lead to direct conflict, they serve to exacerbate more serious issues of conflict and contribute to an atmosphere of mistrust.

CONFLICT WITH IRAQ

The future development of Iraq will have a profound effect on Saudi security. The full picture of Iraq's future will unfold now that U.S. combat forces have withdrawn from the war-shattered country.

The worst scenario for Saudi Arabia would be a government in Baghdad that is controlled by Shia who are closely aligned with Iran. In this worst-case scenario, Iraq's Sunni minority is marginalized or even suppressed. The emergence of a Shia-dominated Iranian ally on Saudi Arabia's northern border would present the Saudis with several options, all unpalatable. The most likely Saudi reaction would be to use the close relationships it has built with Sunni militant groups in Iraq to support and arm an insurgency against the Shia government. The goal would be to keep the Iraqi government—and, by extension, Iran—occupied with internal security and thus unable to foment unrest among Saudi Shia or pose a threat along the Saudi border. Most likely, however, Iran and the Shia government in Iraq would respond by increasing efforts to destabilize the Saudi kingdom by supporting Shia dissident groups.

Only slightly less problematic from Saudi Arabia's perspective would be an Iraq that disintegrates into three separate entities: a Shia state in the south, a Sunni state in the center, and a Kurdish state in the north. Under this scenario, Saudi Arabia likely would become the de facto guarantor and defender of the Sunni state. While this would provide the Saudis with a foothold in Iraq, it also would create a situation of almost constant tension between the various Iraqi entities as well as between Saudi Arabia and the Shia state, which would most likely become a client of Iran.

The most acceptable outcome for Saudi Arabia would be a unified Iraqi state—even if the majority parties are Shia based—in which all sects have guaranteed political and economic rights. As the RAND study put it: "It is important to note here that Riyadh is probably resigned to living with a Shiites-controlled government but wants it to be one that is relatively nationalistic in orientation, free from Iranian influence, inclusive of Sunnis, and unable to threaten its neighbors with reconstituted power projection."[16]

It is also important to Saudi Arabia that the future Iraqi state be firmly a member of the Arab camp and not be overly influenced by Iran. This outcome could in fact be preferable to the pre-2003 situation, in which Iraq continued to be ruled by the Baath, who, although severely weakened by the Gulf War and ensuing sanctions, remained an essentially hostile force.

Whatever Iraq's future orientation turns out to be, the Iraqi people will require massive investment to rebuild their shattered nation (or three nations, in the event of dismemberment). This means that Iraq will more likely side with Iran on OPEC issues and could find itself at odds with Saudi Arabia over pricing and production policies.

TERRORIST THREAT FROM YEMEN

Even if Iran were not involved in the fighting in northwestern Yemen, the political and security situation in Yemen always has been a major concern of the Saudis, and much of the two countries' historical relationship has been characterized by border conflict and war.

After decades of war, Saudi Arabia and Yemen reached a border agreement in 1934 that demarcated their border between the Red Sea and the mountains—farther east, the desert border was left undemarcated. Saudi Arabia's King Abdul Aziz had earlier annexed territories to the north of Yemen, and the two countries had fought a war over control of the Asir region before the Saudis prevailed. The 1934 agreement was to be reconsidered in 20 years' time, but both sides let that timetable lapse.

In 1962, the government of Yemen—which had been an imamate generally conducive to good relations with the neighboring Saudis—was overthrown by military officers who declared the establishment of a republic. A bloody civil war ensued, with the Saudis providing assistance to the monarchists, and Egypt—then under the control of the pan-Arabist socialist leader Gamal Nasser—sent troops to back the rebellious republicans. When the war ended in 1969, Yemen was divided into two states: The Saudis now recognized north Yemen as the Yemen Arab Republic. The southern part of Yemen, which had been a British protectorate until 1967, became the Marxist Peoples Democratic Republic of Yemen (PDRY).

The Saudis became important financial supporters of the Yemen Arab Republic in an attempt to prevent the PDRY from expanding its influence. Scores of north Yemenis crossed the border to work in Saudi Arabia, whose economy started to boom after the price increases in the early 1970s. Although the PDRY provided military facilities to the Soviet Union, the Saudis were satisfied to see Yemen divided. A unified Yemen would have a population equal to or greater than Saudi Arabia's and, with its internal problems resolved, might seek to reclaim parts of Saudi Arabia that were once in Yemeni hands. Nevertheless, in 1990—with global communism on the wane—the north and south declared their unification as one republic.

Saudi fears seemed justified in 1991, when Yemen appeared to support Saddam Hussein's invasion of Kuwait. Some Saudis believed that their country was the victim of a coordinated plot, in which Saddam would grab the eastern oil fields and then support Yemen's claims to much of southwestern Saudi Arabia.[17] The Saudis cut off aid to the Yemeni government and expelled over 1 million Yemeni workers from the kingdom, an act that caused tremendous economic disruption in Yemen. There were reports of sporadic border clashes over the next several years. By the late 1990s, however, the two countries were once again discussing a permanent border treaty.

An agreement was reached in 2000, based essentially on the existing border that was demarcated in 1934. The agreement included a clause prohibiting the stationing of troops in a 26-mile-wide swath straddling the border, clearly an attempt to avoid potentially explosive clashes, as had occurred in the early 1990s. Four years later, however, Saudi Arabia began construction of a security barrier along the 1,500-mile border. The Saudis claimed that arms were being smuggled across the border and making their way to extremist elements inside the kingdom. Moreover, Saudi Arabia's harsh crackdown on domestic extremists after the terrorist attacks in September 2001 had driven many al-Qaeda members and supporters into northern Yemen, where they were able to hide easily in the difficult terrain. The government of Yemen strongly criticized the barrier.[18]

Saudi Arabia's concerns about border security seemed justified when, in 2009, fighting broke out in northern Yemen between Shia rebels and government troops. Hundreds were killed in the fighting, and tens of thousands were rendered refugees, many of who sought to cross into Saudi Arabia. The Shia claimed that Saudi troops and planes were involved on the side of the government—and, as noted above, the Saudis claimed that Iran was providing aid to the Shia.[19]

Popular protests in Yemen against the regime of President Ali Abdullah Saleh in 2011 caused further concern for Saudi Arabia. Seeing Saleh as a source of instability, the Saudis supported calls for his ouster but wanted to ensure that it occurred in such a way as to prevent Yemen from descending into chaos and intensified civil war. The prospect of Yemen becoming a failed state poses an immediate and serious security threat to Saudi Arabia. The Saudis' priority will be to prevent terrorist elements in Yemen—including many Saudi citizens affiliated with al-Qaeda—from gaining access to the kingdom. Tight border security will be the minimum Saudi requirement; the possibility of Saudi military involvement is very high. The more Yemen descends into chaos, the greater the chance of direct Saudi intervention, which risks dragging the kingdom into a proxy war with Iran on its southwestern border.

SYRIA

Saudi Arabia and Syria have been essentially at odds on regional policies ever since the socialist, secular Baath Party took power in Syria in 1963. The Baath's radical ideology and close ties to the Soviet Union were anathema to Saudi Arabia, as was Syria's support for rejectionist and leftist Palestinian organizations. Moreover, the al-Assad family that has effectively ruled Syria for the past four decades are followers of the Alawite sect of Islam, which is seen by Wahhabist purists in Saudi Arabia as being too close to Shiism at best, and heretical at worst. While Saudi Arabia publicly supported Syria in its wars against Israel in 1967 and 1973, and has even provided billions of dollars in economic aid over the years when the Syrian government seemed on the verge of economic crisis, the relationship never has been characterized by genuine warmth or a commonality of views.

Saudi suspicions of Syrian intentions have been deepened by Syria's ties with Iran. The Syrian-Iranian alliance has multiple causes, including a shared mistrust of Iraqi Sunnis (especially during the period of Saddam Hussein but also during the post-2003 civil disorder in Iraq), a non-Sunni religious leadership, a hard-line approach toward Israel, and anti-Americanism. On each of these issues, Saudi Arabia and Syria are in opposition.

The late Syrian leader Hafez al-Assad was astute at managing the Saudi-Syrian relationship, despite the fundamental differences between the two countries. On several occasions, Saudi aid helped to prop up the Baathist regime against economic challenges and internal Islamic extremism; as much as the Saudis disliked the Baathists, they feared a power struggle in Syria even more. Bashar al-Assad, however, has been less tactful about provoking the Saudis and has formed a stronger connection with Iran than his father had done. As a result, Saudi-Syrian relations started to deteriorate almost as soon as Bashar took office in 2001.

Syria was implicated in the assassination of Lebanese prime minister Rafik Hariri in February 2005, an act that caused serious concern in Riyadh. Hariri was a close Saudi ally (prior to entering Lebanese politics, he had made his fortune in Saudi Arabia and had close personal ties to many prominent Saudis). The Saudis had relied on him to keep Lebanon stable—which, in their eyes, meant limiting the influence of both Syria and Israel. Riyadh interpreted the assassination as an attempt by Syria to enhance its power over Lebanese politics—and perhaps, the Saudis feared, open a door for greater Iranian involvement. To pressure Syria, Saudi Arabia joined the United States and other Western governments in supporting the United Nations' special tribunal set up to investigate the assassination and identify its perpetrators.

The 2006 Israeli invasion of Lebanon, which was provoked in part by Hezbollah, the Iranian-supported Lebanese Shia party, caused further alarm in Saudi Arabia. Riyadh was notably mild in its rebuke of Israel, and Saudi officials suggested that Hezbollah held some responsibility for the ensuing destruction of Lebanese property and loss of life. With relations souring, Saudi Arabia withdrew its ambassador from Damascus in February 2008 and sent only a low-level diplomatic representative to the Arab League summit hosted by Damascus later that year.

In late 2009, a thaw took place in Saudi-Syrian relations as Saudi Arabia sent a new ambassador to Damascus. This move may have been in part due to Syria's acceptance of Lebanon's election outcome in June 2009, elections in which Hezbollah fared less well than many had expected. The fact that the United States, under the new Obama administration, launched a détente with Syria may also have encouraged

Riyadh to temper its hostility. But despite the new approach, the fundamental elements of competition and disagreement remain—and will, as long as Syria is aligned with Iran's interests in the region.

The possibility of a direct military conflict between Saudi Arabia and Syria is almost nonexistent—the two countries do not share a common border. This conflict is more likely to remain at the level of diplomatic exchanges and support for proxy actors. However, both countries in the past have accused the other of supporting domestic opposition forces and even terrorist elements (Syria, in particular, has accused Saudi Arabia of supporting elements of the extremist Muslim Brotherhood in Syria), and both countries have intelligence services that are capable of such support.

The revolt in Syria against President Bashar al-Assad, which erupted slowly in 2011 but soon became widespread following the regime's violent response and Assad's inadequate response to calls for reform, would appear to be welcomed by Saudi Arabia, because the events will lead to a weaker Syria, at least in the short term. In fact, however, the kingdom does not wish to see Syria descend into civil war, and especially a war whose lines are sectarian-drawn. The Saudi desire for regional stability overrides any advantage that may result in a weakened, or destroyed, Baath regime in Syria. While the Saudis may prefer a Sunni-dominated government in Damascus, they also know that the process of getting to that end result is fraught with dangers.

ISRAEL

Historically, Saudi Arabia has publicly been one of the strongest advocates for the Palestinians and has rigidly refused to maintain any connections or exchanges with Israel. Despite the official animosity, Saudi and Israeli military forces never have engaged in direct conflict (although the Saudis reportedly sent token forces to Syria to support the Arab cause in the 1973 war). Saudi Arabia is not a front-line state (i.e., it shares no borders with Israel), and Saudi leaders are aware that their armed forces, while extensive and modern, are no match for Israel's. As for Israel, its leaders have respected the fact that Saudi Arabia has traditionally maintained a close relationship with the United States; an overtly aggressive action against the kingdom would risk causing a rupture in U.S.-Israeli relations.

Indeed, the fact that both nations enjoy close ties with the United States (which is the primary arms supplier to both states) has served to temper their hostility. Moreover, many of Israel's most implacable foes in the Arab world—Syria, Iraq under the Baath, Egypt under Nasser, revolutionary Iran—also have been foes of Saudi Arabia, to varying degrees. Thus, Israel and Saudi Arabia have long shared a common ally (the United States) as well as common enemies. At several points in history, U.S. and Israeli policy makers have attempted to create an Israeli-Saudi partnership. For example, during the Reagan administration, Secretary of State Alexander Haig envisioned a Saudi-Israeli "strategic consensus" (along with other moderate Arab states, such as Egypt) to counter Soviet threats to the Middle East.[20] More recently, several senior officials in the administration of President George W. Bush attempted to create a de facto alliance among pro-U.S. states, including Saudi Arabia and Israel, against Iran.

Neither of these—or similar—initiatives have taken hold, however, because the underlying Arab-Israeli conflict, which is centered on the plight of the Palestinians, has proven too strong to allow this commonality of interests to forge a positive relationship between Saudi Arabia and Israel.

In 1981, Saudi Arabia's King Fahd proposed an eight-part comprehensive peace plan designed to bring an end to the Arab-Israeli conflict. Fahd's plan called for the recognition of all states in the region and their right to live in peace, which most observers interpreted as a Saudi pledge to recognize Israel once peace was achieved. In 2002, then crown prince (and later king) Abdullah put forward another peace plan at the Arab League summit in Beirut. Abdullah's plan called more specifically for normalized relations between the Arab world and Israel in exchange for a complete Israeli withdrawal from territory occupied in 1967. Israel responded coolly to both proposals, although, after the 2002 initiative, Israeli leaders proposed an open dialogue with Saudi Arabia, which the Saudis refused.

The scenario that poses the most serious potential for direct conflict between Saudi Arabia and Israel would be an Israeli preemptive military strike against Iran in which Israeli warplanes reached their targets by traversing Saudi airspace. Not only would this in itself be an act of war, but from Riyadh's perspective, it would implicate Saudi officials in the attack, thus incurring the wrath (and probable retaliation) of Iran. As a result, Saudi Arabia might feel the need to challenge such an attack militarily or, more likely, diplomatically. In 1981, Israeli warplanes struck an Iraqi nuclear facility by flying unchallenged over Saudi airspace, so there is a precedent for such an Israeli action, although the consequences of striking Iran would be considerably greater for both Israel and Saudi Arabia.

NOTES

1. Central Intelligence Agency, *The World Fact Book 2009*.

2. Ibid.

3. For a full description of the seizure of the Grand Mosque, see Robin Wright, *Sacred Rage* (New York: Simon & Schuster, 2001).

4. Turki al-Hamad, "Terrorism: A Cultural Phenomenon," *Al Sharq Al Awsat* (April 2009).

5. See Thomas Kean and Lee Hamilton, *Without Precedent: The Inside Story of the 9/11 Commission* (New York: Knopf, 2006).

6. Robert Worth, "Saudis Retool to Root out Terrorist Risk," *New York Times* (March 21, 2009).

7. For a thorough discussion of Saudi Arabia's soft counterterrorism tactics, see Christopher Boucek, "The Counseling Program: Extremist Rehabilitation in Saudi Arabia," in *Leaving Terrorism Behind: Disengagement from Political Violence,* ed. Tore Bjørgo and John Horgan (New York: Routledge, 2008).

8. See Human Rights Watch, "The Ismailis of Najran" (September 22, 2008).

9. For a good discussion of this period, see David E. Long, "The Impact of the Iranian Revolution on the Arabian Peninsula and the Gulf States," in John L. Esposito, *The Iranian Revolution: Its Global Impact,* ed. John L. Esposito (Miami: Florida International Press, 1990, 100–115.

10. See Mohsen Milani, "Iran's Gulf Policy: From Idealism and Confrontation to Pragmatism and Moderation," in *Iran and the Gulf: A Search for Stability,* ed. Jamal S. al-Suwaidi (Abu Dhabi, United Arab Emirates: Emirates Center for Strategic Studies and Research, 1996).

11. See Michael Slackman, "Possibility of a Nuclear-Armed Iran Alarms Arabs," *New York Times* (October 1, 2009).

12. Frederic Wehry et al., *Saudi Iranian Relations since the Fall of Saddam* (Santa Monica, CA: RAND Corporation, 2009), 88.

13. Jeffrey Fleishman, "Fighting in Yemen Escalates," *Los Angeles Times* (August 24, 2009).

14. Ibid.

15. John Lyons, "Saudis Set Stage for Mid-East Nukes Race," *The Australian* (August 22, 2009).

16. Wehry et al., *Saudi Iranian Relations,* 90.

17. See Michael Collins Dunn, "The Yemeni Saudi Border Treaty," *The Estimate* (June 30, 2000).

18. Brian Whitacker, "Saudi Security Barrier Stirs Anger in Yemen," *The Guardian* (February 17, 2004).

19. Roula Khalaf, "Forgotten Yemen Slides towards the Brink," *Financial Times* (September 28, 2009).

20. Laurence Barrett, "The Alexandrian Strategic View," *Time* (March 30, 1981).

11 SYRIA

Syria has been at the fulcrum of Middle East politics and conflict for most of its existence as an independent country. In early 2012, Syria's future as a stable and unified state was at serious risk, and the possible outcomes of the intense popular unrest that raged throughout the country ranged from civil war and the collapse of the Syrian state to renewed assertion of autocratic control, either by Bashar al-Asad or a new leader from within the Baathist ranks. But whatever the outcome, Syria's strategic location, its historic links to Lebanon and Palestine, its more recent alliance with Iran, and its traditional aspirations to pan-Arab leadership virtually assure that Syria will continue to play a significant role in most Middle Eastern events.

Syria's ancient capital, Damascus, was one of the political and intellectual centers of the Arab nationalist movement in the 19th and early 20th centuries. When the Ottoman Empire collapsed after World War I, Sherif Hussein, the Hashemite family's custodian of Mecca, sent his son, Emir Feisal, to capture Damascus and drive out the remaining Ottoman Turkish forces. Sherif Hussein had sided with the British during the war, hoping that the defeat of the Ottoman Empire would lead to Arab independence (and, indeed, the British promised him that it would). Emir Feisal entered Damascus victoriously in October 1918.

Little known to Sherif Hussein and his son, the Western powers had secretly agreed in 1916 to divide the Ottoman dominions into spheres of influence; only the Arabian Peninsula would be granted independence. Under the terms of this arrangement—known as the Sykes-Picot Agreement—France was given the mandate over Syria, an area that included Lebanon as well. In July 1920, French troops drove Emir Feisal from Damascus. The British subsequently installed the scion of the Hashemite family as monarch in Iraq. Feisal's brother, Hussein, took the helm in Jordan. The Western powers' betrayal understandably created great bitterness among Arab nationalists as well as an attitude of distrust of Western powers that exists to this day. While the Sykes-Picot

Agreement is all but forgotten in the West, Syrian schoolchildren are well versed in the colonial powers' machinations in the Middle East.

Following decades of anticolonial resistance, France relinquished its Middle East mandate after World War II, and in 1946 Syria was granted independence. To the dismay of Arab nationalists in Damascus, however, Lebanon also was granted independence as a separate state, something that most Syrians refused to recognize. Syria would not officially recognize Lebanon's independence until 2008.

The first 25 years of Syria's independence were politically tumultuous, as the new state sought to find its way among the competing trends in the postwar Middle East. Established as a republic, Syria flirted with parliamentary democracy. But the first of a string of military coups came in 1949, in the wake of the Arabs' unsuccessful war against Israel (in which Syria participated). Democracy was restored in 1954, and elections brought to power a coalition of Arab nationalist and leftist forces that aligned with the Soviet Union and Nasser's Egypt. Fearful of the new state of Israel and the strong U.S. alliances with Jordan and Iraq, Syria elected in 1958 to merge with Egypt and form the United Arab Republic (UAR).

The UAR was short-lived. It came apart in 1963 when yet another coup brought the Baath Party to power in Damascus. The Bath Party, founded in Syria in 1947, was a revolutionary pan-Arab nationalist movement with branches in Jordan, Lebanon, and Iraq. Its principal tenets were socialism, secularism, and Arab unity. The Baath movement was harshly anti-Israel and mistrustful of the West. Baath ideology and rhetoric were among the factors that led to the 1967 Six-Day War, a disaster for the Arab world. In six days, Israeli forces captured Egypt's Sinai Peninsula, the West Bank of the Jordan, and Syria's Golan Heights. The loss of these Arab lands to Israel remains the core element of the Arab-Israeli conflict, and the loss of the Golan Heights in particular has left Syria and Israel at odds for over 40 years.

Hafez al-Asad seized power in Damascus in November 1970. A military leader and Baathist, al-Asad set out to improve Syria's relations with the rest of the Arab world (especially the more traditional states of the Arabian Peninsula, which had been repelled by the Baath Party's secular radicalism). Al-Asad was a member of Syria's minority Alawite sect, which accounts for about 15 percent of the population.[1] He placed many other Alawites in key positions but maintained the pan-Arab, secular ideology of the Baath. Many Sunni Muslims, however, consider Alawites to be a schismatic sect related to Shiite Islam, and some do not consider it to be Islam.

In part due to al-Asad's Alawite faith and in part due to growing pan-Islamic trends in the region, Syria witnessed an increase in activity by Muslim extremists, including bloody terrorist attacks in Damascus during the late 1970s designed to weaken the control of the Baath government. Al-Asad responded harshly. After insurgents from the Syrian Muslim Brotherhood declared the city of Hama to be liberated from the Baathists in 1983, al-Asad ordered the Syrian army to effectively raze the city of 300,000. The exact death toll is unknown but almost certainly was above 20,000.[2] The Brotherhood never again threatened the al-Asad regime.

Syria was involved in two wars in the 1970s. In 1973, Syria joined Egypt in launching a war against Israel to regain the territory captured in 1967. The Arab armies performed respectably—Syria won back a small part of the Golan—before a cease-fire and U.S. mediation brought an end to the fighting. Unlike Egypt's Anwar Sadat, however, al-Asad did not use the 1973 war to launch a peace process with Israel. Still committed to the Palestinian cause—and with continuing pretensions to pan-Arab leadership—Syria became the leading Arab opponent of the Camp David peace process that eventually led to peace between Egypt and Israel. Syria broke diplomatic ties with Egypt and resumed its standoff with Israel.

In 1976, Syria intervened militarily in the Lebanese civil war that had broken out in 1975. Syria's intervention was motivated by a desire to prevent any single party from securing dominance in Lebanon and by the fact that Syria considered Lebanon to be, at a minimum, within its sphere of influence and, at a maximum, an integral part of the Syrian nation. The presence of Syrian troops in Lebanon led to several direct confrontations with Israel when the Jewish state invaded Lebanon in 1982. But both Israel and Syria were careful to ensure that the Golan front remained quiet.

In the 1980s, Syria became increasingly occupied with developments in Iraq. Although both Syria and Iraq were ruled by Baathist regimes, the two governments were bitter enemies. Both countries vied for leadership of the pan-Arab movement, and the personal animosity between Hafez al-Asad and Iraq's Saddam Hussein ensured a tense relationship. Syria quietly supported Iran during that country's war with Iraq (1980–1988), and, to the surprise of the world, Syria joined the U.S.-led coalition to drive Iraq out of Kuwait in 1991. Al-Asad was well aware that his superpower ally, the Soviet Union, was tottering, and he saw the Gulf War as an opportunity to get on the United States' good side (and to deal a blow to Saddam in the process).

After the Gulf War, Syria resumed its demands on Israel for a full return of the Golan. For decades, Syria had taken the position that peace would come only when Israel had returned *all* Arab lands, and al-Asad had harshly criticized Egypt's Sadat for striking a separate deal. Al-Asad also was critical of the Oslo Accords and the Palestine Liberation Organization's (PLO's) decision to recognize Israel. To al-Asad, pan-Arabism required a common and steadfast position vis-à-vis Israel. But Arafat's agreement with Israel, combined with his own declining health, prompted him to seek a separate deal of his own with Israel.

In late 1999 and early 2000, Israel's prime minister Ehud Barak and Syrian foreign minister Farouk al-Shara held talks in the United States under the mediation of President Bill Clinton. By several accounts, the two sides came very close to an agreement, but the talks collapsed in the end over questions related to the exact delineation of the new border between the two countries.[3] Hafez al-Asad died a few months later.

Al-Asad was succeeded by his son, Bashar, a British-trained ophthalmologist. Many Syrians hoped that Bashar would introduce desperately needed economic reforms and bring about a degree of political opening, and initially he appeared to make moves in this direction. But after the September 2001 terrorist attack on the United States, which launched a new era of U.S. involvement in the Middle East, Bashar moved to secure his grip on power. He consolidated support within the Alawite community and relied on many of his father's former allies, especially within the military forces. The tentative political opening all but ended.

Bashar al-Asad professed to support the United States' war on terrorism, but Syria maintained close ties with the Lebanese group Hezbollah and the Palestinian group

Hamas, both of which were considered terrorist organizations by the United States. After the initial U.S. victory over Saddam Hussein's forces in the 2003 invasion of Iraq, several prominent Bush administration officials started to suggest that Syria would be next on the list of states to face regime change. Bashar responded by offering clandestine support to insurgents in Iraq (taking advantage of the long and porous Syrian-Iraqi border) and by strengthening Syria's ties to Iran.

Syria also took steps to strengthen its hold on Lebanon, where it had based troops since the Lebanese Civil War. But after being implicated in the assassination of Lebanese prime minister Rafik Hariri in February 2005, Syria succumbed to international and popular Lebanese pressure and withdrew its troops in April 2005. But Syria maintained its close relationship with Hezbollah and continued to play a significant role in Lebanese affairs.

As the United States became increasingly bogged down in Iraq—thus reducing the chances that Bashar would face a U.S. campaign to overthrow his regime—Syria found itself with greater room to maneuver. In 2008, working through Turkish mediators, Syria and Israel began discussions about renewing their aborted peace negotiations. French president Nicolas Sarkozy paid a high-profile visit to Damascus in the summer of 2008—the first such visit by a Western leader in decades—which granted the Bashar government a degree of enhanced international legitimacy.

The popular protests that broke out in Syria in 2011, on the heels of the overthrow of Tunisia's Ben Ali and Egypt's Mubarak, were met by a strong response from the regime. Unlike in Tunisia and Egypt, the Syrian army remained loyal to the government, and special forces (such as the Republican Guards) also joined in the battle. Syria under al-Asad has been a much more closed society than Egypt was under Mubarak, so violently repressive actions by the regime were often hidden from international view. In the first three months of unrest, over 1,300 people had been killed—more than were killed in the entire Egyptian revolution several months before.

Like the uprisings in Egypt and Tunisia, the Syrian unrest derived from years of autocratic rule under the al-Asad family and the tightly controlled Baath regime, corruption among cronies of the regime, and poor economic prospects, especially for the young. Also as in Tunisia and Egypt, the protests began with an unfocused objective but very quickly transformed into a call for the regime's overthrow (especially after the regime responded with violence). President al-Asad periodically flirted with the idea of offering a program of serious reforms to assuage the unrest, even suggesting in June 2011 that he would be willing to launch a national dialogue with the opposition with the goal of establishing a multiparty democracy. But in the meantime, the repression continued, and thousands of Syrian refugees fled to neighboring Turkey. The prospects of al-Asad being able to offer a degree of reform that would both satisfy the protesters and guarantee his regime's hold on power are slim.

Syria will remain, however, a central player in the hottest conflicts in the region. It is hard to envision a lasting Arab-Israeli peace without Syria's participation, and Lebanon's ongoing internal turmoil is unlikely to be resolved as long as Syria enjoys powerful leverage over the outcome. Iraq's future as a peaceful, stable, and unified nation will depend in part upon relations with Syria, as Damascus has proven that it has the ability to promote insurgency in Iraq. And as Iran's only real Arab ally, Syria's current rulers know they can rely on the support of a nation that is rapidly becoming a regional power.

CONFLICTS

Islamist Internal Dissent

The al-Asad family, supported by its Baath Party and Alawite allies, have ruled Syria for nearly four decades with little visible opposition. Like his father, Bashar al-Asad has enjoyed the support of the military and security forces, which conduct extensive internal intelligence operations and have never hesitated to clamp down quickly and brutally against opposition, as demonstrated throughout 2011. The peaceful transfer of power to Bashar upon the death of his father attests to the level of control the al-Asads and their allies enjoyed.

But opposition groups do exist, and, like all authoritarian regimes, the Syrian government is inherently vulnerable to unrest. Because the Syrian population has been given few outlets to participate politically, anyone who actively opposes the government or its policies has no choice but to affiliate with banned or outlawed groups. Because these groups by necessity operate in secrecy, it is never easy to determine with complete accuracy the true level of opposition and dissent in Syrian society.

It is possible, however, to identify the three principal sources of opposition: Islamists, Kurdish nationalists, and the secular (sometimes democratic) opposition. Of these, Islamist extremist groups pose the greatest potential threat to the Syrian regime. As is the trend in the entire Arab world, Syria has witnessed an increase in Islamist affiliation and identity among its citizens. In large part, this is because the Islamists have offered the most clearly defined alternative to the Baath leadership—it is thus the most attractive outlet for those who oppose the regime.[4]

Moreover, the Baath regime is especially vulnerable to Islamist opposition. The Baath is an avowedly secular party that has pursued socialist economic policies and at one time was aligned with the "godless" Soviet Union. Even more offensive to devout Muslims is the fact that the al-Asad family, and its closest allies in the government, are members of the Alawite sect. Sunni Muslims—who make up the majority in Syria—consider the Alawites to be, at best, closet Shia and, at worst, heretics. Thus, the most accurate way to view Syria is as a majority Sunni society ruled by a secular political party and a government that is in the hands of a minority sect. This fact makes Syria uniquely vulnerable to Islamist extremism.

From the earliest days of independence, the largest Islamist organization in Syria was the Muslim Brotherhood, a Sunni movement that is affiliated with the Brotherhood organizations in Egypt, Jordan, and Palestine (Hamas). Hafez al-Asad initially allowed the Brotherhood to operate and even held a dialogue with its leadership. This was consistent with al-Asad's overall policy of religious tolerance, a long-cherished Syrian tradition (it was also self-serving: as a member of a minority religious group, it was in al-Asad's interest to support religious tolerance). But sensing an opportunity to challenge the government for power, the most radical followers of the Brotherhood began adopting more violent tactics in the late 1970s, inspired in part by the successful

Islamic revolution in Iran in 1979. After a series of attacks against regime targets and representatives, al-Asad in 1982 ordered the now infamous assault on the Syrian city of Hama, a Brotherhood stronghold.

The Brotherhood has not posed a serious threat to the regime since the Hama massacre, and its leadership lives in exile in Jordan. Membership in the organization is forbidden, and it maintains nothing more than a few underground cells. Under Bashar al-Asad, the Syrian government has attempted to co-opt partially the Brotherhood's supporters by building more mosques, approving more imams (all Islamic religious leaders in Syria must operate with government approval), and generally adopting a more Islamist tone. In the first year of his rule, Bashar also released many imprisoned Brotherhood members—perhaps an indication that he no longer viewed the group as a threat.[5]

But the rise of Hamas within the Palestinian movement and the legalization in February 2011 of the Egyptian Brotherhood have been positive developments in the eyes of the Syrian branch of the movement. In any event, the Islamist extremist threat to Syria is not limited to the Brotherhood. The rise of the al-Qaeda organization in the 1990s reverberated in Syria, leading to the rise of a distinct group of Sunni Muslims known as salafists. Salafism is based on the belief that Islam has diverged from its origins and must return to its pure form. Although salafism is not inherently violent, it does contain an element that supports jihad—or holy struggle—against nonbelievers. Al-Qaeda is at its essence a salafist organization.

The salafist movement in Syria is centered in the northern city of Aleppo.[6] The movement has gained significant influence since the U.S. invasion of neighboring Iraq in 2003. The Sunni salafists are opposed to the majority Shiite government that was established in Iraq after the overthrow of Saddam Hussein, and salafist fighters from Syria have crossed the border to take part in insurgent attacks in Iraq, often coordinating with Iraqi groups affiliated with al-Qaeda. The massive flow of arms into Iraq after the U.S. invasion, combined with the porous Iraqi-Syrian border, has led to a reverse flow of arms and explosives into Syria.

A number of terrorist attacks in Syria since 2003 have been attributed by the Syrian government to al-Qaeda and its supporters (most likely, Syrian-based salafists). These attacks include a failed car bombing of the U.S. embassy in Damascus in September 2006 and a car bombing near the Damascus airport in September 2008 that killed 17 civilians. Numerous unconfirmed reports of shoot-outs between security forces and insurgents also have been reported.

Syria will remain vulnerable to Islamist extremist activity for the foreseeable future. The chances of an Islamist takeover of Syria, however, are slim, at least as long as the al-Asad family or a successor authoritarian regime maintains a firm grip on power and control over the country's highly trained security forces. Moreover, after three decades of Baath rule, Syria is a largely secular society where Islamist extremists would be unlikely to find great popular support. Any breakdown in order in Syria—such as could occur if the regime were to fall or face a protracted internal power struggle—would provide an opening for Islamist insurgents to increase their activities, and they would find external sources of aid and support from extremist groups throughout the Middle East. In addition, if Iraq were to slip into chaos and insensate violence, the spillover effect would have a profound impact on Syria and would greatly increase the power and capabilities of extremist groups.

Secular Internal Dissent

Syria's Baath regime has always faced a wide range of secular dissent, from prodemocracy activists to left-wing forces. Under Hafez al-Asad, such dissenters were either co-opted into the Baath apparatus or suppressed with varying degrees of harshness, as attested to by Syria's generally poor human rights record.[7] Syria's relative political isolation in the region contributed to Hafez al-Asad's ability to keep secular opposition under control—the average Syrian had less access to foreign travel or outside influences than did the average Egyptian or Jordanian. After Israel captured and occupied Syria's Golan Heights in 1967, the country's leaders were able to use this issue as a rallying point that ultimately bolstered their hold on power.

With Hafez al-Asad's death, Syria's secular opposition perceived a window of opportunity, all the more so because Hafez's successor, his son Bashar, had spent considerable time in the West and was an advocate of computers and the Internet.[8] As chairman of the Syrian Computer Society, Bashar had sought to increase the number of personal computers in the country and expand access to the Internet, despite the fact that this would diminish the regime's ability to control information.

Bashar's accession to power was thus encouraging to those Syrians who desired a more open and liberal political system. Bashar's first months in power saw a rapid increase in informal political dialogues, lively café gatherings, and the formation of new (and the revival of old) civil society organizations. Syrian reformers were encouraged by the young president's inaugural speech in July 2000, in which he pledged to liberalize the economy, expand technology, and fight corruption; he admonished the Syrian people "not to rely on the government to do everything for them."[9] Later that year, a group of reformers published the Manifesto of 99, a document that called for more political freedoms and greater openness but was careful not to call for a change in regime or Western-style multiparty politics.

A more daring document—termed the Manifesto of 1,000—was published in a Lebanese newspaper in January 2001. It went much farther in its calls for political reform and the introduction of democracy.[10] The fact that it was not published inside Syria reveals the degree to which its signers knew that they were pushing the limits. In many ways, the manifesto can be seen as the precursor to the unrest that broke out a decade later. At the time, however, the Manifesto of 1,000 served primarily to rally the conservative elements within the ruling circle who disapproved of any political opening. In effect, its release ended what had become known as the "Damascus Spring." By 2001, Baath officials were warning that the growing civil society movement threatened to tear Syria apart and distract the nation from its true security threat: Israel. The government began to suppress political forums and other gatherings, close down organizations that were not officially registered with the authorities, and arrest outspoken activists.

Bashar was helped in his suppression of reformists by U.S. rhetoric. Neoconservatives within the Bush administration were actively calling for regime change in Syria.

After the initial success of the U.S. invasion of Iraq in the spring of 2003, some U.S. commentators suggested that the overthrow of Syria would be next. The Syrian government was able to use these very real threats to rally support for the regime and justify the suppression of opponents.

Secular opponents of the regime made another effort to garner attention in 2005 with the publication of the Damascus Declaration for Democratic National Change. The declaration, signed by 250 intellectuals and activists, called for real democratic change in Syria.[11] This time, the Baath regime wasted no time in suppressing the opposition leaders. Within a few weeks, dozens of arrests had been made. In 2007, Bashar al-Asad announced reforms to the political parties' law, but the mostly cosmetic changes would do nothing to weaken the supremacy of the Baath Party. Al-Asad won another term that same year in a referendum in which he secured 97 percent of the vote.[12]

But Syria's secular opposition did not disappear and quickly capitalized on the demonstrations that started in March 2011. Traditionally made up of intellectual elites, the secular opposition now had a grass-roots popular uprising to connect with. The clear lines beyond which the regime would not allow the opposition to go have been crossed, but, as of early 2012, the regime maintained sufficient military power to suppress activity it deems to be a threat to its rule. Moreover, the secular opposition is yet to galvanize toward a particular personality or party that could serve as a rallying point.

Antiregime protesters protest after Friday prayers in Damascus in 2011. Thousands of Syrians took to the streets initially demanding reforms but ultimately calling for the removal of the Al-Asad government. (AP Photo/Muzaffar Salman)

Ethnic Internal Dissent

Syria's population of 20 million is not homogeneous. While Arabs make up 90 percent of the population, there is a substantial non-Arab Kurdish community (around 9 percent) and small communities of Armenians, Turkmen, Circassians, and Assyrians. Syria's population is divided religiously among Sunni Muslims (74 percent, including most of the Kurdish community), Alawites (15 percent), Christians (10 percent), and Druze (1 percent). Damascus is home to a very small, and dwindling, Jewish community.[13]

Syria's diversity, and the fact that the country has been ruled by members of a minority religious community for over 30 years, has produced a remarkably tolerant society. Unlike Egypt, where clashes between Muslims and Coptic Christians occur frequently, Syria has rarely experienced open conflict between members of religious communities. The violent acts carried out by religious extremists (the Muslim Brotherhood in the 1970s, al-Qaeda–affiliated groups more recently) have targeted the government, not other religious groups.

The one significant exception to Syria's tradition of tolerance is in the government's relations with the Kurdish community. Syria's Kurds live predominantly in the country's north, along the borders with Iraq and Turkey, which also have substantial Kurdish populations (these areas of Syria, Turkey, and Iraq, along with parts of northwestern Iran, compose the region known as Kurdistan). The Kurds were for decades treated as outsiders in Syria and, being non-Arabs, were effectively excluded from the Baath's pan-Arab nationalist ideology. In the 1970s, the Kurdish language was banned from schools, Kurdish land often was confiscated, and the government of Hafez al-Asad launched an Arabization program to settle Arabs in Kurdish areas.[14] Moreover, hundreds of thousands of Kurds were stripped of their Syrian citizenship; the government argued that they in fact have infiltrated Syria from Turkey and thus were not native inhabitants.[15] Although a small number of Kurds successfully assimilated into Arab culture and even have achieved government positions, the majority have remained relatively isolated from mainstream Syrian society.

Because of the government's effectiveness at suppressing internal opposition, the Syrian Kurds expressed few outward signs of opposition to these restrictive policies, at least in comparison to the Kurds in Turkey, Iraq, and Iran. Turkish political groups have always existed in Syria, but they were traditionally careful not to call for independence or sovereignty. The 1980s and 1990s witnessed a few incidents in Kurdish areas in which expressions of Kurdish nationalism were harshly suppressed, but, for the most part, the region remained quiet during the rule of Hafez al-Asad.

The brief period in the wake of Bashar al-Asad's assumption of power in 2000 brought about heightened activity by Kurdish groups, who started to meet more openly. After a few months, the regime returned to its repressive ways, and a score of Kurdish leaders were arrested. But in 2003, the Kurdish movement in Syria received a renewed boost when the United States invaded Iraq and overthrew the Saddam Hussein regime. In March 2004, the interim Iraqi government granted autonomy to Iraqi Kurds over the Kurdistan region of Iraq, a move that heartened and inspired Kurdish activists throughout the region.

It perhaps no coincidence that soon after the liberation of Iraqi Kurds, unrest broke out in the Syrian Kurdish areas. It began with a confrontation between Kurds and Arabs following a football match in March 2004 and quickly spread to include demonstrations and riots in Kurdish towns throughout Syria. The regime responded harshly—Syrian army tanks and combat helicopters moved into the region—and eventually put down the uprising. Outside observers estimate that up to 40 Kurds were killed and thousands arrested.[16]

Renewed unrest occurred in May and June 2005 following the suspicious death in Damascus of Sheikh Ma'shuq Khaznawi, a respected Kurdish religious leader. Clashes between Kurdish activists and police forces were reported throughout the remainder of 2005.

The Bashar al-Asad regime is clearly concerned about the Kurdish community, especially in light of developments with the Kurdish community in Iraq. In June 2005, the Baath Party announced a plan to grant citizenship to more of Syria's Kurdish citizens and took other steps that indicated an attempt at conciliation.[17] But in pure balance-of-power terms, the Kurdish community is aware that the Syrian regime is not as strong as it was under Bashar's father and that it is facing a number of other security challenges that give the Kurdish community unprecedented maneuvering room. The success of Iraq's Kurdish community serves not only as an example but also a potential source of support, given the porous border between the two nations. However, recent developments to the north might counterbalance the benefit of a Kurdish sanctuary in Iraq. As Turkey and Syria have grown closer diplomatically and economically, they have reportedly coordinated their repression of Kurdish political groups that pose a danger to the ruling elites in both countries.[18]

The Kurdish issue will be the most likely source of internal unrest in Syria in the event that the regime's hold on power begins to slip, and if the country were to descend into civil war—a distinct possibility—the Kurds would likely view this as their chance to sever ties with Damascus. In addition, if the Kurdish region of neighboring Iraq were to fully secede or achieve even greater autonomous powers, the Syrian Kurds would be encouraged to follow a similar path. But even short of civil war, unless a balance is found between Kurdish aspirations and the Syrian government's obsession with internal control, more conflict is likely.

Conflict with Iraq

Syrian-Iraqi relations were for decades marked by rivalry and hostility. Although both countries were ruled by Baath Party leaders, each claimed to be the true reflection of Baath ideology and values. Moreover, both Damascus and Baghdad (along with Cairo) have vied for centuries to be the center of the Arab and Islamic worlds, and neither was willing to cede regional leadership to the other. Compounding the tense relationship was the personal animosity between Hafez al-Asad and Saddam Hussein, which culminated in Syria's support for non-Arab Iran during the long and bloody Iran-Iraq war and its support for the U.S.-led coalition assembled to oust Saddam's forces from Kuwait in 1991.

Bashar al-Asad made an attempt to improve relations with Iraq by reopening the closed border and reactivating an oil pipeline from Iraq to the Syrian port of Baniyas, an action that defied U.S. sanctions against the Saddam government. Bashar's government supported United Nations (UN) Resolution 1441, which authorized UN inspectors to investigate Iraq for weapons of mass destruction, but Syria opposed the U.S. march to war against Iraq.

The fall of the Iraqi Baath and Saddam's overthrow at the hand of the U.S. invasion in 2003 posed a dilemma for Syria. On the one hand, Syria's leadership was not unhappy to witness an end to the rival Baath government in Baghdad. At the same time, however, Saddam's overthrow was a cause of concern to Damascus. The neoconservative U.S. officials who spearheaded the war with Iraq openly declared that Syria also was in their sights, and in fact could very well be the next domino to fall. Long at odds with the United States, Syria's Baath leaders were unnerved by the presence of a U.S. invasion force in neighboring Iraq. The fall of the Iraqi Baath Party—although a hated rival of the Syrian Baath—also created a precedent that Syria's leaders were not happy to witness.

Perhaps an even greater concern to Damascus, however, was the danger that Iraq could descend into the chaos of religious and ethnic violence following the destruction of Saddam's regime. The Syrians feared that an unstable Iraq in the throes of a confessional civil war could easily have spillover effects in Syria. The fact that disorder in Iraq created a fertile ground for al-Qaeda and other salafist terrorist groups was also a grave concern to Bashar al-Asad. Syria was faced with a difficult choice: if Damascus supported insurgents in Iraq to keep the United States tied down (and thus unable to expand its Middle East war to Syria), it risked contributing to instability in Iraq, which, in the longer term, was not in Syria's interests.

In fact, Bashar al-Asad had limited ability to control the flow of people or contraband across his country's 400-mile-long border with Iraq, even if he had wanted to. Not only did insurgents cross into Iraq from Syria, but loyal members of Iraq's former regime crossed the other way and sought refuge in Syria.[19] The United States issued a number of thinly veiled threats against Syria in an attempt to force the Syrian government to tighten its border security, but as the war in Iraq quickly turned more difficult for U.S. forces, the threat of U.S. military action against Syria waned.

By 2006, U.S. military commanders in Iraq acknowledged that the infiltration of insurgents from Syria had slowed, and they admitted that Iraqi insurgents in Syria operated without the approval of Damascus.[20] With the United States tied down in Iraq and facing growing domestic opposition to the war, Syria's concerns focused more on instability in Iraq than on a possible U.S. attack on Syria. In November 2006, Syria and Iraq restored diplomatic relations, an important acknowledgement of legitimacy for the new Iraqi government. Despite the resumption of relations, signs of the old enmity periodically resurface. After a bloody Baghdad bombing in August 2009, Iraqi officials claimed to have found evidence implicating Iraqi exiles in Damascus, claims that Syria denied. Both countries withdrew their ambassadors in the row, only to smooth the rough patch with Turkish mediation.[21] The large population of former high-level Iraqi Baath officials—generally at odds with the Shiite-dominated Iraqi central government—who fled to Syria after the invasion makes continued tension between the countries likely.[22] Although Syria continues to call for the withdrawal of all U.S. forces from Iraq, it is likely that, in private, Damascus does not really want to see this happen until Iraq is on a more stable footing.[23]

Iraq's uncertain future after U.S. withdrawal poses several threats to Syria. First is the danger that insurgents connected to the al-Qaeda/salafist movement could renew their war of terror against the central government. Any successes this movement might have in destabilizing Iraq would embolden and empower its supporters within Syria and would put the Syrian government in the difficult position of having to fight against the very insurgents that it earlier allowed to cross its borders and carry out actions in Iraq.

Second, a deteriorating situation in Iraq could lead to greater Kurdish sovereignty, if not outright independence. Such a development would likely lead to even greater suppression of the Syrian Kurds by the Damascus government and thus create the conditions for intensified internal violence in Syria. Equally complicating would be a situation in which Iraq were to disintegrate into several independent, and mutually hostile, entities. The concomitant risk of civil war would pose a threat to Syria by increasing the numbers of Iraqi refugees seeking a safe haven across the border and by stoking the fires of internal dissent in Syria.

Third, instability in Iraq could lead to growing Iranian influence in the country. Although Syria and Iran have been close allies, Damascus might not welcome a strong Iranian presence in Iraq. The other Arab countries of the region—such as Jordan and Saudi Arabia—would certainly look unfavorably on this situation, and Syria might then be in a position of choosing between its strategic alliance with non-Arab Iran and its long-standing desire to be a leader in the Arab world.

Ironically, a peaceful and stable Iraq also poses some dangers to Syria. If Iraq, post-U.S. withdrawal, were to develop into a stable multisectarian and multiethnic democratic country, pressure would grow (both internally and externally) on Syrians to follow a similar path and begin real democratic reforms.

Israel

Israel has been Syria's principal regional enemy since 1948, when the Jewish state declared its independence. Syria has taken direct part in every Arab-Israeli War and has been indirectly involved in Israel's wars in Lebanon. Syria has traditionally supported the hardest-line factions of the Palestinian resistance movement and has allowed many of these organizations to base their operations—terrorist and otherwise—in Damascus.

Its decades-long conflict with Israel has been costly to Syria. Syria lost the Golan Heights to Israel in the 1967 war. The Golan is a strategic plateau that overlooks the Hauran Plain in Syria and the Galilee Valley in Israel; it also is an important source of water for Israel. Syria attempted unsuccessfully to seize the Golan back in the 1973 war. In 1981, Israel de facto annexed the Golan, which was a violation of international law that infuriated the Syrians. Regaining the Golan remains the central focus of Syrian foreign policy.

Syria's ongoing conflict with Israel has also damaged its economy by forcing it to spend excessive sums on its military. Moreover, Syria's hard-line position vis-à-vis

Syrian demonstrators walk toward the cease-fire line, as seen from the Druze village of Majdal Shams in the Israeli-occupied Golan Heights, on June 5, 2011, marking the 44th anniversary of the 1967 Six-Day War. Israeli troops opened fire on the protestors, killing three. (Uriel Sinai/Getty Images)

Israel has prevented Damascus from developing a positive relationship with the United States and much of Europe, which has had both political and economic consequences. Syria also has found itself at odds with other Arab states—such as Egypt, Jordan, and Qatar—that have pursued more peaceful policies toward Israel.

Syria's traditional hostility toward Israel is an important component of the Baath Party's ideology of Arab unity. Moreover, in order to advance its desired role as the center of Arab nationalism, Damascus has presented itself as the chief defender of Palestinian rights—even when the Palestinians themselves have been more accommodating toward Israel. Syria has maintained the position that peace with Israel can come only after all Arab lands occupied in 1967 are returned, and the Palestinians have been granted their rights—presumably including the right of return of Palestinian refugees.

Nevertheless, in 1999–2000, Hafez al-Asad made an effort to reach a bilateral peace agreement with Israel. As his health was failing, he was motivated perhaps by his desire to bring about a return of the Golan as part of his legacy. Moreover, the Palestine Liberation Organization had launched an official dialogue with Israel in 1993 when PLO leader Yasser Arafat and Israeli prime minister Yitzhak Rabin shook hands on the White House lawn, and Syria feared that if it did not strike a bilateral deal with its historic enemy, it would be left as the last Arab frontline state without an agreement for the return of its territory.

The 1999–2000 talks, mediated by U.S. president Bill Clinton, were unsuccessful, and Hafez al-Asad died soon afterward. The Israeli-Palestinian peace process collapsed later in 2000, and a new Palestinian intifada—or uprising—broke out. With the election of a hard-line government in Israel in early 2001, Israeli-Syrian relations returned to their usual state of hostility. Bashar al-Asad was more focused on securing his new regime's hold on power than on pursuing a bold and potentially risky peace process.

Tensions between Syria and Israel were strained in the summer of 2006, when Israel launched an assault on Lebanon in an attempt to destroy the armed forces of Hezbollah, a Lebanese Shiite party that controlled most of southern Lebanon. Syria was careful to avoid a direct confrontation with Israeli troops but facilitated Iran's efforts to supply Hezbollah with arms and equipment. Israel was also careful to avoid a direct confrontation with Syria, but Israeli forces did bomb a number of roads and bridges that connected Lebanon and Syria in order to hinder supplies reaching Hezbollah.

In September 2007, the Israeli air force attacked a military facility deep inside Syrian territory. Israeli sources claimed that the facility was being used to manufacture weapons-grade material supplied by North Korea and suggested that Iran also was involved in the project. Syria denied this claim but made no effort to retaliate. In fact, despite the Israeli attack, Syria agreed in 2008 to pursue indirect negotiations with Israel, via Turkish mediators, over the return of the Golan and a formal peace agreement.

The ups and downs of Syrian-Israeli relations reflect in many ways changing developments in the Middle East region as a whole. There is little doubt that both nations desire peace, but the costs of peace—for Israel, returning the strategic Golan Heights; for Syria, foregoing the role as the Arab world's stalwart defender of Arab nationalism—have so far been more than either side has been willing to incur. Although Syria and Israel have avoided a direct military confrontation since 1973, as long as their conflict remains unresolved, there will remain a number of hot spots that could erupt.

The Golan Heights is strongly defended by Israel, and another Syrian attempt to recapture the territory is highly unlikely. With the fall of the Soviet Union, Syria lost its principal arms supplier, and its troops would be no match for Israel's army and air force. Syria is well aware of the military balance, which explains why the Golan border has been peaceful for nearly 40 years.[24]

Syria and Israel have frequently acted out their mutual hostility indirectly in Lebanon. By arming and supporting groups such as Hezbollah, Syria has been able to keep pressure on Israel's northern border without risking a direct war. There is even less risk of a direct confrontation since April 2005, when Syria withdrew its armed forces from Lebanon as a result of Lebanese and international pressure. Syria had maintained forces in Lebanon since 1976, when it intervened during Lebanon's civil war, but Syrian troops had always tried to avoid a confrontation with Israel (confrontations did occur, but both sides worked to limit the damage). Nevertheless, Lebanon remains the most likely venue for a Syrian-Israeli confrontation. Neither country could accept the other gaining a dominant position in Lebanon, and each will remain wary of the other's intentions there.

As the home base for several hard-line Palestinian organizations and for the senior leader of Hamas, Syria could find itself drawn into conflict with in the event that the Israeli-Palestinian conflict descends into violence. Israel has demonstrated a willingness to attack individuals and organizations that it perceives to be perpetrators of terrorism; in February 2008, for example, the Israeli government allegedly masterminded the assassination of Hezbollah official Imad Mughniyeh in Damascus.[25] The Israeli military probably would not hesitate to conduct similar operations on Syrian soil in the context of a wider confrontation between Israel and extremist Palestinian groups. A return to violence in the Israeli-Palestinian conflict would also confront Syria with the need to once again assume the role of leader of the Arab world and defender of the rights of the Palestinians.

When Israel launched a harsh attack against Hamas forces in the Gaza Strip in late 2008 and early 2009, however, Syria was careful to prevent an expansion of the conflict to southern Lebanon, despite some evidence that the Lebanese group Hezbollah sought to open a second front. Despite the brutality of Israel's assault on Gaza, Syria clearly wanted to prevent a possible confrontation. Syria did, however, suspend its back-channel talks with Israel that the Turkish government was mediating. The deterioration of Israeli-Turkish relations in the wake of the Gaza flotilla raid in May 2010 suggests that future peace talks between Syria and Israel may require a different mediator.

Syria and Israel could be drawn into conflict over Syria's close relationship with Iran. Israel has declared that Iran will not be allowed to develop nuclear weapons and has threatened to attack Iran if it appears to be on the verge of becoming a nuclear power. In this event, Syria would be called on to come to the aid of its Iranian ally—at least rhetorically—and possibly to play a role in any likely Iranian retaliation. This retaliation could take the form of Hezbollah attacks on Israel from southern Lebanon—a situation that would risk bringing Syria and Israel into direct confrontation.

Finally, any evidence that Syria is attempting to develop weapons of mass destruction, and especially nuclear weapons, would likely be met by a quick and violent Israeli response, as occurred in September 2007. However, Israel probably would act in a surgical way designed to destroy suspicious facilities and not start a full-scale war.

Syria's leaders have and will continue to use the perceived threat from Israel as an argument against popular opposition—and, in fact, the al-Asad government suggested that the unrest was provoked by Israeli provocateurs—but this argument is unlikely to persuade opposition forces to leave the streets (unless, that is, Israel were to make the mistake of conducting an aggressive action against Syria or Lebanon, but in the early months of Syria's unrest, Israeli leaders very cautiously avoided any provocative actions).

Jordan

Syrian-Jordanian relations never have been close. Syrian nationalists have always regarded Jordan (along with Lebanon and Palestine) as part of greater Syria. Moreover, Jordan has been from its founding a monarchy ruled by the Hashemites, while Syria—especially under the Baath—has been one of the Arab world's centers of secular pan-Arab nationalism. To make matters worse (from Syria's perspective), Jordan has been a traditional ally of the West and looked first to Britain and later to the United States for support. For many years, the Syrian-Jordanian border was a virtual line of confrontation in the Cold War, as Syria relied on Moscow for arms and support.[26]

The tensions between Syria and Jordan led to direct conflict on several occasions. In 1970, Syrian troops crossed into Jordan to aid Palestinian resistance fighters who were battling the Jordanian army. Virtually the only thing the two countries agreed on was opposition to Israel: they fought as allies in the 1967 war, and Jordan sent a few thousand troops to bolster Syria during the 1973 war. But even on the issue of Israel, there was tension. Constant rumors of secret negotiations between Jordan's King Hussein and Israeli leaders (rumors that later were proven to be true) infuriated Syria.

The Iran-Iraq War and the Gulf War further divided the two countries during the 1980s. Syria supported Iran, while Jordan strongly backed Iraq (and served as a channel for U.S. assistance to Iraq). Syria viewed Saddam Hussein's regime as a rival and threat and saw revolutionary Iran as a potential source of support against the United States and its regional allies. Conservative and pro-Western Jordan, on the other hand, saw Iran as a regional threat. Jordan again supported Iraq during Saddam Hussein's invasion of Kuwait and subsequent war with the U.S.-led coalition, while Syria uncharacteristically aligned with the United States and participated in the coalition.

Syria was adamantly opposed to the Israeli-PLO accords reached in Oslo and to the subsequent recognition of Israel by the PLO. Jordan, however, took advantage of the Israeli-PLO dialogue to reach its own peace agreement with Israel in 1994, an agreement that Syria condemned. But when Jordan's King Hussein died in 1999, the new King Abdullah paid a visit to Damascus in an attempt to improve relations. Syria began its own dialogue with Israel in 1999, which, although ultimately unsuccessful, was supported by Jordan. For a few years, the two countries appeared to be on a more peaceful path.

Once again, issues involving Iraq drove a new wedge between Syria and Jordan in 2003. Jordan offered lukewarm support for the U.S. war effort to overthrow Saddam Hussein, while Syria stridently opposed the invasion. Once Saddam's regime was removed, Jordan's concerns focused on growing Iranian influence in the region as a result of the new Shiite-dominated government in Iraq. Syria, however, continued to cultivate its alliance with Iran. In 2005, Jordan's King Abdullah warned of a growing Shiite "crescent" in the Middle East that posed a threat to Sunni governments. He was referring to an arc running from Iran (the largest Shiite nation), through Iraq, and including Syria and Lebanon.[27] King Abdullah's words, by describing Syria as part of a threatening crescent, further solidified the mutual antagonism between Jordan and Syria. In 2006—perhaps in response to Abdullah's warning—Syria and Iran signed a defense pact. Even with signs of a U.S.-Syrian rapprochement in 2010, Iranian officials have emphasized the strength of the Syrian-Iranian relationship.[28]

The core elements of Syrian-Jordanian tension remain in place. Jordan is still a conservative monarchy seeking to preserve Sunni dominance in the Middle East; Syria remains a proponent of secular nationalism, although it combines this with an alliance with the Islamic Republic of Iran. Jordan maintains its military and political alliance with the West, and the United States in particular; Syria has been the object of Western sanctions and even veiled threats of attack.

Nothing on the horizon suggests that Syrian-Jordanian tensions may ease in the near future. The chances of a direct military confrontation, however, also are unlikely. First, the countries have no significant border issues or disagreements that could lead to war. Second, Jordan's position as an ally of the United States, as well as a country whose stability is in Israel's interests, means that a Syrian attack on the Hashemite kingdom would be extremely risky.

If tensions were to intensify, however, it is possible that the two countries could become engaged in an indirect conflict via terrorist attacks and subversion. Syria's alliance with Iran and the Lebanese group Hezbollah provide it with the resources to conduct a terrorist campaign, and Jordan's highly effective intelligence services also are capable of conducting cross-border actions. Scenarios that could trigger such an indirect conflict include the coming to power of a strongly pro-Iranian government in Iraq and a subsequent increase in Iranian power throughout the region.

But despite their history of tension and animosity, Jordan would prefer a stable al-Asad government to a Syria in the throes of civil war. The latter scenario could create a refugee problem for Jordan (as Iraq's civil conflict did). Moreover, as Jordan's King Abdullah tries to negotiate power with various opposition forces, he would not want to see neighboring Syria serve as an example of regime change.

Lebanon

Syria never fully accepted Lebanon's independence as a separate country. The country known today as Lebanon had for centuries been considered a part of greater Syria but was granted its separate independence by France, which wanted to both protect the interests of the Christian Maronite community and maintain a sphere of influence in the Levant. Despite their close historical bonds, the two countries developed in starkly divergent ways: while Syria emerged as one of the centers of secular Arab nationalism and was ruled by a succession of authoritarian regimes, Lebanon evolved into a free-wheeling and prosperous laissez-faire society with strong ties to the West. But Lebanon's image as the playground of the Middle East—a place where people were too busy making money to engage in conflict—was misleading, for beneath the surface were a host of tensions and sectarian rivalries that erupted into civil war in 1975.

Syria—which regarded Lebanon as, at a minimum, in its sphere of influence and, at a maximum, as an integral part of greater Syria—sent military forces across the border soon after the civil war broke out. The Syrian intervention was generally welcomed by the world (including the United States) and helped to bring about a cease-fire. But for the next 15 years, Syrian forces would pursue a Machiavellian policy of supporting various sides in order to prevent any single force from gaining the upper hand.

Israel also considered at least southern Lebanon to be in its sphere of influence and was concerned about the presence of PLO fighters in Lebanon, a factor that had contributed to the outbreak of civil war. Israel invaded Lebanon in 1978 and again in 1982 in an attempt to destroy the PLO's infrastructure; each time, Syrian forces kept their distance to avoid a direct confrontation with Israel.

At the same time, however, Syria began forging ties with Shiite groups in southern Lebanon (where the Shia make up the majority of the population). Syria viewed these groups as a natural buffer with Israel and as a means to resist Israeli moves in southern Lebanon without risking a direct Syrian-Israeli confrontation. Syria's allegiance with the Islamic Republic of Iran, which also sought to forge ties with Lebanon's Shiite community, was mutually reinforcing.

In the late 1990s, Hezbollah and Israel fought a series of battles, which Syria carefully avoided becoming engaged in. But the pressure on Israel was such that, by May 2000, all of its forces had been withdrawn, opening the way for near complete Hezbollah domination of southern Lebanon. Syria regarded this as a victory and repositioned its own troops in Lebanon's Bekka Valley. But many Lebanese, especially among the country's Christian community, felt that Syria and its Hezbollah allies effectively controlled the southern part of the country and threatened to bring the entire nation under their sway.

In April 2003, after years of internal political turmoil, Lebanese prime minister Rafik Hariri formed a new government that was strongly pro-Syrian. It appeared that Syria had succeeded in solidifying Lebanon's position as a satellite state. In fact, Syria had overplayed its hand. With the encouragement of the United States, which was now pursuing a more aggressive policy toward the Middle East, the United Nations in May 2004 passed UN Resolution 1559, which called on all foreign troops to withdraw from Lebanon. The United States also imposed economic sanctions on Damascus.

In October 2004, Hariri resigned to protest the heavy Syrian meddling in Lebanese affairs, and opposition to Syria's continued presence in Lebanon began to grow more widespread and more vocal. Under pressure, Syria agreed in December 2004 to withdraw its intelligence forces from Lebanon (it had never previously even admitted that it maintained such forces in Lebanon). But the opposition to Syria's military presence continued to grow, and Hariri had taken on the mantle of chief opposition leader.

In February 2005, Hariri was assassinated in a car bomb attack. Most Lebanese—as well as the international community—accused Syria of carrying out the attack, despite Damascus's fervent denials. Whoever was responsible, the assassination of Hariri sparked a massive opposition movement with huge demonstrations in Beirut and other cities. The movement, which became known as the Cedar Revolution, brought immense pressure on Syria to withdraw all of its forces from Lebanon, which it did by June 2005.

Lebanon was now free of Syrian forces but not of Syrian influence, as the ties between Damascus and Hezbollah were, if anything, rendered even stronger. In the summer of 2006, Israel and Hezbollah fought a 34-day war in southern Lebanon after Hezbollah forces kidnapped two Israeli soldiers along the border. This war—which Israel extended via aerial bombardment to include most of the country—created further division and uncertainty in Lebanon but was seen as a Syrian-Hezbollah victory after Israeli troops withdrew without having accomplished their stated goal of destroying Hezbollah. Once again, Lebanon had been the scene of a proxy war between Israel and Syria.

Syria continues to play a powerful role in Lebanese political developments through its alliances and, most certainly, the continued presence of intelligence officials. Several anti-Syrian politicians have been assassinated since the Hariri killing, even as the United Nations investigated Syria's role. Syria's continued involvement in Lebanese affairs became clear when Syria's concerns were taken into account when Lebanon chose a new president in May 2008.

Later in 2008, Syria and Lebanon exchanged ambassadors for the first time in their history—the first formal indication that Syria accepted Lebanese sovereignty.

But Damascus agreed to this move only after the Lebanese government conceded that Hezbollah would not be disarmed—as the United States, Israel, and many Lebanese were demanding. The new Lebanese government formed in June 2008 also gave Hezbollah and its allies effective veto power over major government decisions. In December 2009 and July 2010, Lebanese prime minister Saad Hariri visited Damascus, symbolizing the significant improvement in relations between the two countries.[29] It appears likely that Hezbollah members—rather than Syrian officials, as many had initially expected—will be indicted on charges of Saad's father's assassination, removing a major stumbling block in Lebanese-Syrian relations; Saad had previously accused Syria of his father's assassination.[30] However, such events could also push Lebanon into deeper political paralysis or even outright civil war.

Syria has most likely given up on the old dream of including Lebanon in a greater Syrian nation, but its fundamental goals vis-à-vis its smaller neighbor remain the same: to prevent Lebanon from ever coming under control of a hostile state (especially Israel) and to ensure that Lebanon is never used as a route to attack Syria. Syria would undoubtedly go to war—either directly or through its well-armed Hezbollah proxies—to prevent either of these events from happening.

Syria also is concerned about Lebanon's internal stability. This goal may seem ironic, given that Syria's past meddling in Lebanese affairs was one of the sources of Lebanon's instability. But Syria is extremely sensitive to the dangers of sectarian violence within Syria and thus fears that a chaotic political situation in Lebanon could spread across the border. Syria desires Lebanon to be weak but stable and under the general oversight (if not outright control) of Damascus. Syrian troops could once again be dispatched to Lebanon if Damascus felt this was necessary to ensure a balance of power among Lebanese sects and groups.

Finally, Syria and Lebanon maintain a close economic interdependence. Syria is Lebanon's largest trading partner, and thousands of Syrian laborers work in Lebanon. A number of high-ranking Syrian government officials have been involved in very profitable cross-border smuggling. As Syria faces U.S. and Western sanctions, Lebanon to a degree serves as an economic lifeline for the al-Asad regime. It is likely that Syria would intervene militarily—despite the risks involved—if it felt this relationship were threatened by either Lebanese politicians or outside powers.

If the al-Asad government is overthrown, or if it is required to devote its resources to internal control over the long term, Syria's position in Lebanon will weaken, as will that of its principal ally there (Hezbollah). But in the long run, geography and history will ensure that any government in Damascus will take a strong interest in, and attempt to affect, developments in Lebanon.

Palestinian Resistance Groups

Syria's relationship with Palestinian resistance movements has been complex and characterized by periods of close cooperation as well as fierce mutual antagonism. Palestine was traditionally included in the concept of greater Syria, and as a result Syrians have felt a responsibility—as well as a right—to play a role in Palestinian affairs. Moreover, thousands of Palestinian refugees fled to Syria during the 1948 war;

today, Syria is home to around 450,000 Palestinian refugees and their descendents (over 120,000 of whom live in refugee camps).[31] Following the creation of Israel and the first Arab-Israeli War, Syria offered support to Palestinian guerillas (known as fedayeen) who staged raids into Israel, including raids across the Syrian-Israeli armistice line. Such raids were one of the precipitants of the 1967 Arab-Israeli War.

In 1964, Palestinian resistance leaders formed the Palestine Liberation Organization to coordinate and spearhead their goal of liberating Palestine through armed struggle. Almost immediately, the PLO became "a diplomatic football between Cairo and Damascus and other Arab capitals . . . in their respective attempts to gain more control over the Palestinian movement."[32] At the same time, the PLO's leader, Yasser Arafat, became adept at playing the Arab powers against each other in order to gain the greatest advantage and support.

When PLO guerillas threatened the stability of Jordan in 1970, Syria sent troops to back the Palestinian fighters, even at the risk of provoking war with Israel. But this represented perhaps the last example of unambiguous Syrian support for the PLO. After Jordan subdued the PLO fighters, the guerillas and the PLO leadership moved to Lebanon, where thousands of Palestinians already lived in refugee camps. The sudden influx of armed fighters who were determined to wage war with Israel not only upset Lebanon's delicate confessional balance, it also complicated Syria's long-standing strategic goal of controlling Lebanese political developments.

When Lebanon's civil war broke out in 1975, Syria initially sided with the Christian Maronite militias, the PLO's arch enemy in Lebanon. Syria feared that a PLO-dominated Lebanon could provoke another war with Israel, and Syria wanted any war with Israel to be waged on Damascus's terms, not the PLO's.[33] Syria's fears came true: in 1982, Israel launched a massive invasion of Lebanon to deal a death blow to the PLO. Two years later, PLO fighters and the PLO leadership agreed to withdraw from Lebanon. The PLO's new base of operations would be in Tunisia, far from the battlefield; Syria was not unhappy with this outcome.

By the late 1980s, the Tunisia-based PLO leadership began sending peace feelers toward Israel, to Syria's dismay. Syria always had favored a unified Arab approach to the struggle with Israel—ideally, led by Damascus—and feared that the Palestinians, following Egypt's model, would try and broker a separate deal. Syria responded to the PLO's peace overtures by opening up to the anti-Arafat factions of the PLO, both those on the ideological left—such as the Popular Front for the liberation of Palestine—as well those that were motivated by Islam—such as Hamas.

Syria was adamantly opposed to the 1992 Oslo Accords and the PLO's subsequent negotiation process with Israel. Syria not only criticized Arafat and the other PLO leaders for seeking a separate deal with Israel, it also argued that the Oslo agreement did not protect the interests of the Palestinian people and would never succeed. Syria maintained its position that a unified Arab approach was the only way to deal with Israel.

The collapse of the Oslo process and the eruption of the second intifada in 2000 appeared to validate Syria's views. These developments also bolstered the power and influence of the more radical and Islamist Palestinian groups who had made Damascus their base of operations. A slight thaw in Syrian-Palestinian relations occurred in 2000, when Arafat, to the surprise of many observers, attended the funeral of Hafez al-Asad and met afterward with Bashar al-Asad. But mutual suspicions remained high.

Syria looked on as Arafat was placed under virtual house arrest by Israel and as a new Palestinian leadership—one regarded as more moderate by the United States and more pliable by Israel—began to emerge. Damascus strongly protested, however, when in 2003 this new leadership agreed to the so-called road map for peace, a plan developed by the United States in close consultation with Israel's hard-line prime minister Ariel Sharon. As always, Syria opposed peace initiatives that did not take its own considerations and demands into account.

Bashar attended Arafat's funeral in 2004 after the iconic PLO leader died in Paris under suspicious circumstances. Syria then began to reach out to the new Palestinian leadership, and especially the new president Mahmoud Abbas, who paid an official visit to Damascus in December 2004. Although Abbas was a favorite of both the United States and Israel, he had grown up in Syria and attended the University of Damascus; the Syrian leadership felt a certain comfort with him.[34]

But Syria also remained the home base for some of Abbas's fiercest opponents within the Palestinian movement, especially the top leadership of Hamas. Khaled Mashal, one of Hamas's founders and its titular leader, operates out of Damascus. Mashal's presence in Damascus provides Syria with some leverage over Abbas as well as Israel and ensures that Syria will play a role in any future negotiations over internal Palestinian political reconciliation or any indirect negotiations between Israel and Hamas. It is unlikely that Syria would allow Mashal's presence—or that of any other extremist Palestinian leader—to provoke open conflict with Israel.

Tensions with Turkey

Syria and Turkey share a long and mostly difficult history. Syria was dominated by the Turkish-run Ottoman Empire for centuries, and Damascus was the center of the anti-Ottoman Arab nationalist movement in the early 20th century. Relations remained tense even after the fall of the Ottoman Empire in 1918. In 1939, the French—who governed Syria under a League of Nations mandate, negotiated with Istanbul to cede the Syrian province of Alexandretta to Turkey, an action that embittered Syrian nationalists and further soured relations with the Turkish Republic, the successor government to the Ottomans.

Syrian-Turkish relations became further strained in the 1950s and 1960s as a result of Cold War alliances. Turkey, pursuing a path of westernization, joined NATO and became a key U.S. strategic ally in southern Europe and the Middle East region. Syria had moved closer to the Eastern Bloc, to the point that the Turkish-Syrian border was regarded as a potentially explosive Cold War front. On numerous occasions, each country massed troops along the border.

But ideological differences and Syria's resentment over the loss of Alexandretta were not the only issues of conflict. In the 1980s, Syria offered support to the Kurdish Workers Party (PKK), a Kurdish nationalist group that was spearheading a guerilla war in Turkey's heavily Kurdish eastern provinces. Turkey regarded the PKK as a terrorist organization and threatened Syria with military retaliation if its assistance to the

Kurdish group continued. In 1998, Turkey threatened to attack Syria if Damascus did not turn over the PKK's leader, who was living in exile in Damascus. Eventually, Hafez al-Asad partially relented—he forced the Kurdish leader to leave Syria, and he was later arrested in Kenya and deported to Turkey.

Another source of friction between the two countries derives from Turkey's economic development plans in the east, which include the construction of dams along the Tigris and Euphrates Rivers. Much of Syria's water supply comes from the Euphrates, and the Damascus government accused the Turks of purposefully trying to control the water supply as a means of exerting influence over Syria.

Relations between Syria and Turkey improved dramatically after 2000, in part because of the Cold War's end and in part because the PKK had ceased being a major threat to Turkey's stability. In 2004, Bashar al-Asad paid a state visit to Turkey, the first time a Syrian leader had ever visited the Turkish Republic. Both countries found themselves on the same side as the United States prepared for war against Iraq in 2003— both opposed the Bush administration's policies. Both countries also feared that the U.S. campaign in Iraq would strengthen the Kurdish nationalist movements in their own countries. This confluence of interests did a great deal to ease the historical tensions between the two neighbors.

Relations improved further in 2008, when Turkey offered to mediate informal Syrian-Israeli talks on a permanent peace agreement. Turkey, one of the few Muslim nations on good terms with both Israel and the Arab states, took advantage of this unique status to facilitate dialogue. Although the dialogue abruptly ended as Turkish-Israeli relations declined through 2009 and 2010, the Turkish-Syrian relationship has only improved. A series of measures in October 2009 easing border restrictions between the countries has facilitated booming trade.[35] As hostility has grown between Turkey's ruling Justice and Development Party and Israel—perhaps culminating in the Gaza flotilla raid of 2010—Turkey and Syria have often found themselves in accord.

Potential conflict still exists between Syria and Turkey, especially over the water resources of the Euphrates. The Kurdish nationalist issue also could reemerge, although by 2003 Damascus and Ankara were essentially aligned on the issue and appeared to be coordinating their operations. Syria's close relationship with Iran could become a source of tension, but so far Syria has been adept at maintaining positive ties with both Iran and Turkey. Moreover, Turkey appears keen on nurturing its own relations with Iran, perhaps heralding a new tripartite alliance in Middle Eastern politics.[36]

United States

The U.S.-Syrian relationship has been characterized by discord and conflict, interspersed with brief periods of diplomatic cooperation over the Arab-Israeli peace process and the 1991 Gulf War. Although the United States supported Syria's independence from France in 1946, relations soured soon afterward as Syria staked out a claim to leadership of the Arab nationalist movement and took an extremely hard line against Israel's establishment in 1948. Syria's de facto alliance with the Soviet Union further inhibited the development of good relations with the United States.

Syria broke diplomatic relations with the United States following the 1967 Six-Day War, and relations remained severed until 1974, when Syria negotiated with U.S. secretary of state Henry Kissinger to bring about a separation of forces after the 1973 Arab-Israeli War. Several years later, the United States supported Syria's military intervention in Lebanon's civil war, seeing it as a factor for stability and at least a temporary end to the fighting. But even during this period of diplomatic thaw, relations were never close or warm; in many ways, U.S.-Syrian relations during the 1970s mirrored the ongoing U.S.-Soviet relationship of détente: cooperation where possible and mutually beneficial, but continuing competition in other arenas. For example, in 1979 Syria was placed on the U.S. list of state sponsors of terrorism (primarily for its support to radical Palestinian organizations), a designation that severely restricted bilateral commercial and trade relations. Even as relations with the United States appeared to thaw in 2010, Syria remained on the list.

In 1991, Syria surprised many observers by joining the U.S.-led military coalition to drive Iraqi forces out of Kuwait. Syria's alliance with the United States probably had more to do with its conflict with Saddam's regime in Iraq, but it nevertheless marked a dramatic change in U.S.-Syrian relations. Following the Gulf War, Syria agreed to participate in the U.S.-led Middle East peace conference in Madrid, the first time Syrians and Israelis sat together at a negotiating table.

Relations soured once again, however, in 1992, when Syria strongly rejected the Israeli-PLO accord reached in Oslo and formalized in a public meeting on the White House lawn between Yasser Arafat and Israeli prime minister Rabin. Syria returned to its more traditional position of rejecting any peace process that was not "comprehensive"—that is, that did not deal with Syria's demands concerning the return of the Golan Heights. But by 1999, Syria had accepted President Bill Clinton's offer to broker a peace agreement with Israel, and high-level meetings took place in West Virginia. The talks eventually collapsed, and the death of Hafez al-Asad and resumption of the Palestinian intifada in 2000 ended the U.S. mediation effort.[37]

The year 2000 also saw the election of George W. Bush as president of the United States. Bush and several influential members of his administration—including Vice President Richard Cheney and Secretary of Defense Donald Rumsfeld—viewed Syria as a "rogue state" that was at the root of the Middle East's problems. This attitude gained strength in administration circles after the terrorist attacks of September 11, 2001. No one in the Bush administration seriously considered that Syria might have been in any way responsible for the attacks, but they lumped Syria together with Iraq, North Korea, and Iran as regimes that were antithetical to U.S. interests. In the case of Syria, U.S. officials cited Syria's support for Hezbollah in Lebanon and Hamas in Palestine and its close relationship with Iran.

After the initial success of the U.S. invasion of Iraq in 2003, some Bush administration officials began to speak openly of the need for regime change in Damascus.[38] Needless to say, the Syrian government was alarmed by this rhetoric, and its policy of allowing foreign fighters to transit Syria on their way to Iraq may have been based in part on trying to ensure that the United States became bogged down in Iraq. Eventually, that is indeed what happened, and talk of forcible regime change in Syria came to end.

The Bush administration did, however, tighten sanctions against Syria under the 2003 Syria Accountability Act, which restricted virtually all U.S. trade except for food and medicine, and in 2005 withdrew the U.S. ambassador from Damascus, effectively cutting off all dialogue with the al-Asad government.[39] When Syria was implicated in the 2005 assassination of Lebanese prime minister Rafik Hariri, the Bush administration expressed further outrage and pushed for a UN inquiry into the assassination. By this time, however, the Iraq war was going badly and the threat of U.S. military action against Syria was considerably diminished.

By 2006, Syrian officials were quite open about declaring that they expected no improvement in U.S.-Syrian relations until after the Bush administration left office. Syrian officials also were pleased by presidential candidate Barack Obama's campaign pledges to open dialogue with countries such as Iran and Syria, with whom the United States had been at odds. There were credible reports that the Obama administration began back-channel talks with Syria as soon as it came into office in January 2009.[40] In February 2010, the administration nominated the first U.S. ambassador to Syria in five years.[41]

The United States and Syria are entering a phase in their relationship in which diplomacy plays a more significant role. This does not mean, however, that the sources of tension and conflict have been removed. The chances of a direct U.S.-Syrian military confrontation—or attempt by the United States to bring about regime change in Syria—are slim. President Obama has pledged to withdraw U.S. forces from Iraq, thus removing the forces that would be best situated to attack Syria.

The United States also took a cautious approach to the Syrian uprising that began in March 2011. There was no possibility of U.S. or NATO forces becoming involved (as they did in Libya), and calls for al-Asad's resignation or removal were muted. Like most countries in the region, initially the United States was not eager to see Syria collapse as a state. The somewhat predictable al-Asad seemed a safer option than a completely unpredictable civil war or internal collapse. But as the repression against antiregime protesters became more violent, and as global human rights groups demanded a response, the United States imposed financial sanctions on a number of Syrian officials, including al-Asad and many of his family, and openly called for his removal.

But many issues of conflict remain and could be exacerbated at any time. These include Syria's support for organizations that the United States regards as terrorist groups and Damascus's friendship with Iran. A resumption of internal conflict in Lebanon—or a renewed confrontation between Israel and Hezbollah—could lead to a deterioration in the U.S.-Syrian relationship. Any indications that Syria is trying to follow Iran's path toward the development of a nuclear program would also exacerbate tensions with the United States, although the United States probably would rely on Israel to conduct any military operations. Years of ingrained U.S.-Syrian animosity, as well as serious policy differences over Middle East peace, will mean that virtually any government that assumes power in Syria post-al-Asad will maintain political distance form the United States.

NOTES

1. Central Intelligence Agency, *The World Fact Book 2008,* https://www.cia.gov/library/publications/the-world-factbook/.

2. See Robert Fisk, *Pity the Nation* (London: Touchstone, 1990), 181–87, for a description of the Hama massacre.

3. Dennis Ross, who participated in the U.S.-led mediation effort, provides a firsthand account in *The Missing Peace: The Inside Story of the Fight for Middle East Peace* (New York: Farrar, Straus and Giroux, 2004).

4. See Lucy Ashton, "Syrian Repression Drives Opposition into the Arms of the Islamists," *Financial Times* (May 6, 2005).

5. David Lesch, *The New Lion of Damascus: Bashar al-Asad and Modern Syria* (New Haven, CT: Yale University Press, 2005), 142.

6. See Ghaith Abdul-Ahad, "Outside Iraq but Deep in the Fight," *Washington Post* (June 8, 2005).

7. See Middle East Watch, *Syria Unmasked: The Suppression of Human Rights by the Asad Regime* (New Haven, CT: Yale University Press, 1991).

8. Lesch, *The New Lion of Damascus,* 73–74.

9. Khaled Dawoud, "Between Chapters," *Al-Ahram Weekly* (July 20–26, 2000).

10. Lesch, *The New Lion of Damascus,* 87.

11. For the full text of the Damascus Declaration, see http://www.Syriacomment.com, November 1, 2005.

12. "Syria's Assad Wins Another Term," *BBC News* (May 29, 2007), http://news.bbc.co.uk/2/hi/middle_east/6700021.stm

13. Central Intelligence Agency, *The World Fact Book 2008*, https://www.cia.gov/library/publications/the-world-factbook/.

14. Robert Lowe, *The Syrian Kurds: A People Discovered* (London: Chatham House, 2006), 3.

15. Ibid., 3.

16. Amnesty International, "Kurds in the Syrian Arab Republic One Year after the March 2004 Events (March 2005), http://www.amnesty.org/en/library/info/MDE24/002/2005/en

17. Lowe, *The Syrian Kurds,* 6.

18. "Syria Detains 400 Kurdish Rebels in Raids—Report" *Reuters Africa* July 1, 2010), http://af.reuters.com/article/worldNews/idAFTRE6601W820100701.

19. Lesch, *The New Lion of Damascus,* 183–89.

20. Ferry Biedermann, "U.S. Colonel Sees Cut in Fighters Coming to Iraq from Syria," *Financial Times* (February 9, 2006).

21. "Iraq and Syria at Talks in Turkey," *BBC News* (September 17, 2009), http://news.bbc.co.uk/2/hi/middle_east/8261805.stm.

22. Natalya Antelava, "Iraqi Baathist Resentment Simmers in Syria," *BBC News* (March 5, 2010), http://news.bbc.co.uk/2/hi/middle_east/8552106.stm.

23. Ferry Biedermann, "Iraq and Syria Agree to Restore Relations," *Financial Times* (November 6, 2006).

24. See Anthony H. Cordesman, *The Israeli and Syrian Conventional Military Balance* (Washington, DC: Center for Strategic and International Studies, 2008).

25. Lisa Sinjab, "Damascus in Shock over Killing," *BBC News* (February 14, 2008), http://news.bbc.co.uk/2/hi/middle_east/7245313.stm.

26. For a classic analysis of this era, see Malcolm Kerr, *The Arab Cold War* (London and New York: Oxford University Press, 1971).

27. David Hirst, "Arab Leaders Watch in Fear as Shia Emancipation Draws Near," *The Guardian* (January 27, 2005).

28. "Mahmoud Ahmadinejad Insists Ties with Syria Are 'Deep,'" *BBC News* (February 25, 2010).

29. "Lebanon, Syria Sign Accords as Hariri visits Damascus," *Agence France Presse* (July 18, 2010).

30. Robert Worth, "Hezbollah Looks for Shield from Indictments' Sting," *New York Times* (July 24, 2010), http://www.nytimes.com/2010/07/25/world/middleeast/25lebanon.html.

31. United Nations Relief Works Agency, http://www.un.org/unrwa/publications/index.html.

32. Lesch, *The New Lion of Damascus,* 25.

33. Ibid., 39.

34. Sami Moubayed, "Thaw in Frosty Syria-Palestine Ties," *Gulf News* (July 13, 2005).

35. "Has It Won?" *Economist* (November 28, 2009).

36. Sabrina Tavernise, "For Turkey, an Embrace of Iran Is a Matter of Building Bridges," *New York Times* (June 12, 2010), http://www.nytimes.com/2010/06/13/world/middleeast/13turkey.html.

37. For an excellent and comprehensive overview of U.S.-Syrian relations through 2005 that also provides a regional perspective, see William Quandt, *Peace Process: American Diplomacy and the Arab-Israeli Conflict since 1967* (Washington, DC: Brookings Institution, 2005).

38. Walter Pincus, "Bush Aides Eye Regime Change in Syria," *Washington Post* (April 9, 2003). See also Tom Regan, "Is U.S. Planning an Iraq Style 'Regime Change' in Syria?" *Christian Science Monitor* (November 9, 2005).

39. For the text of the act, see http://www.fas.org/asmp/resources/govern/108th/pl_108_175.pdf.

40. See "Obama Talks with Syria Begun," *Agence France Presse* (February 1, 2009).

41. "Obama Nominates First US Ambassador to Syria since 2005," *BBC News* (February 17, 2010), http://news.bbc.co.uk/2/hi/middle_east/8519328.stm.

12 YEMEN

Yemen has suffered a politically turbulent history for much of the past 200 years, and its future as a unified state is highly problematic. Yemen occupies the southwestern corner of the Arabian Peninsula, separated from the Horn of Africa by the Bab al-Mandeb, the strategic strait that separates the Red Sea and the Gulf of Aden. Since the opening of the Suez Canal in 1869, all ship traffic between the Mediterranean Sea and the Indian Ocean has passed through the 18-mile-wide Bab al-Mandeb Strait—including over 3 million barrels of oil per day—and, as a result, developments in Yemen have been a serious concern of great powers.

Yemen also has been a concern of Saudi Arabia, with whom it shares the Arabian Peninsula. The Saudis have never been hesitant to intervene if they believe that instability in Yemen—which has been frequent—could lead to threats against the kingdom. At the same time, Saudi rulers also have feared a strong and unified Yemen; it long has been rumored that King Abdul Aziz Ibn Saud's dying words to his sons were "keep Yemen weak."[1] Apocryphal or not, subsequent Saudi leaders have behaved as if it were true, and Yemenis long have resented Saudi behavior, beginning with Ibn Saud's conquest in the early 20th century of three regions to the north of Yemen that Yemenis historically believed to be part of Yemen.

Yemen's turbulent history was exacerbated by the fact that the nation was divided into two until 1990, and has never truly shared one dominant political culture. Tribalism and family networks have played far greater roles in political and social life than have institutions of state. The northern part of Yemen came under Ottoman rule in the 16th century, and in 1839 Britain occupied and colonized the strategic southern Yemeni city of Aden and created a buffer around it; Aden and its buffer zone were known as South Yemen. When the Ottoman Empire collapsed after World War I, North Yemen became an independent country under a conservative and rather xenophobic monarchy. A military coup in 1962, however, established a republic under a leadership that espoused a pro-Nasser, pan-Arab ideology. A civil war between monarchists and re-publicans ensued, with Saudi Arabia coming to the aid of the monarchists and Egyptian troops fighting alongside the republicans. The ensuing civil war became a proxy war between the forces for pan-Arab secular social nationalism, as advocated by Nasser, and the traditional conservative regimes exemplified by the Saud dynasty.

The two sides agreed to end the war in 1972; North Yemen would remain a re-public, but members of the former royal family would be allowed to play roles in government. Sporadic fighting and political assassinations continued for several more years, however, until Ali Abdullah Saleh came to power in 1978 in North Yemen. Saleh clamped down on the most radical left-wing elements of the regime and developed a closer relationship with Saudi Arabia. Although Saleh maintained a military relation-ship with the Soviet Union, he also adroitly managed to stay on friendly terms with the United States.

Meanwhile, the British withdrew from South Yemen in 1967 after several years of armed struggle against resistance fighters and as part of Britain's general withdrawal from former colonial enclaves. The National Liberation Front, which had spearheaded the anti-British resistance, seized power and established the People's Democratic Re-public of Yemen, a socialist state modeled after (and allied with) the Soviet Union. In 1978, the National Liberation Front transformed into the Yemeni Socialist Party (YSP). The late 1970s witnessed periodic border wars with North Yemen and the es-tablishment of a Soviet naval presence at the port of Aden.

Infighting within the YSP led to a civil war in South Yemen in 1986—a war that was in fact a bloody battle between different YSP elements vying for power. Exhausted by internal fighting, weakened by economic collapse, and facing the global decline of its Moscow ally, South Yemen's leaders agreed in 1989 to the North's proposal for uni-fication of the two countries. Ali Abdullah Saleh, the leader of North Yemen, headed a presidential council composed of three northerners and two southerners, with its capi-tal in Sanaa, the former capital of North Yemen. Despite unification, however, Yemen remained one of the poorest countries in the world, and its tribal social structure and heavily armed population almost ensured a less than peaceful future.

Yemen's Saudi neighbors watched the country's unification with trepidation; the Saudis were not keen to see a unified Yemeni nation that might oppose Saudi policies. These concerns were borne out in 1991, when Yemen refused to support the Saudis and their U.S. allies in the war against Saddam Hussein. Yemen had multiple reasons for remaining officially neutral in the war, but the nation paid a high cost for not joining the coalition forces. The United States drastically reduced economic aid to the impov-erished nation, and the Saudis expelled nearly 1 million Yemeni workers from Saudi Arabia. The latter blow was especially severe, as Yemen relied heavily on foreign ex-change earned by its workers in Saudi Arabia to sustain its fragile economy.

The resulting strains on Yemen's political system led to a brief civil war, in which troops loyal to Saleh attacked Aden—the former capital of South Yemen—and effec-tively eradicated the remaining elements of the YSP. Ironically, Saudi Arabia supported the YSP, not because of any sympathy for the radical party but rather out of a desire to weaken Saleh's government and keep it focused on internal issues. During this time, a few border clashes occurred between Yemeni troops and Saudi troops, raising the risk of a regional war. But Saleh knew well that such a development would not be in Yemen's interests, so he began negotiations with Riyadh on an agreement to define, once and for all, the two countries' borders. An initial agreement was reached in 1995, and in 2000 a permanent agreement was signed in which Yemen recognized Saudi sovereignty over the lands that had been historically a part of Yemen before being seized by Ibn Saud, and diplomatic relations between the two countries finally were normalized.[2]

In 2004, a rebellion erupted in the northern Yemeni province of Sa'da involving government forces and local tribal groups. Because many residents of northern Yemen are Shitte Muslims, the conflict has risked becoming a Shitte-Sunni battle, which is why it attracted the interest and involvement of Saudi Arabia and, purportedly, Iran. As of mid-2010, the instability and conflict in the north simmered, while challenges to the government from al-Qaeda members and discontented southerners threatened to boil over.

Throughout it all, the Yemeni economy continued to sink to the point of despair, leading to a serious refugee and humanitarian problem. Indeed, almost all of the security issues confronting Yemen derive in large measure from the country's economic woes, as described by Ginny Hill in a 2008 study:

> The poorest nation in the Arab world struggles with 27% inflation, 40% unemployment and 46% child malnutrition. Half of its 22 million citizens are under sixteen and the population is set to double by 2035. Seven million people live in poverty and the country is heavily dependent on food imports, making it especially vulnerable to global price shocks. Reserves of groundwater and oil are rapidly diminishing.[3]

When the revolutionary movement in the Arab world in the spring of 2011 reached Yemen, it did not face an ossified authoritarian regime that nevertheless had maintained order, as in Egypt, Tunisia, Libya, and Syria. Rather, the uprising against the Saleh government occurred against a backdrop of many years of internal conflict, the potential for terrorism, and dire economic collapse. As a result, the unrest in Yemen was less of a surprise to the international community—concerns about Yemen's stability had been apparent in Western policy making for at least a decade.

The popular demands for Saleh's removal from power followed the uprisings in Egypt and Tunisia but took on a more violent form, especially after Saleh loyalists fired on and killed over 50 protesters in Sanaa in March 2011. Even many prominent Saleh supporters in the armed forces called for his resignation after this attack, but he refused to do so, and divisions within the army accelerated the trend toward violence. In subsequent weeks, Saleh at times appeared to accept an offer of resignation in exchange for immunity from prosecution, but in the end he refused to relinquish power. In June 2011, Saleh was seriously injured in an attack on the presidential palace and was flown to Saudi Arabia for medical treatment. But September 2011 saw his return to Sanaa, and with it a return to ever more violent protests and counterattacks.

While the Yemen uprising followed closely behind those in Egypt and Tunisia, the consequences are far greater, given Yemen's essential fragility as a unified state, lack of experience with democracy, and violent history of tribal and clan warfare. It was highly unlikely that any central authority would be able to secure control in the wake of Saleh's departure, and the prospects for Yemen's political future are bleak.

POTENTIAL CONFLICTS

Internal Conflict in Sa'da Province

The rebellion that broke out in Sa'da province in 2004 has deep roots. The conflict centers on fighting between government forces and a rebel group known as the Huthis. The Huthis represent followers of Zaydism, a form of Shiite Islam practiced in Yemen. Prior to the 1962 military coup that established the republic of North Yemen, the country had been ruled for over 1,000 years by a Zaydi royal family; their supporters, also mostly Zaydis from Sa'da province, led the decade-long civil war against the new republican government. Although members of the family were allowed to play a role in the North Yemen government according to the terms of the peace agreement reached in 1972, the province of Sa'da—a mountainous region along the Yemeni-Saudi border—remained somewhat marginalized, and many of its tribal leaders never fully supported the republican government, which, in turn, never fully trusted the Zaydi community (although there are exceptions; President Ali Abdullah Saleh, for example, hails from a Zaydi Shiite group in the north).

Moreover, beginning in the 1970s, Sunni Wahhabists from Saudi Arabia began to seek followers in Yemen, including in Sa'da, the Zaydi stronghold. Wahhabism, the dominant Sunni interpretation in Saudi Arabia, was doctrinally hostile to Zaydism. Many Zaydi leaders believed that the Yemeni government in Sanaa was secretly supporting the Wahhabists in exchange for financial aid from Saudi Arabia.[4]

The violence that broke out in 2004 was triggered by the government's attempted arrest, and later killing, of a prominent Zaydi from Sa'da who was a former member of parliament. Opposition rapidly grew and spread among Sa'da's tribal groups and Zaydi community, and before long the conflict expanded to include others with grievances against the government. As the International Crisis Group reported:

The war expanded because it became a microcosm of a series of latent religious, social, political and

An armed Yemeni fighter takes position next to an army post at the battle front in the rebellious northern province of Sa'da. (Khaled Fazaa/AFP/Getty Images)

economic tensions. It can be traced to the decline of the social stratum led by Hashemites, who claim descent from the Prophet Muhammad, and legitimised by Zaydism; lack of investment in Zaydi strongholds like Sa'da; failed management of religious pluralism; permeability to external influences and the emergence of new political and religious actors, particularly Salafis. It has variously and at times simultaneously taken the shape of a sectarian, political or tribal conflict, rooted in historical grievances and endemic underdevelopment. It also has been shaped by the regional confrontation between Saudi Arabia and Iran.[5]

By most reports, the violence was extensive and brutal; the destruction of entire rebel villages not only increased resentment against the government, but also led to a growing refugee problem in the north; by one estimate, over 130,000 were internally displaced by 2008.[6] Over the course of the fighting, the Huthis became more radicalized; although they initially declared their support for a unified Yemen, by 2008 they were openly calling for the demise of the regime.[7] The government's tendency to employ tribal groups to assist in the fighting exacerbated local rivalries and expanded the scope of the conflict.

The Huthi forces were well armed—many Yemeni government officials, as well as the Saudis, accused Iran of supplying the rebels—and by 2008, rebel forces were on the outskirts of Yemen's capital city of Sanaa. The government declared a unilateral cease-fire in July 2008, which the rebels respected, but isolated outbreaks of fighting continued, and the government violated its own cease-fire by staging a major assault in August 2009. In November 2009, Saudi warplanes attacked rebel positions in Sa'da, and, although the Yemeni government denied any coordination with the Saudis, both governments clearly have the same objectives and the same concerns about Iranian influence within the Huthi movement.[8] The subsequent conflict, which lasted until a February 2010 cease-fire agreement, resulted in extensive civilian casualties and an internally displaced population of 250,000.[9] Despite the cease-fire, the conflict has continued sporadically since February 2010, with fighting periodically taking place between the Huthis and local tribes allegedly backed by the Yemeni government.[10]

As these outbreaks of violence suggest, negotiated peace will remain fragile as long as issues underlying the conflict are not addressed. The possibility of increased involvement by both Iran and Saudi Arabia is high and will result in a prolongation and intensification of the conflict. Indeed, the prerequisite for a calming in Sa'da province may very well be a regional rapprochement—or at least détente—between Saudi Arabia and Iran.

The principal risk posed by the crisis in Sa'da province, combined with the upheaval against the Saleh government, is that Yemen becomes a failed state, in which case it could serve as a base for terrorist groups (the country's dire economic situation already is consistent with that of failed states). While Yemen could officially remain a unified sovereign state, it more likely will become a fragmented entity ruled at the local level by militias and tribal groups, all heavily armed and easily susceptible to outside influence and control.

Antigovernment protestors chant slogans during a demonstration demanding the resignation of Yemeni president Ali Abdullah Saleh. (AP Photo/Hani Mohammed)

Internal North-South Conflict

As noted, in 1994 a brief civil war between northern and southern forces was won by the northerners, and Yemen remained unified under the government in Sanaa. But disgruntlement among some southerners over the 1990 unification did not come to an end, and in fact many southerners considered themselves to be under northern occupation.

In the summer of 2007, demonstrators took to the streets in Aden, the former capital of South Yemen, to demand higher pension payments for former military officers of the South Yemeni army. Led by the Southern Movement—or Hiraak—the protests soon turned into a demand for southern secession, and protestors waved the flag of the former state. At the root of the protests is widespread sentiment among southerners that government patronage favors residents of the north and that the south does not benefit equally from the country's oil resources, which are located mostly in what was formerly South Yemen. As these oil resources become depleted (as they are expected to do over the next decade), the struggle for economic growth will likely exacerbate the secessionist tendencies in the south.[11]

The protests eventually transformed into violent attacks, often aimed at symbols of central government authority (such as military checkpoints and police stations). In October 2009, the Yemeni interior ministry banned all street demonstrations in Aden, the south's largest city, but according to some analysts, the government's radical crackdown on the broad movement appears to have only strengthened secessionist tendencies.[12] Moreover, while Hiraak's leadership has done much to distance itself from al-Qaeda's violent challenges to the Yemeni government, the southern group clearly benefits from popular displeasure at the heavy-handed tactics employed by the government to fight the terrorist group. In addition to these powerful domestic factors, the movement is also bolstered internationally by expatriate Yemenis in Europe and the United States who left the country after unification with the north in 1990. Combined with the rebellion in Sa'da, the southern secessionist movement further pushes Yemen toward the category of failed state. Moreover, each conflict feeds on and to a certain degree reinforces the other, as they both operate to weaken the government in Sanaa.

The refusal of President Saleh to step down—and his defiant return to Yemen after months of medical treatment in Saudi Arabia—has further convinced Hiraak and many southerners that secession is the only viable option. The prospects for civil war—in effect, a new round of previous north-south wars—are high.

Internal Threat from al-Qaeda and Related Jihadist Groups

Yemen first attracted world attention as a potential terrorist stronghold in 2000, when the USS *Cole,* docked in Aden for refueling, was approached by a small manned craft loaded with 1,000 pounds of explosives. The ensuing suicide attack blew a hole in the *Cole*'s hull and killed 17 U.S. sailors. Osama bin Laden's al-Qaeda organization took credit for and boasted about the attack. Although subsequent investigations suggested that the terrorists may have been based and trained in Sudan, the attack on the *Cole*—which was followed by an attack on a French oil tanker in Aden in 2002—focused attention on the significant al-Qaeda presence in Yemen.

The bin Laden family has deep roots in Yemen. Osama bin Laden's father, Mohammed bin Awad bin Laden, was born in southern Yemen and emigrated to Saudi Arabia early in the 20th century. Following the Soviet withdrawal from Afghanistan in 1989, many former mujahideen—the Islamist fighters who provided fierce resistance against the Soviets—relocated to Yemen to consider the next steps in their global jihadist movement. Among them were many members of al-Qaeda, an organization that Osama bin Laden had established during his stint fighting the Soviets in Afghanistan (bin Laden himself, however, returned first to Saudi Arabia, and in 1992 to Sudan; he eventually would return to Afghanistan after the Islamist extremist Taliban took control of the country).

The number of al-Qaeda supporters in Yemen grew in the early 2000s, when Saudi Arabia, following the dramatic terrorist attacks against the United States in September 2001, launched a major crackdown on Islamist extremists in the kingdom. In March 2008, a Saudi financier of al-Qaeda and affiliated groups declared that al-Qaeda had been effectively defeated inside the kingdom and encouraged its supporters to move to Yemen.[13] In January 2009, al-Qaeda in Saudi Arabia and al-Qaeda in Yemen officially merged to form al-Qaeda in the Arabian Peninsula.

The porous border with Yemen proved to be an excellent escape route. Indeed, Yemen provides a particularly suitable site for terrorist groups due to the vast areas of desert and mountain terrain—especially in the northern parts of the country, along the border with Saudi Arabia—combined with a weak central government that exercises only minimal control over much of the country. And because of Yemen's history of civil wars and tribal violence, the country has a large supply of weapons and ammunition.

The terrorist and terrorist sympathizers who arrived in Yemen in the 2000s found fertile ground. Over the years, Saudi Arabia had funded Islamist schools in Yemen, all of which were based on the strict Sunni Wahhabist traditions and doctrine. Thus, many Sunni Yemenis already were inclined to support the objectives—if not necessarily the methods—of the jihadists. Several indigenous jihadist organizations and militias already were active in Yemen when the influx of Afghan veterans and Saudi exiles began to arrive (one such group, the Aden-Abyan Islamic Army, had been implicated in the kidnappings of Western tourists in 1998 and the 2000 bombing of the British consulate in Aden).[14] More recently, an influx of potential insurgents appears to have occurred from the opposite direction, as thousands of Somalis—some with connections to the violent Islamist militia known as the Shabab—have fled to Yemen as the situation in Somalia has deteriorated.[15]

Although it is difficult to determine with certainty, it appears that al-Qaeda and its supporters enjoy a certain degree of popular support in Yemen, especially during episodes of Israeli military activity in the region or in response to U.S. policies that appear to be directed against the Muslim world or in favor of Israel.[16] These pan-Arab sentiments among the population have made it difficult for Yemen to provide the degree of support in the U.S.-led war on terrorism that many officials in Washington would like to see. Another concern is that al-Qaeda has aggressively sought to appeal to Yemeni tribes, seeking a relationship much like that between the extremist group and tribes in Pakistan.[17] As a result, the group enjoys a modicum of sanctuary in some areas of Yemen where the central government holds little power.

Al-Qaeda has capitalized on these favorable conditions to establish extensive networks within Yemen capable of inspiring, if not always executing, attacks far beyond Yemen's borders. Failed attempts at bombing an airliner in Detroit in December 2009 and detonating a car bomb in New York's Times Square in May 2010 both possessed a Yemeni connection, namely to a U.S.-born imam of Yemeni descent—Anwar al-Awlaki—who is believed to have resided in Yemen since 2004. The links to Yemen in each case have renewed the interest of U.S. government officials in supporting the Saleh regime's campaign against the terrorist group. One early measure was the U.S. suspension of transferring Yemeni prisoners from Guantanamo Bay back to Yemen, for fear that the prisoners might become involved in terrorist activities upon returning to their native country.[18] Additionally, the Obama administration succeeded in assassinating al-Awlaki in September 2011, and coordination between Yemeni and U.S. intelligence has increased.[19] There was a notable uptick in fighting between the government and al-Qaeda militants throughout much of 2010, including a brazen al-Qaeda attack on government intelligence headquarters in Aden that freed several prisoners.[20] Clearly, al-Qaeda poses a danger to the Saleh government; however, so too do any actions by the central government that might alienate the Yemeni population, such as appearing overly subservient to U.S. interests or engaging in operations that result in significant civilian casualties. With such narrow space for operating combined with the dire economic situation, the ongoing civil war in the north, and persistent secessionist tendencies in the south—all in the context of a heavily armed tribal society—it seems likely that the country will remain an ideal base of operations for terrorist organizations for years. Moreover, the ouster of Saleh will complicate matters for Western intelligence and antiterrorism operations

Saudi Arabia

Saudi Arabia has maintained an ambivalent relationship with Yemen and has traditionally pursued mixed-motive policies toward its southern neighbor: On the one hand, Riyadh fears a strong and unified Yemen. But at the same time, the prospect of a chaotic and violent failed state in Yemen is also worrying to the Saudis, especially in light of the fact that Yemen hosts a powerful offshoot of al-Qaeda, known as al-Qaeda in the Arabian Peninsula. Evidence of Iranian influence in Yemen causes further concerns for the Saudis.

Saudi Arabia's mixed-motive strategy on Yemen has generated policies that at times have seemed contradictory. For example, the stridently anticommunist Saudis supported North Yemen in an attempt to bolster Sanaa against the Marxist South Yemen. But after the two Yemeni states unified in 1990, Riyadh supported the southerners in their 1994 uprising against the central government, in part as punishment for Yemen's neutral position during the Gulf War but also to keep the central government off balance.

Some observers—including many Yemenis—have accused Saudi Arabia of trying to prevent major international oil companies from investing in Yemen, presumably out of a desire to prevent Yemen from becoming a significant oil power.[21] Saudi leaders also are wary of Yemen's more open political system, which features competing political parties, a relatively free press, and women's suffrage.[22]

Saudi Arabia's ambivalence about Yemen was apparent during the anti-Saleh uprisings in 2011. Ultimately, Riyadh supported calls for Saleh's removal, but preferred that this be done in the context of a Gulf Cooperation Council–coordinated process. Saudi Arabia will likely continue its policy of supporting a unified central government in Yemen when doing so bolsters Riyadh's perceptions of its security interests, but undermining the central government if it deems that Yemen is becoming too powerful or unified. Clearly, Riyadh has not in the past and probably will not in the future take into account the interests of Yemen or Yemenis. The result of this mixed-motive strategy could drive Yemen further down the road to state failure, in which case the Saudis may find themselves with a chronically unstable situation on their southern border.

NOTES

1. Quoted in Ginny Hill and Gerd Nonneman, *Yemen, Saudi Arabia and the Gulf States: Elite Politics, Street Protests and Regional Diplomacy* (London: Chatham House, May 2011), 5.

2. For an excellent overview of this period of Yemen's history, see Paul Dresch, *A History of Modern Yemen* (Cambridge, UK: Cambridge University Press, 2000).

3. Ginny Hill, *Yemen: Fear of Failure* (London: Chatham House, 2008), 2.

4. Shelagh Weir, "Clash of Fundamentalisms: Wahabbism in Yemen," *Middle East Report* 204 (1997): 22–23, 26.

5. International Crisis Group, "Yemen: Defusing the Saada Time Bomb," Middle East Report No. 86 (May 27, 2009), i.

6. "Invisible Civilians: The Challenge of Humanitarian Access in Yemen's Forgotten War," Human Rights Watch (November 2008), www.hrw.org/en/reports/2008/11/18/invisiblecivilians-0.

7. International Crisis Group, "Yemen: Defusing the Saada Time Bomb," 5.

8. For an analysis of the motivations of involved actors, see Joost Hilterman, "Disorder on the Border: Saudi Arabia's War Inside Yemen," *Foreign Affairs* (December 16, 2009), http://www.foreignaffairs.com/articles/65730/joost-r-hiltermann/disorder-on-the-border.

9. "A Bloody Blame Game," *The Economist* (February 6, 2010), 52.

10. "Yemen Fighting Kills Dozens," *Al-Jazeera English* (July 21, 2010), http://english.aljazeera.net/news/middleeast/2010/07/201072134622962696.html.

11. Hill, *Yemen: Fear of Failure,* 5.

12. Stephen Day, "The Political Challenge of Yemen's Southern Movement," Carnegie Endowment for International Peace: Middle East Program No. 108 (March 2010), http://carnegieendowment.org/files/yemen_south_movement.pdf.

13. "Why Al Qaeda in Yemen Is Wooing the Saudis," *Khaleej Times* (May 10, 2008).

14. International Crisis Group, "Yemen: Coping with Terrorism and Violence in a Fragile State," Middle East Report No. 8 (January 8, 2003), 11.

15. Raghavan, Sudarsan, "Somalis fleeing to Yemen prompt new worries in fight against al-Qaeda," *Washington Post.* 12 January 2010. http://www.washingtonpost.com/wp-dyn/content/article/2010/01/11/AR2010011103929.html

16. International Crisis Group, "Yemen: Coping with Terrorism and Violence in a Fragile State," 22.

17. Sarah Phillips, "What Comes Next in Yemen? Al-Qaeda, the Tribes, and State-Building," Carnegie Endowment for International Peace: Middle East Program No. 107 (March 2010), http://www.carnegieendowment.org/files/yemen_tribes.pdf.

18. Peter Finn, "Return of Yemeni Detainees at Guantanamo Bay Is Suspended," *Washington Post* (January 5, 2010), http://www.washingtonpost.com/wp-dyn/content/article/2010/01/05/AR2010010502850.html.

19. Scott Shane, "US Approves Targeted Killing of American Cleric," *New York Times* (April 6, 2010), http://www.nytimes.com/2010/04/07/world/middleeast/07yemen.html.

20. Patrick Cockburn, "Al-Qa'ida Boosted by Hit on Yemeni Secret Police," *The Independent* (June 21, 2010), http://www.independent.co.uk/news/world/middle-east/alqaida-boosted-by-hit-on-yemeni-secret-police-2006120.html.

21. See Richard Schofield, "The Last Missing Fence in the Desert: The Saudi-Yemeni Boundary," in *Yemen Today: Crisis and Solutions,* ed. E.G.H. Joffé, M.J. Hachemi, and E.W. Watkins, 213–68 (London: Caravel Press, 1997).

22. International Crisis Group, "Yemen: Coping with Terrorism and Violence in a Fragile State," 22.

SELECTED BIBLIOGRAPHY

Abrahamian, Ervand. *A History of Modern Iran.* New York: Cambridge University Press, 2008.

Al-Aswany, Alaa. *On the State of Egypt: A Novelist's Provocative Reflections.* Cairo: American University in Cairo Press, 2011.

Allan, Tony. *The Middle East Water Question: Hydropolitics and the Global Economy.* London: I. B. Tauris, 2002.

Allin, Dana, and Steven Simon. *The Sixth Crisis: Iran, Israel, America, and the Rumors of War.* New York: Oxford University Press, 2010.

An-Na'im, Abdullahi Ahmed. *Islam and the Secular State: Negotiating the Future of Shari'a.* Cambridge, MA: Harvard University Press, 2008.

Bayat, Asef. *Life as Politics: How Ordinary People Change the Middle East.* Stanford, CA: Stanford University Press, 2009.

Beinin, Joel, and Frederic Vairel, eds. *Social Movements, Mobilization, and Contestation in the Middle East and North Africa.* Stanford, CA: Stanford University Press, 2011.

Blumi, Isa. *Chaos in Yemen: Societal Collapse and the New Authoritarianism.* New York: Routledge, 2010.

Byman, Daniel. *A High Price: The Triumphs and Failures of Israeli Counterterrorism.* New York: Oxford University Press, 2011.

Calvert, John. *Sayyid Qutb and the Origins of Radical Islamism.* New York: Columbia University Press, 2010.

Caplan, Neil. *The Israel-Palestine Conflict: Contested Histories.* Hoboken, NJ: Wiley-Blackwell, 2010.

Caton, Steven C. *Yemen Chronicle: An Anthropology of War and Mediation.* New York: Hill & Wang, 2006.

Clark, Victoria. *Yemen: Dancing on the Heads of Snakes.* New York: Nation Books, 2010.

Cleveland, William L., and Martin Bunton. *A History of the Modern Middle East,* 4th ed. Boulder, CO: Westview Press, 2008.

Coleman, Isobel. *Paradise Beneath Her Feet: How Women Are Transforming the Middle East.* New York: Random House, 2010.

Crane, Keith, et al. *Future Challenges for the Arab World: The Implications of Demographic and Economic Trends.* Santa Monica, CA: RAND Corporation, 2011.

Davis, Eric. *Memories of State: Politics, History and Collective Identity in Modern Iraq.* Berkeley, CA: University of California Press, 2005.

Ebadi, Shirin. *Iran Awakening: A Memoir of Revolution and Hope.* New York: Random House, 2006.

El Fadl, Khaled Abou. *Islam and the Challenge of Democracy.* Princeton, NJ: Princeton University Press, 2004.

Fawcett, Louise, ed. *International Relations of the Middle East,* 2nd ed. New York: Oxford University Press, 2009.

Fisk, Robert. *The Great War for Civilisation: The Conquest of the Middle East.* New York: Vintage, 2007.

Fisk, Robert. *Pity the Nation: Lebanon at War.* New York: Oxford University Press, 2001.

Fromkin, David. *A Peace to End All Peace: The Fall of the Ottoman Empire and the Creation of the Modern Middle East.* New York: Holt, 2001.

Gause, F. Gregory. *The International Relations of the Persian Gulf.* New York: Cambridge University Press, 2010.

Gelvin, James. *The Modern Middle East: A History,* 3rd ed. New York: Oxford University Press, 2011.

Hegghammer, Thomas. *Jihad in Saudi Arabia: Violence and Pan-Islamism since 1979.* New York: Cambridge University Press, 2010.

Henry, Clement Moore. *Globalization and the Politics of Development in the Middle East.* New York: Cambridge University Press, 2010.

Hirst, David. *Beware of Small States: Lebanon, Battleground of the Middle East.* New York: Nation Books, 2010.

Hodges, Tony. *The Western Sahara: The Roots of a Desert War.* Chicago: Lawrence Hill, 1983.

Howe, Marvine. *Morocco: The Islamist Awakening and Other Challenges.* New York: Oxford University Press, 2005.

Hunter, Robert E. *Building Security in the Persian Gulf.* Santa Monica, CA: RAND Corporation, 2010.

Jones, Toby Craig. *Desert Kingdom: How Oil and Water Forged Modern Saudi Arabia.* Cambridge, MA: Harvard University Press, 2010.

Keddie, Nikki R. *Women in the Middle East: Past and Present.* Princeton, NJ: Princeton University Press, 2006.

Kemp, Geoffrey. *The East Moves West: India, China and Asia's Growing Presence in the Middle East.* Washington, DC: Brookings Institution Press, 2010.

Kepel, Gilles. *Beyond Terror and Martyrdom: The Future of the Middle East.* Cambridge, MA: Belknap Press, 2010.

Khalidi, Rashid. *Palestinian Identity.* New York: Columbia University Press, 2010.

Khalidi, Rashid. *Sowing Crisis: The Cold War and American Dominance in the Middle East.* Boston: Beacon Press, 2010.

Khan, Saira. *Iran and Nuclear Weapons: Protracted Conflict and Proliferation.* Hoboken, NJ: Routledge, 2010.

Lacroix, Stephane. *Awakening Islam: The Politics of Religious Dissent in Contemporary Saudi Arabia.* Cambridge, MA: Harvard University Press, 2011.

Laqueur, Walter, and Barry Rubin, eds. *The Israel-Arab Reader: A Documentary History of the Middle East Conflict,* 7th ed. New York: Penguin Books, 2008.

Lawrence, Quil. *Invisible Nation: How the Kurds' Quest for Statehood Is Shaping Iraq and the Middle East.* New York: Walker, 2009.

Louer, Laurence. *Transnational Shia Politics: Religious and Political Networks in the Gulf.* New York: Columbia University Press, 2008.

Lynch, Marc. *Voices of the New Arab Public: Iraq, al-Jazeera, and Middle East Politics Today.* New York: Columbia University Press, 2007.

MacFarquhar, Neil. *The Media Relations Department of Hizbollah Wishes You a Happy Birthday.* New York: PublicAffairs/Perseus, 2009.

Milton-Edwards, Beverley and Stephen Farrell. *Hamas: The Islamic Resistance Movement.* Cambridge, UK: Polity Press, 2010.

Nasr, Sayyed Hossein. *Islam: Religion, History, and Civilization.* New York: HarperOne, 2002.

Nasr, Vali. *The Shia Revival: How Conflicts within Islam will Shape the Future.* New York: W. W. Norton, 2007.

O'Connell, Jack. *King's Counsel.* New York: W. W. Norton, 2011.

Osman, Tarek. *Egypt on the Brink: From Nasser to Mubarak.* New Haven, CT: Yale University Press, 2011.

Polk, William R. *Understanding Iran: Everything You Need to Know, From Persia to the Islamic Republic, From Cyrus to Ahmadinejad.* London: Palgrave Macmillan, 2011.

Primakov, Yevgeny. *Russia and the Arabs: Behind the Scenes in the Middle East from the Cold War to the Present.* New York: Basic Books, 2009.

Quandt, William B. *Peace Process: American Diplomacy and the Arab-Israeli Conflict since 1967.* Berkeley, CA: University of California Press, 2005.

Richards, Alan, and John Waterbury. *A Political Economy of the Middle East: State, Class and Economic Development,* 3rd ed. Boulder, CO: Westview Press, 2008.

Ricks, Thomas. *Fiasco: The American Military Adventure in Iraq.* New York: Penguin Group, 2006.

Roberts, Hugh. *The Battlefield Algeria, 1988–2002.* London: Verso, 2003.

Rouhana, Nadir N. *Palestinian Citizens in an Ethnic Jewish State.* New Haven, CT: Yale University Press, 2007.

Ruedy, John. *Algeria: The Origins and Development of a Nation,* 2nd ed. Bloomington: Indiana University Press, 2005.

Sachar, Howard. *A History of Israel: From the Rise of Zionism to Our Time.* New York: Knopf, 2007.

Savir, Uri. *The Process: 1,100 Days that Changed the Middle East.* New York: Vintage, 1999.

Segev, Tom. *1967: Israel, the War and the Year that Transformed the Middle East.* New York: Picador, 2008.

Sorenson, David S., ed. *Interpreting the Middle East: Essential Themes.* Boulder, CO: Westview Press, 2010.

Takeyh, Ray. *Guardians of the Revolution: Iran and the World in the Age of the Ayatollahs.* London: Oxford University Press, 2009.

Tessler, Mark. *Public Opinion in the Middle East: Survey Research and the Political Orientations of Ordinary Citizens.* Bloomington: Indiana University Press, 2011.

Tripp, Charles. *A History of Iraq.* New York: Cambridge University Press, 2007.

Vassiliev, Alexei. *The History of Saudi Arabia.* New York: New York University Press, 2000.

Wright, Robin. *Rock the Casbah: Rage and Rebellion across the Islamic World.* New York: Simon & Schuster, 2011.

Yergin, Daniel. *The Prize: The Epic Quest for Oil, Money and Power.* New York: Free Press, 2008.

Ziadeh, Radwan. *Power and Policy in Syria: Intelligence Services, Foreign Policy and Democratization in the Modern Middle East.* London: Tauris Academic Studies, 2011.

INDEX

IDF. *See* Israeli Defense Forces

International Court of Justice (ICR), 24

Iran: alliance with U.S., 7; attack against GCC, 50; background on, 37–41; Bahrain, tensions with, 21; civil unrest in, 50–51; Egypt relations with, 6–8; ethnic insurgencies in, 45–47; external sources of conflict in, 47–55; Green Movement in, 43–44; Guardian Council in, 42–43; Hamas influenced by, 7–8, 93; internal sources of conflict in, 41–47; intervention in Iraq, 51; Iraq conflict with, 51–52, 72–74;-Iraq war, 52, 59, 168–69; Israel conflict with, 50, 52–54; Israeli-Hezbollah confrontation, 53; Israeli military strike against, 53; Israel threatened by, 96–97; Jordan, relations with, 117–18; Jundullah, Baluchi in, 46–47; Kurdish Pajak in, 45–46; Kuwait, relations with, 127–28; Lebanon, relations with, 141–42; Mujahedine-e-Khalq in, 44–45, 73; nuclear weapons in, 48–49, 50, 54, 96–97, 128, 172; Oman attack on, repercussions, 25; Qatar, potential conflict with, 27–28; regime infighting and succession in, 42–43; Saudi Arabia, competition with, 168–73; Saudi Arabia, U.S., and, 172–73; Saudi Arabia and GCC conflict with, 54–55; Syria's political instability relating to, 53–54; United Arab Emirates, nuclear ambitions relating to, 31–33; United Arab Emirates, tensions with, 29–33; United Arab Emirates, territorial dispute with, 30–31; U.S. conflict with, 47–51, 73–74

Iranian Islamic Revolution, 21

Iranian Revolution: Egypt and, 3, 6; Jordan and, 116

Iranian Revolutionary Guard Corps (IRGC), 62

Iraq: agriculture in, 80; armed struggle in, 60–64; Article 140 of, 67–68; background on, 57–60; Badr Brigade, 62; Basra, 65, 72; constitutional flaws in, 64–66; corruption in, 66–67; CPA in, 63; flag representing, 66; instability in, impacting United Arab Emirates, 33–34; Iran conflict with, 51–52, 72–74; Iranian intervention in, 51;-Iran war, 52, 59, 168–69; Israel threatened by,

98–99; Jordan, relations with, 116–17; Karbala, 65; Kirkuk, 67–69; Kurdistan, 69–71; Kuwait, relations with, 74–75, 125–27; Mahdi Army, 60–62; militias in, 60–63; Najaf, 65, 72–73; Obama on, 76; Office of Special Inspector General for Iraq Reconstruction, 66; oil in, 71–72; Ottoman Empire and, 57; al-Qaeda in, 78–79; refugees of, in Jordan, 75, 110; relations with neighbors, 72–76; religion in, 77; Saudi Arabia, relations with, 75, 170–71, 173–74; sectarian tensions in, 77–79; Shia community in, 23, 77; Sons of, 62; Sunni community in, 62, 77; Syria, relations with, 75, 190–92; Turkey, relations with, 74; U.S., relations with, 7, 76–77, 169; water in, 79–81

IRGC. *See* Iranian Revolutionary Guard Corps

Islamic Action Front (IAF), 113–14

Islamic Jihad, 3

Islamic law, 5

Islamic Republic of Iran: creation of, 41–42; Hussein, S., war against, 39, 98, 117–18. *See also* Iran

Islamic Resistance Movement, 92

Islamic Revolution, 168–69; with Iran, 21; Sadat government relating to, 5

Islamic Salvation Front (FIS), 146

Islamic Tendency Movement (MTI), 155–56

Islamist radicalism: Egypt's conflicts with, 8–10; Mubarak on, 10; Muslim Brotherhood, 3, 5, 8–10, 92; resurgence of, 7

Ismaili community, 166–67

Israel: Arab-, peacemaking, 2–3; Arabs in, 102–3, 104–5; background on, 83–91; delegitimization in, 103–4; Egypt, renewed conflicts with, 13–15, 104; Egypt, wars with, 13, 84–85; Fatah Party relating to, 94; governments in, 99; Hamas in Gaza Strip relating to, 87–90, 91–94; Hezbollah as threat to, 88, 94–96;-Hezbollah confrontation in Iran, 53; internal conflict in, 99–102; Iran as threat to, 96–97; Iran conflict with, 50, 52–54; Iraq as threat to, 98–99; Jewish settlements in, 99, 101; Jordan conflict with, 114–15; Lebanon, relations with, 85, 95–96; Lebanon, war with,

ABOUT THE AUTHORS

MAIN AUTHOR

WILLIAM MARK HABEEB is an adjunct professor at Georgetown University's School of Foreign Service and an international consultant specializing in conflict resolution and the Middle East. He received his PhD from the Johns Hopkins University School of Advanced International Studies.

GUEST AUTHORS

RAFAEL D. FRANKEL covered the Middle East and Southeast Asia for the *Boston Globe, Chicago Tribune,* and *Christian Science Monitor,* among other news organizations. He is currently conducting PhD research on nonstate militant groups at Georgetown University, from which he also holds an MS degree in foreign service.

MINA AL-ORAIBI is the assistant editor in chief of *Asharq Alawsat*, the international daily newspaper. She was previously Washington, D.C., bureau chief for Asharq Alawsat, where she was based from 2009 until November 2011. Among her recent work is a series of articles on Iraqi refugees, the development of American military doctrine, along with high profile interviews including Iraqi prime minister Nouri Al-Maliki. She was awarded an MA degree with distinction from University College London.